LIBERTY AND PROPERTY

LIBERTY AND PROPERTY

A Social History of Western Political Thought
from Renaissance to Enlightenment

ELLEN MEIKSINS WOOD

VERSO
London • New York

First published by Verso 2012
© Ellen Meiksins Wood 2012

1 3 5 7 9 10 8 6 4 2

Verso
UK: 6 Meard Street, London W1F 0EG
US: 20 Jay Street, Suite 1010, Brooklyn, NY 11201
www.versobooks.com

Verso is the imprint of New Left Books

ISBN-13: 978-1-84467-752-8

British Library Cataloguing in Publication Data
A catalogue record for this book is available from the British Library

Library of Congress Cataloging-in-Publication Data
A catalog record for this book is available from the Library of Congress

Typeset in Sabon MT by Hewer UK Ltd, Edinburgh
Printed in the US by Maple Vail

For Ed

CONTENTS

ACKNOWLEDGEMENTS

I am finding it more difficult than usual to thank all the many people who have, in one way or another, helped me with this book. The 'early modern' period covered in this volume has been a special preoccupation of mine since I first started reading, then writing and teaching, the history of political thought nearly half a century ago; and everything I have written about contemporary capitalism, imperialism and democracy has been informed by my reflections on that earlier historical moment and by years of conversation with colleagues, friends and students who may never have seen a single page of this book. My greatest debt remains to Neal Wood, who died some years before I started working on it.

My particular thanks must go, of course, to those who read the whole manuscript: Perry Anderson and George Comninel, whose comments have, as on other occasions, been no less generous than trenchant, and Ed Broadbent, to whom this book is dedicated, who again superbly played the role of 'intelligent general reader' with his customary insight and unflagging support.

I also owe thanks to Frances Abele, Robert Brenner and David McNally, who have read parts of the manuscript or allowed me to try out bits of it on them. And then there are those who advised me on (and who were acknowledged in) previous related works, including editors who commented on and/or permitted me to use some of my earlier publications, parts of which have inspired or been absorbed into this book: 'The State and Popular Sovereignty in French Political Thought: A Genealogy of Rousseau's "General Will" ', *History of Political Thought* IV.2, Summer 1983, pp. 281–315; 'Locke Against Democracy: Representation, Consent and Suffrage in the *Two Treatises*', *History of Political Thought* XIII.4, Winter 1992, pp. 657–89; 'Radicalism, Capitalism and Historical Contexts: Not Only a Reply to Richard Ashcraft on John Locke', *History of Political Thought*, XV.3, Autumn 1994, pp. 323–72; *A Trumpet of Sedition: Political Theory and the Rise of Capitalism, 1509–1688* (London: Pluto Press, and New York: New York University Press, 1997 – this book was coauthored with Neal Wood, although the sections on the seventeenth century used in the present volume were written by me); 'Capitalism or Enlightenment?', *History of Political Thought* XXI.3, Autumn 2000, pp. 405–26; 'Why It Matters', *London Review of Books*, vol. 30, no. 18, 25 September 2008.

Finally, a note on sources: I have tried to keep the number of footnotes under control and make it easier for readers to locate citations from the political thinkers discussed in this book. Instead of footnoting page numbers from one particular edition or translation I have, wherever possible, cited the original chapter, section and paragraph numbers that can be found in any standard editions of the works quoted. Where such citations may not be specific enough, I have included footnotes with page numbers (as in the case of works by Bodin and Rousseau in Chapter 6); and, for readers who would like to identify specific translations, here is a list of the translated works that, in subsequent chapters, will be cited without footnotes in the body of the text:

John Calvin, *Institutes*, transl. H. Beveridge (Edinburgh: Calvin Translation Society, 1845).

Niccolò Machiavelli, *The Prince*, transl. W.K. Marriott (London and New York: Everyman's Library, 1992); *The Discourses*, transl. L. Walker (Harmondsworth: Penguin Books, 1983); *History of Florence and the Affairs of Italy* (New York: Harper Torchbook, 1966).

Charles-Louis de Secondat, Baron de Montesquieu, *The Spirit of the Laws*, transl. T Nugent (New York: Hafner, 1962).

Benedict Spinoza, *The Political Works*, transl. A.G. Wernham (Oxford: Oxford University Press, 1958).

Francisco Vitoria, *Political Writings*, eds. A. Pagden and J. Lawrance (Cambridge: Cambridge University Press, 1991).

1

TRANSITIONS

The decline of feudalism and the rise of capitalism, from its agrarian origins to the early phases of industrialization; the religious ruptures of the Reformation; the evolution of the nation state; the growth of modern colonialism; cultural landmarks from the Renaissance to the Age of Enlightenment; modern philosophy and a scientific revolution, rooted in the empiricism of Francis Bacon or the rationalism of Renée Descartes – all these momentous historical developments, punctuated not only by wars among states but by popular uprisings, rebellions and revolts of various kinds, up to and including civil war, have been ascribed to the so-called early modern period.

It may not be surprising, then, that the canon of Western political thought is disproportionately populated by 'early modern' thinkers. While historians may differ about the inclusion of this or that name, the period has more than its share of towering figures – from Machiavelli or Hobbes to Locke and Rousseau – whose canonical status is as unassailable as that of Plato or Aristotle. Yet all the historical landmarks that mark out the era and even their conventional names – Renaissance, Reformation, Enlightenment, to say nothing of 'feudalism' or the 'rise of capitalism' – regularly provoke controversy among historians. So, for that matter, does the designation 'early modern' itself. It seems, on the face of it, a fairly innocent, if imprecise, descriptive label indicating rough chronological boundaries, somewhere between the middle ages and full-blown modernity. We shall use the label here in that more or less neutral sense, just for the sake of simplicity and for lack of anything better. But there is more at issue than chronology. Whatever dates we settle on – let us say approximately 1500 (or 1492?) to 1800, or maybe 1789 or even 1776 – the early modern presupposes an idea of the modern, as distinct from the ancient, the medieval or at least the 'pre-modern', an idea of modernity that raises questions of its own.

Much intellectual effort has been expended on clarifying the idea of 'modernity', and we shall, in what follows, have occasion to confront some of the questions it poses. For the moment, it is enough to say that, although there has been disagreement about what exactly constitutes the 'modern' and whether it is good, bad or morally neutral, there is, in 'Western' culture, a deeply rooted and tenacious conception that cuts across divergent schools of thought which may agree on very little else. Even when sharp distinctions are made among various national histories, there remains a single, overarching narrative of European history and the advent of modernity, a narrative defined by discontinuities and at the same time transitional processes, passages from one age to another marked by fundamental transformations.

In that narrative, the modern era, whatever else it may be, is a composite of economic, political and cultural characteristics, uniting capitalism (what classical political economists liked to call 'commercial society'), legal-rational political authority (perhaps, but not necessarily, with a preference for its liberal democratic form), and technological progress – or 'rationalization' in its various aspects as manifest in markets, states, secularism and scientific knowledge. Emphases or causal primacies may vary, and different balances may be struck among the factors of modernity, economic, cultural or social. There may be fierce dispute about the processes of transformation that produced the modern age. The critical transition may be defined as a passage from feudalism to capitalism, the rise of the bourgeoisie, the forward march of liberty, a destructive rupture from tradition, and much else besides. But it is difficult to find a notion of the modern in which the culture of 'rational' inquiry, advances in technology, the market economy and a 'rational' state are not, in one way or another, for better or worse, inextricably connected.[1]

In recent years the lines between the early modern and the modern have been more sharply drawn in some historical accounts, as the early modern has tended to merge with the 'late medieval'. Among historians of political thought in particular, there are those who question the idea of an early modern period, on the grounds that there was no significant rupture between medieval thinkers and those described as early modern. Political ideas, in this account, remained strikingly consistent throughout the historic transformations that brought the 'middle ages' to an end. But even here, the concept of modernity, and the conventional narrative associated with it, have been remarkably persistent.

There are, to be sure, those who reject the very idea of modernity. It makes some people uneasy because of its association with conceptions of progress, which smack of teleology or, after the horrors of the twentieth century, appear in questionable taste. Others are opposed to 'grand

---

1   The issue here may be confused by debates about the late nineteenth- and early twentieth-century cultural phenomena described as 'modernism'. But whatever may be meant by 'modernism' (or, indeed, 'postmodernism'), whether it is treated as an intensification or, on the contrary, a repudiation of the 'modern' and its cultural forms, this much-disputed concept leaves the conventional idea of modernity essentially intact.

narratives' of any kind and prefer to discard the *longue durée* in favour of a focus on the local, the particular and the contingent. Since 'modernity' implies a very long historical sweep from ancient to modern, with at least implicit explanations of how one led to the other, this refusal of a longer view makes it hard to sustain an idea of the modern.

Yet, these controversies notwithstanding, the notion of modernity is rarely challenged from a vantage point that, while systematically questioning the conventional paradigm, still takes a longer view of history. The most influential 'grand narratives' – from Enlightenment conceptions of progress, to Marxist or Whig interpretations of history or Weberian historical sociology, and all their varied legacies – have tended to leave the conventional composite portrait of the modern era fundamentally intact, however divergent their judgments of modernity have been. The challenge to the standard story of modernity has more often come from various kinds of disconnected or fragmented history, 'postmodernist' or 'revisionist' accounts with no long view and little explanation of historical causality or, indeed, historical process – though even then the stubborn concept of the modern has tended to return through the back door.

Early Modern Europe?

What, then, does it mean to speak of early modern political thought? The growth of the 'modern' state, with its entrenchment of national boundaries, political, economic and cultural, is certainly a central feature of the early modern period; and, in one way or another, it affected all forms of political organization that came within its field of force. But the canon of Western political thought, which is the subject of this book, was in that period also shaped by political forms as diverse as the city-states of Italy, the bewildering variety of German jurisdictions, and the commercial republics of the Netherlands – to say nothing of the Holy Roman Empire, simultaneously a self-conscious throwback to imperial antiquity and an aspiring if ultimately unsuccessful nation state, in constant tension with all other claimants to sovereignty, secular and ecclesiastical. The concept of the early modern encompasses not just the early manifestations of the modern state or the modern economy but cultural and intellectual developments rooted in very different, and not conspicuously modern, social and political forms, such as the Italian city-states in which the Renaissance came to fruition or the Electorate of Saxony where Martin Luther, at least according to historical convention, launched the Reformation.

These cases differed not only in their political form but in the particular interactions among public power, private property, and the producing classes; and these differences would give rise to distinctive traditions of political discourse. This was true even among the city-states and principalities joined at one time or another under the rule, however tenuous, of the Holy Roman Empire: the Germans and the Spanish, the Italians and the Dutch. To be sure, Italians and Germans, Spanish and Dutch, or, for that matter, English and French, all shared a common cultural legacy; and our period begins at a moment of particular cultural unity, manifested in the Latin that united Western European scholars, the whole apparatus of Christian theology, the revived Greek classics of political philosophy, the 'republic of letters' constituted by European humanism. Yet this common intellectual vocabulary simply makes the variety of national traditions that much more striking. The inherited languages of Western political theory have been remarkably flexible in their adaptation to varying contextual circumstances; and, as each specific historical form has posed its own distinctive problems, the same traditions of discourse have been mobilized not only to give different answers but in response to different questions.[2]

Is there, nonetheless and despite all these divergences, a sense in which it is meaningful to speak of 'early modern Europe', or, more particularly, does it make sense to think of Western Europe as an entity distinct from other regions, which is, in the period covered by this book, experiencing a pattern of historical development that distinguishes it from others? In what follows, there will be much emphasis on the specificities of national development, but let us for the moment consider the common foundations.

In the first volume of this social history of political thought, it was argued that Western political theory, in all its variations, has been shaped by a distinctive tension between two sources of power, the state and private property. All 'high' civilizations have, of course, had states, and some have had elaborate systems of private property; but developments in what would be Western Europe, with roots in Greco-Roman antiquity and especially the Western Roman Empire, gave property, as a distinct locus of power, an unusual degree of autonomy from the state.

Consider, for instance, the contrasts between the Roman Empire and the early Chinese imperial state. A strong state in China established its power by defeating great aristocratic families and preventing their appropriation of

---

2   *The Cambridge History of Political Thought: 1450–1700* (Cambridge: Cambridge University Press, 1991), without, to be sure, dismissing national differences and certainly acknowledging the variety of national discourses, adopts what it calls 'a more illuminating approach to the subject as a whole', choosing, for the most part, a thematic rather than a national mode of organizing the material. It does so mainly on the grounds that not only the survival of the *res publica christiana* but the humanist 'republic of letters' produced an intellectual community that transcended national boundaries (p. 5). Whatever its virtues, this approach fails to do justice to significant differences in the application and elaboration of precisely this common European discourse in response to different questions posed by divergent patterns of political and economic development among the European states.

newly conquered territories, which were to be administered by officials of the central state.[3] At the same time, peasants came under the direct control of the state, which preserved peasant property as a source of revenue and military service, while ensuring the fragmentation of landholdings. Rome, by contrast, achieved imperial expansion without a strong state, governed instead by amateurs, an oligarchy of landed aristocrats, in a small city-state with a minimal government. While peasants were part of the civic community, they remained subordinate to the propertied classes; and as the empire expanded, with the help of conscript peasant soldiers on military service far from home, many peasants were dispossessed. Land was increasingly concentrated in the hands of the aristocracy, much of it – at least in Roman Italy – worked by slaves. When the republic was replaced by an imperial state with its own structure of office, the landed aristocracy continued to amass huge properties; and, while in China great riches were typically derived from office in the central state, in the Roman Empire land remained the only steady and secure source of wealth. Even at its height, the imperial state was, by comparison with China, 'undergoverned', administered through a vast network of local aristocracies.

The Roman Empire represents the first known example of a strong imperial state combined with strong private property. This powerful, if sometimes uneasy, partnership is expressed in the Roman concepts of *imperium* and *dominium*. The Roman concept of *dominium*, when applied to private property, articulates with exceptional clarity the idea of private, exclusive and individual ownership, with all the powers this entails, while the *imperium* defines a right of command attached to certain civil magistrates and eventually the emperor himself. While, in the history of Western legal and political thought, the distinction between private property and public jurisdiction would not always be so clear, the Romans certainly did break new ground in distinguishing between the public power of the state and the private power of property, in both theory and practice. In contrast to China, where there was a direct relationship between the state and the peasants whose labour it appropriated, in Rome the primary relation between appropriators and producers was not between rulers and subjects but between landlords and subject labour of one kind or another, whether slaves or peasants exploited as tenants and share-croppers. When the empire disintegrated, what remained was this primary relationship, which would survive as the foundation of the social order for centuries to come.

The existence of two poles of power, the state and strong private property, together with a mode of imperial rule dependent on propertied classes with a substantial degree of local self-government, had created a tendency

---

3   See Jacques Gernet, *A History of Chinese Civilization* (Cambridge: Cambridge University Press, 2nd edn, 2005), Chs 3–5.

to fragmentation of sovereign power even in the Roman Empire. In the end, the tendencies towards fragmentation prevailed, leaving behind a network of personal dependence binding peasants to landlords. When the empire disintegrated, and after several attempts at recentralization by the Merovingian monarchy, the Carolingian empire and the successor states, the autonomy of landed aristocracies asserted itself in what might be called the privatization of public authority, the feudal 'parcellization of sovereignty',[4] with the devolution of public functions to local lords and various other independent powers. This devolved public power was at the same time a power of appropriation, the power to command the labour of producing classes, appropriating its fruits in rent or in kind, in particular from peasants who remained in possession of land but worked in political and legal subjection to lords. We can, for lack of a better term, apply the much-disputed concept of feudalism, or 'feudal society', to this specifically Western parcellization of sovereignty, which invested private property with public power in historically distinctive ways. The 'medieval' period for our purposes is roughly marked out by the dominance of that distinctive configuration and its decline.[5]

This feudal parcellization existed in various forms and to varying degrees. Feudal monarchies were stronger in some places than in others; and parts of Europe were in varying degrees under the sway of higher authorities, the Holy Roman Empire or the papacy. But political parcellization affected even European political entities that did not conform to the model feudal system. Italy, for instance, has been called the 'weak link' of European feudalism because, especially in the north, urban patriciates were dominant, in contrast to seigneurial landed classes elsewhere. Yet, not only did the city-states of northern Italy have their own fragmented governance – what might be called a kind of urban feudalism – but the great commercial centres like Florence and Venice were what they were in large part because they served a vital function as trading links in the fragmented feudal order.

Wherever we choose to place the dividing line between the 'medieval' and the 'early modern', we can, by the late fifteenth century, identify a new configuration of political power, with new relations between property and state different from feudal parcellized sovereignty. Lords and autonomous corporate bodies did, to be sure, continue to play a prominent role; but centralizing monarchies – especially in England, France and the Iberian peninsula – were now taking centre stage, imposing a new political dynamic

4   The phrase 'parcellization of sovereignty' appears in Perry Anderson, *Passages from Antiquity to Feudalism* (London: Verso, 1974), p. 148.

5   For a discussion of the much-debated concept of feudalism, see Ellen Meiksins Wood, *Citizens to Lords: A Social History of Western Political Thought from Antiquity to the Middle Ages* ((London: Verso, 2008), Ch. 4.

even on different political forms, such as the Italian city-states or German principalities. While northern Italy, for instance, had been a battleground for rivalries between the Holy Roman Empire and the papacy, the challenge to the autonomy of city-states was increasingly coming from the territorial ambitions of monarchical states such as France and Spain.

Many explanations have been offered for the decline of feudalism. Some historians have argued that, just as the emergence of feudalism was marked, or even caused, by a contraction of trade, commercial expansion and the growth of the money economy inevitably brought feudalism to an end; while others have persuasively argued that trade and money were very much part of, and not intrinsically inimical to, the feudal order. Much is often made of the demographic collapse that occurred in the time of the Black Death, the pandemic that affected Western Europe in the 1340s; and it has been argued that the relationship between lords and peasants was fundamentally transformed as the drastic decline in population gave peasants an advantage in bargaining with lords in need of labour. Peasants, according to some historians, may have had yet another bargaining advantage, an escape route provided by the growth of urban centres as commerce expanded. Popular rebellions of various kinds were then provoked by the efforts of lords to reimpose and intensify peasant dependence; and, though rebellions in the West were successfully suppressed, the feudal order was effectively dead.

The development of the modern nation state may be attributed to the needs of landed aristocracies for a stronger central power to maintain order against the threat of rebellion, or – and perhaps at the same time – feudal monarchies may have been under greater pressure to consolidate their positions, as revenues derived from peasants became more precarious and the competition with landlords for access to peasant labour became more intense. The pressures became that much greater when aristocratic rivalries spilled over into wars between aspiring territorial states, as happened most dramatically in the Hundred Years' War, which began as a dynastic struggle over the monarchy in France and continued as a battle over the territorial boundaries of the French and English states. The incentive to consolidate centrally governed territorial states was further intensified by the commercial and geopolitical challenge of the growing Ottoman Empire, which made deep incursions into Europe and commanded east–west trade routes.

Yet, however important any or all of these factors may be, this cannot be the whole story. Commercial expansion, plague and demographic changes, peasant revolts and dynastic conflicts occurred in various parts of Europe; and we may even accept, as a very general principle, that all of them played a part in the decline of feudalism. But, quite apart from the variety of 'feudalisms', there was a wide variety of outcomes; and the feudal order gave way to more than one 'transition'. Serfdom, for instance, ended in

Western Europe, while Eastern Europe saw what has been called the 'second serfdom'. Even in Western Europe, which is our main concern here, relations between landlords and peasants turned out to be very different in, say, England than in France; and these differences were associated with divergent paths of state-formation. In England, where the monarchy had developed in cooperation with an unusually united aristocracy, lords had gained control of the best land, including properties left vacant by the demographic collapse. In France, the monarchical state, which consolidated the dominance of one aristocratic family against its rivals, helped to ensure that peasants remained in possession of by far the most land, as a vital source of tax revenues for the centralizing state.

In these different contexts, commercial expansion, too, had divergent effects. All the major Western European states, to say nothing of the highly developed economies of Asia and the Arab Muslim empire, were very much engaged in trade, both domestic and international; but a distinctively *capitalist* 'commercial society' arose 'spontaneously' only in England and produced a historical dynamic unlike any other, even in the most commercialized societies.[6] Capitalism, as it emerged in England, was not simply more of the same, more trade and more expansive commercial networks. The 'rise of capitalism' cannot be explained as just a quantitative process, 'commercialization' approaching some kind of critical mass. England, indeed, was very far from being the dominant commercial power in Europe when its economic development began to take a distinctive turn, giving rise to something different from traditional modes of commerce, the old forms of profit on alienation or 'buying cheap and selling dear'. English capitalism, which was born in the countryside, produced a new kind of society, with an economy uniquely driven by compulsions of competitive production, increasing labour productivity, profit-maximization and constant capital accumulation. When other European economies later developed in a capitalist direction, they were in large part responding to military and commercial pressures imposed by English capitalism.

Which 'Modern' State?

In the following chapters, we shall look at various distinctive patterns of development in Western Europe as they affected national 'traditions of discourse'; but for the moment, and to illustrate the contextual history proposed in this book, we can concentrate on the one overarching

6   See Robert Brenner's two contributions to *The Brenner Debate: Agrarian Class Structure and Economic Development in Pre-Industrial Europe*, eds T.H Aston and C.H.E. Philpin (Cambridge: Cambridge University Press, 1985). See also Ellen Meiksins Wood, *The Origin of Capitalism: A Longer View* (London: Verso, 2002).

development that had effects on all of them: the evolution of the 'modern' state, especially in England and in France.

Quentin Skinner, in his *Foundations of Modern Political Thought*, tells us that in the period from the late thirteenth century to the end of the sixteenth, 'the main elements of a recognizably modern concept of the state were gradually acquired.' He goes on to elaborate his definition of the modern state in terms derived, as he acknowledges, from Max Weber:

> The decisive shift was made from the idea of the ruler 'maintaining his state' – where this simply meant upholding his own position – to the idea that there is a separate legal and constitutional order, that of the State, which the ruler has a duty to maintain. One effect of this transformation was that the power of the State, not that of the ruler, came to be envisaged as the basis of government. And this in turn enabled the State to be conceptualized in distinctively modern terms – as the sole source of law and legitimate force within its own territory, and as the sole appropriate object of its citizens' allegiances.[7]

The elements of this modern state, Skinner explains, were by the sixteenth century visible at least in England and in France. The transition to a modern discourse of the state, he suggests, 'first appears to have been accomplished in France'. This was so not only because the intellectual preconditions were present – inherited from Italian humanism – but because 'the material preconditions' were more fully developed in France: 'a relatively united central authority, an increasing apparatus of bureaucratic control, and a clearly defined set of national boundaries'.[8] 'The next country in which the same fundamental conceptual shift took place', Skinner continues, 'appears to have been England', where, by the 1530s, 'a similar set of material as well as intellectual preconditions for this development had been achieved: an increasingly bureaucratic style of central government, together with a growing interest amongst English humanists in the problems of "politics" and public law.'[9]

This formulation obscures a wealth of differences between the two cases, both in the nature of their states and the forms of 'discourse' they engendered. Those differences also cast doubt on some other standard conventions about 'modernity' and especially about the connections between the capitalist economy – or 'commercial society' – and the 'rational' state. In subsequent chapters, we shall look more closely at the varying traditions of political discourse that emerged out of divergent patterns of historical development;

---

7 Quentin Skinner, *The Foundations of Modern Political Thought, Volume 1: The Renaissance* (Cambridge: Cambridge University Press, 1978), pp. ix–x.

8 Skinner, *Foundations, Vol. 2: The Age of Reformation*, p. 354.

9 *Ibid.*, p. 356.

but a broad preliminary sketch of the differences between England and France will serve to illustrate the 'social history' on offer here.

The story begins at least as early as the Middle Ages, at a time when the Frankish empire was disintegrating while the Anglo-Saxon state was the most effective centralized administration in the Western world.[10] Medieval Europe was generally characterized by what we have called a 'parcellization of sovereignty', the fragmentation of state power, as feudal lordship and other autonomous powers took over many of the functions performed in other times and places by the state, combining the private exploitation of labour – typically the labour of peasants – with the public role of administration, jurisdiction and enforcement. Yet England, for all the power of the barons – and, in some ways, precisely because of it – never really succumbed to parcellized sovereignty, while France never completely overcame it, even under the absolutist monarchy; and the centralizing project of the state remained on the agenda to be completed by the Revolution and Napoleon.

This meant, too, that there were major differences between England and France in the relations between state and dominant classes. In England, even at a time when English law was at its most ostensibly feudal and the manorial system was at its height, the process of state centralization continued. The Norman Conquest, when it brought feudal institutions with it from the Continent, also, and above all, brought a military organization, which vested power in a central authority and built upon the foundations of a centralized state that already existed in England. The Normans established themselves in England as a more or less unified ruling class, a conquering army that imposed itself as both a dominant class of great landholders and a governing power; and the central state was always its instrument. Thereafter, the centralization of the post-feudal state would remain a cooperative project between monarchy and landed aristocracy. This certainly did not rule out fierce dynastic rivalries; and, though some historians have questioned the very existence of, for example, the 'Wars of the Roses', there certainly were powerful incentives for battles over control of an already well-established central state. When, in the sixteenth century, the Tudor monarchy embarked on a programme of state-centralization, which has (controversially) been described as the 'Tudor revolution', it was not inventing but building on a long-standing unified state apparatus, which, when the Reformation came to England under Henry VIII, would have the added strength of a state Church.

This centralizing project was cooperative not only in the sense that the central state would develop as a unity of monarchy and the landed class in

---

10   These points are discussed at greater length in *Citizens to Lords*, as are the differences between feudal societies in England and France, among others. For an important discussion of those differences, see George Comninel, 'English Feudalism and the Origins of Capitalism', in *The Journal of Peasant Studies*, July 2000, pp. 1–53.

Parliament, nicely summed up in the old formula 'the Crown in Parliament'. The cooperative project also took the form of a division of labour between the central state and private property. As legislation and jurisdiction were increasingly centralized, the aristocracy would increasingly depend for its wealth on modes of purely *economic* exploitation. Recent scholarship has shown that smallholders may not have disappeared from the English countryside as completely as historians have sometimes suggested; but the fact remains that lords in England, while lacking some of the jurisdictional powers enjoyed by their counterparts elsewhere in Europe, had control of the best land, which was concentrated in the hands of large landholders to a greater degree than in France, where peasant property prevailed. When feudalism experienced its crisis throughout Europe, and serfdom declined in the West, English landlords were in a uniquely favourable position to exploit the purely economic powers that they still enjoyed, even as the state became increasingly centralized.

The English landed class was, in this respect, markedly different from those Continental aristocracies whose wealth derived from 'extra-economic' power, or what has been called 'politically constituted property', of one kind or another, various forms of privilege, seigneurial rights and the fruits of jurisdiction.[11] The concentration of landed property in England meant that land was worked to an unusual extent by tenants – increasingly on economic rents subject to market conditions – while landlords without access to politically constituted property came to depend on the productive and competitive success of their tenants. The result of this distinctive development was agrarian capitalism, which was 'capitalist' in the sense that appropriators and producers were dependent on the market for their own survival and the maintenance of their positions, hence subject to the imperatives of competition, profit-maximization and the need constantly to improve labour productivity.

Because of uniquely English relations between large landowners and tenants whom we might call capitalist farmers, English agriculture began to respond to new requirements of market competition with no historical precedent. The particular relations between landlords and tenants, in the context of a distinctive kind of domestic market, meant that already in the seventeenth century both parties were compelled to enhance the land's productivity for profit – to promote what they called *improvement*. Improvement and profitable production became the preferred strategy for the ruling landed class. What this meant was not – at least in the first instance – mainly technological innovation. It had more to do with methods and techniques of land use; but it also meant, and more fundamentally, new forms and conceptions of property. Agricultural

---

11   The phrase 'politically constituted property' has been used by Robert Brenner in various historical works.

improvement and the enhancement of profit for capitalist agriculture ideally called for a concentration of property; but above all, they required the elimination of various customary rights and practices that interfered with capital accumulation. Improving landlords and capitalist tenants needed to be free of obstructions to the productive and profitable use of property.

Between the sixteenth and eighteenth centuries, there was growing pressure to extinguish customary rights – for instance, disputing communal rights to common land by claiming exclusive private ownership; challenging customary tenures which granted smallholders rights of possession without outright legal title; eliminating various use rights on private land; and so on. This meant the establishment of property that was literally *exclusive* – excluding other individuals and the community, eliminating various kinds of restrictions on land use imposed by custom or communal regulation.

The detachment of economic from 'extra-economic' powers meant that the processes of state-centralization and capitalist development, although sometimes in tension, were closely intertwined. There were obviously conflicts between the landed class and the monarchy, which would come to a head in the Civil War. But those conflicts had a particular character and intensity precisely because of the underlying partnership between dominant class and monarchical state. The interests of the English ruling classes were, from very early on, deeply invested in a unitary Parliament, with legislative powers, which was very much a part of the centralized state. The aristocracy was also committed to a national system of law, and jurisdictional conflicts between king and the nobility ended quite early. Even in the early thirteenth century, at a time of violent tension between monarchy and barons, when Magna Carta claimed the rights of the barons to be tried by their peers, it did not assert their rights of jurisdiction over other free men. The common law – which was, in the first instance, the king's law – became the favoured legal system for the aristocracy as well as for free peasants who could seek protection from the Crown, while the rule of law was understood to mean that the monarchy itself was subject to the law.

This uniquely unified system of law, in an unusually centralized state, produced a distinctive type of 'free' man, subject only to the king and to no other, lesser lord. Landlords enjoyed great local powers, but outside the manor they acted as delegates of the Crown in relation to free men. There remained land subject to manorial lordship; but the 'free' Englishman, with an individual 'interest' in freehold property recognized in common law and free of lordly claims or obligations, was a unique formation. In France, for example, even charters of freedom did not dissolve seigneurial obligation; and even free peasants with access to royal protection could still be subject to seigneurial jurisdiction.[12]

---

12   See Comninel, 'English Feudalism'.

The English common law did eventually come to represent parliamentary power *against* the Crown, with Parliament asserting its supremacy as the interpreter of common law. In the Civil War in the seventeenth century, the conflict between monarch and Parliament, common lawyers tended to side with Parliament, against the prerogative courts allied with the king. But this was not a case of parcellized jurisdictions asserting themselves against the central state. On the contrary, it was an assertion of the aristocracy's essential role in the partnership that constituted the central state, at a time when that partnership was being challenged by the monarchy. At the same time, while the ruling class was claiming its share in the public sphere of the central state, it was also asserting its power in the private sphere of property, as landowners rather than as officers of state. From this point of view, the issue was less an assertion of public jurisdiction than of private rights, intended to protect the ruling class against the Crown's violation of its partnership and the division of labour between property and state.

The English Revolution – the whole period from the Civil War in the 1640s to the so-called Glorious Revolution of 1688–9 – saw major upheavals, and, as we shall see in a subsequent chapter, it produced uniquely radical ideas. But it did not fundamentally transform social property relations in England, which were hardly less capitalist before the Revolution than after. Nor, for that matter, did it fundamentally transform – bar the 'interregnum' – the relation between Parliament and monarchy. Even if we attach great importance to the settlement of 1688 in establishing parliamentary supremacy, it did little more than consolidate what was already on the table before the Revolution, before the Stuart monarchy attempted, unsuccessfully, to establish a Continental-style absolutism in a society where there was little political support and even less social foundation for any such project. If the old cooperative enterprise between monarchy and Parliament was increasingly giving way to parliamentary supremacy (and we should not exaggerate the extent to which this was true even in the eighteenth century), what remained was the characteristic division of labour between state and property, the separation of economic and extra-economic powers, which had marked out Britain from its neighbours.

The long history of partnership between aristocracy and central state, and the role of Parliament as the public face of private property, has meant that the ruling class in Britain has, on the whole, been consistently committed to parliamentarism. But the other side of the coin is that the dominant historical narrative and mainstream political culture have marginalized the truly revolutionary and democratic traditions that emerged during the English Revolution, the tradition of the Levellers, Diggers and other radical movements. Democratic popular forces were defeated by the parliamentary oligarchy; and, though their legacy has never completely disappeared from the British labour movement, the dominant parliamentary tradition owes more to the victorious propertied classes.

The process of state-formation in France was quite different. If in England there was a transition from feudalism to capitalism, in France it was rather a transition from feudalism to absolutism – absolutism not simply as a political form but the absolutist state as a form of politically constituted property, a means of enriching office-holders by exploiting the peasantry. The monarchy emerged out of feudal rivalry, as one aristocratic dynasty established itself over others in a context of parcellized sovereignty. The monarchical state continued to confront the challenge of feudal parcellization, not only opposition from dynastic rivals but claims to independent powers and privileges by the aristocracy and various corporate entities, guilds, estates, provinces and towns.

The monarchy certainly did pursue a centralizing strategy with some success; and royal courts did emerge, which, among other things, could be used to protect peasants from lords (not least, in order to preserve the peasantry as a source of state taxes). But the dominant class continued to depend to a great extent on politically constituted property – that is, on means of appropriation deriving from political, military and judicial powers, or 'extra-economic' status and privilege, in contrast to the English landed classes and their dependence on competitive production. In France, in contrast to England, even in the eighteenth century peasants still dominated agricultural production, and relations between landlords and tenants had very different effects. There was, for instance, nothing like the culture of 'improvement' nor the improvement literature that had been so important in seventeenth-century England. Village regulation of production and restrictions on land use continued to be important in agriculture even beyond the Revolution. For French landlords, extra-economic strategies – political and legal – for enhancing their power to squeeze more surplus out of peasants were still more important than agricultural improvement. This meant, among other things, that peasants were more plagued by taxes than by attacks on their property rights.

The state developed as a competing form of politically constituted property, a primary resource, a mode of direct appropriation for state office-holders by means of taxation, which some historians have called a kind of centralized rent. If the absolutist state was able to undermine the independent powers of the aristocracy, it did so in large part by replacing those powers with the lucrative resource of state office for a segment of the aristocracy. An elaborate bureaucracy developed not just for political and administrative purposes but as an economic resource for office-holders, proliferating state offices as a form of private property.

Nor was there anything in France like England's long parliamentary tradition. No such tradition existed before the Revolution. There was, to begin with, a stark historical contrast between the unitary national Parliament in England, with its early legislative role, and the fragmented estates in France. The estates had no legislative function and were divided by locality – even on the rare occasions when they met on the national plane of the Estates General. They were also divided by corporate hierarchy, above all the division between, on the one hand, the two privileged estates, the nobility and the Church, and, on the other hand, the Third Estate, which encompassed both bourgeoisie – the more prosperous non-privileged classes, often urban notables – and peasantry. The emergence of a representative legislative body in France had to await the Revolution; and one of the most striking differences between England and France is that, in France, even when estates were replaced by a national assembly, important sectors of the dominant classes remained opposed to the Republic. The revolutionary transformation created both a new parliamentary tradition, even a radical republicanism, and at the same time a dangerously anti-parliamentary, anti-republican formation, which persisted well into the twentieth century and explains much that would happen in France in the Second World War.

The French legal system also developed in ways sharply different from the English. Not only was there a long-standing division between the Roman law which survived in the south and the Germanic customary law of the north, but in addition, on the eve of the Revolution there were still approximately 360 different law codes in France, with various seigneurial, local and corporate powers contesting jurisdiction with the monarchy, and customary law challenging the supremacy of state legislation. Although the absolutist state succeeded to a considerable degree in limiting seigneurial and local jurisdiction, jurisdictional conflicts remained a constant feature of the ancien régime and a major preoccupation of French courts. The aristocracy and corporate bodies clung to their autonomy and independence from the national state, while the monarchy continued its efforts to co-opt and integrate them.

When monarchical absolutism gave way to Revolution, the centralizing project of the state continued. The French *état légal* evolved not as a defence of private rights against public incursions but as a means of asserting the power of the central state against fragmented jurisdictions and independent local powers. This limited the independence of the judiciary, effectively absorbing it into the civil service. It remained for Napoleon to complete the project begun by the Revolution. While the judiciary would regain some of its autonomy in the Fifth Republic of 1958, the historic function of the law in asserting state sovereignty against autonomous jurisdictions remains a powerful legacy.

Relations between central state and landed aristocracy, then, were quite different from the English case. In contrast to the close English partnership between the aristocracy and monarchy, in France the tensions between aristocratic privilege and monarchical power, between different modes of extra-economic exploitation, persisted until the Revolution. At the same time, the aristocracy itself was divided between those with power in the central state and the many who remained dependent on their privileges and local powers; and this division continued to be fluid. The centralizing project of the state can be understood as in large part an attempt to overcome that division by replacing autonomous aristocratic powers with perquisites and privileges deriving from the state – for instance, by granting privileged exemption from royal taxation in place of seigneurial jurisdiction.

As for the bourgeoisie, throughout the ancien régime and beyond, state office would be a favoured career. Notwithstanding the conventional conflation of 'bourgeois' with 'capitalist', the French bourgeoisie was not in essence capitalist. While France was certainly a major trading nation, the majority of 'bourgeois' were urban notables or functionaries of various kinds, office-holders, professionals, intellectuals; and even those engaged in commerce (who might also be inclined to use their wealth to buy ennobling office) were operating on familiar principles of non-capitalist commercial profit-taking.[13] When the Revolution came, the revolutionary bourgeoisie – typically consisting precisely of those office-holders, professionals and intellectuals – was less concerned with breaking the shackles impeding the development of capitalism, as is often suggested by the notion of the 'bourgeois revolution', than with preserving and enhancing their access to the highest state office, 'careers open to talent'. It was, indeed, a threat to the access they already enjoyed under the absolutist monarchy that probably more than anything else provoked the bourgeoisie into revolution and a confrontation between bourgeoisie and aristocracy.

Although private property in office was abolished by the Revolution, state office remained a lucrative career, in which office-holders appropriated the surplus labour of peasants through taxation. Even after the Revolution, even after Napoleon, the state continued to serve this economic function for the bourgeoisie. The peasantry, which remained in possession of most land in France, continued to be exploited by extra-economic means, through the medium of state taxation. The Revolution did not radically transform the social property relations between the state and small agricultural producers which had prevailed in absolutist France.

While the Revolution may have been 'bourgeois', then, there was little that was 'capitalist' about it. If, in its political principles and in its legacies it went far beyond the 'bourgeois' impulses that first set it in motion, there remained strong continuities between the ancien régime and the post-revolutionary state. What is so striking about the post-revolutionary period,

---

13   For a discussion of this point, see George Comninel, *Rethinking the French Revolution: Marxism and the Revisionist Challenge* (London: Verso, 1987), esp. pp. 180ff.

throughout much of the nineteenth century in France, is the persistence of the tax/office structure, in which appropriation took the form of direct exploitation of peasant producers by the state through taxation. Not only did the economy continue to be based on small-scale agricultural production, but the state continued to relate to that production as a primary exploiter of direct producers through the medium of taxation, for the benefit of office-holders.

One has only to read Marx's account of nineteenth-century France in the *18th Brumaire* to see how persistent this formation was. He speaks of the 'immense bureaucratic and military organization', a 'frightful parasitic body', in which the '*material interest* of the French bourgeoisie is most intimately imbricated. It is that machine which provides the surplus population with jobs, and makes up through state salaries for what it cannot pocket in the form of profits, interest, rents and fees.' This bourgeois tradition would continue well into the twentieth century, if not until today, in a culture where state office would remain the highest career, with a tradition of mandarinism, dominated by a hereditary elite of office-holders and their exclusive academies.

Economic development in a capitalist direction was, in France, largely driven from without, in particular by military pressures. After the Revolution, the defeat of Napoleon not only made clear the military advantage that a victorious Britain had gained from the economic growth and wealth created by capitalism but also opened the former Napoleonic empire to the purely economic pressures of British capitalism in unprecedented ways. The state responded to those external imperatives by bringing about a state-led development of the economy. In a sense, the development of capitalism preceded social transformation; and, in contrast to England, capitalist class relations were more a result than a cause of industrialization.

Modern Political Thought?

It is certainly true that the emergence of national states with clear territorial boundaries and a more or less unified sovereign power created conditions for new developments in Western political thought – but perhaps not quite in the ways that Skinner has suggested. It does make sense to identify the rise of territorial states in Europe as a major historical development, a departure from the parcellized sovereignty of previous centuries; but it helps very little to describe these states as 'modern' if that label disguises important historical differences, such as those we have already observed between England and France. Is absolutist France more modern because of its elaborate bureaucracy, the sign of a 'rational' state? Or should we give the prize to England, because its centralized state, however 'irrational' in Weberian terms, has more completely asserted its sovereignty against autonomous powers of various kinds and has largely ceased to be a form of property?

It also makes sense to single out the rise of the 'market economy' as a critical development, but what precisely makes a market 'modern' as distinct from 'ancient'? There were vast commercial networks in various parts of the world long before the advent of 'modernity', and it is not at all clear that the trade we see in 'early modern' Europe is operating on significantly different principles, the age-old practices of buying cheap and selling dear. It cannot be simply a matter of scale, or else why should Europe in the sixteenth century be more modern than India or China even centuries before? If there is a fundamental rupture in the age-old pattern of commercial exchange, it occurs in England (a point to which we shall return in later chapters), with the rise of agrarian capitalism; but England is at first a fairly minor player in the global trading network compared to, say, Venice or Portugal; so which of them is more modern? If we try to identify a uniquely modern complex of a rational state, a 'rational' economy, and a culture of 'reason', where, if anywhere, did it exist?

If the notion of the modern state conceals as much as it reveals, what does it mean to speak of modern political thought? There seems to be an irresistible temptation among historians of political thought to identify the first modern political thinker in the Western canon. Pride of place is commonly awarded to Hobbes or Machiavelli. The reasons for selecting Hobbes may have to do with his theory of government, grounded in a systematically secular, materialistic account of epistemology, human psychology and morality. Or the reason may be that, however ambiguously, he bases his theory of politics on a conception of individual freedom and rights. Or it may simply be that, by elaborating a definitive conception of sovereignty, he best represents the triumph of territorial monarchies, or even 'nation states', over medieval forms of governance. Hobbes has even been called a 'bourgeois' thinker, an exponent of a 'possessive individualism' associated with a modern market society.

If Machiavelli is chosen, with or without denouncing his 'Machiavellian' amorality, it is likely to be on the grounds that he, before Hobbes, gave an account of politics divorced from moral or religious principles, or even that he is the first political *scientist,* on the side of the 'empirical' instead of the 'normative' study of politics, 'facts' rather than 'values'. Or it may be on the grounds that his republicanism, albeit more visible in the *Discourses* than in his most famous work, *The Prince,* mobilizes ancient ideas of civic autonomy against feudal hierarchies and in support of more modern conceptions of liberty and citizenship, a pivotal moment – as in John Pocock's 'Machiavellian moment' – in the development of modern republican ideas. Or at least, it might be said, if he has one foot in the ancient world, he is a 'transitional' figure; and, even if the city-state of Florence that produced him fails to fit the model of a modern nation state, it was, after all, a centre of commerce, which is supposed to be a prelude to a modern capitalist economy.

The Cambridge School, which dominates the field of early modern political theory in the Anglo-American academy, may have muddied the waters – making it harder to award the modernity prize to any one thinker – by eschewing the very idea of a 'canon' and replacing it with discursive contexts that include a host of not-so-canonical writers who have in their various ways contributed to language 'situations'. This approach certainly has its advantages, but it may – as we have seen in the case of Quentin Skinner – simply shift the question to which political language or discourse represents a modern break from ancient or medieval precedents. The conventional language of ancient and modern persists even when traditions of discourse span centuries of historical change, indeed even when ancient and modern languages of politics are allowed to coexist in historical time, in conflict or in paradoxical unity – as in the notion of 'civic humanism' or, for that matter, 'republicanism'.

But whether applied to a single major thinker or to a collective 'discourse', the concept of modernity, in all its conflicting forms, is loaded with assumptions that shed little light on historical processes. Might it not be better to look for historic transformations, even ruptures, without being obliged to define them as breakthroughs to modernity? And what kinds of transformations might we find if we set aside the elusive search for modernity? In particular, what significant changes would we find in the discourse of politics in the era we are exploring here?

During the medieval period, at the height of 'parcellized sovereignty', there scarcely existed a distinct political sphere.[14] The elaborate feudal network of competing jurisdictions, bound together – when not in open conflict – by a complex apparatus of legal and contractual relations, meant that the boundaries of the 'political' were ill-defined and fluid. The main 'political' agent was not the individual citizen but the possessor of some kind of secular or ecclesiastical jurisdiction, or a corporate entity with its own legal rights, a degree of autonomy and often a charter defining its relation to other corporations and superior powers. Legal and political thinking was preoccupied not, as ancient political philosophy had been, with portraying the political transactions among citizens within a civic community, but with mapping out the spheres of authority among overlapping and competing jurisdictions or negotiating interactions among them. The emergence of territorial states in the early modern period would change these conditions (though, as we shall see, we should not exaggerate the speed or degree of these transformations), creating a new political domain, new political identities, and new political ideas to suit them.

Among the most significant developments were new conceptions of individual rights in relation to political authority. Although there has been

---

14   There is a detailed discussion of these themes in my *Citizens to Lords*, Ch. 4.

much debate about when and how the concept of 'subjective' rights originated, the idea of rights inherent in the person, prior to and independent
of civic authority or positive law, certainly had roots in the Middle Ages,
in the writings of canon lawyers and philosophers. The very idea of a
Christian conscience, for instance, presupposed a human capacity for
understanding principles of right (in the 'objective' sense, as 'what is
right') and a responsibility to follow them.[15] That responsibility implied
both a moral obligation and a certain individual autonomy, the capacity to
disregard the principles of right no less than to respect them. From that
individual autonomy it was possible to deduce a notion of individual freedom from which followed certain entitlements – which might include a
'right' to be free of enslavement, or a 'right' of self-preservation and self-
defence; and it also entailed respect for the same entitlements in others, if
only on the basis of the Golden Rule.

These principles of right did have some implications for political
thought. An insistence on individual autonomy or natural freedom
seemed, for instance, to require an acknowledgement that civil authority
is constituted by consenting individuals – which was consistent with the
prominent role of contractual relations in the feudal order. But none of
this had any necessary implications for the rights of individuals in relation
to the state, once established. As long as the central category of political
thought remained not citizenship but jurisdiction, and as long as the principal political agent was not the individual citizen but the bearer of some
jurisdictional authority – a feudal lord, perhaps, or some corporate entity
endowed with legal rights and liberties – there was no obvious connection
between individual rights and limitations on the state, nor, indeed, any
need to demonstrate by systematic argument that individual rights do not
preclude almost unlimited civil power.

A monarch might, for instance, invoke a doctrine of consent, based on
rights, to buttress his own authority against the claims of popes or emperors. What may look to us like a paradox seemed to medieval thinkers not so
paradoxical. The creation of the body politic was quite distinct from the
conditions of rule. The idea that civil authority is constituted by the 'people'
(typically conceived as a corporate body) was perfectly consistent with the

---

15 The history of 'rights' is difficult to trace not least because the Latin *ius* has such
variable meanings, denoting both 'objective' principles of right or justice, established
by positive or natural law, and 'subjective' rights in the sense of entitlements inherent
in the individual person. Some of the same complexities exist in modern European languages, as in the German *Recht* or the French *droit*. Since the principles of 'objective'
right derive their moral force from their availability to the same rational, responsible and
autonomous individual who is the subject of 'subjective' rights, it is that much harder to
draw a neat line between 'objective' and 'subjective' right in the development of Western
political thought.

view that such authority was almost unconditional – not least because the right of resistance to illegitimate authority, if it existed at all, was typically vested not in individual citizens but in jurisdictional authorities. Even in the 'early modern' period, there would continue to be doctrines of resistance in which the right to resist civil authority was not a right of private individuals or citizens but an attribute of office, the authority of one jurisdiction pitted against another.

A right of private property might be emphatically acknowledged; but even that right was conceived in the context of competing jurisdictions, typically to assert lordly autonomy or to mark out a domain of private power, the power of the head of the household over his family and possessions, or perhaps the remnant of jurisdictional authority construed as a right of *dominium*, against some higher *imperium*.

If the universal possession of natural rights and natural liberty did not guarantee universal entitlements to full political rights, much the same can be said about notions of natural equality. It is, as we shall see in subsequent chapters, a striking characteristic of Western political thought throughout much of its history that ideas of natural equality among men did not rule out the unequal distribution of political rights; and elaborate arguments have been constructed to legitimate relationships of rule and domination among naturally equal men. Men might all be equal under God or natural law, but some might be entitled to rule others nonetheless. The determinants of property and class could trump all natural equalities.

It has even been possible for political thinkers to go some distance in conceding the equality of women, while taking for granted their complete exclusion from the political domain – for example, on the grounds of their child-bearing functions or men's monopoly of coercive force. Few thinkers exceed Thomas Hobbes in acknowledging the natural equality of men and women, just as few go beyond him in insisting on natural equality among all men; yet none of these concessions to equality pose any obstacles to his convictions on the legitimacy of absolutist rule. Nor is John Locke inhibited in his views on the unequal distribution of political rights among men by his belief in their natural equality, or the total exclusion of women from politics by his denial that God decreed the subjection of Eve to Adam or women to men.

The compatibility of natural equality with political inequality would remain a persistent theme in Western political thought. But the emergence of a sovereign state in which the contest among jurisdictions ceased to play a central role undoubtedly created, as we shall see, conditions for new conceptions of 'natural right'; and, in that respect, the rise of sovereign territorial states clearly had a bearing on the development of Western political theory. Yet the differences among the European states were no less decisive in shaping 'traditions of discourse'. If we look beyond the most formal characteristics of a centralized state, the 'material' conditions in the two cases identified by Skinner as the sources of 'modern' ideas of the state look very different. It is not unreasonable to identify those cases as, in one way or another, emblematic of the 'modern' state, in theory and in practice; and, largely for that reason, the chapters devoted here to England and France will be longer than the others. But, even if we ignore the fact that it was England more than France that first experienced a centralization of the state unencumbered by 'parcellized sovereignty', while French absolutism even at its height remained in constant tension with various competing jurisdictions, their patterns of political and economic development are strikingly divergent.

This is not to deny that France and England shared a common intellectual legacy and, indeed, important material roots traceable at least to imperial Rome, its mode of imperial rule and its system of property. Nor is it to deny that their national histories were always inextricably intertwined, by virtue of proximity, shifting territorial boundaries, war, trade, commercial rivalries, and even recurrent alliances. But the historical moment we are exploring here – the moment of rising territorial states and national economies – is precisely the period of diverging national histories, with their distinctive patterns of development.

As we shall see in what follows, the national differences we have already observed had fundamental implications for the development of political thought. When, for instance, French political theory, especially in the person of Jean Bodin, clearly and systematically articulated a 'modern' conception of state sovereignty, it was not because the French had already established one clear and undisputed centre of political authority but, on the contrary, because the centralizing power was still contending with competing jurisdictions. Bodin's political theory, in other words, reflected not the reality of undivided sovereignty in France but its absence. He was proposing his idea of a single, indivisible and absolute power in order to support the king's claims to authority over the nobility and other autonomous powers, at a time, during the Wars of Religion in the sixteenth century, when the monarchy was being challenged by rebellion and radical ideas about the right of resistance.

Those ideas of resistance were themselves deeply rooted in the persistent tension between the central state and the remnants of parcellized sovereignty. When the French *monarchomachs* insisted on the people's rights of resistance to the monarchy, the people they had in mind were not private citizens. They were corporate bodies, provincial aristocrats and local magistrates, who claimed a right of resistance in their capacity as office-holders. The main resistance tracts – which will be discussed in a subsequent chapter – were expressing the interests of local aristocracies and various corporate entities. When they invoked some kind of popular sovereignty, they did so as officers asserting their jurisdictional rights against the central state; and, when the absolutist monarchy invoked the concept of state sovereignty against them, it was professing to represent a more general interest, as opposed to the particularities of these fragmented jurisdictions. It claimed to be acting on behalf of a more universal corporation than the particularistic corporate bodies that were challenging its sovereignty. Even as late as the eighteenth century, when revolutionaries challenged the existing hierarchy of corporate power and privilege, they purported to act on behalf of the corporate 'nation'. The concept of equality that has figured so prominently in French political discourse and the revolutionary tradition owes much to the Third Estate's struggles over corporate privilege and its battle for access to office, 'careers open to talent'.

In England, where there was no such fundamental conflict of jurisdiction between the monarchy and ruling classes, there was no strategic need to assert the power of one against the other with a clear idea of indivisible sovereignty. In fact, the English tended to avoid the issue of sovereignty altogether (a thinker like Thomas Hobbes was one striking exception, and even he formulated an idea of sovereignty significantly different from the French). The idea of a 'mixed constitution' – anathema to Jean Bodin – conformed very nicely to English conditions and the interests of the ruling class. The partnership between Crown and Parliament had created a delicate balance which neither side was anxious to upset by claiming ultimate authority. Even when the conflicts between them came to a head, as the king threatened the partnership with Parliament, parliamentarians were very slow to invoke their own sovereignty as representatives of the people. To assert the sovereignty of Parliament against the king and on behalf of the people threatened to unleash more dangerous claims to popular sovereignty from the truly radical forces mobilized by the Revolution, without the protection of intermediate powers between Parliament and people. A degree of vagueness seemed prudent even among republican elements in Parliament.

The particular formation of the state, the distinctive relation between aristocracy and monarchy, the unity of Parliament and Crown, the evolution of a unified system of law on which the ruling class depended to sustain its property and power, meant that political conflict did not in general take the form of jurisdictional disputes among fragments of sovereignty. It also meant that corporate principles were weak. From early on, the relation between state and individual was not mediated by corporate entities, and political rights were vested in the individual rather than in corporate bodies.

In England, where the primary political relation was not among competing jurisdictions but between individual and state, the idea of individual rights was bound to have different implications than it did elsewhere in Europe. It is significant, as we shall see, that the first systematic discussion of the relation between individual rights, the rights of private individuals, and sovereign power was produced by an English theorist, Hobbes, though not in defence of individual rights against the state but in favour of absolute sovereignty. At the same time, any theory of resistance or popular sovereignty would, in that context, represent a greater challenge to the power of propertied classes than did the French resistance tracts. When such theories did emerge in England, they effected a revolution in political thought – as, for instance, when the Levellers in the English Civil War insisted that consent to government, on which freedom depends, must be given not only once in a single transfer of power but continuously, and by a multitude of individuals, the people outside Parliament, not by some corporate entity which claims to represent them.

The differences between England and France are visible, too, in conceptions of the relation between state and economy. We are accustomed to associating 'political economy', in the tradition of Adam Smith, with the development of 'commercial society' in its Anglo-Scottish mode. Yet the very first writer to use the term 'political economy' in the title of his work was a Frenchman, Antoine de Montchrétien. Already in the early seventeenth century, as we shall see in Chapter 6, he elaborated an idea of commerce as a means of harnessing private interests and passions to the public benefit, so that civic virtue was no longer necessary. In his *Traité de l'économie politique,* published in 1615, he insists that selfish passions and the appetite for gain, far from threatening the common good, can be its very foundation, without any reliance on virtue or benevolence. But his argument was critically different from what followed in Britain, and French arguments would continue to be different for a long time thereafter. French thinkers who, like Montchrétien, extolled the benefits of *le doux commerce* took for granted that the necessary condition for the positive effects of trade was a forceful monarchy to integrate and harmonize particular interests and transform private vices into public benefits. This assumption is rooted in the realities of absolutist France, a society in which there is still no integrated market or competitive capitalism, and where the polity is still fragmented by a welter of corporate entities and privileges. French thinkers were bound to look, as the English were not, for ways of dealing with this structural divisiveness when they reflected on the replacement of virtue by commerce.[16]

In the eighteenth century, the same assumptions are present in

---

16 The fact that monarchy is regarded as the necessary unifying principle should be enough to distinguish these views from modern conceptions of the state as simply a means of 'articulating' and 'aggregating' interests. It is true that the idea of private passions and 'vices' producing public benefits would emerge in a different form in the Netherlands, as we shall see in a later chapter, with roots in the philosophy of Spinoza and culminating in Bernard Mandeville's *Fable of the Bees*. While a Dutch thinker like Spinoza might still feel the need for political harmonization of private vices, in the context of the Dutch commercial republic, a republican form of government might seem more practicable than an absolutist monarchy. Yet this is not because Dutch republicans had in mind the 'invisible hand' of the market but largely, as will be suggested in the discussion of Spinoza in Chapter 5, because a republic can bind private greed to public office.

Montesquieu's views on monarchy. Unlike republican government, he tells us, monarchy has the advantage of making it possible to promote the common good with minimal virtue or self-sacrifice. Private interests can be the source of public benefits. But, while Montesquieu is less convinced than some of his contemporaries that commerce among nations need be a zero-sum game, this is not because he imagines that the common good will emerge naturally out of the interplay of private interests through an autonomous market mechanism. On the contrary, the monarchy must play that harmonizing role. Even the physiocrats, who most admired English agrarian capitalism and held it up as a model for France, shared classic French assumptions about the primary role of the state in harmonizing particular and corporate interests; and heavy traces of that view are still visible even in post-revolutionary France, in Napoleonic conceptions of the state.

The English – or, more precisely, the Anglo-Scottish – argument proceeds on the basis of different social and economic conditions. In the Anglo-Scottish version of *le doux commerce* in the eighteenth century, the burden of harmonizing private interests falls much more heavily on the market, on the discipline of competition in organizing production. The state, to be sure, plays a critical role in producing and maintaining the conditions for commercial development; but the purpose of the state is not to impose harmony on competing private interests. On the contrary, its role is to facilitate the operations of the market, which has that integration as its primary object.

What is critical, then, is not that commerce is presented as a substitute for civic virtue (more on this in a later chapter) but rather that commerce itself is conceived in new ways, in practice no less than in theory. We are now dealing with a competitive national market far more integrated than any other in Europe, and this market has a dynamic completely different from old forms of trade. The old forms of profit on alienation in transactions between separate markets really do look like a zero-sum game which inevitably leads to conflict. But the new dynamic of England's economy allows Adam Smith, for instance, to regard competition as itself an integrative force. It is precisely the discipline required to keep self-interested commercial classes in check.

The state undoubtedly plays a vital part in Smith's economy, above all to ensure that the market mechanism operates as it should – which seems to include, among other things, protection against employers combining to drive down wages. He also believes firmly in the importance of education for the lower classes. He does, to be sure, make debatable assumptions about the role of market mechanisms not only in advancing general prosperity but also in enhancing a more equitable distribution of wealth, which is, for him, a major reason for advocating free markets (in sharp contrast to our contemporary 'neoliberals', who may acknowledge that markets are more likely to increase inequality but regard that as a fruitful outcome). The freedom of the market that Smith has in mind requires intervention by the state to sustain it; and he does indeed believe that merchants lack the moral fibre or traditions of the landed classes, though concentrations of landed property represent a danger too. But the solution is not to find some kind of counter-weight to commerce. On the contrary, the solution must be sought in commerce itself. The market imperatives that come with a mature commercial society impose their own discipline on all the participants, and it is not the function of the state to counteract them. Intervention by the state is necessary to sustain the mechanisms of the market; but its purpose is not to suppress or to lessen but to intensify the imperatives of competition – against, for example, the monopolistic inclinations of merchants.

Smith's analysis of market mechanisms certainly owed much to the French and particularly to the physiocrat Quesnay (more in Chapter 6). But this debt makes even more striking the differences between the French and the Anglo-Scottish views on what is required to ensure the proper functioning of the 'invisible hand'. Both regard a stable social order as a necessary precondition of a prosperous economy, and for both this requires interventions by the state. But Smith not only takes for granted a new form of commerce, such as already exists in England, but a unitary state with a unitary representative, while Quesnay assumes the need for a politically constituted integrating force, a kind of 'legal despotism', to deal with the fragmented system of estates and corporate bodies; and this kind of state, according to physiocratic doctrine, is needed not only to sustain but to create a new form of economy, which exists in English agrarian capitalism but not in France.[17]

The different patterns of 'political economy' in English capitalism and French absolutism would continue to have implications in the realm of ideas, in what many historical narratives depict as the age of 'Enlightenment'. But, even while it has become fashionable to acknowledge national differences by speaking of 'Enlightenments' in an ever-proliferating plural, the very idea of 'Enlightenment(s)' has tended to obscure some critical divergences – which will be explored in the concluding chapter of this book.

A Social History of Political Thought

The purpose of this book is not to enlarge the canon or to argue for a more inclusive canonical literature that does justice to popular or democratic forces. It will confine itself largely to political thinkers who are most typically regarded as 'canonical', or who have had substantial influence on

---

17   For an important discussion of these points, see David McNally, *Political Economy and the Rise of Capitalism: A Reinterpretation* (Berkeley and Los Angeles: University of California Press, 1990), esp. pp. 121–9.

thinkers more generally included in the canon, particularly for their ideas on legitimate rule and domination. Like any other survey of this kind, this one will, if only for reasons of space, leave out or briefly summarize the ideas of thinkers who may, in their various ways, be no less important than are the major figures treated here at greater length. Even major philosophers like David Hume, whose work belongs to the philosophical canon but for whom political theory was a more marginal concern, will get short shrift. We shall not, in general, deal with theorists best known for their theories of relations among states, with the notable exception of Grotius, whose views on private property and public jurisdiction are especially germane to our main themes. The primary aim of this study is to illustrate our social–contextual approach, and how it differs from others, by applying it to major thinkers whose status in the canon of political thought has been accepted by convention.

It should already be clear that the 'social history' of political thought on offer in this book departs from other accounts of Western political theory in the 'early modern' period, not least because it is based on a historical narrative that questions the conventional story of modernity. It aims, among other things, to disentangle the disparate threads of the 'modern'. For example, it distinguishes 'bourgeois' from 'capitalist'; it seeks to detach the culture of 'reason', or what postmodernists call the 'Enlightenment project', from the development of capitalism; it suggests that there was not just one overarching historical trajectory but several 'transitions' in the Western European passage to 'modernity', which have shaped divergent traditions of political thought; and it puts in question some fairly conventional wisdom, but also recent scholarship, on what it means to speak of 'modern' states and 'modern' ways of thinking about politics.

To those interested in the arcana of the discipline, it will also be clear that this social history departs from other contextual approaches not only in substance but in form and method. Like other modes of 'contextualism', it requires us not only to decipher texts but also to situate them in their specific historical contexts. Yet it entails an idea of 'context' that differs from others, in particular the school of contextualism that, in the Anglo-American academy, has dominated the history of political thought and especially the study of the early modern period, the so-called Cambridge School.

Both the Cambridge approach and our social history start from the premise that, to understand the ideas of political thinkers, we must know something about the questions they are seeking to answer. Both approaches treat those questions as constituted by specific historical conditions. Yet, while both accept that thinkers are likely to respond not only with a cool intelligence but with a sense of urgency and often passion, neither form of contextualism assumes that ideas can be simply 'read off' from a thinker's situation within a given context. Great thinkers, indeed, are likely to be those who shed light on their historical setting by thinking at an unpredictable angle from it, often as uncongenial to their friends as to their enemies – such as Hobbes, an absolutist whose works were burnt by the monarchy. The Cambridge School would on the whole agree with our social history that even when thinkers offer idiosyncratic answers or seek to transcend the specificities of time and place, the questions confronting them are posed in specific historical forms. Where the two contextual approaches differ is in their conceptions of what form these questions take and how they are configured by the specificities of history.

For the Cambridge School, contexts are 'discourses', utterances or 'language situations'. Social relations and processes are visible only as either literary and theoretical conversations, or the discursive transactions of high politics. A Cambridge School historian like Skinner is, to be sure, concerned with what theorists were 'doing' and why, given the range of political vocabularies available to them, they chose specific languages and strategies of argumentation, in the specific political circumstances of their own time and place and often for very specific political purposes. But the social conditions in which words were deployed are deliberately excluded. The period covered by Skinner's history of political thought was marked by major social and economic developments that loomed very large in political theory and practice, yet he tells us virtually nothing about them. We learn little, if anything, about – for instance – relations between aristocracy and peasantry, about agriculture, land distribution and tenure or disputes over property rights, about urbanization, trade, commerce and the burgher class, or about social protest and conflict. John Pocock is generally more interested than is Skinner in the languages of civil society and political economy, not simply in the discourses of formal political theory; but his subject remains discourse and language. Social relations, if they are visible at all, appear in the form of conversations among literate elites.

The social history of political thought raises questions about how the political sphere itself is constituted by social processes, relations, conflicts and struggles outside the political space – producing, for instance, different patterns of state-formation in England and France and different traditions of political discourse, even while sharing common languages of politics. It raises questions about how social conflicts set the terms of political controversy – as, for example, in England, conflicts over property rights and even the very definition of property were playing themselves out between landlords and commoners before they reached debates in Parliament, philosophy or classical political economy.

It is not here simply a matter of attending to popular voices as distinct from, or in addition to, elite conversations. No one can deny that subordinate classes have tended to be voiceless in the historical record. To be sure, even when there remains no record of their discourse, if we are attentive we can detect their interactions with dominant classes in the great theoretical efforts devoted by their masters to justifying social and political hierarchies, and, of course, in theories of property. But the principal question is where we should look to discover the meanings and motivations of discourses, whether popular or dominant.

For the social history of political thought, it is not enough to track relations among thinkers, their utterances and texts; but nor is it enough to situate them in the historical context of very specific political episodes, such as the Engagement Controversy in which Hobbes may have sought to intervene (see below, p. 242) or the Exclusion Crisis, in which Locke was almost certainly engaged (see below, p. 256). There is no doubt that such historical moments may have far-reaching consequences in shaping political languages – as the revolutionary crisis of the Exclusion controversy shaped Locke's political ideas. But for the social history of political theory, the questions confronting political thinkers are framed not only at the level of philosophy, political economy or high politics but also by the social interactions outside the political arena and beyond the world of texts.

To identify these questions is likely to require greater attention to long-term historical processes of a kind the Cambridge approach eschews altogether. We might, for example, situate Locke not only in the context of the Exclusion Crisis but also in the context of a long-term process like 'the rise of capitalism'. This is not to enlist him as an advocate of the system we now know as capitalism, nor to attribute to him a kind of supernatural prescience about the eventual development of a mature industrial capitalism, nor even to credit him with anything like an idea of a 'capitalist' economy. The point is rather that a process of transformation in the property regime (the development of 'agrarian capitalism' discussed here in this chapter and in Chapter 7) was being contested in Locke's own time and place, and was generating conflicts over the definition of property. We are much more likely to discern the issues at stake if we observe them, as it were, in the process of becoming, as existing social forms are being challenged or displaced.

Whether we choose to call the new property regime 'agrarian capitalism' or something else altogether, we may wish to point out that it had some bearing on what came after, not least on the emergence of 'commercial society', which figures very prominently in Cambridge School accounts of eighteenth-century England. But even if we choose to abstract Locke's brief historical moment from any longer processes of social transformation, the least that can be said is that these social transformations generated conflicts over property in Locke's own time and place; and the issues at stake were very much the stuff of his ideas.

There are certainly moments when history intrudes with special urgency into the dialogue among texts or traditions of discourse, when long-term developments in social relations, property forms and state-formation episodically erupt into specific political–ideological controversies that

meet the requirements of the Cambridge School; and it is certainly true
that political theory tends to flourish at times like this. But it is not enough
to identify those moments; and we cannot get the measure of a thinker like
John Locke if we fail to acknowledge the questions that were posed to him
not just by this or that political episode but by larger social transformations and structural tensions, which made themselves felt beneath the
surface of high politics.

Without in any way dismissing the importance of specific political
moments in shaping ideas (which are often admirably covered by exponents
of the Cambridge School), this book, and the social history of political
theory it offers, will place more emphasis on the kinds of social contexts
and historical processes commonly overlooked, if not explicitly discounted,
by other modes of 'contextualization'. Consideration of what might be
called deep structural contexts and long-term social transformations does
not in the least imply a neglect of historical specificities, including national
differences. On the contrary, we shall in the following chapters be keenly
attentive to such differences; and the chapters will be organized along these
lines, exploring certain historical landmarks in the development of Western
political thought in their varied political and social contexts. If anything,
the social history of political theory is more attuned to historical specificities than is a mode of contextualization devoted to 'language situations' in
which common vocabularies may disguise important historical differences.
Despite the Cambridge School's insistence on the specificity of every historical moment, its conception of linguistic contexts and their detachment from
social conditions occludes all kinds of historical specificities, the differences
of meaning that even common languages may have in different social
contexts, not only giving different answers but posing different questions.

As we track the various Western traditions of discourse in the early
modern period, it is nonetheless important to keep in mind that, for all the
variations, the tension between two sources of power – the state and private
property – and the complex three-way relations between state, property and
the producing classes, had clear implications for the development of political thought throughout Western Europe and its colonial dependencies. If
there is in this book a single overarching theme, it has to do with certain
distinctive transformations in the relation between private property and
public power that took place in our period. Earlier in this chapter, and at
greater length in *Citizens to Lords*, the first volume of this social history, we
traced the development of the relation between property and state from
classical antiquity to 'feudal' society and took note of the very particular
effects of Roman property, the privatization of public authority with the
devolution of public functions to local lords and other autonomous powers.
This volume deals with a period when fragmented sovereignty was giving
way to more centralized states, and new tensions emerged between property

and state. It is also a period in which, with the advent of capitalism, property and political power, *dominium* and *imperium*, became structurally disentangled in historically unprecedented ways.

In what follows we shall be especially attentive to the distinctive tensions between private property and public power in Western Europe. We shall also emphasize their national divergences. But for now, and as a general rule, we can say that appropriating classes, even when they were competing with the state for access to surpluses produced in the main by peasants, also relied on the state to maintain order, conditions for appropriation and control over the producing classes whose labour sustained and enriched them; yet they also found the state a burdensome nuisance, as a threat to their property or as a competitor for the wealth derived from subject labour. Propertied classes, in other words, were always fighting on two fronts; and the Western canon of political thought has always reflected this three-way relation.

Challenges to authority have come from two directions. Subordinate classes have resisted oppression by their overlords. But overlords themselves, while always looking over their shoulders for threats from their subordinates, have sought to protect their autonomy, their 'liberties', privileges, jurisdictions and properties, against intrusions from the state. This has meant that, even while the canon has generally been the work of ruling classes or their clients, and even when social and political hierarchies have been at their most rigid, there has been a continuous and vigorous tradition of interrogating the most basic principles of authority, legitimacy and the obligation to obey.

The canon of Western political thought has owed much of its vigour to the fact that the discourse of liberty has belonged to ruling classes asserting their mastery, no less than to those resisting oppression by their masters. One objective of examining the canon in its social context is to suggest that even – or especially – now that capitalism has decisively transformed relations between property and power, our conceptions of freedom, equality, rights and legitimate government are constrained by their roots in the defence of ruling-class power and privilege; and even ideas of democracy have been distorted by this complicated legacy.

2

THE RENAISSANCE CITY-STATE

It has been said that 'one of the most essential factors separating Renaissance from later philosophy [is] its fully international character, based on the use of Latin as an almost universal language of scholarship', not divided by modern linguistic or national boundaries.[1] Yet this period is precisely the age in which territorial states, defined by national boundaries, were becoming the dominant political force in Western Europe. It is certainly true that these states were not the homeland of the cultural phenomenon called by convention the Renaissance (a convention often questioned by historians these days); but this international culture was born in an even more particularistic setting, the Italian city-states most fiercely attached to their local autonomy.

The poet and scholar Petrarch, who, for his recovery of ancient classics and his Latin writings, is often called the 'father of humanism', or even of the Renaissance itself, is also, by virtue of his Italian poetry, considered one of the principal founders of a national language and literature. His revival of antiquity appealed not only to philosophers but to princes, emperors and popes who were keen to invoke Italy's glorious past for their own political purposes. 'Humanism' would become the discourse of thinkers who have come to be called 'civic humanists', in defence of civic liberty and of their city-states' autonomy. Yet the Renaissance would flourish as the city-states were in decline, and civic humanism would reach its pinnacle when the political independence and economic prosperity of the major city-states were most severely threatened by a new world order of 'national' states.

Whether we call this period the 'Renaissance' or something else, the dichotomy of 'ancient' and 'modern' cannot help us very much to understand these paradoxes. It is far more trouble than it is worth to determine whether civic humanism – if it exists at all as a distinct and coherent body

---

1 *Cambridge History of Renaissance Philosophy,* eds C.B. Schmidt et al. (Cambridge: Cambridge University Press, 1988), p. 2. This insight, or at least full justice to it, is credited to the German philosopher and intellectual historian Ernst Cassirer.

of thought (about which more in a moment) – partakes of the ancient because it resists the trend towards large territorial or national states and because it adopts an ancient Greco-Roman discourse, or whether it is more modern than ancient because it supports the principles of civic liberty against monarchical or feudal rule. Nor, for that matter, is it particularly useful to describe this cultural form as transitional, or even as a synthesis of contradictions. We can, and clearly should, take note of the discourses available to thinkers; but we can better understand the particular ways in which political theorists chose to exploit them not by locating them along some abstract continuum from ancient to modern but by situating them in very specific historical processes.

Renaissance City States

The medieval city-states of northern Italy (which were discussed in the first volume of this history) represented an exception to the Western feudal model of seigneurial domination. Landed aristocracies certainly existed and in some city-states continued to play a prominent role; but urban concentrations which had survived the collapse of the Roman Empire, together with landholding patterns that preserved a free peasantry in contrast to the serfdom that had emerged elsewhere, produced a distinctive configuration: more or less autonomous city-states, governed by urban elites, often – as in the case of Florence – exercising what has been described as a collective lordship over the surrounding countryside, the *contado*. Some developed into prosperous commercial centres, serving a fragmented feudal Europe as trading links, providing goods to landed aristocracies and offering financial services to kings and popes.

But, if these city-states departed from seigneurial patterns of lordship, they had their own forms of parcellized sovereignty. The civic communes were always fairly loose associations of patrician families, factions, parties and corporate entities with their own liberties, organizations, jurisdictions and powers. In the Middle Ages, they were also battlegrounds for larger temporal authorities. In particular, they were caught up in struggles between the papacy and the Holy Roman Empire, which conducted their rivalries through the medium of factions within the civic commune – most notably, the infamous battles between Guelf (papal) and Ghibelline (imperial) factions, which typically, though not always, coincided with divisions between merchant classes and landed *signori*. These self-governing cities were, on the whole, oligarchies; and even when more effective republican governments came to power, they never succeeded in overcoming their internal fragmentation. Still later, even the most centralized Renaissance kingdoms continued to be divided by party, privilege and competing jurisdictions. For all the talk of civic humanism, the civic order never marked out a clearly defined public sphere detached from private corporate powers of various kinds.

Nor did the commercial activities of the civic communes mark a significant departure from feudal economic patterns. Their commercial success depended not, in the capitalist manner, on cost-effective production and enhanced labour productivity, in a market driven by price competition, but rather on 'extra-economic' factors, that is to say, factors external to the 'economic' transactions of production and exchange: not just the quality of goods but political power, monopoly privileges, sophisticated financial techniques, and military force. In external trade, which was the most lucrative economic activity for a major commercial centre like Venice, success clearly depended on military power and a symbiotic connection between commerce and war. Venice's command of east–west trade required control of eastern Mediterranean sea routes, no less than rivers and mountain passes on the Italian mainland. To maintain that control, the Venetians developed a powerful military force, which itself became a marketable commodity, as Venice offered military aid to other powers – notably the Byzantine Empire – in exchange for commercial privileges and rights to trading posts.[2]

In general, economic rivalries took the form of power struggles among merchants, cities or states over direct control of markets; and city-states were constantly at war with one another. The major centres such as Florence and Venice consolidated their commercial dominance by forcibly incorporating their less powerful neighbours into larger city-states. It is certainly true that Venice, and even more Florence, traded in commodities produced in their own cities, such as Florentine textiles; and great merchant dynasties did invest in production. But substantial wealth and power depended on command of trading networks, which in turn depended not simply on the quality or price of goods produced at home but on superiority in controlling and negotiating markets, to say nothing of dynastic connections, patronage, personal networks among patrician families, and leading positions in ruling oligarchies.

Even where, as in Florence, wealth was heavily invested in production, it was no less dependent on 'extra-economic' factors, not least on office in the city-state's administration. The career of the Medici speaks volumes: they began in the wool trade, then moved on to achieve their greatest wealth, with the help of family connections and personal networks among the Florentine patriciate, not as producers but as bankers to European princes and popes. Three Medici themselves became popes. The dynasty finally reached the summit of its ambition as effectively rulers of the Florentine republic, leaving the wool trade far behind.

---

2 For more on these points, see Ellen Meiksins Wood, *Empire of Capital* (London: Verso, 2005), pp. 54–61.

In Renaissance Florence, in other words, political and economic power were inextricably connected in the feudal manner; and this was true not only for city elites. The guilds that organized the wool trade and other occupations were principal players not only in the economic sphere, protecting the interests of their members and sheltering them from competition, but also in the political domain. The guilds themselves had autonomous corporate powers, governed by charters and systems of rules that had the force of law. It may even be misleading to speak of *citizenship* in the republic, since active membership in the civic community did not reside in individuals but in these corporate entities.

Internal conflicts in the city-states were shaped by this unity of political and economic power. Economic rivalries among merchant families could never simply take the form of competition in the marketplace but were always political rivalries at the same time. The pursuit of high office and the dominance of any family depended on its standing in a complex network of patrons and clients, inevitably embroiled in factional struggles, often with support from foreign powers. It has even been suggested that this helps to explain the remarkable cultural richness of these city-states and their patronage of the arts, creating not only great wealth but a climate of competitive achievement and conspicuous consumption – especially in times and places where, as in the Florentine republic, artisanal guilds played a major political role.

In Venice, which remained an oligarchy even when ostensibly ruled by one man, the Doge, it was largely a matter of rivalry among noble families. In Florence, other strains and conflicts were also at work. Patrician family connections or membership in major guilds afforded the only consistent access to the political sphere; and political battles throughout the history of Florence often revolved around the political standing of lesser guilds. There were constant struggles over access to the political domain among *signori,* rich merchants and guildsmen, as well as between major and lesser guilds. Outside the guilds, the *popolo minuto,* the 'little people' or labouring classes, including large numbers of skilled and unskilled workers in the wool trade, were completely excluded from the political sphere, except for one brief democratic moment, the Revolt of the Ciompi in 1378, one of the most famous incidents in Florentine history. The *ciompi* rebels briefly seized control of the government and then, with support from some members of the minor guilds, obtained guild privileges, which meant access to the political domain – only to lose it soon thereafter when the *popolo grasso,* their wealthy 'fat' compatriots, now with the help of the minor guilds, deprived them of guild and political privileges.

This episode would long remain, for better or worse, a vivid memory in the consciousness of the republic, not least for Machiavelli; and it illustrates most dramatically the distinctiveness of the civic domain in the Italian city-states. When, just three years later, the English peasant revolt erupted, its leader, Wat Tyler, is reported to have said, 'No lord should have lordship save civilly', and all men should be equal but the king. He was advocating not the peasant's access to the civic domain but rather certain rights of property against the claims of lords and, perhaps, access to common-law courts to protect those property rights. The contrasts between this English case and the Revolt of the Ciompi are striking. For English peasants the issue is lordship, not citizenship; but, while the Italian case may seem in this respect less 'feudal', it is distinctive not because it presages some modern principle of individual autonomy and citizenship. The issue for the *ciompi*, no less than for the English peasantry, is the exclusive extra-economic powers and privileges, or 'politically constituted property', of their superiors. We might even be tempted to say that the English assertion of property rights against the claims of lordship have more in common with modern conceptions of citizenship than do the demands of Florentine labouring classes for a share in corporate privileges.

What singles out the Italian case, and what helps to explain the particularities of Renaissance Italian political thought, is that 'politically constituted property' is indeed political – that is to say, the extra-economic rights and privileges upon which economic power rests derive from the civic community, depending not on individual powers of lordship but on membership in the civic corporation. Social conflicts play themselves out on the civic terrain, not only in open struggle or organized rebellion but in the daily transactions of civic life, in an urban setting where all contenders, as individuals and as collective entities, are always face to face as citizens or aspirants to civic status. The inextricable connection between economic power and 'extra-economic' force means that economic rivalries, or social conflicts over property and inequalities of wealth, are inseparably struggles over civic power, always on the brink of open war.

'Civic Humanism' and Machiavelli

This very particular configuration of the civic domain produced distinctive traditions of political ideas. The designation 'civic humanism' to describe the main currents has become conventional among many historians of political thought. For the German historian Hans Baron, who coined the phrase, 'civic humanism' was a specifically Florentine conjunction of cultural humanism, with its educational ambitions, and the city republic's defence of civic liberty against imperial domination. This, in his view, marked a decisive break from medieval religion and feudal hierarchy, towards modern ideals of political liberty, economic progress, secularism and intellectual creativity. Although he would, over several decades, develop and modify his views on civic humanism – and would later be more inclined than he was at first to include Machiavelli in that tradition – his original intention in identifying this historic rupture was not only historiographical but also political. He was seeking to promote a conception of modernity as the advance of human autonomy, at a time when, in Weimar Germany, such ideas were under threat from anti-democratic strains of German nationalism.

Baron's idea would later find its way into the anglophone academy, adapted to various Anglo-American 'republican' traditions (the most notable example being John Pocock's 'Machiavellian moment'). Recent scholarship has, nonetheless, tended to correct Baron's exaggeration of the rupture between medieval and Renaissance political thought. More attention has been given to the continuities between scholasticism and humanism, indeed their coexistence and revival in the later Renaissance. Yet these corrections have failed to dispel the notion that 'republican' political theory, especially in its humanist mode, somehow points us towards the modern world. We shall in subsequent chapters raise questions about the very idea of 'republicanism', especially in its application to seventeenth-century English thinkers; but, for the moment, it is enough to say that, even if we acknowledge the existence of something like a 'civic humanist' tradition, it is profoundly misleading to characterize the political ideas of the Italian Renaissance – and of Machiavelli in particular – as a breakthrough to modernity. The very characteristics that give a 'modern' appearance to ideas like Machiavelli's are rooted in a dying political form that would soon give way to 'modern' states. These states would generate their own political predicaments, together with modes of discourse designed to confront them in ways that 'civic humanist' or 'republican' ideas were unable to do.

There are, to be sure, significant differences between Machiavelli and, say, Marsilius of Padua two centuries before.[3] These differences can even be characterized, without too much exaggeration, as having something to do with the contrasts between scholasticism and humanism. But much depends on whether we define those differences as products of transformations in language and discourse or place our emphasis on social relations and historical processes. It may be true that civic humanism had introduced a new language of politics, quite different from that of medieval scholasticism. It may even be true that Machiavelli belongs to the humanist tradition in a way that Marsilius did not. Yet both political thinkers were deeply rooted in the Italian city-state; and the differences between them have as much to do with changes in the circumstances of the city-states as they do with transformations in discourse.

The differences between Marsilius and Machiavelli also have to do with their differing relations to the social conflicts of their day. Marsilius was preoccupied not with the survival or autonomy of city-states but the

---

3   Marsilius of Padua is discussed at greater length in *Citizens to Lords*, pp. 218–25.

factional struggles between papal and imperial parties. It can even be argued (as was done in the first volume of this study) that his defence of imperial power was driven less by fear of the papacy and its threats to civil peace than by his support for great aristocratic families like the Visconti of Milan and the della Scalas of Verona, who had strong imperial (Ghibelline) loyalties (as was typical among the landed nobility) and in whose service Marsilius worked. This allegiance to signorial power is masked by interpretations of Marsilius's doctrine that treat him as a forerunner of modern republicanism, which also obscure the immediate issues confronting this late medieval thinker.

For Marsilius the problem, in the medieval manner, was a complex network of competing jurisdictions. When he outlined his idea of a single unitary jurisdiction, the civic corporation, he was certainly departing from the medieval norm of parcellized sovereignty; but he was by that means quite consciously supporting one claim to temporal authority against another, not so much the civic commune against all other jurisdictions but the Empire against the papacy, and Ghibelline *signori* against their civic rivals. He showed no concern for the threat to civic unity and jurisdiction posed by the feudal powers of the landed nobility, while his notion of a single unitary civic corporation represented a clear challenge to autonomous guilds and their anti-signorial powers. His notion of one undivided civic corporation simply trumped the claims of lesser corporate bodies.

Machiavelli's Florence presented different problems, and his responses to them were shaped by different allegiances, perhaps more truly republican and certainly less inclined to the interests of the *signori*. The very survival of the city-state as anything like an autonomous entity was indeed at stake; and the immediate challenge was coming not from various fragmented jurisdictions, or from struggles between papal and imperial authorities, or between the civic factions they sustained, but from increasingly centralized and expanding states. The most powerful external forces were now rising territorial monarchies like France and Spain; and internal disorders in Florence were shaped by this new political reality.

The Italian city-states had already suffered from the general European crises, famine and plague of the fourteenth century. But even in good times their prosperity and success had depended on the fragmented governance of European feudalism and could not long survive the rise of strong territorial states. In constant rivalry and often open war with one another, the Italians were especially vulnerable to the territorial ambitions of the European monarchies. The role of commercial centres such as Venice and Florence as indispensable trading links in feudal Europe declined as feudal fragmentation gave way to centralized state powers, sustained by military superiority and the commercial advantages of imperial expansion.

By the fifteenth century, Venice and Florence stood almost alone as independent city-states. The Ottoman Empire deprived Venice of its dominance in east–west trade, capturing Constantinople in 1453, while European monarchies challenged both the political independence and the economic prosperity of the remaining city-states. Portugal extended its commercial reach to India, Spain gained access to the wealth of the New World, and France invaded Italy in 1494. Economic stagnation, social unrest and political upheaval in the city republics were immensely aggravated by years of war following the French invasion, as France, Spain, and the Holy Roman Empire battled for control of Italian territory – even while culture flourished in the city-states at the very moment of decline, when wealthy patrons of the arts, now more rentiers than entrepreneurs, engaged in ever more passionate conspicuous consumption.

It was the military disasters facing Italy, in 1494, and the political instability associated with them, that more than anything else concentrated the minds of Italian political thinkers, particularly in Florence. They were forced to reflect not only on the conditions of civic success and decline but also on the fundamental human traits that encouraged or impeded them. Niccolò Machiavelli's generation was formed in this context, and its shadow looms over everything he wrote. He was born in 1469, the son of a distinguished lawyer, at a time when republican government had given way to Medici rule. Although of moderate means, his family seems to have belonged to a long line of Florentine notables. Machiavelli, who received a classic humanist education, began his career of public service as a clerk in 1494, the very year of the French invasion and the expulsion of the Medici from Florence, and would go on to serve the restored Florentine republic in various civil, diplomatic and military functions from 1498 to 1512.

When the Medici returned, Machiavelli was thrown out of office. In 1513, accused of conspiracy against the Medici, he was imprisoned and tortured. On his release, expelled from the centre of power, he retreated to the countryside outside Florence, where, as he would famously write in a wistful letter to his friend Vettori, he whiled away the time in idle rural pursuits all day and

> When evening comes I return home and go into my study, and at the door I take off my daytime dress covered in mud and dirt, and put on royal and curial robes; and then decently attired I enter the courts of the ancients, where affectionately greeted by them, I partake of that food which is mine alone and for which I was born; where I am not ashamed to talk with them and inquire the reasons of their actions; and they out of their human kindness answer me, and for four hours at a stretch I feel no worry of any kind; I forget all my troubles, I am not afraid of poverty or of death. I give myself up entirely to them. And because Dante says that understanding

does not constitute knowledge unless it is retained in the memory, I have written down what I have learned from their conversation and composed a short work *de Principatibus*[4]

And so he produced his most famous work, *The Prince,* though it was published only later, in 1532. His advice to princes has been variously described – for instance, as an effort to ingratiate himself with the Medici, in an attempt to revive his career; or even as a coded message to opponents of the Medici, and others like them, exposing their methods of obtaining and retaining power. Whatever his intentions, Machiavelli remained confined to his rural retreat, where he also wrote the *Discourses,* which more clearly expressed his republican convictions. The Medici would eventually call again on his services, but his later career was less notable for his official duties than for his work in other fields, such as his great *History of Florence* and his play *La Mandragola.* He died in 1527.

The rising monarchical states, and the French monarchy in particular, would figure prominently in the formation of Machiavelli's political thought. He was sent several times on diplomatic missions to the court of Louis XII to enlist the aid of France in various battles on Italian territory, not least the rivalry between Florence and Pisa, or to ensure that Florence would not be implicated in territorial wars among the European monarchies. His early missions inspired a growing conviction that Florence should free itself of dependence on foreign powers by mobilizing its own citizen army, in sharp contrast to the Italian tradition of mercenary soldiers. Machiavelli supervised the formation of the Florentine army in the restored republic, which won a famous victory against Pisa in 1509; and a strong commitment to citizen militias would lie at the heart of his political thought. When Spain supported the Medici in their efforts to recover their power in Florence, the republic turned for help again to France, to no avail – with dramatic consequences for Machiavelli's career. Whatever else he may have intended when he wrote *The Prince,* one bitter inspiration may have been Louis XII's betrayal of the Florentine republic. Machiavelli would invoke the example of the French king as a primary lesson to princes not for his successes so much as for his failures, which, in Machiavelli's eyes, had brought such tragedy to Italy.

European territorial monarchies, then, would always be in Machiavelli's line of sight as he elaborated his political ideas. In the conclusion to *The Prince,* with its passionate call for the liberation of Italy from the 'barbarians', his main target is patently obvious. Yet it would be a mistake to interpret this call for a strong and united Italian defence against expanding

---

4   Quoted in Roberto Ridolfi, *The Life of Niccolò Machiavelli* (London: Routledge & Kegan Paul, 1963), p. 152.

territorial states as a demand for the unification of Italy – or even its north-central regions – into a 'modern' nation state like France. These developing territorial states were already becoming the dominant force in Europe, but for Machiavelli they represented not so much models to be emulated as external threats to be resisted. He does, to be sure, cite France as the best monarchy, for its lawfulness and apparently for its suppression of the nobility. But it cannot be said that he sheds much light on the nature of the rising monarchies. He can speak of the French king in terms hardly different from those he uses to describe the infamous Cesare Borgia. Machiavelli remained rooted in the city-state of Florence. Although he certainly shared his city's expansionist ambitions and would have welcomed an extension of Florentine rule over its neighbours, of the kind the republic had enjoyed in its more prosperous days, he retained a firm commitment to the city-republic. Visible even in *The Prince*, this is the very essence of the *Discourses*.

Machiavelli was deeply rooted in the civic corporation; and the very particular force of his 'modern' approach to political 'science' derives from his attachment to the independent city-state at a very specific historical moment. Conditions were very different from what they had been in Italian city-states when his great predecessor, Marsilius of Padua, devised his theory of the civic corporation. It is the threat to the very survival of the city-state that gives Machiavelli's political thought its particular edge. Renaissance conceptions of human autonomy and civic liberty may seem to presage modernity even while reviving ancient ideas; but the 'modern' sensibility attributed to Machiavelli derives from a particularly archaic feature of the Italian city-state, the characteristic blend of civic and military values that sustained it.

In Machiavelli's political works, as distinct from his history of Florence, there is no evidence that the context in which he was writing was one of the great commercial centres of Europe. Commercial values are nowhere visible, and commercial activity barely figures at all. Yet the spirit of his work is very much the spirit of the Italian commercial city, the city-republic in which a commercial economy existed under a highly militarized urban rule, armed to withstand external threats, to dominate the *contado,* to defeat commercial rivals and extend the city-state's commercial supremacy, in what might be called an urban and commercial feudalism.

Political and economic power, as we have already observed, were inextricably conjoined in the commercial republics, which in this respect had more in common with medieval social forms than with modern capitalism. Governed by collectives of urban elites, whose political and economic rivalries were never far from violent struggle, these cities relied on armed force not only to dominate their neighbouring territories but to defeat commercial rivals and expand their own supremacy in trade. Even conflicts between rich and poor, or between the *popolo minuto* and *popolo grasso*, had the character of power struggles always on the verge of violence. In the late fifteenth century, the immediate threats from foreign powers, which also exacerbated internal conflicts, added a particular urgency to military questions. In these circumstances, Machiavelli was not alone to see the civic domain in military terms.

It was not unusual to ascribe the success of commercial republics to the warrior mentality of urban elites, nor to blame commercial decline on a loss of martial spirit. Republicans who decried the corruptions of Medici rule were likely to share the view of Machiavelli's friend and critic Francesco Guicciardini, that 'the Medici family, like all narrow regimes, always tried to prevent arms being possessed by the citizens and to extinguish all their virility. For this reason we have become very effeminate, and we also lack the courageousness of our forefathers.'[5] This assessment might be shared by all kinds of republicans, whether they subscribed to a less restrictive republican citizenry, a *governo largo*, as Machiavelli did, or, like Guicciardini, to a *governo stretto*, a republic in which the aristocracy played a more important role. It may even be possible to say that a certain martial spirit, as much as any other quality, sets civic humanism apart from scholastic philosophy.

The humanists are noted above all else for reviving the literature of classical antiquity, both Greek and Latin; but in civic humanism there is no mistaking an inclination towards Rome. The novelties of humanistic discourse, in contrast to the scholastic tradition, are akin to the Roman departures from Greek philosophy, the characteristically Roman interest in the active life, in rhetoric and ethics for its own sake, less systematically grounded in theories of the cosmos, metaphysics or psychology. If Aristotle was the prophet of scholasticism, in civic humanist discourse he was displaced, or at least supplemented, by Cicero, whom Petrarch called 'the great genius' of antiquity. Aristotle may have been no less attached to the life of the polis than to the life of the mind; but Cicero, the consummate politician and orator, spoke more directly to the spirit of republican activism. It is Cicero who was likely to be invoked to counter Christian, and especially Augustinian, fatalism about the possibilities of human excellence and action in attaining a good life in this world; and it is Cicero who guided republican views on the education needed to achieve that excellence, especially the skills of rhetoric so vital to the active public life.

But the Roman example meant something else, too. When Aristotle spelled out his classic characterization of man as a political animal, and his theory of the polis as the terrain of human excellence, he was not concerned to defend the city-state from external threats to its very survival. The polis,

---

5 Francesco Guicciardini, *Dialogue on the Government of Florence*, ed. Alison Brown (Cambridge: Cambridge University Press, 1994), p. 34.

after the Macedonian conquest, was already effectively dead as an independent political form. But the philosopher embraced, and even served, the
Macedonian hegemony; and he envisioned a new life for the polis under
imperial rule, in keeping with Alexander's distinctive mode of imperial
governance, through the medium of local aristocracies in ostensibly self-
governing municipalities. Macedonian hegemony had the added advantage,
for Aristotle, of supplanting radical Athenian democracy, enhancing the
power of the aristocracy against unbridled rule by the demos. This delicate
balance of class power required the suppression of social strife, especially
the conflicts between rich and poor, the philosopher's main practical
concern. The ideal Athenian citizen, then, governed by Macedonian agents
under the watchful eye of imperial garrisons, was not a man of struggle or
of military virtues.

The Roman case could hardly be more different. The republic was itself
an imperial power, whose conquests had created a huge territorial empire
with what would become the largest military force the world had ever
known. While Roman thinkers such as Cicero were no less committed than
Aristotle to a 'mixed' constitution in which the common people were subordinate to aristocracy, in Cicero's Rome the civic culture was at heart a
military ethic. Against the background of the threat to Florentine autonomy, it was this above all that spoke to Machiavelli, who took the civic
humanist idea of 'virility', or *virtù*, to the limits of its martial spirit.

The Prince

In his most famous, not to say notorious, work, *The Prince*, Machiavelli lays
out his 'Machiavellian' challenge to any conception of political power that
invokes moral principles to distinguish between legitimate and illegitimate
uses of power. There is, evidently, no such thing as rightful authority, and
power is to be maintained by any means necessary. How far Machiavelli
meant to push this principle remains a matter of dispute. Whatever his
motivations, whether he was seeking the approval of the Medici or was
simply driven by a bitter sense of irony in his exile from politics, commentators who regard him as a 'realist' are no doubt closer to the truth than those
who treat him as the emblematic advocate of political evil. There is, at any
rate, no mistaking the differences between *The Prince* and the *Discourses on
the Ten Books of Titus Livy*, which almost certainly expresses Machiavelli's
own disposition more precisely, displaying a preference for republican
government that requires him to make the kinds of judgments about good
government that he refuses in *The Prince*.

Much has been written about Machiavelli's relation to, and divergences
from, the civic humanist tradition; and, more specifically, about where to
situate *The Prince* within a genre familiar to his contemporaries: humanist

THE RENAISSANCE CITY-STATE

advice-books to princes. For Machiavelli, as for other writers in the genre, writes Quentin Skinner, 'the prince's basic aim, we learn in a phrase that echoes through *Il Principe,* must be *mantenere lo stato*, to maintain his power and existing frame of government. As well as keeping the peace, however, a true prince must at the same time seek "to establish such a form of government as will bring honour to himself and benefit the whole body of his subjects"'.[6]

Where Machiavelli significantly and famously departs from other humanists, as Skinner observes in his account of what it means to *mantenere lo stato*, is in his insistence that the willingness to use force is essential to good princely government, in contrast to the conventional humanist distinction between *virtus* or manliness, and *vis,* that is, brute force, and in his dissent from humanist accounts of princely virtues, which require both the highest standards of personal morality and a strict adherence to principles of justice.[7] But this departure may have less to do with differing views about how best to maintain what Skinner calls 'the existing frame of government' than with Machiavelli's concentration on external military threats, which puts war at the centre of his doctrine.

What Machiavelli means when he speaks – as he so often does – of *lo stato* remains a subject of scholarly debate. Yet again, the issue turns on whether he has in mind a 'modern' concept of the state as an impersonal legal and political order, or a pre-modern idea of political authority as a personal possession or *dominium*, or something in between and 'transitional'. There is still much of the pre-modern personal in Machiavelli's *stato*, with its emphasis on the personal power and honour of the prince. But if there is also an element of the impersonal, it may have less to do with a 'modern' conception of the state than with Machiavelli's military preoccupations and the threats that loom from without.

In *The Prince* Machiavelli tells us that

> A prince ought to have no other aim or thought, nor select anything else for his study, than war and its rules and discipline . . . there is nothing proportionate between the armed and the unarmed; and it is not reasonable that he who is armed should yield obedience willingly to him who is unarmed, or that the unarmed man should be secure among armed servants . . . He ought never, therefore, to have out of his thoughts this subject of war, and in peace he should addict himself more to its exercise than in war. (XIV)

---

6 Quentin Skinner, "Political Philosophy," in *Cambridge History of Renaissance Philosophy*, p. 431.

7 *Ibid.,* pp. 432–3.

Machiavelli's military model goes beyond the art of war. In *The Prince* he not only identifies war as the prince's main concern. His conceptions of leadership, political morality, and the conditions for sustaining a successful civic order are at bottom the conditions of a successful military power. Ideally, in his view, this is best achieved by a difficult balance between ruthless leadership and popular support, a capacity for cruelty and frequent departures from conventional morality, combined with an ability to mobilize the loyalties of the rank and file. The fact that Machiavelli has no use for a traditional military aristocracy and that his ideal military organization is a citizens' militia makes the conditions of success even more exacting – and, as becomes clearer in the *Discourses,* at this point his views on military success become inseparable from his republicanism.

Machiavelli's views on religion are also a subject of controversy, not least because, especially in the *Discourses*, he suggests that conventional Christianity has had the effect of weakening the manly vigour, the *virtù*, required for the active civic life. Yet his attitude has much in common with that of other humanists in his challenge not to Christian faith in general but to scholastic Christian fatalism, which requires submission to the blind power of fate and fortune and views the frivolous goods of this world – wealth, power, honour, fame and glory – as useless and unworthy of pursuit. Again like other humanists, he challenges these beliefs not by denying that much of human life is determined by circumstances beyond our control – the dictates of *fortuna* – but by emphasizing the scope of human action within the limits imposed on us by fate or fortune or God's will. Fortuna can be a friend to the man of *virtù*, instead of a pitiless enemy beyond the reach of human capacities and action. Every civic order will, to be sure, inevitably decline; and then a new order will have to be founded, which will make even greater demands on *virtù*. On this score, too, Machiavelli is not so distant from other humanists. Where he departs from humanist conventions is in his insistence that *virtù* may run counter to conventional morality; that political stability is possible despite – or even because of – humanity's most stubborn defects; and that men of *virtù* must often commit acts of violence, especially in the foundation of new states.

Machiavelli's views on the conditions for the creation and maintenance of a successful civic order depend, of course, on certain convictions about the possibilities available to human action; and his military principles are supported by more fundamental assumptions about history and human nature. He never precisely spells out his conception of human nature, though he certainly assumes the worst by emphasizing the insatiable desires of human beings, their short-sightedness and envy, even their general untrustworthiness. But the important point for him is that, because human nature remains essentially immutable, we can learn from historical experience, imitating successful actions while avoiding those that have failed. Human beings can adapt to varying circumstances. They can indeed, up to a point, shape those circumstances and, in so doing, shape themselves; and the very qualities that seem to militate against stability and social order can be channelled to positive ends.

Machiavelli's military model of political order, then, encompasses his most familiar 'Machiavellian' strictures on the necessity of force and violence in creating and sustaining the body politic; the importance of fear in the maintenance of leadership (it is best, of course, for a leader to be both loved and feared, but if he has to choose, fear must prevail); the need for ruthless treatment of one's adversaries, even if that means violating the most cherished principles of conventional morality; and so on.

The opposition of the armed and the unarmed lies at the very heart of Machiavelli's political theory. In *The Prince*, one of his principal criticisms is levelled against a man who was also one of the most famous leaders of the Florentine republic, Girolamo Savonarola. A Dominican friar, preacher and prophet, Savonarola led Florence when the Medici were expelled in 1494; but, says Machiavelli, he was an 'unarmed prophet', in sharp contrast to others who had founded a new order but who, unlike the prophet unarmed, were able to maintain their positions: 'armed prophets' such as Moses or leaders like Cyrus, Theseus and Romulus. The whole of Machiavelli's political theory is in many ways directed at the failings of the unarmed prophet.

Savonarola had predicted the French invasion, placing the blame on the corruption and decadence of Florence in the era of Medici rule. He began, in fact, by predicting the downfall of the city, doomed by the will of God as punishment for its own sins; but he would go on to extol the Florentine republic, which would, he declared, restore itself by banishing moral corruption. When the Medici fled and the French withdrew, the preacher's credibility was vastly enhanced, and his vision of an incorruptible Christian republic held sway for a few years, finding its most emblematic moment in a 'bonfire of the vanities'. Since his attacks on moral corruption included the clergy, he had powerful enemies in the Church. Having lost the support of the Florentine people who had tired of his moralistic rule, he was excommunicated by Pope Alexander VI and executed in 1498.

Savonarola's defence of the republic was essentially scholastic in its mode of argumentation. Humanistic speculations about human autonomy and excellence, while certainly not alien to Christianity, were less congenial to the preacher's uncompromising convictions about the primacy of divine will. While he extolled republican liberties, they were to be preserved not by struggle but by banishing corruption and suppressing conflict within the civic order. After his execution his followers, who remained a significant political force in Florence, would prefer the example of aristocratic Venice ruled by its Great Council, or of Florence in the era of *governo stretto*, the restricted civic order that governed the republic on the eve of Medici rule and was advocated by the Florentine aristocracy.

On these scores, Machiavelli disagreed with Savonarola and his supporters on every count. There has been much debate about Machiavelli's attitude towards Savonarola. Some commentators have suggested that he respected the preacher as much as he condemned him; and he certainly does praise him, for instance in the *Discourses*. But Machiavelli's doctrine of struggle, conflict and military prowess is in direct antithesis to the 'unarmed prophet', in opposition to Christian fatalism and the invocation of God's will as responses to disasters like the French invasion.

The *Discourses*

Machiavelli's conviction that every state will eventually decline suggests, on the face of it, that he shares the views so typical of his contemporaries and predecessors about the cyclical processes of history and the inevitable decline of even the most stable and powerful political order, however well endowed with *virtù* their leaders may be. In the *Discourses* he also – at least pro forma – draws on his ancient predecessors, especially Polybius, in outlining the different forms of government and the conditions of their rise and decline. But it soon becomes clear that he has something else in mind. He tells us that others who have written about such matters have said that there are three principal forms of government: principality or monarchy, aristocracy and democracy. Moreover, he continues, they have said that there are actually six, three good forms and three bad, each good form having a tendency to degenerate into a pernicious variant: principality can easily become tyranny, as aristocracy can readily become oligarchy, and democracy anarchy. Machiavelli then ascribes to the classics the view that all six forms are actually pernicious, the 'bad' because they are bad in themselves and the 'good' because they can so easily corrupt. To avoid the inevitable evils of these basic forms, he tells us, classical writers tend to opt for a mixed constitution.

Machiavelli goes through the motions of summing up the early history of Rome as a process of transition from monarchy to aristocracy to democracy. But it soon emerges that he differs fundamentally from his predecessors, because he is addressing a rather different problem. He is not primarily concerned with the forms of constitution as defined by the ancients. He is interested in the forms of state that immediately affect his own time and place: above all the city-republics of Italy, governed by civic bodies that range from the oligarchic to the more inclusive, though never democratic, as well as (up to a point) the rising monarchies, such as France or Spain, by which the city-states are threatened. He offers – without systematically spelling it out – a classification different from the ancient one, a simple opposition between principalities and republics, the latter either democratic or aristocratic; and his principal objective in exploring these two forms is even more specific: to consider the conditions for maintaining liberty. That, when all is said and done, is the main theme of the *Discourses*. In this respect, it already asks questions different from those that concerned Plato in his account of political rise and decline, or even Polybius, whose idea of the 'mixed constitution' Machiavelli appears to adopt. But, if his concerns with republican liberty have more in common with his contemporary civic humanists than with ancient ideas on political cycles, he makes an observation that sets him on a rather different path; and in retrospect, it also sheds light on *The Prince*.

Describing the cycle of rise and decline, he writes:

This, then, is the cycle through which all commonwealths pass, whether they govern themselves or are governed. But rarely do they return to the same form of government, for there can scarce be a state of such vitality that it can undergo often such changes and yet remain in being. What usually happens is that, while in a state of commotion in which it lacks both counsel and strength, a state becomes subject to a neighbouring and better organized state. Were it not so, a commonwealth might go on for ever passing through these governmental transitions. (I.2.13)

This observation is not simply a prelude to the remarks that follow it about the advantages of a constitution that can claim to combine – as did the Roman republic – the three major forms, monarchy, aristocracy and democracy, in a way that enhances stability. On this score, Machiavelli appears to have much in common with other advocates of a 'mixed' constitution. At the same time, he departs from convention by insisting that, in Rome, 'it was friction between the plebs and the senate that brought this perfection about'. He departs from the classic view of the mixed constitution as a mode of consolidating oligarchic rule. In the context of Florentine politics, he has little use for the nobility. While he is no democrat, he prefers *governo largo* to *governo stretto;* and, given a choice between democracy and oligarchy, his preference would seem to be democracy.

Yet his comments suggest that he is less concerned with classifying governments, or with the internal conditions that preserve or destroy particular forms of government, or with the mechanisms of transition from one form to another, than with the maintenance of the commonwealth itself and above all its capacity to resist threats from without. The cycles of governmental change could, for better or worse, go on forever, were they not cut short by conquest. The fundamental criterion of political stability is not the quality or duration of any specific political form but the capacity of the state, whatever its form, to withstand external military threats.

This is not to say that Machiavelli is interested only in military readiness and not in the general conditions of a stable civic order or the well-being of the people; but, even when he departs from the amorality of *The Prince*, his preoccupation with external threats colours everything he says about political success. In the *Discourses* he remains concerned with the survival of states in the face of foreign invasions, and he is as direct and uncompromising as ever in his advocacy, when necessary, of violence and deception. Here, too, domestic conflicts are conceived in terms not very different from wars between states. But now he extends his analysis beyond the most basic conditions of *mantenere lo stato* against external threats; and his demands are more exacting than in *The Prince*, because the issue is no longer mere survival, or even the preservation of the state's liberty from external domination, but also the preservation of civic liberty within the state. This requires more than the absence of tyranny. The fundamental condition is still the city-state's autonomy, its freedom from foreign conquests and, not least, from dependence on foreign powers; but there is more at stake. While he certainly discusses the conditions for maintaining principalities, his chief concern is the foundation and preservation of a free republic.

It is, nonetheless, striking how much of the *Discourses* is devoted to military matters, and how much his preference for republican governments itself is cast in military terms. Republican liberty may be good in itself, but popular government also generally gives rise to more reliable armies and to better soldiers – even if they must submit themselves to leadership. It could even be said that, for Machiavelli, what makes a republic on the whole a better bet than princely government is that it tends, as Roman history so clearly demonstrates, to produce a more effective fighting force.

It is here that Machiavelli's military preoccupations merge with his republicanism. His military ideal, the citizen's militia, certainly requires leadership, but it is leadership that can inspire loyalty and love among the rank and file. Ordinary soldiers cannot simply be obedient cannon fodder but must enjoy the respect of their leaders and must themselves partake of military virtues. While a mercenary army is typically led by a traditional military aristocracy, a citizen's militia requires the subordination of the aristocracy to the larger civic community. When Machiavelli extols the benefits of social conflict, untypically for his time and in sharp contrast, for instance, to Aristotelian principles, he has in mind not simply its effects in maintaining the militant spirit of the citizens but also the necessity of constant struggle to keep the aristocracy in check. On this score he departs even from Cicero, who shared Aristotle's predisposition to aristocratic dominance and the kind of social harmony required to sustain it.

Yet even if Machiavelli's preference for republican liberty is in large part shaped by a conviction that it produces better armies, the military cast of his arguments is not just a matter of defending against external threats. If he were simply writing about the art of war – as he does in his book of that name, which he regarded as his greatest achievement – his characteristic 'Machiavellian' principles would be less startling than they are when applied to the daily transactions of politics. What he has to say about violence and deception would hardly seem alien to a military strategist. Nor would his insistence on the need to adapt oneself to the times and to existing circumstances – which commentators have singled out as a particularly significant departure from the standard views of his contemporaries and predecessors, who measured politics against some universal moral standard. The advocacy of deception and the necessity of adapting to changing conditions were, after all, central to one of the earliest masterpieces of military literature: *The Art of War,* attributed to Sun Tzu in China in the sixth century BC. What is new in Machiavelli is the application of these military principles to politics; and this is rooted in the very specific conditions of Renaissance Florence.

The military model of politics belongs to the essence of the *Discourses* no less than to that of *The Prince.* Maintaining a republic, he insists, requires ruthless leadership, which is prepared to violate conventional morality – as his friend and mentor, Piero Soderini, failed to do when he led the Florentine republic, with, as Machiavelli tells us, disastrous results. But understanding Machiavelli's preoccupation here with domestic liberty and order demands something more, a closer look at the conditions of civic disorder and decline. In his *History of Florence*, he recounts at some length the story of the *ciompi* rebellion, presenting it as a turning-point in the history of his city, the culmination of its endless factional and social conflicts. In a speech attributed to a *ciompi* militant, he sums up in the most dramatic terms what is at stake. Just as the economic rivalries of the urban patriciate played themselves out in political factions, so, too, did the economic grievances of the urban poor over inadequate remuneration for their labours turn into conflict over guild privileges and then a struggle for political power. Power struggles of this kind all too readily took on the character of war:

> [O]ur opponents are disunited and rich; their disunion will give us the victory, and their riches, when they have become ours, will support us. Be not deceived about that antiquity of blood by which they exalt themselves above us; for all men having had one common origin, are all equally ancient, and nature has made us all after one fashion. Strip us naked, and we shall all be found alike. Dress us in their clothing, and they in ours, we shall appear noble, they ignoble – for poverty and riches

make all the difference . . . [A]ll who attain great power and riches, make use of either force or fraud; and what they have acquired either by deceit or violence, in order to conceal the disgraceful methods of attainment, they endeavour to sanctify with the false title of honest gains. Those who either from imprudence or want of sagacity avoid doing so, are always overwhelmed with servitude and poverty . . . Therefore we must use force when the opportunity offers; and fortune cannot present us one more favourable than the present, when the citizens are still disunited, the Signory doubtful, and the magistrates terrified; for we may easily conquer them before they can come to any settled arrangement. By this means we shall either obtain the entire government of the city, or so large a share of it, as to be forgiven past errors, and have sufficient authority to threaten the city with a renewal of them at some future time. (III.3)

This dramatically captures the realities of Florentine politics and, perhaps more than any other passage in Machiavelli's writings, starkly sums up his understanding of the problems his political theory is meant to confront. He is not here advocating the violence proposed in the speech, but he sees how and why things have come to this pass. He even suggests that it was inevitable and, in the circumstances, preferable to what the *signori* had done. Yet in the *Discourses* a bloody outcome like this is precisely what he sets out to avoid in his recommendations for a successful republican order – that it be, at the same time, an effective military force.

The balance at which he aims is difficult. Civic liberty requires that the aristocracy be kept in check and that the people have some role in politics. Military success, which is far more likely to be achieved by a citizens' militia than by untrustworthy nobles and their mercenary armies, also depends on some kind of equilibrium among the social classes; and this requires some degree of civil strife, a fruitful tension between people and patriciate. The problem is that civil strife can always descend into outright war. It was the Romans who, at least for a time in the days of the republic's imperial expansion, struck the right balance. They built their empire not by simple oligarchic rule and the suppression of the common people – as in ancient Sparta or in Venice. They found a middle way between oligarchy and democracy by giving the people a voice through the tribunate, which institutionalized and channelled social strife. Contrary to all conventional opinion, which condemns the quarrels between the nobles and the plebs, says Machiavelli, it was those very quarrels that preserved Roman liberty.

If Machiavelli seems to be a political 'scientist' or even a political 'realist' *avant la lettre*, these qualities have more to do with his grounding in the political realities of his city-state, with its military civic culture and the immediate dangers it confronted, than with any modern conception of the state or some affinity to scientific methods.[8] His military model of politics conformed to the realities of domestic politics in Florence, where political rivals and factions were always on the verge of war, no less than to the threats that faced his city from without. More than other civic humanists, he proceeded unambiguously on the premise that the object of war, foreign or domestic, is to win, in conformity with moral principles if possible but with cruel violence, deceit and stratagem if not. Machiavelli's military model was, in the context of Florentine realities and the culture of civic humanism, a relatively small change of perspective; but it was enough to shift the focus away from the just political order or the virtuous prince to the means of seizing and maintaining power, pure and simple. Especially when cast in Machiavelli's vivid and uncompromising prose, that seemed a shocking innovation.

It is, then, precisely his commitment to a practically defunct political form that produced what many commentators have interpreted as Machiavelli's most 'modern' political ideas. His views on governance, on how to achieve and maintain power, on relations among citizens and even between princes and their subjects, are steeped in the conditions of the city-state. It is the city-state that for Machiavelli defines the political terrain. This affects his military model of politics, which gives his political theory the aura of 'realism' that to some commentators seems distinctly modern; but it also produces a conception of civic liberty that gives his ideas a flavour in some ways more familiar to modern audiences than political ideas

---

8 A different understanding of Machiavelli's lasting insights, if not his 'modernity', is offered by Louis Althusser in *Machiavelli and Us*, transl. Gregory Elliott (London: Verso, 1999). What is distinctive about Machiavelli, he argues, is not a 'scientific' approach that seeks to discover general laws but rather his concentration on political 'conjunctures'. There are indeed constants that recur in various cases, and they must be clearly understood; but they manifest themselves in different ways in different cases, which means that the general and the particular combine in different ways in each specific historical 'conjuncture'. Machiavelli's particular strength, according to this argument, is not that he proposes certain universal laws but that he grasps conjunctural particularities and the 'aleatory' nature of political practice. Whatever his own political preferences might be, his primary concern is the conjunctural conditions in which political action must take place, which will require different responses. This argument (though it may exaggerate the absence of 'conjunctural' considerations in the history of Western political thought) certainly captures something distinctive about Machiavelli's approach; but, as has already been suggested here, a 'conjunctural' approach as uncompromising as Machiavelli's might have seemed more familiar to military strategists and was expressed in terms not so fundamentally different in China many centuries before. Machiavelli's originality in this respect may, again, lie in his application of such military principles to politics, for reasons that are not particularly 'modern'.

emanating from the rising territorial monarchies that would shape the new world order of modern nation states.

In the classics of sixteenth-century French political thought, for example, the political domain is not a civic community, a community of citizens. It is a contested terrain among various competing jurisdictions: the monarchy, the nobility, local magistrates and various corporate bodies. When Jean Bodin outlined an argument in favour of an 'absolutist' monarchy and devised a theory of sovereignty that has been called a landmark in the evolution of the modern state, he was addressing the position of the monarchy in relation to various corporate powers with varying degrees of autonomy. Even the anti-absolutist arguments of, say, the Huguenot resistance tracts, had little to do with the rights and powers of citizens. Instead, when they asserted the rights of the 'people' against the centralizing monarchy, they were asserting not the rights of citizens but the autonomous powers of various office-holders, 'lesser' magistrates, the provincial nobility, urban corporations and other corporate powers.

In England, which had long before become the most effective centralized administration in Europe, corporate powers were weaker than in France; and even at moments of the greatest tension between monarch and nobility, from Magna Carta to the Civil War, the issue was not jurisdictional disputes of the kind that defined the political terrain in France. Yet the political sphere was typically conceived as a partnership of Crown and Parliament, and the English were slow to formulate the tensions between these two partners in terms of popular sovereignty. We shall return to the peculiarities of England in a later chapter and to the radical ideas that challenged the prevailing wisdom; but for now it suffices to say that, even when royalists and parliamentarians came to blows, the English were, for their own distinctive reasons, disinclined to conceptualize a political domain defined by the rights and powers of citizens as distinct from the rights and powers of Parliament. Even 'republicans', as we shall see, did not always make clear that citizenship meant something more than the right to be (actually or 'virtually') represented by Parliament – which did not necessarily entail the right to vote for it.

By contrast, the Renaissance city-republics extended corporate principles and corporate autonomy to the civic community as a whole; and this produced something more ostensibly akin to modern ideas of popular sovereignty, the sovereignty of citizens, in contrast to the discourse of territorial monarchies. We are, in today's liberal democracies, accustomed to thinking of citizens' rights as a hallmark of a truly modern politics. That, among other things, is what allows some commentators to identify 'civic humanism' or even Renaissance 'republicanism' as a window to the modern world. But it may be misleading to describe membership in the civic corporation in medieval and Renaissance Italy as 'citizenship', since it vests political rights in corporate bodies and not individual citizens, while the republican discourse has less to do with the advent of the 'modern' state (unless it is as a threat to the survival of city-republics) than with the distinctive unity of civic, commercial and military principles in a political form that would not survive modernity.

3

THE REFORMATION

Martin Luther is one of very few, even among canonical thinkers, for whom a persuasive case can be made that, had he never been born, history would not have unfolded as it did. He may, for this reason alone, seem to present a special challenge to a social-contextual history like this one. If the ideas of one man can seem to change the course of history in such dramatic ways, must we not reconsider the primacy of discourse? Yet to ask the question in this way would be to misunderstand what is entailed by the kind of contextualization proposed in this book. Whatever doubts we may have about the decisive role of this or that historic figure, the social history of political theory does not require us to denigrate the creativity or world-historic influence of individuals. It does not oblige us to think that a Protestant movement would have emerged more or less in the form that it did with or without Martin Luther, nor does it suggest that if Martin Luther had never existed he would have had to be invented, or, for that matter, that Protestantism had no significant effects on the truly 'basic' processes of history.

How, then, should we pose the question? We shall certainly want to ask how the particularities of Luther's time and place shaped the particular configuration of problems he sought to resolve; and we shall want to consider how it came about that the same ideas were mobilized so differently, to such divergent purposes, in different contexts. But in the case of Luther more than most other thinkers, we are compelled to ask how a conceptual shift in the realm of ideas could have had such massive historical consequences; and it may turn out that the greater the world-historic effects we claim for Luther's ideas, the more – not the less – we must appeal to a contextual explanation.

The Roots of Reformation

Some historians have questioned the very existence of a Reformation conceived as a radical discontinuity in Christian dogma and reactions to it. The ideas of Luther and other major Protestant thinkers, they point out,

were deeply rooted in the medieval Church, which was already alive with
debate and projects for internal reformation; and there had long been heresies to challenge the institutions, no less than the theological orthodoxies, of
the Catholic Church. Conflicts in the Church had been vastly aggravated by
geopolitical rivalries among rising territorial states, as the papacy at Avignon
had increasingly come under the influence of the French monarchy, and
competing papal claimants in Avignon and Rome became embroiled in
inter-state rivalries between France and its European neighbours. In the late
fourteenth century, these rivalries produced the so-called Western Schism,
which would last for decades and helped to generate a climate of reform and
outright heresy.

The conciliar movement, which flourished in the fourteenth and fifteenth
centuries, elaborated the idea that it was not the pope but the corporate
body of Christians in the form of a general Church council that held ultimate authority in spiritual matters. While the movement would give way to
a revived papal dominance, its influence remained alive, even if more as a
model for secular theories of constitutional government than as a programme
for reform of the Church. More scathing attacks on the papacy, as well as on
the abuses and corruptions of the Church, would come from the Englishman
John Wycliffe (1330–84) and, most importantly, from the Bohemian Jan Hus
(1369–1415), whose influence on Luther would run very deep. Both Wycliffe
and Hus denied that the ecclesiastical hierarchy, from pope to cardinals to
priests, constituted the Church; and both called on secular rulers to initiate
reform of the Church. They even demanded that ecclesiastical possessions
should be subject to secular rule, on the grounds that the Church did not
enjoy ownership but only use rights conditional on good behaviour.

Renaissance humanism, too, played a critical part. Indeed, there may be
something artificial about distinguishing the 'Reformation' from 'Christian
humanism'. The humanist preoccupation with ancient texts would be
extended to the Bible, encouraging theologians to mobilize scripture in challenging the current practices of ecclesiastical authorities. The spread of
printing, needless to say, gave a new force to this kind of textual challenge.
Christian humanism, especially in the person of Erasmus, may have
remained committed to internal reform of the Church and deeply suspicious
of the Lutheran 'reformation'; but it also encouraged, if not necessarily
outright anti-clericalism, at least the subjection of Church rituals and orthodoxies to critical scrutiny and the moral judgment of the individual. All
these challenges to clerical authority, both Christian humanist and
'Protestant', would at the same time, directly or by implication, affect attitudes towards the powers of secular rulers.

Ideas such as these – not only criticism of the Church and its abuses but
also, and not least, the elevation of secular authority – would be central to
the Reformation. Yet even if we acknowledge that the institutions of the

Church were in the end resistant to the necessary changes, and even if we treat Luther's ideas as a profoundly revolutionary transformation in theology, the magnitude of the Lutheran rupture seems incommensurate with the novelty of his theology. There is also a massive disparity – which, of course, there often is with major thinkers but which, in Luther's case, is particularly striking – between the meaning or intentions of his doctrine and the direction of the changes that emerged in its wake. It will be argued in what follows that the scale and consequences of the break had less to do with the originality and revolutionary import or intent of Luther's ideas than with the geopolitical and social conflicts into which they were drawn.

That Luther challenged some of the beliefs and practices of Roman Catholicism with drastic effect is beyond question, as is, needless to say, the separation of 'Protestants' – in all their various and often antithetical guises – from the Catholic Church. We shall look at the nature and implications of Luther's challenge to medieval Catholicism, but Luther's doctrine was something else too. Inextricably connected with his attacks on the Church, not only its corruptions but its very claims to jurisdiction, are his views on secular government. For all Luther's occasionally stinging attacks on German princes, there hardly exists in the Western canon a more uncompromising case for strict obedience to secular authority; and this, as we shall see, belongs to the essence of Lutheran doctrine no less than does the attack on the medieval Church's practice of indulgences or Luther's idea of justification by faith.

Yet, while this fundamental aspect of Protestant doctrine was certainly not lost on German princes or on European kings, it was also somehow transformed into its opposite, a doctrine of rebellion. The question, then, must be how such a rigid doctrine of obedience could have such revolutionary effects and, beyond that, how a doctrine that seems far better suited to defending than to challenging the supremacy of princely power could be transformed into a doctrine of resistance. The answer lies in specificities of context, which both impelled Luther to formulate his doctrine of obedience and also permitted it to be transformed into its opposite.

Martin Luther

If the sixteenth century was a period of rising territorial states in Western Europe, Germany, like Italy, represented an exception. While in other cases the crisis of feudalism had meant a growing challenge to parcellized sovereignty from centralizing monarchies, in Germany it gave new life to the fragmentation of governance. Feudal lordship may have given way to princely government, and the feudal powers of the lesser nobility may have been weakened; but German principalities and duchies vigorously resisted the kind of monarchical centralization that was taking place elsewhere in Western Europe and produced in its stead a new kind of parcellized sovereignty.

In the Holy Roman Empire, which was the nearest thing to a national state in German territories, the emperor's authority was severely and explicitly limited by the autonomous powers of local duchies, principalities and cities. In the thirteenth century, Frederick II – partly in a fruitless effort to maintain the presence of the Empire in northern Italy – had ceded even more powers to local German lords, including princes of the Church. Although German landed classes in the west were never able to consolidate their powers over peasants in a 'second serfdom' as their eastern counterparts would do, the Empire had effectively transformed them from feudal lords into local rulers, territorial princes with state-like powers of their own, not least the power to tax. This gave them access to increasing revenues from peasants, especially from more prosperous peasant farmers who, even while freed from feudal dependence, bore the greatest burden of taxation. This would become a major source of grievance in the peasant war of 1524–5.

Secular authority had been further fragmented, especially from the twelfth century, with the foundation of cities by both emperors and dukes, for administrative or commercial purposes. These cities would challenge the powers of both emperor and local princes. Like the Italian city-states, German cities often governed their surrounding villages, exacting taxes from the peasantry by means of a collective urban lordship; but they stood in a different relation to landed aristocracies and princes than did the Italians. In northern Italy, the major city-states could trace their urban lineage back to imperial Rome, and the landed aristocracy was, in general, weaker than it was elsewhere in feudal Europe. The German cities, by contrast, owed their late foundations to superior lords. Even as they built upon the independence granted by higher authorities, they were obliged to defend their autonomous powers, inseparably political and economic, against other claimants within the imperial hierarchy, from emperors to princes.

Here, as in Renaissance Italy, political struggles were difficult to disentangle from economic rivalries and conflicts. Just as German princes relied on their political and military dominance for access to the revenues derived from cities and especially from peasant labour, so too was the success of the commercial cities dependent on their 'extra-economic' powers and privileges. The commercial dominance of the Hanseatic League in Northern Europe, for instance, relied on the League's coercive powers, the capacity to enforce monopolies, embargoes and blockades, which might require military interventions up to and including outright war. The League's dominance was threatened not so much by the purely 'economic' superiority of its commercial rivals – the kind of competitive advantage enjoyed by cost-effective capitalist producers – as by their more effective geopolitical reach and military power.

In 1519, the Habsburg King Charles I of Spain became the Holy Roman Emperor Charles V. His reign would be marked by intense and varied conflicts with German princes and municipal authorities, to say nothing of the peasant revolt. Charles was constantly distracted by the Empire's rivalries with other rising states, as well as Spain's project of imperial expansion, revolt on Spanish soil and the ever-present Turkish threat. He never succeeded in subduing local powers in the German territories. His reign would play a decisive role in the life of Martin Luther and in the Reformation, which flourished in the context of the Holy Roman Empire, not only because the emperor's attacks on Luther helped to concentrate the theologian's mind but because Lutheran doctrine proved so useful to various protagonists in the rivalries among competing powers.

Born in 1483 into a reasonably comfortable family, Luther was intended for the law; but he soon gave up his legal education for the Church and became an Augustinian monk. The monastic life seems to have generated little but doubt and despair. The Christianity he had learned from preachers and a very pious mother was obsessed with sin, repentance and the wrath of God. It did, to be sure, suggest that repentant sinners can make some contribution to their own salvation; and theology appeared to teach that, even if salvation is a matter of God's grace and not just a simple reward for a virtuous life, believers can and must engage in a constant struggle to cooperate with God – always, of course, with the help of the Church. But, to Luther, this appeared to mean that, torn between virtue and sin, between God and the devil, we can in this life never know whether all our efforts are enough to please God. Not even the extreme asceticism he adopted in the monastery could offer any certainty or comfort. As he described his own experience, it only turned his soul upon itself. He began to break free from this tormented struggle when his superior, Johann Staupitz, convinced him that repentance is not a matter of seeking God's love, which is already evident in the sacrifice of Christ, but, on the contrary, begins with our own love of God.

Luther was also persuaded by Staupitz, who was dean of the new University of Wittenberg, to pursue an academic career in biblical theology; and it was not as any kind of activist but as professor of theology that Luther launched his attack on the corruptions of the Church. He would later attribute his theological innovations to a transformative moment, a rebirth, which came to him while grappling with the doctrine of St Paul. 'For therein is the righteousness of God revealed from faith to faith:' said Paul in Romans 1: 17, 'as it is written: the just shall live by faith.' Luther would later recount that, while lecturing on the Psalms, he finally came to understand this passage to mean that the righteousness of God was not revealed by punishment. Instead, in his grace, he declared the sinner righteous – or 'justified' him – by means of faith alone. Salvation was not, in other words, the uncertain outcome of a lifelong human effort but a free and loving gift of God.

Luther never resolved the question of predestination, and debate still rages about what he meant on this score. Lutherans would come to distinguish themselves from Calvinists on the grounds that, while both theologians believed in election by God, only Calvin insisted on a 'double' predestination, according to which God also chose those who are damned. Luther, they maintain, never taught that some were predestined to eternal damnation. Yet, if this is so, some would argue, Luther remained caught in an irreducible contradiction, which undermined belief in God's total sovereignty. It might be better simply to accept that Luther deliberately refused to confront the conundrum of predestination, because preoccupation with this issue was, in his eyes, a distraction from acknowledging our sinfulness and from unwavering faith in God's grace and salvation through Christ. This would also, as we shall see, have the effect of strengthening Luther's doctrine of obedience to secular authority.

Whether or not Luther's revelation was as sudden as he later made it out to be, the doctrine of 'justification by faith' represents a revolutionary moment in the history of Christianity. It is true that St Augustine had elaborated a doctrine of salvation that seemed to leave very little scope for repentance and good works as the road to salvation. For him, too, salvation was a free and unearned gift of God through grace; and he had a particularly uncompromising view of predestination. But Luther, as influenced as he was by St Augustine, was convinced that, once he had experienced his revelation on St Paul, he had put Augustine behind him.

For Augustine, justification by God's grace was not something that happened all at once. It was a process that occupied a lifetime in this world and could only be completed in the next, while, for Luther, it was God's immediate and unconditional gift in this life. Augustine may have been no less intent than was Luther on emphasizing that salvation was an unearned gift from God; but his formulation may have seemed open to the interpretation that human beings could in their lifetime, at least in some small way, cooperate in their own transformation by divine grace. In any case, whatever St Augustine had intended, the authority of the Catholic Church clearly depended on maintaining the sinner's role in achieving salvation, with, of course, the necessary help of sacramental interventions by the Church; and Augustinian theology would be interpreted by medieval popes, such as Gregory the Great (590–604), in just this way. Luther would have none of that – not on the grounds that Christian virtue and good works meant nothing to him, but on the grounds that, while they should be undertaken freely for the love of God, they had nothing to do with earning God's love and the free gift of justification. Sinners are saved not by their own righteousness but, all at once and in this life, by the righteousness of God, which means that, even while remaining sinners, they are 'justified' by faith alone. This doctrine had fatal implications for the sacramental functions of the Church, but its implications for obedience to secular authority may have been even greater.

Whenever Luther's doctrine of justification by faith reached maturity – and commentators disagree on when and how it happened – Luther's challenge to the authority of the Catholic Church did not at first depend on it. The most famous moment in his career, which is conventionally depicted as the Reformation's true beginning, was his attack on the corruptions of the Church, and especially the practice of indulgences, in his *Disputation on the Power and Efficacy of Indulgences,* commonly called the 95 *Theses,* which he issued in 1517, nailing them, as tradition (if not historical evidence) tells us, to the door of the Castle Church in Wittenberg. His target was the pope's claims to powers that were, for Luther, God's alone: the power to award salvation or to affect the scope and duration of penance in the after-life. This attack on the pope did not require, nor did Luther invoke, the doctrine of justification by faith as he would later formulate it.

Luther would soon be threatened by a papal ban, which would lead to his excommunication; and his personal fate became enmeshed in public conflicts between the Church and secular authorities over the distribution of tempo-ral power. His immediate response to papal threats was a series of treatises in 1520, the first of which was his *Address to the Christian Nobility of the German Nation.* Here, his theological preoccupations shifted, significantly, from the disposition of power between God and the pope to the conflicts between the Church – specifically the pope, together with the Holy Roman Emperor – and German secular authorities.

This would be followed in rapid succession by two other treatises, laying the groundwork for his mature theology: *On the Babylonian Captivity of the Church,* which, written in strongly vituperative terms, attacked the papacy and challenged the sacramental functions of the Church; and *On the Freedom of a Christian,* which, though framed in more conciliatory language and even dedicated to Pope Leo X, outlined the principles that would constitute the doctrine of justification by faith. Luther here elabo-rated on the dualism, or the paradox, at the root of his theology: the simultaneity of human sin and divine justification, the nature of humanity as irreducibly sinful yet saved.

Human beings, Luther argued, are at once sinners by nature and saints by faith. Redeemed by God, they may freely undertake service to others; but, while Luther can be interpreted to mean that justification by faith is simultaneously a free commitment to good works, he insists that ordinary human beings are free as any lord or king and subject to no overlord in matters affecting the soul. Yet, at the same time, as he would soon make clear, the irreducible sinfulness of humanity requires temporal authorities to whom all Christians owe obedience. It is true that, in these early works, Luther not only challenged the division of the world into temporal and spiritual jurisdictions but established the principle that all baptized Christians are equally priests; and the idea of a universal priesthood would be taken up by radical forces as a justification of rebellions far beyond anything envisaged by Luther himself, including the peasant revolt. But this radical appropriation of Lutheran doctrine should not disguise the fact that Luther's account of the simultaneous duality of sin and justification entailed both a denial of ecclesiastical jurisdiction and an insistence on strict obedience to secular authority.

In 1521, Luther was called before an assembly of the estates of the Holy Roman Empire at the Diet of Worms; and, refusing to recant the views expressed in the *95 Theses* and other writings, he was outlawed by the emperor, Charles V. Under threat of arrest, he disappeared for a time. Despite imperial orders for his apprehension and punishment, declaring it a crime to shield him, he was offered protection at Wartburg Castle in Eisenach by a leading German prince, Frederic III, Elector of Saxony. It was then that he began his translation of the Bible into German, which would be printed in 1534 and can reasonably be regarded as his most far-reaching accomplishment, with influences well beyond the German language or Lutheran theology.

The Doctrine of Obedience to Secular Authority

In Luther's treatises of 1520, ideas essential to the Reformation, challenging the spiritual authority of the Church, its monopoly on the interpretation of scripture and its sole right to call a council of the Church, were formulated with direct reference to the relation between ecclesiastical and secular authority. Whatever effects these treatises may have had in undermining ecclesiastical authority, their implications for obedience to secular government were very different. To challenge the claims of the Church as privileged mediator between humanity and God, it might have been enough to reject, as Luther did in the *95 Theses,* its efforts to usurp divine powers of punishment and absolution. Challenging the Church's claims to temporal power and its usurpation of secular authority required something more, and even that would not suffice to impose on Christians a strict obedience to secular government. The doctrine of justification by faith would achieve all these effects.

Commentaries on Luther's theology have tended to identify his greatest innovation as his challenge to the Church's sacramental, sacerdotal powers. By the late Middle Ages, they say, a clear distinction had been established between the sacramental powers of the Church and its jurisdictional authority in the temporal domain, its coercive powers in the public realm (*in foro exteriori et publice*), its 'plenitude of power'. Indeed, others before Luther, such as Marsilius of Padua, had challenged its temporal authority. But Luther took the extra step.

No one had yet gone quite so far in questioning not just the Church's temporal authority but even its powers over the souls of the faithful.

Yet, if we follow the logic of Luther's theological development, it is striking that it proceeds in the opposite direction. He begins by questioning the Church's power to punish sins, to excommunicate or to confer benefices and indulgences, and then advances from there not simply to attack the temporal authority of the Church but to support secular governments and their claims to almost unconditional obedience. It is at this point that the doctrine of justification by faith becomes truly essential. That doctrine may have contributed even more to the defence of secular authority, and the necessity of obedience to it, than to the attack on the sacramental powers of the Church.

The Lutheran creed of obedience looks back to St Augustine and St Paul, who had, at different moments in the history of the Roman Empire, enunciated doctrines of obedience to secular authority.[1] In the first volume of this history, it was argued that the defining principle of Western Christianity was the rendering unto Caesar and God their respective domains of law and obedience. The 'universal' Catholic Church was born when what had been a Jewish cult detached itself, in accordance with the doctrines of St Paul, from Judaism's all-embracing religious law, which applied to both matters of faith and the mundane practices of everyday life. The distinction between Caesar and God, each with his own proper sphere of obedience, would perhaps more than anything else set Christianity, especially in its Western form, apart from the other monotheistic religions.[2] It was this, above all,

<hr/>

1 St Paul and St Augustine are discussed in my *Citizens to Lords*, pp. 144–63.

2 There has been much confusion about Islam and the consequences of its belief in a single divinely revealed system of law, encompassing the whole range of human practice, secular as well as religious. We have become familiar with a strain of Islam for which this view of the law requires an 'Islamist' state, replacing secular governance with a fundamentalist theocracy. But this was certainly not characteristic of medieval Islam. The belief in a single divinely revealed law meant not the dominance of *mullahs* but, on the contrary, the absence of an institutional power comparable to the Christian ecclesiastical establishment, with its own distinct claims to authority and obedience. There was no autonomous Islamic power such as the Catholic Church for policing theology, let alone laying claim to authority over the whole temporal domain. There were no jurisdictional claims and disputes of the kind that characterized Christianity; and this permitted, among other things, an openness to the idea that truth could be arrived at in various ways – for example, by means of secular philosophy no less than by means of Islamic theology (see vol. 1 of this history for a discussion of the relation between Islamic theology and classical philosophy). By the same reasoning, a secular government could be perfectly consistent with Islamic theology – and perhaps without all the tensions engendered by jurisdictional conflicts of Western Christianity. Christian theology did not prevent secular governments from claiming their authority as divinely ordained; and, if anything, the jurisdictional dualism of Christianity could easily accommodate, indeed invite, a doctrine of strict obedience to secular authority imposed on sinful human beings, in the manner of Augustine and Luther.

that permitted Christianity to become an imperial religion, which relin-
quished to Caesar the right to rule this world.

Before the Constantinian conversion, St Paul had already invoked this
principle to impose upon Christians a need to obey imperial authority. After
Christianity had become the official religion of empire, St Augustine elaborated the principle of obedience to secular power into an even more
uncompromising doctrine, which still included submission to pagan rulers.
He accomplished this by transforming the old Christian dualism into a
rather more complex dichotomy. Instead of a simple distinction between
earthly and heavenly realms, or secular and spiritual authority, or even the
sacred and the profane, Augustine proposed a dichotomy between the divine
and earthly 'cities', which are antithetical but inextricably united in this
world: the one representing the saintly, holy, elect, pious and just, the other
representing the impure, impious, unjust and damned, which runs through
every human society and every human institution, including holy institutions of the Church. Since all human beings and all human institutions are
tainted by unholiness and sin, no truly just and rightful order is possible in
this world; and they must all subject themselves, by divine ordination, to the
earthly powers whose purpose is not to achieve some higher principle of
holiness or justice on this earth but simply to maintain peace, order and a
degree of physical comfort.

For early Christian theologians under imperial rule, a doctrine of obedience to Caesar may have been a relatively simple matter. The issue became
infinitely more complicated when empire gave way to the medieval fragmentation of temporal power, in which ecclesiastical authorities were major
players. Now theologians had to confront not only a division of labour
between Caesar and God, with their respective claims to obedience, but also
between Empire and Church, or princes and popes, among a bewildering
variety of other autonomous powers, from feudal lords to civic corporations. It is not surprising that much of Christian theology soon took the
form of legalistic arguments on jurisdiction.

No philosopher or theologian could ever have decisively resolved the
boundary disputes between ecclesiastical jurisdiction and secular governments, especially between the papacy and rising feudal kingdoms, which
increasingly plagued Western Christendom in the later Middle Ages; but
medieval Christian theology was at least obliged to confront the question in
a way that early Christianity was not. It may have been enough in the time
of St Paul to elaborate the principle of rendering unto Caesar and God their
respective domains; and it may have been enough in St Augustine's time to
construct a theology of other-worldliness, like Christian Neoplatonism,
which allowed obedience to Caesar to coexist with a devaluation of earthly
existence and a philosophy of mystical release from the material world. But,
in the age of Thomas Aquinas, theologians were compelled to contend with,

and even to justify, the preoccupation of medieval Christians with the intricacies of worldly governance and conflicts among competing claims to temporal power.

This was a time when rising kingdoms like France were contending with other temporal powers, such as the German princes of the Holy Roman Empire and above all with the papacy. Christian theologians confronted not only the contests between spiritual and secular domains but ecclesiastical powers that laid claim to temporal authority on the grounds of their privileged access to the spiritual domain. Aquinas himself never systematically spelled out in practical terms his views on the relation between spiritual and temporal powers; but, drawing on the rediscovered Aristotle, he did find a way of situating the secular sphere in the cosmic order, retaining for the Church its own rightful domain while securing the position of secular governments. Although he placed the secular political sphere in a descending hierarchy from the divine to the mundane, he ascribed to it a positive function in the greater scheme of things, not simply in the role of necessary evil, as it had been for Augustine. The spiritual realm still reigned supreme in the cosmic hierarchy, and the Church still had its privileged position in that sphere; but secular government, which was granted substantial autonomy, could, on Thomistic principles, be treated as the highest of Christian concerns in this world.

Here, too, the cosmic order was defined in legalistic terms, as Thomas distinguished among various kinds of law, divine, eternal, natural and positive. Natural law was that aspect of divine regulation and the cosmic order accessible to human reason and hence available to secular governments no less than to ecclesiastical authorities. Political society was not directly instituted by God but by natural law as mediated through positive law. This doctrine went some distance in sustaining the authority of secular princes against ecclesiastical powers claiming temporal supremacy. While Aquinas himself remained aloof, his doctrines were soon deployed in favour, for instance, of Philip IV of France in his struggles with Pope Boniface VIII.[3]

Lutheran theology disrupted this neat Thomistic structure. The hierarchy of the cosmic order was replaced by a particularly rigid separation of spiritual and temporal domains, which denied any temporal jurisdiction to the Church. As we have seen, Luther took this further than ever before by denying the jurisdiction of the Church *in foro interno*, no less than *in foro externo*, not only depriving it of authority in matters temporal but restricting even its formal sacramental functions, divesting the Church's officers, the priesthood, of their role as humanity's only and official channel to God.

---

3   Thomas Aquinas is discussed in greater detail in *Citizens to Lords*, as is the preoccupation with jurisdiction in medieval theology.

The powers of coercion belonged solely to secular government, to which Christians owed their obedience.

In spiritual matters affecting the soul, Christians were, to be sure, obliged to follow their Christian conscience; and, if commanded to act in ungodly ways, they might be obliged to disobey. Yet this obligation did not constitute a right to resist or rebel. If Christians felt compelled in conscience to disobey, they were obliged simply to accept the punishment for disobedience. True Christian liberty belongs to the soul and is perfectly consistent with bodily imprisonment. The right of refusal was reserved to the individual Christian conscience and could not be translated into active, collective and organized resistance to secular authority. A radical reading of Luther might seem to suggest that civil authority could not reside in ungodly princes, and more radical resistance theories would interpret Lutheran doctrine in this way. But the master himself would make very clear, most emphatically during the peasants' revolt, that the ungodliness of rulers is no warrant for rebellion.

Luther would, in his later years, reluctantly accept – at the strong and repeated urging of German princes – a right of resistance that went beyond his earlier convictions; but the issue then was whether the princes had a right, even a duty, to form a league to resist the emperor, which Luther had earlier opposed. Some supporters even appealed to Roman civil law in support of the right to resist force with force and to disobey unjust judges. There were those who argued, invoking 'private law', that an unjust ruler might forfeit his public authority and effectively become a private person subject to resistance on the grounds of self-defence. Even Luther himself with great hesitation accepted the 'private law' doctrine; but, while some did indeed interpret the doctrine as implying a more radical right of individual resistance, for Luther the narrowly circumscribed issue was the right of lesser authorities like German princes actively to resist the higher authority of the emperor.[4] The argument developed by rebellious princes to justify resistance to the imperial power was intended, from beginning to

---

4   See Skinner, *Foundations, Vol. 2: Age of Reformation*, esp. pp. 199–202. While Skinner argues that Luther's change of mind was indeed a real one, he also takes pains to emphasize that the Lutherans were 'of course' 'anxious to avoid at all costs' any interpretation of the private-law doctrine as implying that private individuals had a right of violent resistance to public authority or any confusion between private individuals and public office (p. 200). See also Cynthia Grant Bowman, 'Luther and the Justifiability of Resistance to Legitimate Authority', *Cornell Law Faculty Publications*, Paper 151, 1979. 'It is important to note that in voicing this new position Luther based his stand solely upon the cautious, tightly circumscribed grounds of constitutional law', on the question of whether lesser authorities could resist higher ones. Private citizens could refuse to obey their emperor and to participate in the war on his side; but 'only those who had public authority to do so, and that seemed in the light of the jurists' arguments to include the princes, should actively oppose the Emperor' (pp. 11–12).

end, to be formulated in such a way as to ensure that resistance was not conceived as a general right residing in the people. It was meant, from the start, to be a constitutional argument about the rights of princes and other officials to resist the higher authority of the Empire, especially in matters of religion, and even to repel the emperor with military force. Even if the emperor had become a private person by governing unjustly, his punishment remained a public duty, performed by proper authorities, and not a private right.

Other Christian theologians had devised theories of obedience to secular authority, but Luther faced specific problems that no other theologian had effectively confronted. Unlike, for instance, Marsilius of Padua, who attacked the papacy on behalf of the Holy Roman Empire and its allies in Italian civic communes, in particular the Ghibelline nobility, Luther was asserting the authority of secular rulers, sometimes kings but in particular local princes, who were in conflict with both pope and emperor. To establish that Christians owed obedience to German princes, it was not enough to declare that the Church had no jurisdiction, public or private. This might suffice to shift the balance of authority in worldly affairs from Church to secular government, but princes whose authority was in no way derived from divine associations – such as even the Holy Roman Emperor enjoyed – would seem to have a tenuous claim on the strict obedience of Christian believers. Augustine had gone a long way in establishing the principle that secular and even pagan rulers could command the obedience of Christians; but there remained some loopholes, which were closed by Luther's doctrine of justification by faith.

Augustine had certainly argued that temporal government is providentially ordained by God to deal with a fallen humanity. Since the purpose of government was simply to maintain peace, order and a fair degree of comfort among sinful human beings who could expect no justice in this world, even pagans could fulfil this modest purpose and could command obedience on the same grounds as did a Christian ruler. The principle of obedience was underwritten by his doctrine of predestination, which seemed to leave little, if any, scope to human effort in achieving salvation. At the same time, as we have seen, Augustine's view of salvation appeared, in the eyes of some interpreters, to leave room for human effort in cooperating with the grace of God, while his attitude to heresy and his support for its brutal suppression by the state might be understood to imply that Christians did, after all, stand in a different relation to secular authority than did heretics or nonbelievers. Some might even be inclined to interpret the distinction between the sinful mass of humanity and the elect, rooted in the doctrine of predestination, to mean that secular government was necessary to control the many but that the few might somehow be exempt.

Luther decisively closed all the doors left ajar by Augustine. The

Reformation would, to be sure, produce sects, in particular the Anabaptists, who believed that true Christians were subject only to the Word of God and not to the temporal sword. But Luther's theology is emphatically on the side of obedience to secular government and the need for Christians to submit to it. Whatever he may have believed about predestination or the division between damned and elect, his doctrine of justification by faith effectively rendered them irrelevant to the question of obedience to secular authority, while at the same time giving secular government an unambiguous claim to divine ordination.

Luther accepted the Augustinian opposition between the realm of God and the earthly realm, or the devil's; but that antithesis was trumped by another distinction, between temporal and spiritual realms, with their corresponding modes of authority, both of which are divine. The antithesis of divine and diabolic 'kingdoms' remained important; but it figured in the argument on divinely ordained temporal and spiritual realms only in the sense that it reflected the dual nature of humanity, the simultaneous unity of sin and justification that characterizes Christians, whose human sinfulness requires the temporal sword.

The distinction between temporal and spiritual realms, or between the kinds of order to which they are respectively subject, does not, then, correspond to the antithesis of God's realm and the devil's, because, as we have seen, both orders are divine. Nor does Luther situate temporal and spiritual orders in some kind of Thomistic hierarchy. Each has its rightful and inviolable domain and its own mode of governance: the spiritual realm is the domain of the Word, with no business in the sphere of jurisdiction or coercion, which is the preserve of secular government. The line of demarcation between the two domains is clear, and any confusion between them is the work of the devil. This formulation puts paid to the temporal pretensions of the Church, while elevating secular authority to a status no less divine than the spiritual order.

Obedience Transformed into Resistance

Despite the doctrine of obedience, there was always a danger that attacks on abuses of clerical power might put in question any religious legitimation of secular authority; and Lutheran theology was – selectively – invoked by radical Protestants to justify rebellions of a kind Luther himself vehemently opposed. In his absence from Wittenberg after the Diet of Worms, some of his followers promoted more radical reforms of the Church than he had envisaged; and their rebellion did not stop with ecclesiastical authorities but extended to the government of civic magistrates. Luther responded, already in 1521, with *A Sincere Admonition to All Christians to Guard Against Insurrection and Rebellion*. He was, to be sure, critical of German princes; but even in his treatise *Temporal Authority: To What Extent It Should Be Obeyed* (1523), which most clearly expresses his reservations about how princes are actually using their divinely ordained power, he never abandons his call to obedience. Luther admonishes the princes – without much hope, it must be said – to behave like Christians; and he also appears to suggest that true Christians are obliged to sustain the powers of secular government only out of Christian love and service to others who are more in need of coercive correction. Yet his principal message is that, while the Christian soul is governed by the Word, Christians, whether because of their own sinfulness or in service to others, are in the temporal domain no less subject than anyone else to the sword of secular authority and the obligation to obey.

On his return to Wittenberg, Luther managed to subdue his most radical followers; but this did not prevent others – notably the Anabaptist Thomas Müntzer, who had broken with him – from supporting and leading the peasant rebellion. While Müntzer certainly had Luther in his sights when he excoriated a view of the world in which all things and creatures have been turned into property, support for the peasants' revolt did not require anything quite as radical as an attack on the very institution of private property. But even short of that, given Luther's unambiguous insistence on obedience to secular authority, it may not be immediately obvious how Lutheran doctrine could lend support to a popular uprising.

Luther's attack on the Church could be more readily mobilized against the ecclesiastical hierarchy, princes of the Church and the imposition of tithes, which were indeed a major grievance. But during the peasant revolt the challenge to authority went beyond ecclesiastical jurisdiction to include secular authorities, the ever-increasing burden of taxation and gross inequalities of property and power. To justify rebellions such as these in Lutheran terms required a considerable stretch. If Luther advocated the personal and passive disobedience of Christians when commanded to act in an ungodly way, his radical followers transformed that principle into militant collective rebellion against 'ungodly' rulers, in a way Luther never intended. His doctrine of a universal priesthood or the equality of all baptized Christians before God had to be translated, in distinctly un-Lutheran ways, into principles of social equality and challenges to any kind of earthly lordship.

If some peasant rebels were driven by Lutheran ideas and expected support from the master, they were soon disillusioned. In *Against the Robbing and Murdering Hordes of Peasants,* Luther left no ambiguity at all about the obligation to obey the secular authorities, however ungodly their behaviour. Whatever legitimate grievances the peasants may have had, they were in the very act of rebellion guilty of terrible sins against God and man; and for that they must be brutally suppressed. 'Therefore let everyone who can, smite, slay and stab, secretly or openly, remembering that nothing can be more poisonous, hurtful or devilish than a rebel. It is just as when one must kill a mad dog; if you do not strike him, he will strike you, and a whole land with you.'[5]

This invitation to princely brutality may seem a far cry from Luther's earlier admonitions to misbehaving princes, and there can be no doubt that the peasant revolt aroused his anger as never before; but his strictures against rebellion follow seamlessly from the insistence on obedience to secular authority that lies at the heart of his theology. When the rebellion was finally defeated by German princes and their troops, there remained a sharp rupture between radical sects that challenged the temporal sword, and Luther's Reformation, which supported secular powers and enjoyed their protection. In the end, he would even compromise his basic principles about the sharp dividing line between temporal and spiritual authority, allowing secular governments to invade the spiritual domain in order to defend true religion, even, when needed, by force.

The doctrine of obedience that lay at the heart of Protestantism was certainly a boon to German princes, and this advantage was certainly not lost on other European kings. Where territorial monarchs were already far advanced in their centralizing projects and (unlike, say, the Spanish monarch, who was also Holy Roman Emperor) not dependent on attachment to the Catholic Church, Protestant doctrine could easily be deployed in support of monarchical power. This was particularly true in England. Henry VIII in his earlier, orthodox years wrote an attack on Luther that earned him a papal endorsement as 'defender of the faith'. But, while his attitude towards Lutheranism remained at best ambivalent, Protestant doctrine was soon enlisted in the cause of royal supremacy, which granted the monarch command of state and Church at once. The same ideas would be no less serviceable to James I when he claimed the divine right of kings.

The irony is that, while (mis)interpretations of Lutheranism were used to justify the peasant revolt, the most systematic and influential Protestant doctrines of resistance emerged not from radical rebellion but from assertions of power by secular authorities. It should be no surprise that this transformation first took place in the Holy Roman Empire, with its intricate web of competing jurisdictions. Rivalries among various claimants to secular authority spawned new ideas of resistance to power quite different from those that drove radical sects or the peasant revolt. It was one thing for peasants to rebel against their superiors. It was quite another for princes to rebel against Holy Roman Emperors, or civic magistrates against both emperors and princes. When princes challenged the emperor, or civic magistrates

---

5 Luther, *Against the Robbing and Murdering Hordes of Peasants*, in *Martin Luther (Documents of Modern History)*, eds E.G. Rupp and Benjamin Drewery (London: E. Arnold, 1970), pp. 121–6.

resisted princes, they were certainly pursuing their own economic interests by defending or augmenting their hold on political power, just as burghers and guildsmen fought urban patriciates to gain the material advantages deriving from a greater share in civic governance, or peasants rebelled against princes to free themselves of tithes and taxes. The difference was that, in their resistance to higher authorities, princes or civic magistrates could claim to be acting not in their private interests but in defence of their own public powers.

Luther's theology proved well adapted to these conflicts; and its success must be at least in part explained by its capacity to serve the interests of secular powers in various ways, depending on the balance of forces in any given principality or city at any given time. The complex of ideas that combined separation from the Catholic Church with a doctrine of obedience to secular authority served princes and civic authorities particularly well. The adoption of Lutheranism, however genuine the spiritual motivations, had distinct political and economic advantages. It freed principalities and cities from papal jurisdiction and taxation, while also challenging imperial authority and the diversion of German resources to other imperial territories.

So, while Luther himself was quick to denounce the peasant revolt against princes and other secular powers, his doctrine of obedience did not prevent princes themselves from mobilizing Lutheran theology – nor did it prevent Luther from supporting them – against the Holy Roman Empire. Their resistance could remain consistent with the doctrine of obedience because they launched their opposition not as private citizens resisting authority but rather as one competing temporal jurisdiction against another. Much the same would be true of Protestant urban elites, who challenged higher authorities not to defend the liberties of citizens so much as to assert the rights and jurisdictions of 'lesser' authorities against emperors and princes. At the same time, princes and civic elites could invoke the doctrine of obedience to secular authority in countering threats of rebellion from below.

In 1531, when Emperor Charles V threatened to suppress Lutheranism by military means, a group of principalities and cities, led by two powerful German princes, the Landgrave of Hesse and the Elector of Saxony, formed the Schmalkaldic League to defend the Protestant faith. A theory of resistance was devised, which invested in 'lesser magistrates' – the lower levels of imperial government, such as local civic officials – a right to resist by military force. It was made very clear that no such right belonged to private citizens: never again should there be such a thing as a peasant revolt. Indeed, the right to resist was less a right than an official duty.

Luther himself – belatedly and reluctantly – had come around to this point of view, having been repeatedly called upon by the Elector of Saxony and others to write in support of the princes' political moves against the

Empire or the Catholic Church. At first, he supported the princes on narrowly constitutional grounds, saying that if the lawyers were right in their interpretation of the imperial constitution and the rights of lesser officials, then the princes were entitled to resist the emperor. Even then he narrowly defined the right of those public authorities and explained his change of mind on the grounds that imperial law itself, that is, law imposed by the emperor himself, called for resistance to a notorious injustice wrought by government. For German princes and their supporters, resistance remained a prerogative of office, and the right of other authorities to repel force with force rested on the emperor's having himself become a rebel – whose punishment was clearly a duty of office. Even when the argument expanded from purely constitutional principles to arguments from natural law, the issue was still the rights of princes, or at least the right to disobey the orders of the emperor to take up arms against Protestants.[6] For Luther, if the private citizen had any rights, they almost certainly did not go beyond the citizen's right to join his prince's army against the emperor.

Later, under the influence of Calvin, who was himself – as we shall see – a strong advocate of secular obedience, this defence of Protestant religion against imperial threats would be transformed into a doctrine of secular resistance against any overweening royal power; but even then it remained – as in the Huguenot resistance tracts in France – not a declaration of individual freedom but, above all, an assertion of autonomous powers belonging to provincial nobles and civic officials.

John Calvin

The city of Geneva, where John Calvin would find his spiritual home, had, like other cities in the Holy Roman Empire, long been a battleground for power struggles among bishops, counts and dukes. In the Middle Ages, the bishop of Geneva had been a prince of the Empire; but there were constant battles between the bishops and other princely claimants, eager to gain

---

6 Luther was not above invoking natural law, if only on rhetorical grounds, but his theology did not lend itself to – and he avoided – a systematic theory of natural law. Lutheran theology, from its very first premise, makes appeals to natural law – for instance, in judging the legitimacy of any government – very problematic, since no Christian doctrine can, in Luther's view, be constructed on the assumption that a fallen humanity is capable of following, or even comprehending, divine will or natural law. Christian theology must always proceed from the premise of humanity's innate sinfulness. That is why, in his doctrine of justification by faith, salvation relies on a free gift of God and not on adherence to principles of Christian virtue. His doctrine of obedience to secular authority was constructed on the same premise, making it difficult to argue that obedience to secular authority depended on the virtue of the ruler.

access to the fruits of the city's commercial success. When the House of Savoy sought to turn Geneva into a duchy, the city countered the threat by joining the Swiss federation in 1526; but this union would soon be disrupted by a division between Catholic and Protestant cities. When Geneva finally asserted its autonomy as a republic in 1536, it did so under the banner of Protestantism, for obvious practical and economic no less than spiritual reasons, and managed to maintain its independence as a city-state against prevailing trends.

Calvin would arrive in Geneva the year of its establishment as a Protestant republic, and – except for a period of exile from 1538 to 1541 – he would stay there until his death in 1564. Born in France in 1509 as Jean Cauvin, he began his career as clerk to a bishop; intended for the priesthood, he studied philosophy in Paris, but then gave up the Church for the study of law. At the University of Bourges, he came under humanist influences. The exposure to humanism clearly played a major part in his religious conversion; and like other humanist reformers, he would soon abandon the Catholic Church. On his return to Paris, caught up in conflicts between the reformers and the orthodox Catholics, he was compelled to flee and in 1535 settled for a time in the Protestant city of Basle.

It was during his stay in Basle that Calvin, in 1536, published the first edition of his major life's work, the *Institutes of the Christian Religion*, a catechism of his faith and the principles of reformation to which he subscribed. Written first in Latin, it would later appear in French editions, which would have an enormous influence not only on theology but also on the French language. He would continue to edit and amplify this work throughout his life. On his return to Paris from Basle, finding his reforming views unwelcome in his native France, he set out for the free imperial city of Strasbourg; but, forced by circumstances to take a detour, he arrived in Geneva, and there he would remain.

Calvin settled in Geneva at the urging of another Frenchman, who invited him to join in reforming the Church. Their proposals for ecclesiastical reform, undertaken at the behest of civic authorities, were immediately accepted by the city council. Although Calvin would find himself in conflict with the council in 1538 and yet again forced into exile, the civic authorities of Geneva invited him to return in 1541 to carry on his project of reform. In November of that year, the council amended and passed the Ecclesiastical Ordinances drafted by Calvin, which spelled out the organization and functions of the Church in what amounted to a blueprint for a division of labour between civic and ecclesiastical jurisdictions in governing the city. The Ordinances struck a difficult balance between separating the functions of Church and state, allocating each its proper domain, and at the same time establishing a partnership between them in governing the city according to the principles of the reformed religion. There would be other moments of conflict and danger for Calvin, especially when some Genevan notables challenged the Ordinances, in opposition to the strict discipline imposed on them by both civic and ecclesiastical jurisdictions. But in the end, the so-called *libertines* were defeated and their leaders banished or executed.

It is difficult to disentangle Calvin's theological development from the evolution of his political consciousness. His first book, a commentary on Seneca's *De Clementia*, which he began writing while still a law student, was not a work of theology but a humanist essay on a classical text. Seneca's work, addressed to the emperor Nero, has been called a forerunner of what would become the humanist genre of 'mirrors for princes'. While it would be too much to say that Calvin's commentary was intended as a comparable lesson to Francis I, some of the essential principles of his later views on civil government already make an appearance here. There is, for instance, a significant note citing St Paul's Romans 13 to demonstrate that Christianity requires obedience to princes; and there are several references to princes as the vicars or delegates of God, an idea that would play a central part in his mature political theology. By the time he wrote the first edition of the *Institutes* after his conversion, his theological principles were already bound up with his views on civil government; and, whichever came first, Calvin's political ideas are securely grounded in the most fundamental tenets of his theology. The inextricable connection would be firmly sealed by his career in Geneva.

The first edition of the *Institutes* was introduced by an epistle dedicatory to Francis I of France, which presents the catechism that follows as a defence of the reformed religion against threats faced by French Evangelicals. In his effort to demonstrate that the reformed faith poses no threat to the king's authority, Calvin proceeds on two fronts: he seeks to show that the Roman Church, in its usurpations of temporal power, represents a more sinister challenge to the monarch's authority, while at the same time the theologian opposes radical reformers, notably the Anabaptists, who deny the legitimacy of civil governance. The book ends with a long chapter on civil government, which may be read as a continuation of his letter to the king; but it also confronts a different set of questions, posed not by the threat of the Catholic Church but by the distinctive relations between civic authority and a reformed Church within the free Protestant city.

It has been said that Calvin's theology, like that of Zwingli and Bucer, is 'the result of the Reformation message filtered through the actuality of the free city'.[7] It is true that the very specific relationship between secular and spiritual spheres that characterized the Protestant cities, where civic and ecclesiastical authority were both separate and intertwined in such

---

7   Bernd Moeller, *Imperial Cities and the Reformation* (Philadelphia: Fortress Press, 1972), p. 89.

distinctive ways, posed different problems for theology than those that preoccupied Luther. When Calvin wrote the first edition of the *Institutes,* he was certainly concerned with the fate of French Evangelicals under threat from the Catholic Church; but he was also compelled to address a very different set of questions, which did not have to do with the rival claims to temporal authority in conflicts between kings or German princes and the Holy Roman Empire or the papacy. While maintaining a distinction between secular and spiritual realms, he could not rely, as Luther did, on denying any jurisdiction to the Church; but nor could he simply assert the authority of secular government over the Church. He was obliged to explain the division of labour between secular and ecclesiastical authorities, both of which had an essential role in sustaining the reformed faith and both of which played a central role in governing the earthly city.

Political life in a city like Basle or Geneva thus placed a special burden on Protestant theology. For Luther, in a different context, it was enough to confine the functions of the Church to preaching the Word and administering certain sacraments, while asserting the exclusive jurisdictional claims of secular government against ecclesiastical pretensions, yet asking little more of earthly government than that it rein in a sinful humanity. His theology achieves this effect by stressing the simultaneous duality of sin and justification: God's loving grace 'justifies' humanity as a free and unearned gift, even while the sinfulness of human beings, their implication in the devil's 'kingdom', requires submission to secular government, which is divinely ordained.

Calvin may have been more reluctant to give secular governments a dominant authority over the Church; but within its own domain he demanded more of secular power than did Luther, and his views on civil government therefore required a different theology. He certainly shares the principal tenet of Lutheranism, the doctrine of justification by faith; but his emphasis is less on God's loving grace than on his total sovereignty.[8] While justification remains an unearned gift, which is not a reward for virtue, good works, or freedom from sin, the godly life of the Christian community is not just a matter of service and good works freely undertaken by the Christian faithful in answer to God's loving grace. It follows from God's unconditional will that Christians must in this world live a life of godly discipline.

Calvin's theology underwrites a partnership between secular and spiritual authorities, in which both, equally under the sovereignty of God, exercise temporal jurisdiction. This not only restores to the Church its own temporal authority but also elevates the role of civil government. Its function is not simply to maintain civil peace and good order among sinful human beings but, in a joint project with the Church, to impose a godly discipline on the

---

8 Francis Oakley, 'Christian Obedience and Authority', in *Cambridge History*, p. 182.

Christian community in recognition of God's total sovereignty. Civil government, in other words, is not just a divinely ordained institution to cope with the 'kingdom' of the devil as it manifests itself in human sinfulness. Civic authorities act together with the Church in the fulfillment of God's sovereign will. This means that, even while the Church ministers to the soul as civil government takes care of more mundane concerns (which include defending the true faith), there can be no clear distinction between the godly standards upheld by the Church and some kind of lesser, more modest, less divine criteria applied to civic life.

Calvin's doctrine of predestination may seem to complicate the issue. After all, if human beings are damned or saved through no fault or virtue of their own, what can it mean to demand of them that they live according to the dictates of a godly discipline? Yet if we start not with predestination but with God's sovereign will, the logic of Calvin's argument may be easier to trace: the doctrine of predestination – the idea that our fate depends entirely, without condition, on God's determination – follows directly from the notion of God's total and unconditional sovereignty, as does the idea of godly discipline and the role of both jurisdictional spheres in maintaining it.

It is almost as if Calvin arrives at his doctrine of predestination less because it expresses his deepest convictions than because it seems an unavoidable consequence of God's total sovereignty, which is central to his views on the role of the Church and civil government. In the *Institutes,* the argument for predestination – the predestination of the damned no less than of the elect – comes down to this: we must believe in it, because to do otherwise is to detract from the glory of a totally sovereign God. But, in Calvin's view, there is little to be gained by dwelling on it. Precisely because it represents God's unconditional sovereign will, which cannot be understood or judged by any human standards, it must remain a mystery; and we should not attempt to penetrate God's judgment on our own fate in the afterlife. The best that Christians can do, in their humility and unconditional obedience to God, is to act in this world with confidence in the goodness and generosity of God's justification, proceeding in their earthly callings as if they and their fellows belonged to the elect, with faith that not only their souls but their works are justified by divine grace.

Christians, then, must serve their community in accordance with the principles of godly discipline. This certainly elevates earthly callings to a new respectability and even grants an element of godliness to the most humble human labours. But, while Calvin's idea of the calling, more than Luther's, invites the faithful to take an active part in shaping the social and political conditions of their lives on this earth, it also means that civil governments must be regarded as representatives of God; and this carries with it a strong obligation to obedience: 'When those who bear the office of magistrate are called gods, let no one suppose that there is little weight in that appellation. It is thereby intimated that they have a commission from God, that they are invested with divine authority and, in fact, represent the person of God, as whose substitutes they in a manner act' (IV.20.4). It follows that Christians owe obedience to civil government, and even tyrants must be treated as the delegates of God: 'even an individual of the worst character, one most unworthy of all honour, if invested with public authority, receives that illustrious divine power which the Lord has by his word devolved on the ministers of his justice and judgment, and that, accordingly, in so far as public obedience is concerned, he is to be held in the same honour and reverence as the best of kings' (IV.20.25). Christians should obey secular government not simply out of fear 'but because the obedience which they yield is rendered to God himself, inasmuch as their power is from God' (IV.20.22).

Nevertheless, if Calvin's doctrine of obedience to civil authority seems hardly less, or even more, stringent than Luther's, his roots in the free Protestant city do make a difference. When considering the various forms of government, he expresses a preference for collective governments instead of kings, if only on the grounds that human imperfections make it useful to have magistrates who can keep an eye on one another. The ideal might be a city like Geneva, governed by civic elites through the medium of magistrates and city councillors, who have an official duty to preserve the city's liberty. This means that, on the whole, aristocracy is best, or perhaps a mixed constitution in which aristocracy is leavened by an element of popular government. There is nonetheless, Calvin tells us, no point in discussing which government is best, since that depends on circumstances; and, in any case, we must assume that, whatever the prevailing type of government in any given circumstance, it was decreed by God. While the Lord may take vengeance against 'unbridled domination', 'let us not therefore suppose that that vengeance is committed to us, to whom no command has been given but to obey and suffer' (IV.20 31).

There seems to be no ambiguity in Calvin's views on strict obedience, but here he introduces a qualification that would have major consequences for political theory. 'I speak', he says, 'only of private men'; because there have existed public offices – presumably decreed by God – whose duty it has been 'to curb the tyranny of kings', such as the Ephori in Sparta, the tribunate in Rome, the Demarchs in Athens, and perhaps even the assembled three estates in a kingdom like France (IV.20.31). It has been the public duty of these 'lesser magistrates' to defend the people against the tyranny of rulers. Although Calvin himself would never go beyond the observation that there have existed public offices whose official duty is to represent the interests of the people as a check on princely power, the doctrine of the 'lesser magistrate' would become the basis of more wide-ranging and militant resistance theories.

That doctrines supporting the power of temporal authorities, and even the need for obedience to them, could be mobilized in support of resistance to power and even popular rebellion is a peculiarity of Western culture. Other societies have certainly created doctrines of rebellion, but they took a very special form in Western Europe. The fragmentation of political power in feudal Europe, and the constant jurisdictional battles that followed from it for centuries thereafter, produced quite distinctive effects. The assertion of one jurisdiction against another could be formulated as a right to resist illegitimate power or tyranny. While this meant that ideas of resistance could be adopted and disseminated by ruling classes, landlords and civic elites, it also meant that their interests would shape and constrain Western conceptions of democracy, in ways that persist to this day.

Protestantism and the Rise of Capitalism?

What, then, should we make of the proposition that Protestantism had something to do with the 'rise of capitalism'? It is certainly true that Lutheranism became a powerful force when it established itself in great commercial centres. It is also true that, in some commercial cities, where urban patriciates had become rentiers instead of active merchants and where they restricted access to the political domain, burghers and new merchants without political privileges might use Protestant doctrine to challenge patrician dominance. It may even be true that Protestantism, and Calvinism in particular, removed ecclesiastical constraints on commercial activities, or that Protestant doctrine, and especially Calvin's doctrine of the calling, called into question old verities about the unworthiness of commercial pursuits and the acquisition of wealth, or about work as a curse and simply a punishment for original sin. But, even if we accept that Protestantism promoted a 'work ethic' or that it had certain benefits for merchants, and even if we set aside its equal usefulness to nobles, princes and kings, its bearing on the 'spirit of capitalism' is another matter altogether.

Let us first be clear about what is meant by capitalism and the conditions of its 'rise'. Conventional wisdom – and, indeed, a great deal of scholarly work – treats the rise of capitalism as little more than the quantitative growth of commerce or exchange for profit. Capitalism, in other words, is 'commercial society' as understood by classical political economy, a society in which commercial practices that have existed since time immemorial have, with the expansion of cities, markets and trade, become the economic norm. Human beings have, time out of mind, engaged in profitable exchange, and capitalism is just more of the same. This means that, if the birth of capitalism requires any explanation, all that needs to be explained is the growth of market opportunities and the removal of obstacles to the expansion of commerce.

Yet this understanding of capitalism takes no account of the very specific economic principles that came into being in early modern Europe, principles very different from anything that had existed before even in the most commercialized societies: not simply the growth of market opportunities with the expansion of vast trading networks, but the emergence of wholly new *compulsions*, the inescapable imperatives of competition, profit-maximization, constant accumulation and the endless need to reduce the costs of labour by improving labour productivity. These imperatives did not operate in the age-old practices of commercial exchange even in its most elaborate forms. Traders made their fortunes not by means of cost-effective production in integrated competitive markets but rather by negotiating separate markets, the 'buying cheap and selling dear' that was the essence of pre-capitalist commerce. A revolutionary transformation of relations between producing and appropriating classes, as well as changes in the nature of property, would be required to set in train the imperatives of the capitalist market – as happened in English agrarian capitalism

Once we identify capitalism with market *imperatives*, the search for its origins must take a different form. The question then becomes not how commercial opportunities expanded and economies were freed to take advantage of them, or even how the cultural and moral climate changed to justify pursuit of profit, but rather how social arrangements and the production of basic human needs were so fundamentally transformed as to impose compulsions and necessities unlike any that had governed human social life before.

This is not a question addressed by the most influential advocates of the view that Protestantism in one way or another promoted the development of capitalism – Max Weber and R.H. Tawney – nor, indeed, by their later supporters and critics. Both traced the evolution of Protestantism, especially in its Calvinist form, into a particular variety of Puritanism, especially in England, that encouraged 'capitalist' values and practices; but neither of them actually argued that Protestantism *caused* the emergence of capitalism. It would be fair to say that in both arguments the development of Protestantism into a doctrine favouring capitalism (in the sense they understood it) *presupposes* the existence of certain forms of property and economic practices that, if not already fully 'capitalist' (in their terms), are 'capitalist' in embryo and mark a significant break from feudal forms and principles.

Weber was perhaps more inclined than Tawney to emphasize the growth of cities and the process of commercialization, while Tawney, despite a more or less conventional association of capitalism with the commercial classes, had a greater interest than did Weber in the transformations of landed property which took place in England as a precursor to commercial and industrial capitalism.[9] Tawney may go further than Weber in tracing the transformation of Calvinism into a capitalist-friendly Puritanism, and he certainly is clearer about the ways in which existing economic practices shaped the formation of religious ideas. But both suggest that, if there had not already existed property forms and classes disposed to operate on 'capitalist' principles, Protestant doctrine would not and could not have been – selectively – appropriated and adapted to the 'spirit of capitalism'. Without these pre-existing elements of 'capitalism' there could, by definition, have been no 'elective affinity' (as Weber himself described it) between Protestantism and capitalism.

The argument being offered here departs from both Weber and Tawney not because it gives 'material' factors priority over ideas. Neither the German sociologist nor the English historian treats religious ideas as autonomous and primary, as against material determinants; and both have complex understandings of causality. Nor does the present book deny complex interactions of causation or the efficacy of ideas. Where it differs most fundamentally from other views on the connection between Protestantism and the rise of capitalism is that it insists, in a way the others do not, on the specificity of capitalism, its radical rupture from preceding social forms, including earlier forms of commerce. However much Weber and Tawney emphasize the break from feudal practices and attitudes, they both take for granted that capitalism is an extension of commerce, which already existed in the interstices of feudalism (and, indeed, before). The rise of capitalism, in this view, took place when and because commercial classes and the practices of commerce were liberated and encouraged to grow by the removal of obstacles – institutional, cultural or attitudinal – and/or by the construction of ethical supports for commercial profit-taking that were lacking before.

---

9 More than a decade before the publication of *Religion and the Rise of Capitalism*, Tawney published his great work, *The Agrarian Problem in the Sixteenth Century*, which clearly outlines the new market principles that were already driving English agriculture before the advent of Puritanism. Just as Tawney's work on religion should be read against the background of that book, so too should Weber's *Protestant Ethic and the Spirit of Capitalism* be situated in his whole body of work on economic history and especially his writings on the city. Although Weber sees elements of 'capitalism' even in ancient Rome, the medieval city, in his view, prefigured modern industrial capitalism when and because it became a 'centre of production' and not just of consumption, as it was, he maintains, in classical antiquity. But this development seems to have been for him a natural consequence of the liberation and political elevation of burgher classes in the medieval West. There is a question-begging slippage at precisely the critical juncture in the argument, since the work ethic that, in Weber's account, encouraged modern industrial capitalism is, in his account, nothing more than an elaboration of the age-old principles of profitable exchange, for the first time given free rein and positive ethical support. For more on this point, see Ellen Meiksins Wood, *Democracy Against Capitalism: Renewing Historical Materialism* (Cambridge: Cambridge University Press, 1995), Ch. 5.

The argument in this book, by contrast, starts from the premise that capitalism represents a fundamental break from other forms of commerce no less than from what Weber and Tawney regard as 'feudal' – that is, in their terms, non-commercial – principles and practices.

Seen from this perspective, the historic role of Protestantism looks rather different. On the one hand, whatever we may say about the usefulness of certain Calvinist principles in sustaining a philosophy of life congenial to commercial profit, it tells us very little about the rise of capitalism. We may place our emphasis, as Weber does, on a 'work ethic' more or less directly derived from Calvin's ideas of predestination, 'limited atonement' and the 'calling'; or we may stress, as Tawney does, the revolutionary Puritan modification of Calvinism that discarded one essential aspect of Calvin's own doctrine, its commitment to a godly discipline and even a kind of collectivism, in favour of an economic individualism. Either one or both may tell us something (though even here a certain caution is required) about strategies of self-justification adopted by people seeking to avail themselves of market opportunities or about psychological adaptations to the uncertainties of commerce. But neither tells us anything about the systemic *imperatives* imposed on capitalists, which compel them to maximize profit, whatever their own motivations and values and however limited their greed.

At the same time, if we acknowledge the specificity of capitalist imperatives, we may be more inclined to consider the ways in which Protestantism had less to do with capitalism or even a commercial ethic than with the maintenance of power in distinctly non-capitalist forms. In the case of England, where capitalist social property relations did emerge, it might be possible to speak of an 'elective affinity' between Protestantism and capitalism, if only in the sense that *all* forms of English Protestantism, including High Church Anglicanism no less than Cromwell's Puritanism, were shaped by the specificities of property and state in England. But this specific case should not be allowed to obscure the distinctly non-capitalist origin and substance of the Reformation.

Luther's theology served the purposes of German princes, but it was also deployed by civic magistrates and became a major historical force when adopted by important commercial cities. Yet Lutheranism emerged at a time when Germany's commercial cities were in a process of decline. The Hanseatic League's domination of trade in Northern Europe was giving way to rising powers, such as the Swedish and the Dutch; and the independence of some cities was threatened by territorial princes with stronger military force at their disposal, not least the princes of the Church endowed with the powers and prerogatives of secular rulers. Maintaining civic autonomy became an ever more costly business, which aggravated social tensions between urban patriciates and other classes that were subject to burdensome exactions. Civic magistrates defended their city's autonomy by challenging

the authority of emperors and princes and often pursued anti-clerical policies to avoid the burdens imposed by ecclesiastical jurisdiction. Burghers
demanded a share in civic governance against dominant urban patriciates;
and urban elites asserted their rule against threats from below. In all these
battles Lutheran doctrine proved distinctively useful, for reasons that had
nothing to do with the 'spirit of capitalism'.

Much the same can be said of Calvinism. Calvin's theology was eminently
suited to the needs of civic magistrates, not because of anything to do with
the doctrine of predestination, the calling or the 'work ethic', but rather
because of his elaborate discussion of civil government, to which a large
part of the *Institutes* is devoted, promoting the idea that magistrates are
'gods'. This doctrine had direct and obvious implications for the civic
governance of Calvin's Geneva. Yet the very same principles that made
Calvinist doctrine so useful to civic magistrates could as easily be, and were,
applied to other secular authorities seeking to preserve their extra-economic
powers, at a time when the economic interests of all classes were (in sharp
contrast to capitalism) dependent on political status and privilege, or 'politically constituted property'. Just as Lutheranism could be mobilized in the
interests of princes no less than of civic authorities, so too did Calvinism,
for all Calvin's devotion to his adopted city and its civic institutions, serve
the purposes of French provincial nobles or even English kings.

4

THE SPANISH EMPIRE

In the 1530s, in his lectures at the University of Salamanca, the Spanish Dominican theologian Francisco de Vitoria presented an interesting variation on Western Christianity's defining principle about the rightful domains of Caesar and God. 'In this way and by this title', he said,

> the Roman Empire was enlarged and extended – that is, by taking over by law of war the cities and provinces of enemies from whom they had received any injury; and yet the Roman Empire is defended as just and legitimate by Augustine, Jerome, Ambrose, St Thomas, and by other holy doctors. In fact, it may be seen as approved by our Lord and Redeemer Jesus Christ in that famous passage: 'Render therefore unto Caesar the things which are Caesar's. etc.', and by Paul, who appealed to Caesar (Acts 25: 10) and advised us (Romans 13) to be subject to the higher powers and to be subject to the princes and render them their tributes – all of which princes at that time had their authority from the Roman Empire. (*De Indis et de jure belli*, III.56)

The principle of 'render unto Caesar' was here being invoked not simply, in the customary Western Christian way, as a warrant for obedience to secular authorities but more particularly as, apparently, a defence of empire. Vitoria's stance on Spain's far-flung empire remained ambiguous. He has been variously cited both against the imperial regime and, at least ambivalently, in its favour; but his lectures at the University of Salamanca elaborated doctrines that would have considerable significance for European political thought and its conceptions of natural law, natural rights, the law of war, and international law.

In the decades following Vitoria's lectures, there would be a flowering of Spanish political thought; and, if there is one defining feature that distinguishes this tradition of discourse from others among Spain's European neighbours, it is that the central questions confronted by the so-called School of Salamanca arose not just from jurisdictional disputes between a centralizing state and various 'parcellized sovereignties' but from Spain's distinctive experience of imperial expansion. Reflecting on empire and the treatment of indigenous peoples had the effect, among other things, of putting on the agenda ideas of natural rights residing in the individual that went beyond what the tradition of Western political thought had yet been able to contemplate in its reflections on the state.

State or Empire?

Spain in the sixteenth century has been called Europe's, even the world's, most powerful nation. Yet this claim can hardly be ascribed to its preeminence in forging a 'modern' or unified national state, with more or less unambiguous sovereignty over its domestic territory, or at least a reasonably well delineated sphere of national jurisdiction. It is certainly true that Ferdinand and Isabella challenged the independent powers of the nobility and did much to establish a strong monarchy in Spain, while weakening the *cortes*, descended from what has been called the first Parliament in Western Europe. Not the least of their efforts in strengthening monarchical authority was their institution of the Spanish Inquisition, which, whatever else it may have done, was clearly intended to replace papal hegemony over religious orthodoxy in Spain with control by the Catholic monarchy. Their successors would continue the centralizing project; but even in the imperial golden age of the Habsburg rule of Charles I and thereafter, the Spanish state was still a tenuous national entity. Its constitutive elements were two very distinct and autonomous kingdoms, Castile and Aragon, with their own very distinct political institutions and traditions.

When the two ruling families united to form a single royal state, each kingdom brought to the union its internal jurisdictional conflicts among parcellized sovereignties, corporate, local and regional. The kingdom of Aragon was a federation consisting of several separate realms, not least Catalonia, with its own jurisdictional tensions, a well-developed feudal structure, and the so-called *pactisme,* in which the power of the central authority was constrained by more or less contractual agreements with the aristocracy. The kingdom of Castile, which led the imperial project, had no strong tradition of feudal lordship; but war with the Moors had produced not only a class of warlords with fairly autonomous powers over the kingdom's expanding territories in Spain but also an armed class of small proprietors. The medieval *reconquista*, recapturing Moorish lands in Europe, had been less the work of a powerful kingdom than a partnership not unlike the classic feudal exchange between monarch and military leaders, in which conditional rights of property and jurisdiction had been vested in the lord in exchange for military services. In the early modern period, a very large proportion of Spain remained outside royal jurisdiction: in 1600 two-thirds of its towns and half of its villages were under private control, while the king had no standing army and no bureaucracy or civil service, generally farmed out taxes, and governed his provinces with the cooperation of elites.[1] The royal state would produce bureaucracies both at home and in the colonies, but the weakness of state sovereignty in Spain remained a constant theme throughout our period.

The Spanish nonetheless created the largest overseas empire the world had ever seen. This would become the essence of the kingdom's wealth and power. Its prosperity depended above all else on gold and silver from the colonies; and this wealth, together with growing colonial demand, did for a time fuel the economy at home. Colonial wealth undoubtedly strengthened the position of Spain in its conflicts with other European kingdoms, such as the French. Yet even in its massive empire the weakness of Spain as a national entity, political or economic, was on display. The circulation of colonial wealth in external trade would come to be controlled less by Spanish traders than by merchants in Genoa and Antwerp, and the weaknesses of the royal state were reproduced in colonial governance.

Imperial expansion in the Americas was modelled on the reconquest of European lands from the Moors and its spread into Africa and the Canaries. While it is certainly true that Spanish monarchs always sought to protect their own royal powers and succeeded in preventing the emergence of a hereditary feudal aristocracy in the colonies, they presided over Spain's massive imperial expansion by farming out the tasks of empire to private conquerors in pursuit of private wealth. Just as the process of royal centralization would be constantly dogged by domestic conflicts over jurisdiction, so too would the empire be marked from beginning to end by the tensions between monarchs and private conquerors or their heirs in the colonial landed classes.

Imperial expansion was achieved with a remarkably small military force, and the Spanish military presence in the colonies was never very large. Nor was the conquest intended to exterminate indigenous peoples in order to occupy their lands. With Spain's dependence on gold and silver from mines in the Americas, the imperial rulers had more to gain from preserving the local population and exploiting its labour. The civilizations they encountered ranged from nomadic hunter-gatherers to densely populated, socially stratified and technologically complex empires; and, while the conquest destroyed these advanced civilizations, the conquerors stood to benefit from their technologies, their agricultural skills and their experience of large-scale public projects.[2] Nonetheless, whatever its intentions, the conquest

---

1 Henry Kamen, *Spain 1469–1714: A Society of Conflict* (Harlow: Pearson/Longman, 3rd edn, 2005), p. 160.

2 On the Latin American peoples encountered by the conquerors, see Mark A. Burkholder and Lyman L. Johnson, *Colonial Latin America* (Oxford: Oxford University Press, 4th edn, 2001).

would prove genocidal, spreading disease and imposing a brutally destructive system of exploitation.

The Spanish monarchy may have succeeded in its efforts to prevent the formation of a feudal aristocracy in the colonies and to avoid the emergence of representative institutions like the *cortes*, but there remained the problem of commanding the subject labour force. Here the Spanish state had to strike a difficult balance between controlling local landholders and allowing them the power to exploit the Indians. Having outlawed formal slavery in 1500, the colonial power produced the *encomienda* system, modelled on the settlement of recaptured Moorish lands in Europe.

In theory, the *encomienda* was not a grant of land to colonial settlers. The Indians were subjected to tributary labour, ostensibly in exchange for religious education and military protection by the settlers; but the indigenous people were in principle recognized as owners of the land, even while nearby plantations might belong to the *encomendero* and be worked by the same Indians. Nor did the *encomendero* have formally acknowledged political jurisdiction over the indigenous population. But, in practice, these formal limits on the *encomendero*'s ownership of land and on his jurisdiction had little effect in containing the settlers' control over their subjects or in moderating the harshness of the system. It became a murderously extreme form of exploitation, little short of slavery and responsible for killing huge numbers of Indians. In the Caribbean it destroyed itself within a generation, while its persistence elsewhere continued to arouse opposition both from the Church and, if inconsistently, even from the royal state, which had its own reasons for seeking to check the powers of *encomenderos*. But when laws were passed to modify or abolish the system, they had little effect. The *encomienda* long remained, in one form or another, a defining feature of Spanish imperial rule, leaving its mark on other colonial forms of landownership and labour.

The monarchy did implant local administrations to counteract the power of the settlers. In Peru, for instance, it created an elaborate state bureaucracy in large part for the purpose of regulating forced labour in the mines. But the Spanish state was never able to govern its colonial territories without permitting local landed classes to dominate the land and its people. Even the all-important gold and silver eluded the royal grasp. The Crown, finding it impossible to exploit this source of huge wealth on its own, was compelled to relinquish its hold on the mines, giving them up to local ownership or leasing them out in exchange for a share of the yield.

Spain's growing dependence on bullion imported from the colonies, instead of on domestic agriculture and industry, and even at the cost of colonial production, has often been blamed for the decline of the Spanish economy from the seventeenth century onward. But, however important such factors may be in explaining the dramatic decline of what for a time had been the greatest imperial power the world had yet seen, it is also true that there was from the start an inherent instability in this world empire. It depended for its dominance neither on a powerful political and military force, nor even on commercial strengths, but rather on vesting powers in colonial landed classes. The later rebellions of colonial ruling classes and the wars of independence that were to follow had less to do with the emergence of a revolutionary bourgeoisie in the colonies, as some historical accounts suggest, than with the legacy of the uneasy colonial balance between a distant imperial state, with a tenuous hold on its own domestic sovereignty, and local power based on landed property.

The School of Salamanca

Spain was a world empire long before it was a proper 'nation state'; and that distinctive reality is clearly reflected in Spanish political thought. The usual Western European jurisdictional disputes – between ecclesiastical and secular authorities, or among monarchs, popes, Holy Roman Emperors, aristocracies, and municipal elites – were certainly all present. The historical moment in which the Salamanca School began to flourish was the reign of Charles I, the grandson of Ferdinand and Isabella, who became the Holy Roman Emperor Charles V; and this period, as we have seen, was fraught with tensions between emperor and pope, as well as German princes, to say nothing of the rivalries among the rising European kingdoms and the always looming Turkish threat. But, in Spanish political thought, these conflicts were typically filtered through the preoccupations of empire. Other rulers, like the French or the English, might claim to be 'emperors' in their own kingdoms; and this would shape European conceptions of sovereignty. But, in the Spanish case, the imperial idea had less to do with the sovereignty of the royal state at home, where its powers were limited by various more or less explicitly contractual relations with competing jurisdictions, than with the colonial domination of far-flung territories and their indigenous peoples.

The contested sovereignty that plagued other monarchs, such as the French, certainly encouraged theoretical debates about what constitutes legitimate political authority, but in Spain the empire raised especially sharp questions. It was one thing for the king to claim *dominium* over his kingdom at home as if it were his private household. It was quite another matter to assert his domination over distant colonial territories and their indigenous populations, especially those with their own complex modes of organization and governance. The 'high' civilizations of the Americas made it more difficult to invoke traditional conceptions of domestic lordship or natural hierarchy. Defenders of the empire and the *encomienda* system did, to be sure, appeal to Aristotle's conception of natural slavery; but Indians with elaborate technologies and complex forms of government were not so easily dismissed as slaves by nature or as irrational creatures, subject to the authority of their natural superiors; and claims to empire on these grounds were contested almost from the beginning. Once even their lack of Christian belief had been challenged as a justification for subjecting indigenous peoples to imperial domination, it became that much more pressing to confront fundamental questions about how legitimate rule should be defined. The Spanish mode of imperial expansion had created its own ideological needs, and Spanish political thinkers had particular reasons to reflect on the natural rights of colonial subjects or the limits imposed on their imperial masters by natural law.

The Reformation, and especially the translation of Protestant doctrine into theories of resistance, would pose problems for the Spanish royal state engaged in a contested process of centralization, as it did for other European monarchies, notably the French. But the realities of imperial conquest presented a distinctive challenge. Debate on this subject preceded the Reformation and would help to shape the Spanish Counter-Reformation. The huge influx of silver and gold would have been enough to generate fierce debate among theologians long accustomed to disputes about the rightful attitude of Christians towards property and wealth;[3] and the Spanish would, among other things, produce innovative theories of money and exchange, which have even been credited as the origin of modern economics. But the fact that imperial wealth was acquired by brute force made its defence even more complicated. While the empire was won by relatively small military forces, there was no mistaking Spanish America as anything but an empire of conquest. It may have been less deliberately murderous than the English colonial project in North America, which was shamelessly intended to clear the land for settlers; yet – or perhaps for that very reason – the Spanish, dependent as they were on ruling and exploiting a large and visible mass of indigenous labour, found it harder to disguise the nature of their imperial enterprise.

Defenders of imperial domination were unambiguously explicit that what they were justifying was indeed conquest, in contrast to the peaceful virtues of commerce and agriculture that would be invoked to support (no less bloody) English, and to some extent French, imperial ventures.[4] At the same time, since Spanish imperial rule was being imposed, and by violent means, on high civilizations with their own complex modes of governance,

---

3 See my *Citizens to Lords*, esp. pp. 182–6 for a discussion of medieval debates on property, particularly between Franciscan and Dominican theologians.

4 For an illuminating discussion of Spanish imperialist ideology, in contrast to British and French, see Anthony Pagden, *Lords of All the World: Ideologies of Empire in Spain, Britain and France c. 1500–1800* (New Haven: Yale University Press, 1995).

the defence of conquest was more difficult, raising fundamental questions about the property and sovereignty, indeed the rationality and natural rights, of colonial victims.

The complexities were greatly aggravated by their implication in the usual jurisdictional disputes. Early justifications of the empire were based on donation from the pope, but the uneasy relations between the monarchy and the papacy, especially when Charles became the Holy Roman Emperor and found himself in conflict with the pope, made papal donation an awkward defence. Papal donation was also vigorously challenged by Spain's European rivals, contesting Spanish claims to imperial territories, which made it even more useful to find alternative justifications.

Under Holy Roman imperial rule, the Empire could be presented as something like a mission on behalf of a universal empire or the Christian world order, much as the ancient Roman Empire had claimed to be acting on behalf of a universal world order; but theological arguments against the claims of the papacy, which worked in favour of the monarchy, tended also to argue against the 'universal empire' and against the Spanish conquest. Theologians of the Salamanca School argued that the pope, though he was the spiritual leader of Christendom, had no temporal authority over the world, nor did the pope – or the Church he represented – have authority of any kind over non-Christians. This could be taken to mean that there was no such thing as a universal 'holy' temporal empire, but it also cast doubt on the defence of conquest on the grounds that it was bringing Christianity to infidels or punishing savages for violations of natural law.

The Spanish crown also had other reasons for encouraging such arguments against colonial oppression, with or without its conflicts with the papacy. In its attempts to control the feudal ambitions of colonial settlers and to prevent the emergence of a hereditary aristocracy in America, it had very practical reasons for welcoming attacks on the *encomendero*'s brutality and on the *encomienda* system itself. The restrictions imposed by the monarchy on the growth of slavery and its attempts to abolish the *encomienda* system may have been in part genuinely motivated by ethical and religious concerns, but there can be little doubt that the effort to curtail the independent power of the settlers was an overriding consideration.

Whether motivated by humanitarian revulsion at imperial atrocities or simply defending the monarchy, powerful arguments were launched by theologians and jurists challenging Spanish domination in the Americas; and this forced defenders of empire to change their strategies. It was a particularly delicate business for monarchist defenders of empire, who were obliged to attack the *encomenderos* without undermining the monarch's imperial claims. They might accept that the Church or the papacy had no universal temporal authority, but then turn – as is suggested by Vitoria in his observations about God and Caesar – to less grandiose claims and especially to the concept of 'just war'.

The 'just war' tradition had, from its roots in antiquity, been notoriously elastic, encompassing everything up to and including the most aggressive and predatory imperial adventures. Throughout its various permutations, the doctrine of just war enunciates a few basic requirements for going to war: there must be a just cause; war must be declared by a proper authority and with the right intention, and after other means have been exhausted; there must be a reasonable chance of achieving the desired end, and the means must be proportionate to that end. Yet these apparently stringent requirements would be made compatible with the most aggressive wars of imperial expansion and, later, commercial rivalry. The idea of just war had already done service in the *reconquista*, when the victors elaborated intricate codes for dealing with, and even enslaving, their victims.

Colonialism in the Americas, then, might not be justified on the grounds of papal decree or the Church's temporal authority; but, argued supporters of the conquest, there were various legitimate reasons for waging war. A 'just war' might be necessary to defend the 'innocent' or, much more broadly, to promote the values of 'civilized' life, in self-defence or on behalf of a universal 'human republic' threatened by behaviour that violated standards of peace and good order or impeded free commerce. Any conquest resulting from a just war could establish legitimate domination, which could be defined so broadly as even to justify slavery.

The debate began in the earliest days of the conquest. In 1493, Pope Alexander VI (the infamous father of the even more infamous Cesare Borgia) issued a papal pronouncement that was meant to settle disputes between Portuguese and Spanish claims to imperial lands. By 'papal donation', Spain was granted land in the Americas. From the beginning there were questions about papal jurisdiction; but even for those unwilling to challenge the pope's authority, or indeed the Spanish monarchy's right to rule colonial territories, ambiguities in the pope's proclamation generated passionate debate about whether he was sanctioning colonization by violent means – that is, by means of 'just war' – or simply the peaceful conversion of heathens. In either case, what is unambiguously clear is the pope's assumption that Spain did indeed have the right to establish its colonies and not only a right but an obligation to impose the Christian faith.

This controversy would figure decades later in the most famous debate – the Vallidolid debate of 1550–51 between Bartolomé de Las Casas and Juan Ginés de Sepúlveda – about the Spanish colonial regime. By this time, the debate was taking place against the background of growing controversy over the treatment of Indians. In 1511, a year after the Dominicans arrived in the colonies, a friar of the order, Antonio Montesino, had given a ground-breaking sermon addressed to the settlers and *encomenderos*. 'Tell me', he demanded,

> by what right and justice do you keep these Indians in such cruel and horrible servitude? On what authority have you waged a detestable war on these people who dwelt quietly and peacefully on their own land? . . . Are these not men? Have they not rational souls? Must not you love them as you love yourselves?

Las Casas had himself been an *encomendero;* and even when, partly under the influence of Montesino, he came to oppose the existing system of labour in the Americas, he would for a time support the enslavement of Africans. But, while he never opposed imperial expansion and remained convinced that Indians should be converted to Christianity, he became a forceful and consistent critic of the *encomienda* system and conversion by force of arms. His views certainly had their effects on Spanish opinion and influenced the Laws of Burgos, passed in 1512–13 to regulate the system, but these had little practical effect in improving the condition of the Indians and were still clearly based on the assumption that the conquest was legitimate. The brutal regime of *encomiendas* continued unchecked.

Las Casas would elaborate a powerful argument in support of the view that the Indians were rational beings with a complex civilization and capable of peaceful conversion. His views, although not yet spelled out as systematically as they would be in the Vallidolid debate, clearly influenced Pope Paul III. In 1537 the pope issued a papal bull proclaiming that 'the Indians are truly men and that they are not only capable of understanding the Catholic Faith but, according to our information, they desire exceedingly to receive it . . .' '[T]he said Indians', the pope went on,

> and all other people who may later be discovered by Christians, are by no means to be deprived of their liberty or the possession of their property, even though they be outside the faith of Jesus Christ; and that they may and should, freely and legitimately, enjoy their liberty and the possession of their property; nor should they be in any way enslaved; should the contrary happen, it shall be null and have no effect.

While this did not explicitly revoke Alexander's earlier edict, it could be so interpreted (though battles to persuade the Vatican to revoke it explicitly have continued to this day). At the same time, it could be, and was, understood by some to leave open the possibility of legitimate conquest – that is, a just war – to impose Christianity on those who proved themselves unable or unwilling to receive it peacefully.

Although Las Casas remained convinced that Christians had a duty to convert the Indians, in 1539 he presented to the royal court a shocking account of Spanish brutality. This would lead to the New Laws of 1542, intended to regulate the *encomienda* system more stringently; but these laws would be fiercely opposed by the *encomenderos* and would, in the end, do little to transform the system. If critics like Las Casas had limited effects in practice, they did set the terms of theoretical debate. In the same year that Las Casas reported so dramatically on the condition of the Indians, Francisco Vitoria delivered the lectures at the University of Salamanca that would be published as *On the Indians and the Law of War* (*De Indis et De Jure Belli*, extracts from his *Relectiones Theologicae XII*). Although Vitoria is commonly cited as an opponent of the empire, his argument can be seen as a response to critics of the *encomienda* system like Las Casas. While Las Casas's views on the Indians' rights of dominion went far enough to challenge any colonial claims to their lands, Vitoria may have been seeking to salvage the strongest case possible for imperial conquest, once the humanity and rationality of Indians had been conceded; or, to put it another way, he may have wanted to formulate an argument that would sustain the imperial legitimacy of the Spanish crown while undermining the *encomenderos*. This may help to explain some inconsistencies and ambiguities in Vitoria's arguments; but even if we read him as an apologist for empire rather than a critic, it was precisely this confrontation with the question of empire that pushed the theory of natural rights beyond its medieval limits. The Dominican friar would be credited with pioneering international law on the strength of the *Relectiones*; and the debates on empire impelled him, and others in the School of Salamanca, to elaborate on medieval conceptions of natural law and natural rights in ways that would have significant effects on the development of Western political thought.

It needs to be emphasized that something like an idea of individual natural rights, with medieval roots, was already well established by the sixteenth century. What was not so well established was its effect on questions of state power, or, more precisely, its implications for limiting state power. Medieval theologians and jurists had left a legacy in which it was not the function of individual rights to decide the contest among competing domestic jurisdictions. Nor was the doctrine meant to establish a right of resistance to overweening royal power. There were, to be sure, thinkers prepared, *in extremis*, to countenance tyrannicide committed by individuals; and radical sects would emerge that justified resistance to any princely power. But in the mainstream of European political thought, the normal right to resist or limit monarchical power would still in the sixteenth century typically be based not on individual rights but on the jurisdictional claims of corporate bodies, municipal authorities, or local aristocracies.

The appeal to certain transcendent principles beyond the civic sphere – the assertion of some kind of moral claim available to human beings that was not derived from positive law or civil authority – would later be elaborated in modern theories of resistance or limited government. But the doctrine of right in its medieval form was, if anything, more likely to be used in *defence* of royal power, especially against the papacy. The idea that government derives its authority from the 'people' was compatible with a broad range of political commitments, including the conviction that monarchical power should be virtually unlimited. The idea that the 'people' – as a corporate entity – was the ultimate source of authority was likely to be invoked less as a limitation on state power than in support of monarchical authority, in particular against the papacy. It was precisely on the grounds that the monarch derived his authority from the people that he had jurisdiction over the secular domain, which the pope could not claim.

The right of private ownership could also, in medieval thought, easily coexist with a conception of the political community as constituted by corporate entities. Even when the state was conceived as accountable to individual propertyholders, this could, in medieval terms, still mean that the state was constituted by, and accountable to, the 'people' as a corporate entity, or even a collection of corporate bodies, with official representatives to speak or act for them.[5]

It was possible, then, to go some distance in arguing a case for rights residing in the individual and yet still espouse the idea that political authority derived from the community as a corporate entity. The idea of natural rights inherent in the individual – notably the right to property – might require some explanation of the extent to which they could, or could not, be legitimately violated by the state; but even to say, for instance, that the monarchy must not interfere with the property of its subjects did not by itself have implications for the contest over jurisdiction and political authority. The conceptual problem (if such it was) posed by the doctrine of individual rights did not arise when political authority was invested in a corporate entity that transcended the individuals of which it was composed. It was not the idea of individual rights but the notion of the community as

5 In *Citizens to Lords*, I argued that 'Even feudal property, however conditional it may be and whatever obligations it may entail, is vested in individuals; but these individuals are themselves defined by their juridical or corporate identity. They hold their property not simply as free men but as lords, or as landholders subject to feudal obligations and lordly jurisdiction.' This also had implications for the principle that the royal state is accountable to the 'people': 'Even when the "people" were granted a right to depose kings who failed in their duty, that right was typically vested in a corporate entity or its representatives, not least in feudal magnates of one kind or another' (pp. 216–17). For instance, according to the *Cambridge History of Medieval Political Thought: c. 350–1450* (Cambridge: Cambridge University Press, 1988), 'In France, the people's right to depose kings was normally discussed only in the context of rebutting papal claims to be able to do so' (p. 517).

greater than any single individual, including the king, that was more likely to be invoked in support of limited, constitutional government.

There was, in other words, no obvious contradiction between asserting the inherent rights of (private?) individuals and supporting the monarch's absolute powers in his own political domain. It might be necessary for the monarchy to guarantee his subjects a sphere of private property, but this could be done without ceding royal jurisdiction to some other fragment of sovereignty. If anything, the notion of individual rights – which entailed no claims to jurisdiction or public authority – was, in the Spanish context as in the French, less threatening to royal power than was the idea of corporate rights, rights residing in corporate entities or their official representatives. It would be in England, where competing jurisdictions were not the central issue between the monarchy and those inclined to check its powers, that the idea of individual natural rights would be most unambiguously drawn into controversies on the absolutist state.

In the English case, as we shall see, the doctrine of natural rights residing in the individual would come to have a different meaning. For contextual reasons, having to do with the relatively minor role of corporate bodies and especially of competing jurisdictions in defining the political terrain, the problem of state power and its limitation was more likely to present itself as a question about the relation between the state and the individuals that constituted it. The doctrine of natural rights would then have more obvious and immediate implications for the limitation of state power. Even an ardent defender of the absolutist state like Thomas Hobbes would feel obliged not only to explain how the natural rights of individuals could be compatible with absolute monarchy but to argue that such a state was constituted by individuals, and only by individuals, with inherent natural rights and without corporate mediations.

In the Spanish context, where the contest over royal power was played out on the terrain of corporate jurisdictions, it was the empire, more than the tensions between monarchs and subjects, that shaped the conception of natural rights. Spanish thinkers did, like their medieval predecessors, raise questions about individual rights, in particular the right of property, in opposition to monarchical intrusions; but their elaborations of medieval Thomist ideas were shaped by the imperial experience. The right to liberty as seen through the prism of empire had less to do with the civil rights and liberties of Spanish subjects in relation to the state than with the rights of indigenous peoples to be free of outright enslavement to *encomenderos*; and the right of property was seen from the angle of the competing claims over colonial territory.

In contrast, then, to more familiar conceptions of natural rights that came after it, such as that of John Locke, the purpose of the theory that emerged from the School of Salamanca was not primarily to delineate the proper relationship between the individual and the community or between the state and its citizens or subjects. The Spanish doctrine of natural rights was specifically intended to confront questions concerning the legitimacy of the empire in general and its treatment of the Indians in particular; and it was articulated in ways designed to deal with Spain's imperial dilemmas, without immediate implications for the legitimacy of the monarchical state in relation to its subjects at home.

To establish the imperial rights of the Spanish crown in the Americas – not least its claims to property in the colonies and in particular the mines – required a battle on several fronts: against other European powers and, more particularly, as we have seen, against the papacy and *encomenderos*. One of the ironies in Spanish political thought is that the argument deemed by Spanish theologians to be most effective in sustaining the king's position against the challenges he faced from all directions was one that asserted the rights of indigenous peoples. It might, in their view, even be wise to argue that the Indians had rights of jurisdiction, so that imperial domination might have to be justified on the grounds that they had consented to rule by the Spanish crown;[6] but it was even more important to concede to Indians their rights of property. The idea of papal donation was dangerous not only because of the tensions between the Spanish monarch, especially in his capacity as Holy Roman Emperor, and the pope, but also because rival European claimants to colonial territories persistently challenged the pope's jurisdiction and his authority to 'donate' land in this way. This made it prudent for defenders of the Spanish monarchy to suggest that land in the Americas could belong only to the indigenous rulers, so that they had the same rights as did European princes, whose rights of property the pope could not infringe. It was for that reason useful to find other ways of justifying Spain's colonial dominance – such as the doctrine of 'just war'. Asserting the property rights of the Indians had the added advantage of denying the *encomendero* any autonomous claims to colonial land. At the same time, to grant the Indians their rights of *dominium* was not inconsistent with the claims of foreigners to things – such as gold in the ground – that had not been appropriated by anyone, which (as Vitoria would argue in *De Indis*) by the *ius gentium* will belong to the first taker.

A Spanish thinker like Vitoria, whose *On Civil Power*, an early *relectio*, was a defence of royal power against the threats posed by radical Protestantism, could, in his later reflections on war and indigenous peoples, readily move on to espousing an idea of natural rights residing in the

---

6 See Pagden, *Lords of All the World*, pp. 50–52 for a particularly useful account of why the School of Salamanca chose to argue that Charles could claim jurisdiction over the Indians only on the basis that they had consented to it, as German princes 'consented' to his supra-legislative authority.

individual, without feeling any need to justify the transition or attempting
to demonstrate how natural rights and royal absolutism could coexist. There
was no need for him to perceive individual natural rights as a challenge to
monarchical authority. The challenge was coming from a different direction.
Vitoria had composed *On Civil Power* in 1528, after the Revolt of the
Comuneros, the rebellion of Castilians against Charles V, and after the peasant revolt in Germany. He was particularly keen to defend the authority of
princes against the threats he perceived from radical theology. Although
there are ambiguities in his account of secular authority, his principal strategy in that work is to insist that sovereign power derives not from a
community of men but from natural and divine law. It is true that even in *On
Civil Power* he sometimes suggests – and in his later lectures does so consistently – that kingly power does indeed originally come from the community,
on whose behalf the sovereign reigns. But his emphasis in this *relectio* is on
the origin of civil power in natural law. The coexistence of these divergent
accounts may seem a careless oversight; but the two propositions may not
have appeared so contradictory to Vitoria, since the idea that state power
derives from the people had long been considered perfectly compatible with
the absolute power of kings.

In another *relectio, On The Power of the Church,* Vitoria denounced the
Lutheran view that all Christians are priests and that the power of the
Church inheres in every believer, but his argument on the source of civil
power was not so different from Luther's. Luther himself, as we saw, had
argued for obedience and against resistance to secular authority, which he
treated as providentially ordained by God. It would not, then, have been
unreasonable for Vitoria to think that the real danger posed by Protestant
doctrine to secular rulers resided less in Luther's views on the source of
secular authority than in his conception of the priesthood and the Church,
which certainly was elaborated by radicals to justify resistance to secular
power despite the master's opposition.

Nonetheless, Vitoria was criticized by other Thomists for failing to recognize the threat posed by the Lutheran idea that political authority derives
directly from God's grace. Luther had argued *against* the right of resistance,
partly on the grounds that the legitimacy of secular authority cannot be
judged by the standards of natural law or the principles of justice, since we
cannot assume that a fallen humanity is capable of following, or even
comprehending, divine will or natural law. For him, in other words, appeals
to natural law could offer a dangerous pretext for rebellion. Yet natural law
had quite a different meaning for the neo-Thomist theologians when they
argued that political society was indeed grounded in natural law and that
there was indeed an element of grace and justice in the human soul. Whatever
their benevolent intentions, they had very immediately practical objectives,
too. They were, of course, concerned to salvage a capacity in human beings

to cooperate to some degree in their own salvation by God's grace, without which the Catholic Church had little meaning or authority. But they were no less concerned about the status of secular monarchies in their conflicts with each other and the papacy. They sought their solution in the concept of natural law inherited from Aquinas.

The Thomist distinction among various kinds of law – divine, eternal, natural, and human or positive – provided a means of asserting the autonomy of secular authority without denying its roots in God's will. Divine law, directed to eternal life and humanity's relationship with God, is the subject of divine revelation in scripture. This is conceptually distinct from eternal law, which represents the principles of a cosmic order governed by God. Natural law is that aspect of divine regulation accessible to human reason; but, while it establishes the basic principles of legitimate government, it exists in political society only as embodied in the positive laws enacted by governments on earth. The emphasis here is not so much (and less in some thinkers than in others) on natural law as a standard against which human legislation can be judged. The essential point is rather that, while political society is ultimately grounded in natural law, it exists only by human institution and through the medium of human legislation. Political society, in other words, does not derive directly from God's grace but is created by the human community to fulfil human ends.

Neo-Thomist theologians were far less worried about the subversive possibilities contained in a view of natural law as a standard against which secular power could be judged than they were about the threat to secular rulers presented by a conception of political authority as derived directly from God's grace. Protestant radicals had dangerously elaborated Luther's doctrine, in such a way as to imply that, if secular authority was founded by God's grace to deal with human sinfulness, his purpose could hardly be served by ungodly rulers. The Lutheran principle could be taken to imply that obedience to rulers is conditional on their godliness. This made it possible to argue that rulers could be not only passively disobeyed but actively resisted according to the dictates of the Christian conscience.

No less disturbing was the implication that 'ungodly' rulers could legitimately be deposed by conquest, an idea that was readily mobilized in conflicts among Europe's Christian monarchs. Such notions were particularly menacing at a time when Protestantism was being drawn into the tensions between monarchs or emperors and 'lesser' jurisdictions, such as the conflicts that would eventually issue in the French religious wars, or the rebellion against the Spanish empire in the Netherlands. It was, apparently, far safer to maintain that secular authority was grounded in natural law via human institution.

Thomist theologians therefore expended a great deal of energy on defeating the Protestant conception of political society and the doctrine of justification by faith that underlay it. At the same time, their arguments in defence of secular princes could put at risk the legitimacy of Spain's empire. The idea that political society is grounded in natural law but only via human institution also implied, for neo-Thomist theologians, that the only forms of dominance that follow directly from natural law are the positions of husbands and fathers. While the general principle of dominance derives from natural law, its political form exists only by human institution, simply to preserve a human community. This put in question the Spanish king's position as emperor in the Americas, even in his capacity as Holy Roman Emperor. He could not claim jurisdiction on the grounds of universal empire. He therefore had no better claim to jurisdiction over colonial territories than did other European princes; and indigenous rulers enjoyed the same legitimacy as any other political authority enacted by men to preserve their own community. If the requirements of European princes in asserting their authority at home took precedence over the monarch's imperial claims in neo-Thomist theology, some other justification would have to be found for Spain's imperial expansion.

Vitoria did later abandon the idea that secular authority derives directly from God and with it any notion that political society was implanted directly by nature. In the lectures on the Indians and on the law of war, he proceeded from the classic Thomist view that political authority derives its legitimacy not from direct divine institution but from natural law through the medium of human legislation. Although ultimately emanating from God, natural law is accessible to men through reason and implemented by them through positive law. Men, as individuals endowed with the right of dominion, voluntarily divided property and established civil authority. While man, according to Aristotelian and Thomistic notions, is by nature a 'political' or civil animal, political society is constructed not by nature but by law.

Vitoria goes on to adopt the fairly conventional view that the sovereign power is established by the transfer of powers originally inhering in the people. Yet, while this differs from his position in *On Civil Power*, the transformation may not indicate a significant change of view on the limits of state power. The idea that political society exists by human institution did not, as we have seen, have any necessary implications for limits on secular government. On the contrary, Thomist theologians were more likely to invoke this doctrine in support of secular authority, against the right of resistance or the powers of the papacy; and the idea of civil authority as originally constituted by the people was capacious enough to allow even absolute monarchy.[7]

---

7   Distinctions might be made between the *transfer* of power from the people to their rulers as against the unconditional *alienation* of power; but that distinction is not always so clear, since even in the case of a conditional 'transfer', the conditions that might permit rebellion could be so stringent as to leave the ruler's power all but absolute.

If the idea that individuals were endowed by nature with a right of domin-ion did not necessarily entail the limitation of civil authority, it did imply that Indians should not be enslaved by their colonial masters. Reflecting on the conquest of Peru and the destruction of Inca and Aztec civilizations, Vitoria ruled out any justification that appealed to the natural inferiority of the Indians or to Aristotle's theory of natural slavery. The Indians were, like other human beings, endowed with the right of dominion, with liberty and rights of ownership. This precluded conquest even to achieve their forcible conversion to Christianity. Nor could imperial domination be justified on the principles of 'universal empire'. Since civil authority is grounded in natural law only through the medium of human law, there can be no such thing as a temporal world empire that derives its authority directly from divine or natural law. The laws and institutions of the Indians have the same legitimacy as any Christian polity. If there are any universal expressions of natural law, it can only be in laws and customs that are common to various peoples throughout the world – the law of nature as embodied in *ius gentium* (variously translated as the 'law of peoples' or the 'law of nations').

The effect of Vitoria's argument was to narrow the scope of imperial justification. The only ground remaining was the theory of 'just war'. He was, nevertheless, at best ambivalent (and even inconsistent, from one work to another) about what could be legitimated by 'just war'. On the one hand, he seems to rule out the forcible conversion of unbelievers and conquest on behalf of a universal empire. On the other hand, he does, as we have seen, invoke the Roman Empire as an example of a legitimate form of forcible imperial expansion, approved not only by Church fathers but, in principle, by Jesus Christ himself. Although Vitoria's remarks on Rome are not explic-itly related to the empire in the New World, they had clear implications for the Spanish empire in the Americas. More significantly, even his conception of the *ius gentium* provides a foundation for the justification of conquest. It represents a kind of natural human community, entailing certain universal principles such as the right of movement and free trade, which includes the right to 'trade' the Christian faith. A just war can be fought in defence of these principles against anyone who interferes with them. Vitoria has, then, conceded to Montesino and Las Casas their defence of Indians as rational human beings entitled to their liberty and property, and has also rejected the idea of a universal empire, while justifying conquest nonetheless. We might conclude that he has made an imperialist case against *encomenderos* but for the king of Spain.

Domingo de Soto, who would join Vitoria at the University of Salamanca, had preceded him in declaring the Roman Empire to be based on nothing more than the force of arms. Like Vitoria, he defended secular authority against what he took to be the Lutheran threat; but he would go on to make stronger arguments against the imperial regime, in 1553 undercutting even

the 'just war' defence. Where Vitoria had invoked the authority of the
Church fathers, and Augustine in particular, de Soto rejected this justification. Vitoria had gone some distance in narrowing the grounds of legitimacy
on which the Roman Empire could stand, but de Soto went further by claiming that Augustine, far from approving Rome's imperial expansion by means
of armed force, regarded it as an unjust pursuit of worldly glory, which for
him was not a virtue but a vice. In any case, whatever legitimacy Rome may
have gained in the eyes of later Europeans did not support the principle of a
world empire. Yet even de Soto did not question the need for Christians to
convert the Indians.

In 1545, the Council of Trent was convened. It would lay out the doctri-
nal terms of the official Counter-Reformation, elaborating arguments
against Protestant heresies and setting in motion internal reforms in the
Catholic Church. Charles V, as Holy Roman Emperor, appointed de Soto to
be his theologian at the Council. Among the principal and most fiercely
contested subjects was the doctrine of justification by faith alone.

In 1550, King Charles V summoned a *junta* of theologians and jurists to
Valladolid to debate the legitimacy of the conquest and the conversion of
the Indians by force, with de Soto presiding. Arguing in favour of conversion
by just war was the humanist scholar and translator of Aristotle, Sepúlveda,
who represented the interests of colonial settlers. In 1545, he had published
his *Democrates alter sive de justis belli causis apud Indios* (Concerning the
just causes of the war against the Indians). Although also a Dominican friar,
he had made his arguments on largely secular grounds, rooted in Aristotle's
theory of natural slavery. He was, to be sure, arguing in favour of the Indians'
conversion; but he made his argument on the grounds that Spain was a superior civilization, which had the right to conquer these 'barbarous' people in
order to prepare them for conversion. He would elaborate these arguments
in the debate at Vallidolid, where his opponent was Las Casas, who was
establishing himself as the Indians' principal defender.

In the debate Sepúlveda, invoking the doctrine of natural slavery,
constructed his argument again on the basis that the Indians were a barbar-
ian people governed not by reason but by passion. They were, he maintained,
also guilty of violating natural law, committing 'crimes that offend nature',
such as cannibalism, idolatry and sodomy, contrary to Spanish law and
custom; and this, too, entitled the Spaniards to wage a just war against
them. Moreover, since the Indians were in the habit of oppressing and killing the innocent among themselves, who were regularly offered as human
sacrifices, their victims could be saved only by outside intervention – and
here, Sepúlveda could draw on something like Vitoria's doctrine of *ius
gentium* as a justification for war. Finally, the Christian mission of conversion could only be effected if the ground was prepared by conquest – just as
the Christian emperor Constantine had in the fourth century brought

pagans under Roman rule in order to convert them. Sepúlveda even appealed to scripture to sustain his case for conversion by force.

Las Casas responded to each of these arguments. He dismissed Sepúlveda's invocation of Aristotle not by arguing against the doctrine of natural slavery but by demonstrating that the Indians did not fit the Aristotelian category. Non-Christians they certainly were, but they were clearly rational, possessing elaborate languages and complex civilizations governed by law. Some, though few, communities did commit idolatry and sacrifice; but this had been true of many advanced civilizations throughout history and could not be cited as evidence of their rule by passion rather than reason. As advanced and rational people, the Indians could and should be converted not by force but by persuasion. Nor did Christians have any right to punish them for their wrongs, because neither the king nor the pope had jurisdiction over the Indians, who were not heretics subject to correction by the Church but pagans available to peaceful conversion. Even if idolatry and sacrifice were contrary to the *ius gentium* – and everyone is obliged to prevent such violations – to say that crimes against nature should be punished by force went against the teachings of Church fathers like Augustine. In any case, it was better wherever possible to avoid the greater of two evils, which was war.

Francisco Suárez

The debate had little effect in practice, but it certainly had theoretical implications. However powerful the arguments that challenged the legitimacy of the empire, they still left some room for a justification of conquest based on 'just war' in cases where war could be judged the lesser evil. Having emphatically ruled out the case for universal empire or natural slavery, it had the effect of placing the burden of justification on the doctrine of 'just war', together with the concept of *ius gentium*, the violation of which remained the most convincing case for waging war – and generally a fairly flexible one. These concepts would enter the mainstream of Western political thought not so much, as is commonly suggested, to place limits on the conduct of war but rather to defend the use of arms in pursuit of imperial interests.

Francisco Suárez, a Jesuit theologian and philosopher, would be the most important conduit for this kind of argument. He also elaborated his predecessors' ideas on natural law and natural right, in ways that have earned him credit for founding the early modern tradition of natural right; but here, too, he left an ambiguous legacy. He expressed views similar to those of Vitoria, de Soto and Las Casas on the Indians' right to dominion in their own lands; and his conceptions of natural law and natural right are sometimes interpreted as a more or less 'modern' defence of the individual's rights against the state. Yet if his predecessors had defended indigenous rights without having any wish to undermine the secular authority of European princes at home, Suárez made it even clearer that natural law and natural right were perfectly compatible with something close to absolute monarchy.

The neo-Thomist principle that political society is grounded in natural law through the medium of human legislation was used, as we have seen, in ways that may, to modern eyes, seem counter-intuitive: to buttress, not to limit, secular authority against resistance. The idea that political society exists by means of human institution in pursuit of human ends, while at the same time being subject in some way to standards of justice and natural law, and that certain rights inhere in individuals by nature, might on the face of it seem better suited to a doctrine of resistance than to a theory of political legitimacy not far short of royal absolutism. Yet for sixteenth-century European monarchies, in the specific context of the challenges they faced, a conception of secular authority such as that elaborated by the Spanish neo-Thomists was consistent with strict obedience to secular rulers or even royal absolutism, and the doctrine of natural right did not yet seem particularly threatening.

Suárez wrote as a theorist of law, and he perfected the legalistic neo-Thomist strategy of argumentation. Political society is, he argued, a human creation, constructed by men endowed with a natural inclination to live in communities, who establish polities to fulfil purely human and temporal purposes. Naturally free, individuals relinquish that freedom by common consent, agreeing to form a political body and set up government with legislative power. Political power thus resides not in individuals but in the community. At the same time, Suárez rules out the medieval principle that, even if the king is greater than any other individual, the community as a corporate body is greater than the king. The consent of individuals is not simply a delegation of power to their governors. It is an outright *alienation* of power; and its transfer to the ruler (whether in the person of a monarch or some other form of government) invests him with a full legal title to power, a kind of ownership, which is virtually unconditional. This means that, even while political power is different from the kind of natural dominion that resides in heads of household – the patriarchal authority of fathers and husbands – the ruler's possession of the legislative power, which is the hallmark of political society, cannot be rescinded or limited in the normal course of political events. The only right reserved by the people is the right to preserve the community from imminent destruction. Only in extreme cases, when a ruler threatens the very existence of the commonwealth, is resistance legitimate; but even then that right is a prerogative of public authority, not an individual right. The ruler can be called to account before a 'public' council; but if he is to be deposed, his deposition may, as we shall see in a moment, require papal authority.

In what sense, then, can it be said that natural law and natural right set the terms and conditions of political power? On this, Suárez remains at best ambiguous. In *De Legibus* he defines a right (*ius*) as 'a certain moral power that every man has, either over his property or with respect to that which is due to him' (I.2.5) . This suggests that rights exist by nature and independently of positive law. At the same time, Suárez tells us, this moral right is 'prescribed and measured by law'. The question, then, is whether positive law can be judged by any independent standard of right or justice. The legitimacy of positive law depends, he explains, on the good of the community, on what is rightful or just; and in that sense *ius* appears to be a standard against which human legislation can be judged. Yet in practice the legislative power residing in rulers can be resisted or constrained only in the most extreme circumstances; there is no normal legal instrument or process to limit it; and the ruler can override individual rights in the interests of the community as he defines them, with no recourse against that definition in the normal transactions of political life.

There is a further complication in Suárez's work. His strongest assertion of the right to resist secular authority occurs in his response to James I of England's *Apologie for the Oath of Allegiance,* which appeared anonymously in 1608 and in the king's name in 1609. It was James more than any political philosopher who, in various writings throughout his life, elaborated the doctrine of the divine right of kings, and this in its most extreme form, asserting the absolute authority of kings, its direct and hereditary derivation from God, and hence the immunity of kings to any resistance, secular or religious. The oath of allegiance explained in his *Apologie* was James's solution to the problem that had plagued English monarchs since the Reformation came to England: how to deal with English Catholics. This problem had acquired special urgency when the Counter-Reformation assumed a politically militant form, especially with the collaboration between the Catholic Church and Charles V's son, King Philip II of Spain, in his designs on the English crown. Throughout James I's reign, there remained a party of Jesuit-inspired English Catholics still wedded to that Spanish project; and the oath of allegiance – which had as its underlying premise the divine right of kings – was designed to deal with that threat.

At the behest of Pope Paul V, Suárez launched an attack on the king in *Defensio catholicae fidei contra anglicanae sectae errores.* It is here that he appears least absolutist, and it is here that he most emphatically asserts what appears to be the right of resistance. Yet the right to punish is, according to him, an act of jurisdiction, which is therefore always the act of a superior; and this is no less true in disciplining kings than in the punishment of any other wrongdoer. In this case the only legitimate superior is the pope, and much of Suárez's response to James I is devoted to asserting papal jurisdiction.

The issue for Suárez was not only the conflict between the pope and King James, or between Catholicism and English Protestantism, but also the political contest between the English Reformation and the Catholic monarchy of Spain. His predecessors in the School of Salamanca were still obliged to take account of the frequent tensions between the pope and King Charles I of Spain – especially as Charles V, the Holy Roman Emperor. The reign of Philip II and his son, Philip III, was a time of partnership with the pope. Suárez struck a complicated balance in his argument between sustaining the power of the Spanish king, as had his predecessors, and, at the same time, making an argument for the pope's superior jurisdiction against the king of England's claims. Against the divine right of kings invoked by King James, Suárez mobilizes the well-known neo-Thomist arguments about the source of political authority, arguing not only that political society exists by human institution but also that the authority of rulers derives from the people. Yet what he seems to give with one hand he takes away with the other, insisting not only that the people have alienated their power to their rulers but also that, on the very rare and abnormal occasions when they can act against him, that right is a prerogative of public authority, a jurisdictional matter, with the sanction of the ultimate superior, the pope.

Suárez is often credited with taking an important step in the formation of natural rights theory, which would increasingly situate rights in individual persons, emphasizing the natural freedom of the individual, detaching the moral force of natural rights from religious authority, and vesting it in the mundane requirements of human well-being, according to principles accessible to human reason. The critical step, it is argued, was to move away from Aquinas, for whom *ius* denoted 'the just thing', what was 'right' in an action or a situation, in a sense indistinguishable from what was just, in accordance with natural law. Suárez began to shift the concept of right from the justice of 'things' – actions or situations – to the entitlements of individual persons. Yet to say this may be to disguise some essential differences between his conception of rights and more familiar early modern 'subjective' theories of natural rights.

It must be emphasized first that the definition of right as a certain 'moral power' residing in a person, in relation to property or in respect to 'what is due' to that person, remains bound up with the condition or status of the person and leaves considerable scope for differential rights. Aquinas himself made it clear in his *Summa Theologica* that 'what is due' to an individual will vary according to status: 'A thing is due', he writes, 'to an equal in one way, to a superior in another, and to an inferior in yet another' – and this, in accordance with the principles of natural law, is justice. It would have been perfectly consistent with the master's doctrine of justice and right to say that the right of resistance is 'what is due' to someone not simply by virtue of his humanity but on the grounds of jurisdictional authority. Everyone has a right to his own property, as well as what is 'due' to him in his particular condition; and that means, for example (as Suárez makes clear), that the right of resistance to royal authority is not a universal right but a prerogative of office. It was even possible, given this conception of rights, to conceive of universal rights in such a way that they remained consistent with absolute royal power.

Since the available doctrines of individual rights and even popular sovereignty were still typically mobilized in support of royal power, not against it, when Suárez directs the idea of rights to sustaining monarchical power, rather than to placing limits on it, he is still following the medieval norm. If anything, he can feel secure in forcefully asserting the existence of rights precisely because the idea of rights vested in all men, and even the idea that secular authority derives from the people, belonged to the corpus of Western political thought as a support to royal power and not as a subversion of it. More dangerous to royal powers were claims to jurisdiction by other, 'lesser' public authorities against royal power. Suárez may direct his conception of rights against King James's notion of divine right, but the Spaniard makes sure that the right of resistance is very narrowly defined and ultimately dependent on the pope. If Suárez was restricting secular authority, then, it was by vesting rights in the pope, not in the 'people';[8] but even short of that, and even in the hands of political theorists who had their own reasons – whether in defence of kings or in support of Holy Roman Emperors – for insisting that the pope had no temporal authority, the idea that sovereignty derived from the people could be readily invoked to support monarchical power.

The doctrine of resistance as a right of jurisdiction would reach its height in sixteenth-century France. French constitutionalists took the idea of sovereignty derived from the people and the right of resistance vested in competing jurisdictions, or 'lesser magistrates', as far as it would go. It would be in England that this theoretical strategy became no longer viable. The English were faced with a conundrum that had not affected the French. When the English elaborated doctrines of resistance – most urgently in the seventeenth century – those who were defending the rights of Parliament against the Crown had to confront the possibility that invoking popular sovereignty might open much more hazardous floodgates, endangering not only the state but the whole social order. The right of resistance could not so easily be confined to the official acts of 'lesser magistrates'. The mediations

8   See Skinner, *Foundations, Vol. 2: Age of Reformation*, p. 179, for an argument that Counter-Reformation neo-Thomists like Suárez, while they did adopt some fairly radical and secularized notions of *imperium*, were no less keen to defend the temporal powers of the Church and the pope against theorists like Marsilius of Padua, who denied any coercive power to the Church, or William of Ockham, who denied the pope's right to intervene in temporal affairs.

between state and individuals endowed with rights, if not altogether non-existent, were weaker than they were elsewhere in Western Europe. In the English context corporate identities had become increasingly diluted, while economic power and property rights were increasingly detached from jurisdiction and corporate privilege. This placed an entirely new burden on the doctrine of individual rights. It is not surprising that England would produce more radically democratic ideas, including new ideas of rights such as those espoused by the Levellers. Less radical English political thinkers, whether defending royal absolutism or the primacy of Parliament, would find themselves obliged to construct their arguments in wholly new ways, on a foundation of unmediated free and equal individuals.

5

THE DUTCH REPUBLIC

In 1598 the Dutch child prodigy Huig de Groot, then barely fifteen years old, accompanied the Advocate of Holland, Johan van Oldenbarnevelt, on an extraordinary embassy from the States-General of the United Provinces to the French court. The purpose of the mission was to obtain whatever assistance it could from France against military threats to the Provinces' still precarious independence and stability as a free republic. Since William I (the Silent) of Orange had led a revolt of the Netherlands against Philip II of Spain in 1568, the Netherlands had been embroiled in more or less continuous conflict. Although the Dutch Republic was declared in 1588, the so-called Eighty Years' War with Spain would end only in 1648 with the Treaty of Westphalia; and throughout that period, which saw the Republic rise to extraordinary heights of economic and cultural success, its internal political life continued to be marked by intense civil strife.

Oldenbarnevelt would play a central role in the formation of the Republic's political institutions and, as architect of the United East India Company, in its immense economic success, becoming effectively the leader of the Republic. Hugo Grotius, later known as the pioneer of international law and, according to some commentators, a major theorist of natural rights and even a founder of modern theories of natural law, began his precocious career as protégé and then supporter of Oldenbarnevelt. While his close association with Oldenbarnevelt would, as we shall see, end badly when they fell victim to an especially ferocious factional dispute, his political ideas were rooted from beginning to end in the politics of the Dutch Republic, its civic conflicts and its vast commercial empire. The other canonical Dutch thinker to be considered in this chapter, Spinoza, may not have been as actively engaged in civic politics, but his political ideas are in their own distinctive way grounded in the conflicts of the Dutch Republic and its unique configuration of political and economic power.

The Dutch Republic

The man who bore the titles Charles I of Spain and Charles V of the Holy Roman Empire, who was born in the Low Countries in the Flemish city of Ghent, was always more at home in the language and culture of his birthplace than he ever would be in his Spanish kingdom. During his reign, the Habsburg provinces in the Netherlands looked set to be the European jewel in the imperial crown – or at least its principal cash cow. The commercial cities of the Netherlands had long been major trading links in the European economy. In the south, the city of Antwerp had become the hub of Europe's so-called rich trades, in spices, textiles, sugar and metals; while in the northern maritime provinces, Amsterdam, though its golden age would come after the Dutch Revolt from Spain, was already on the rise, soon to become what some have called the world's richest city as Europe's greatest transshipment point and a world financial centre. Neither Spain itself nor Habsburg Italy – over which the Empire's command had long been tenuous – could match the Netherlands' prosperity; and, as the contests among Europe's rising states intensified, the Habsburg monarchy was bound to increase its dependence on revenues from the provinces in building up its military capabilities. When France began to challenge Habsburg dominance in the Low Countries, Charles responded by bolstering his military strength, supported disproportionately by exactions from the Netherlands' commercial wealth. The more the king of Spain – and Holy Roman Emperor – depended on resources from the Low Countries, the more he was forced to rely on local elites to organize finances and collect taxes, which only served to aggravate the tensions.

For a time, local elites were prepared to play their part in the imperial project, and indeed to profit from it; but there had always been an inevitable conflict between the monarchy's centralizing mission and powerful forces in the Low Countries intent on preserving the provincial and civic autonomy of their city-states. Any effort to subject the provinces to Spain's monarchical administration was likely to encounter resistance from well-established civic institutions in an unusually urbanized society with powerful urban elites. Urban magnates resisted any challenge to their local powers or their networks of patronage; and, especially in Holland, the tensions between the monarch and the local patriciate were intensified by the Habsburg policy of elevating administrators from outside the leading local families, or sometimes officials from other, less dominant provinces. Charles's son Philip II, who broke the close personal ties his father had with the Low Countries, took the centralizing project even further. Aggravating tensions by ever more taxation, he presided over the final breach between Spain and its richest European dependency.

The conflict between local magnates and the Habsburg monarchy became entangled with religious controversies. Confessional divisions varied among the different provinces and cities; and there was no simple correlation between adherence to the Catholic Church and support for the Habsburg state, or between Protestantism and local resistance. But the northern provinces that broke free of Spanish rule were largely Protestant, while Catholicism prevailed in the south; and there is no question that Protestant religious doctrines were mobilized in the Low Countries, as elsewhere in Europe and notably in France, in support of local elites against the centralizing project of the monarchy. After the Revolt, Protestantism would itself become a fierce terrain of battle in the free Republic. Even divergent forms of Calvinism were pitted against one another in the struggles among civic factions. But in the conflicts leading up to the revolt against the Spanish crown, Protestants were united against the Catholic monarchy's attacks on their faith. Philip's fierce assault on Protestant believers was the final provocation.

The dominance of cities in the Netherlands explains a great deal about the Revolt and what followed in the politics, economy and culture of the Dutch Republic. In the absence of a strong central state, the Low Countries, divided among provinces with diverse political traditions and economic interests, had long been governed by relatively independent local rulers and increasingly by local urban elites, enriched by their city's commercial success. The province of Holland was becoming the most highly urbanized society in Europe, with a powerful urban patriciate presiding over the world's most commercialized economy. The urban centres had a vibrant civic life, with active corporate bodies of various kinds, such as guilds and militia companies. There were even 'chambers of rhetoric', which played a large part in literary and cultural life, especially in Holland, and in the 1520s and 1530s had served as a major conduit for humanism, with all its effects on religious and political debate. Well before the establishment of the Republic, city organizations and authorities had been increasingly involved in the maintenance of social order and civic welfare; and particularly in the northern provinces they would play a major role in the Revolt.

In the years following the Revolt, a new form of state would evolve, a confederation of provinces that maintained their autonomy and were governed largely by civic administrations in the cities. There was a supra-provincial governing body, the States-General of the Republic; but in the richest provinces, most notably Holland, powerful factions among the local ruling classes strongly resisted the formation of a centralized state, especially in the person of the stadtholder, an office inherited from pre-Revolt days. Once the sovereign's representative, this office had become the closest thing to a central state official in the free Republic. Particularly in Holland, whose wealth and power generally enabled it to impose its will on other provinces, there would be persistent conflict between the stadtholder – or, more specifically, supporters of the House of Orange, which claimed the office as its own – and civic leaders. Internal tensions were heightened as the urban patriciate, the regents, became increasingly exclusive and their government more oligarchic, driving less privileged classes to support the Orangists.

Civic conflict after the Revolt was exacerbated by its growing confessionalization. Although the Dutch maintained the separation of Church and state, officials were expected to be members of the Reformed Church. The Republic, with its headless and multi-polar government, relied heavily on the so-called 'public' Church to maintain not only communal welfare but civic order and discipline. Yet there were, from the start, divisions between strict Calvinists and more liberal preachers, which would erupt with particular venom in moments of political strife. In the battle between Oldenbarnevelt and his opponents in 1618, political conflicts – which proved fatal for him and disastrous for his supporter Grotius – were reinforced by a struggle between Arminians ('Remonstrants', after they issued their 'Remonstrance' against certain orthodox Calvinist doctrines) and 'Counter-Remonstrant' Calvinists (about which more later).

In the following decades, political factions, with their fiercely competing networks of patronage and clientage controlling access to civic office, sought to avoid such catastrophic confessional disputes. Civil strife continued to grow between Orangists, or followers of the stadtholder, and supporters of provincial and local power against the stadtholder's monarchical pretensions. The former were generally supported by strict Calvinists, the latter by more liberal believers; but both major factions nonetheless agreed on the importance of maintaining the unity of the public Church.[1] By the 1650s, in the years leading up to the next major crisis of the Dutch Republic, unity had broken down; and political divisions were deepened by confessional disputes.

At the heart of Dutch political development and conflicts, even at the height of the Republic's commercial success, was the importance of civic office not only as an instrument of government but as a guarantee of private wealth and power. The decentralized organization of the Republic created a particularly fertile field for public-service occupations, so the proportion of such occupations in the population of Dutch cities was very high. To be sure, while offices of various kinds often provided high incomes, it required substantial wealth from real property or finance to enter the urban patriciate, since to be part of the governing elite increasingly required abandoning private economic activities; but civic elites had good reason to maintain their hold on high office, which sustained their networks of power and patronage. Even in the Golden Age of the Republic's

---

1   Jonathan Israel, *The Dutch Republic: Its Rise, Greatness, and Fall 1477–1806* (New York: Oxford University Press, 1995), pp. 660–62.

commercial dominance, a wealthy landowner or financier would often choose to use his wealth for access to such offices. When, in the later seventeenth century, the European economy suffered a decline, access to office was even more highly prized, as a direct source of income no less than of power and patronage. By the eighteenth century, at a time when Britain was dominated by the wealth of capitalist landlords, among the highest incomes in the Republic were enjoyed by public servants. It is not surprising that political conflict over control of office, and the networks of patronage that sustained it, was particularly fierce.

We have already encountered societies, in medieval and Renaissance Italy, where urban patriciates extracted great wealth from commercial activities but relied for their success in large part on the privileges and powers associated with their status in the city. Here, too, political conflicts took on a particular ferocity and even violence, to say nothing of their regularity, because more was at stake than political interests and rights. Much the same logic applied to the commercial success of the city-state itself. Just as the wealth of civic elites in Italian centres of commerce depended on civic status, privilege and power, the commercial success of their city-states in rivalry with others depended less on competitive production than on 'extra-economic' advantage, up to and including military force.

The Dutch Republic certainly moved far beyond Italian city-states in its commercial reach and power. The Dutch commercial empire was much larger than the Venetian had been – eventually extending from the Baltic to North America, and from the East Indies to southern Africa – and commerce was the basic condition of Dutch life to a degree unprecedented in history. The Republic's domestic economy was dependent to its very foundations on trade and on the commercial empire that sustained it. But the Dutch no less than the Italians relied on 'extra-economic' advantages for their commercial dominance and always owed their prosperity disproportionately to their role as commercial mediators rather than producers. The Republic's great wealth would have been impossible without its pre-eminence in long-distance trade, circulating throughout Europe commodities produced far afield. It is, for example, indicative of where the Dutch Republic's economic interests lay that it gained more from its major role in the slave trade than it did from slave production. Like other commercial leaders in Europe before the commercial dominance of capitalist Britain, the Dutch typically relied not on competitive production in a single market but on superiority in negotiating separate markets: on dominance in shipping and command of trade routes, on monopolies and trading privileges, on the development of sophisticated financial practices and instruments; on an elaborate network of far-flung trading posts and settlements, and so on.

It is a measure of the Dutch economy's dependence on extra-economic power that its levels of taxation were higher than those of its European neighbours, its revenues devoted, above all, to sustaining military superiority. The complex and often disorderly political organization of the Republic did not prevent it from becoming a powerful military machine, a 'fiscal–military' state with an unusually effective mobilization of domestic resources for purposes of war, which made the Dutch Republic 'a model country that set the standard for European armed forces'.[2] Military aggression played a major part in achieving the Republic's commercial dominance, remaining an essential part of its economic strategy throughout the Golden Age and thereafter: in trade wars, in establishing monopolies and trading posts, in capturing strategic fortresses from commercial rivals. A particularly momentous military venture was the seizure by the Dutch East India Company in 1603 of a Portuguese ship containing an enormously valuable cargo of unprecedented proportions, large enough to affect the future course of Dutch economic development.

Nevertheless, during the Republic's 'Golden Age' there was a close linkage between commerce and production. Commerce itself generated needs that had to be met by industrial production and technological innovation, notably in ship-building, to say nothing of military technology; and the Dutch economy gained much from other sources, such as the textile industry and the herring fishery. The 'rich' trades generated significant industrial production for a thriving export trade in goods from tobacco and sugar to luxury textiles. Even agricultural production, in this highly urbanized society, developed in response to commercial opportunities. While an increasing proportion of the labour force had moved from countryside to city, agricultural productivity, enhanced by technological innovation, advanced beyond all European rivals; and the Republic was very close to being a net exporter of food. As the urban population swelled to service the Republic's growing dominance in shipping, trade and eventually finance, the expanding urban sector provided new markets for agricultural goods, as well as new sources of capital to exploit new opportunities for profit. Urban investors in agriculture became a major feature of the rural scene.

Dutch agriculture was constrained by ecological factors, which limited its capacity for the easy production of basic foods like grain. Yet the Republic's commercial dominance, and particularly the command of trade that gave it privileged access to Baltic grain, meant that Dutch farmers could concentrate on the production of semi-luxury commodities – from butter to flowers – sold in a large and prosperous market. A unique imbalance between urban consumers and rural producers created growing opportunities for commercial profit at home. While even agricultural producers became dependent on the market for access to grain and other basic necessities, the productive

---

2   Jan Glete, *War and the State in Early Modern Europe* (New York: Routledge, 2002), p. 141.

capacities of relatively small farmers were disproportionately enhanced by urban investment responding to growing commercial opportunities.

Its commercial successes have led some historians to describe the Dutch Republic as the first 'modern' economy, and there are even those who suggest that the Dutch Revolt was the first 'bourgeois revolution'.[3] Yet, for all its commercialization and impressive advances in production, it continued to operate on familiar non-capitalist principles, above all in its dependence on extra-economic powers. Public offices were, from beginning to end, no less important to Dutch elites than they would be, for instance, in the 'tax/office' structure of French absolutism; and Dutch commercial dominance depended, as we have seen, on various kinds of extra-economic superiority, particularly in shipping and military technology. Dutch producers were generally not, in the capitalist manner, acting in response to cost–price pressures in a competitive market where advantage depends on increasing labour productivity. Innovations in technology that enhanced productivity had less to do with improving competitiveness than with increasing volume to take advantage of a growing market.

As long as foreign and domestic markets were expanding, Dutch producers availed themselves of growing opportunities; and urban elites continued to invest in profitable production. But when, after 1660, the Dutch economy went into decline, as all Western European economies apart from England descended into crisis, wealthy elites disinvested in land and eventually in industrial production and turned even more to 'extra-economic' strategies. The traditional patriciate sought to tighten its grip on office and to restrict access to it (as the French aristocracy would later do, in a moment of crisis that led to revolution), and civic government became even more narrowly oligarchic. Merchants, who derived their profits from circulation rather than production, pursued pre-capitalist commercial strategies, seeking more lucrative means of trading in goods produced elsewhere by, for example, reviving monopoly privileges – such as the re-establishment of the Dutch West India Company or one company's monopoly on navigational charts. While industrial production for the 'rich' trades and export industry in general held on for a time, after 1720 the decline accelerated; and by the mid-eighteenth century non-productive rentiers, especially among the regents, would account for by far the greatest wealth. The disinvestment from land and even production during and after the European economic

---

3   See in particular Jan de Vries and Ad van der Woude, *The First Modern Economy: Success, Failure, and Perseverance of the Dutch Economy, 1500–1815* (Cambridge: Cambridge University Press, 1997). I have relied on this very important work for much of my discussion of the Dutch economy but have come to somewhat different conclusions, as I explain at length in Ellen Meiksins Wood, 'The Question of Market-Dependence', *Journal of Agrarian Change*, Vol. 2, No. 1, January 2002, pp. 50–87.

crisis represented a sharp contrast to England, where crisis and declining agricultural prices spurred an *increase* in productive investment, not least by landlords, to enhance labour productivity and cost-effectiveness, in the manner of capitalist producers responding to imperatives of competition in an integrated market.

The Dutch role in England's so-called Glorious Revolution of 1688 illustrates nicely the direction of Dutch economic development in the later seventeenth century. Here, the massive financial resources of the Republic were directed not at improving production, as they often had been during the Golden Age, but at achieving extra-economic commercial advantage by military means. The province of Holland in particular depended on the profits of commerce and was especially affected by the incursions of French mercantilism in the late seventeenth century, its interference with Dutch ships and its draconian tariffs. The preferred solution to this problem of commercial profitability was to defeat French mercantilism by means of an alliance with England, which seemed possible only with a friend on the English throne. The Dutch Republic committed its resources to supporting William of Orange's bid for the English monarchy. To the English, the Revolution may have seemed 'glorious' and largely bloodless. But from the Dutch point of view, it was nothing more nor less than an invasion, involving the occupation of London by Dutch troops, in full expectation of a war not only with the English but also with the French. Nor was this military venture just a classic case of geopolitical rivalry. It was an unmistakably commercial investment in pursuit of private profit, financed not simply by the public purse but by the Amsterdam stock exchange.

A Culture of Civil Strife

The cultural and intellectual life of the Netherlands was vibrant and creative long before the Dutch Revolt. In the rich commercial cities there was a large market – including, as ever, the Church – for the arts. A strategic location at the hub of international commerce and a highly concentrated urban population encouraged a lively, and not easily controlled, circulation of ideas; and the civic culture had produced an unusually literate public. The Low Countries, and the province of Holland in particular, were already on their way to becoming the relatively open and, within certain limits, tolerant intellectual and religious societies for which the Dutch Republic would be famous, making it a favoured destination for persecuted foreign intellectuals and religious refugees. By the seventeenth century it had become a major centre of innovative European thought. In 1630, for example, René Descartes moved from France to Holland; and his work would not only have profound effects on philosophy and science but would be taken up by thinkers engaged in very immediate political struggles. The other intellectual currents that

shaped our period – the humanism of the late Renaissance and the Protestant
Reformation – had established deep roots, especially in Holland. Humanism
began to permeate the educational establishment; and Christian humanism
was, in effect, a Dutch creation, in the person of the Rotterdam philosopher
Desiderius Erasmus. Between 1490 and 1520, it spread more rapidly in the
Low Countries than in any other part of Northern Europe.[4]

Despite Erasmus's distrust of Luther and a passionate dislike of public
conflict, his teachings played a major part in advancing the Reformation in
the Low Countries. In the Dutch-speaking Netherlands, Lutheran literature
was more widely disseminated than in France, England or Scandinavia; and
unlike elsewhere in Northern Europe, the Reformation in the Low Countries
was not imposed by government but rose up from the bottom, in a population culturally primed to receive it.[5] This kind of popular Protestantism was
a source of some unease not only to the Catholic Church but to local elites.
Whatever attractions the Reformation may have had for them in their opposition to the Catholic monarchy, they clearly had reason to fear the kind of
radical Lutheranism that had inspired German peasant rebels. Calvinism,
though delayed in reaching the Low Countries, would prove much more to
the taste of civic and provincial leaders. It laid a foundation for doctrines of
resistance that could be mobilized against the Spanish crown, while preaching 'godly discipline' to keep the multitude in check.

Calvinist theories of resistance, in the form of Huguenot tracts, would
have their most notable effects during the French Wars of Religion in the
struggle against a rising absolutist monarchy (which will be discussed in the
next chapter). In the Low Countries, too, Calvin's doctrine of the 'lesser
magistrate' had an obvious appeal to civic elites. The doctrine was, after all,
devised with the temporal authority of civic magistrates in mind. Resistance
to encroaching monarchies was not, in the Huguenot resistance tracts, a
right residing in the ordinary citizen or private individual; it was a right of
officers, or 'lesser magistrates', deriving from some kind of jurisdiction
vested in corporate bodies, aristocracies or municipal officials – more a
public duty than a private right. In their struggles against the Spanish crown,
Dutch Calvinists would certainly have been sympathetic to such notions of
resistance; but the local elites of the Low Countries were very different from
the provincial nobles in France who adopted the Protestant faith in their
resistance to the French king's absolutist project. For Huguenot aristocrats,
the principal issue was preserving what remained of feudal lordship, retaining or restoring their own autonomous powers and jurisdictions. That
purpose was adequately served by some variety of constitutionalist doctrine.
The urban elites of the Low Countries, especially in the northern maritime

---

4   Israel, *Dutch Republic*, p. 47.
5   *Ibid.*, pp. 80, 78.

provinces and most notably Holland, were not promoting feudal lordship but civic autonomy and collective – if oligarchic – urban government. This placed a greater premium on what might be called republican ideas of freedom, a concept of liberty identified with civic self-government.

The trope of freedom was invoked by William I of Orange himself in support of the Revolt against Spain. He cited the 'freedoms and privileges' of the provinces in the manner of medieval corporations asserting their autonomy; but he also defended the freedom of the people from enslavement by the Spanish monarchy. In the later conflict between stadtholders and civic elites, the opponents of the stadtholders turned the slogan against the House of Orange, asserting republican liberty against monarchical forces, with an ideology they called 'true freedom'.

This ideology of republican freedom would have a critical effect on Dutch political thought, but its message was at best ambiguous. There was, in the Republic, no simple opposition between an anti-democratic monarchy and a more democratic republicanism. Republican forces generally represented the wealthy civic elites, which had achieved their dominance at the expense of popular elements. While they argued passionately for the active role of citizens in governing themselves, they were likely to be just as passionate in their efforts to limit access to full political rights and especially to office. Civic magnates, as regents, had begun to constitute a self-perpetuating oligarchy in cities with a narrow political base. Craft guilds in the Dutch Republic, for instance, had less influence on urban government than did their counterparts in the Spanish southern Netherlands. This was not simply a matter of wealthy merchants opposing guild restrictions on their commercial activities but also – or mainly – a political conflict between urban elites and more popular forces over political power and access to office. The revolt of guilds, together with civic militias, especially in the city of Utrecht, would be a major source of unrest in the decade of social conflict that led in 1618 to Oldenbarnevelt's expulsion from office and his and Grotius's arrest.

Although this conflict was no less Byzantine in its causes and party allegiances than any other in the convoluted history of Dutch civil strife, it is worth noting that Grotius had by this time established himself as a theorist of a limited and oligarchic republicanism, while the chief engineer and beneficiary of the coup against Oldenbarnevelt, a coup supported by popular forces, was Maurits, the son of William I. As Prince of Orange and stadtholder, he would become the most powerful man in the United Provinces following the death of his father. Later, during the 'stadtholderless' period of 1650–72 – the high point of the free Republic, when the office of stadtholder was left unfilled – the political role of the people was, if anything, even more restricted. While the 'Orangists' were hardly democratic, when the stadtholderate was restored, it was, perhaps not surprisingly, popular forces that put another Prince of Orange back in office.

From one crisis to the next, the underlying reality was what might be called a politically constituted commercial society, a society in which economic interests were inseparable from extra-economic power, political status and privilege. The urban patriciate, with privileged access to office, jealously guarded its civic power and its command of a self-perpetuating governing elite, with its network of patronage and clientage, while the vast commercial empire in which their wealth was rooted depended more on powers of coercion than production. This accounts not only for war with rival states but also for fierce and frequent civic conflict. It also tells us much about Dutch political theory, in its own golden age from the Revolt and the establishment of the Republic to the crisis of the late seventeenth century.

Hugo Grotius

The Dutch Republic's distinctive configuration of political and economic power found its quintessential theorist in Hugo Grotius. Born in Delft in 1583 to a regent family replete with office-holders, he began his political career very early, as we have seen, and would devote himself throughout his life, in both theory and practice, to defending the interests of the Dutch commercial empire and its urban patriciate. At the age of sixteen, shortly after returning from the mission to the French court with Oldenbarnevelt, he was admitted as a lawyer to the provincial court of Holland and then to the supreme court of the provinces of Holland and Zeeland. In 1601, he became official historiographer for the states of Holland and was commissioned by Oldenbarnevelt to write a history of the Dutch struggle against Spain.

When ships of the Dutch East India Company famously seized the treasure-laden Portuguese ship *Santa Catarina* in 1603, the Company commissioned Grotius to write its defence against strong opposition to this legally questionable act. Although his treatise, *De Indis*, was never published fully in his lifetime, part of his deliberations, published in 1609 as *Mare Liberum,* was the work that would launch his reputation as a theorist of international and natural law. The issues he was compelled to address were not only legal – though the legality of the seizure by the Company and its retention of the prize without state authorization was questionable – but also moral, in response to objections raised even by Company shareholders, not least by Mennonites among them. Grotius's response to this range of legal, moral and religious objections was an argument based crucially on the doctrine of natural law.

Grotius went on to hold various public offices and in 1613 became Pensionary of Rotterdam, which placed him among the ranks of Holland's regents. In the meantime, Oldenbarnevelt had concluded a truce with Spain, widely supported in Europe and among regents in Holland but provoking fierce factional disputes and popular opposition. These political disputes became entangled with a major theological controversy between followers of Arminius, the head of the theological faculty at the University of Leiden, and strict Calvinists, who simultaneously opposed the Republic's policies of religious toleration under Oldenbarnevelt and the truce with Catholic Spain. Remonstrants came to represent the faction of the regents, particularly in Holland, with its view of the public Church as a partner with, if not a subordinate to, civil government. Counter-Remonstrantism became a rallying point for opposition to the regents' regime, uniting a mixed coalition of the regime's opponents, ranging from the old nobility and Orangists to small artisans and craft guildsmen.

Grotius had already established himself as a major spokesman for the Oldenbarnevelt regime and the idea of an oligarchic Republic. In several of his writings between 1602 and 1610, he spelled out a limited republican doctrine, arguing that the best way of preserving liberty, stability and virtue was a consultative government, but one restricted to a closed oligarchy, manned by people like Dutch regents, with the means to devote their time entirely to public business.[6] The stadtholder might have a limited role, in what could be called a type of 'mixed constitution'; but the urban oligarchy clearly reigned supreme. It was this kind of patrician Republic that Oldenbarnevelt was defending against stadtholder and Calvinist critics. The controversy between Arminians (Remonstrants) and Counter-Remonstrants posed an immediate danger when the latter called for English intervention to protect the Dutch Church from Arminian doctrines. Oldenbarnevelt called on Grotius to head a delegation to London both to negotiate the disputes over the East Indies between England and the Dutch Republic and to dissuade King James from supporting the Counter-Remonstrants.

Grotius's position in the theological controversy was carefully calibrated. On the one hand, he fully supported the Oldenbarnevelt regime and its policies of (limited) toleration, against the strict Calvinist position. In the battle between Arminians and Counter-Remonstrants, he and Oldenbarnevelt were certainly closer to the Arminian view that, while salvation is granted by grace, human beings have free will and can accept (or deny) the offer of salvation through faith in Jesus Christ – in contrast to strict Calvinist convictions about predestination. Since salvation in that sense depends on faith, it seemed to follow that religious toleration should extend to anyone of faith, irrespective of confessional differences. On the other hand, while supporting liberty of conscience, he was careful not to extend it too far. In the end, the public Church, as an ally of government, remained supreme as both an arbiter of faith and an instrument of social order. Freedom of conscience and expression might have to be limited in order to maintain stability, if necessary by coercion.

The Oldenbarnevelt regime remained precariously in power for the next

---

6 See *ibid.*, pp. 421–2.

few years, but by 1616 social unrest had reached a dangerous peak. Economic pressures affecting manufacturing cities were aggravating opposition to the oligarchic regime, especially from artisans and immigrant textile workers. High bread prices, as in so many other cases of revolt in medieval and early modern Europe, stirred some to protest (including, significantly, the wives of artisans); but, as always in the Dutch Republic, economic grievances could not be divorced from protests against restricted access to civic government. There emerged a militant popular movement of Counter-Remonstrance, which at the same time challenged the exclusive power of the regents.

Grotius yet again entered the fray, elaborating his brand of Christian oligarchic republicanism to mobilize humanist scholarship in support of the public Church as understood by the regents, against those who claimed their doctrines were inconsistent with the truths of Christianity. In the following months, the religious and political controversy came to a head in a final battle over state sovereignty, with the States-General of the Republic, represented by Maurits, commander of the Republic's army and soon to be the Prince of Orange, pitted against the provincial estates, or, more particularly, the province of Holland and its regents. Maurits won that battle. Oldenbarnevelt was arrested, later to be executed for treason, and Grotius was sentenced to life imprisonment and all his property confiscated.

Grotius would escape from prison, with the help of his wife, in a manner that has made him famous among Dutch schoolchildren even today. Carried out in a chest supposedly containing books, he fled to France, where he wrote the second major work on which his modern reputation rests, *De Jure Belli ac Pacis,* in the hope of returning to Holland and government service. In this work, written at a time when much of Europe was more or less constantly at war – in the series of conflicts called the Thirty Years' War – his defence of Dutch commercial imperialism took account of events in the intervening period, in which the Dutch East India Company was engaged in various military ventures to capture not just ships but rival trading posts and fortresses. Forced to leave France when he angered Richelieu by refusing to support the French against Holland, he did eventually manage to return to his homeland; but unable to resist involvement in current disputes, he was forced to flee yet again, this time to Sweden, where he became a Swedish citizen and even Swedish ambassador to France. He died in 1645 without ever resuming his career in Holland.

Grotius's major works elaborated an ideology well suited to 'extra-economic' strategies for establishing commercial supremacy; and they were transparently constructed to defend the very particular practices of the Dutch in their quest for commercial domination, not least by means of war. To build his case, he not only produced a theory of war and peace but elaborated conceptions of right and natural law, which, it has been claimed by some commentators, laid the foundation for modern theories of natural law.[7]

In *Mare Liberum*, Grotius was defending the East India Company's seizure of the Portuguese ship and its treasure. The Company, founded in 1602 , had been granted by charter a monopoly of trade in the East Indies, together with the right to establish trading posts and fortresses commanding trade routes and, significantly, among other state-like powers, the right to form its own military force, to be used, in principle, for defensive purposes. But the doctrine of 'just war', for all its flexibility and its history of imperial justification, was not so easily adapted to accommodate the pursuit of profit by a private enterprise, let alone a brazen act of piracy, which was hard to describe as a defensive action. Grotius would later, in *De Jure Belli ac Pacis,* elaborate the theory of war more systematically; but in *Mare Liberum,* he set out to demonstrate that this military aggression, committed by a private trading company and not a sovereign state, not simply in self-defence but for no other reason than commercial profit, was undertaken in accordance with natural law and the law of nations.

To justify the Company's act of war, he set out to demonstrate that all nations must have access to the East Indies, on the grounds that the law of nations requires the freedom to trade; that papal donation does not create a legitimate claim, because infidels have rights of ownership, public and private, of which they cannot be divested simply because they are infidels; that the sea and rights of navigation cannot become anyone's private domain, as the Portuguese were treating it; and nor can there be an exclusive right to trade with another nation. He starts from the premise that there is a universal human community, governed by certain universal principles of sociability required for survival, grounded in natural law accessible to human reason. God created the regions of the world with different and incomplete resources for survival; and, since the world is so constructed that no region has the means of self-sufficiency, it is a principle of reason that there must be free commerce among the regions and that obstruction of free commerce violates the law of nations.

In the course of his argument, Grotius begins to lay out a theory of property; but, although he raises such questions as those addressed by Vitoria concerning the right of *dominium* in the Americas, he is, in *Mare Liberum*, less concerned with rights of settlers than with the access of Dutch traders to the seas, to trade routes and to the fruits of commerce. This was in keeping with Dutch commercial strategies. Unlike their imperial rivals, the Dutch were not primarily interested in original colonization in newly discovered territories; and their strategies had less to do with establishment of settler colonies than with commercial supremacy. Even when they did establish

---

7 For a provocative, and persuasive, interpretation of Grotius, see Richard Tuck, *The Rights of War and Peace: Political Thought and the International Order from Grotius to Kant* (Oxford: Oxford University Press, 1999).

colonies, as they would later do, for example, in southern Africa, it was in the first instance for the purpose of provisioning commercial ships. In any case, Grotius's intention in *Mare Liberum* was not to justify colonization; and there was no need to elaborate a theory of property that could underwrite a claim to captured territory. All that was needed was a justification for the Company's act of armed aggression on the high seas.

Between 1603, the year of the *Mare Liberum*, and 1625, when Grotius wrote *De Jure*, the Dutch would embark on a series of military actions to seize trading posts, fortresses and colonial bases from other imperial powers like the Spanish and the Portuguese. It was then no longer simply a matter of maintaining the freedom of the seas but of contesting the power of rival states by capturing territory already claimed by them. Even while the seizure of territory was less for the purposes of wealth-producing settlement than for the promotion of commercial supremacy, it required a more positive theory of property rights, which Grotius would develop in his later work. But in *Mare Liberum*, where he is defending not the seizure and retention of colonial territory but the commercial movements of the Dutch East India Company against the trade monopolies of rivals, he is more concerned with what is *not* property than what is.

Like others before him, he begins with the world as common property, which is divided by human institution to deal with a growing division of labour, as well as the consequences of human sinfulness. Grotius certainly accepts that this institution, although created by human convention, conforms to the law of nature and the *ius gentium*, on the grounds that it is necessary to maintain the social order. It has even been argued by some commentators that he depicts property as an institution so ingrained in human nature and the needs of social life that it approaches a theory of property as a natural right.[8] Nevertheless, his objective in *Mare Liberum*

---

8 There has been much debate among commentators about whether Grotius is arguing that there is no right of property in the state of nature and that property depends entirely on agreement, or whether he does indeed posit something very close to a natural right, which requires agreement only to acknowledge, but not to create, the right of property, so that he makes a major advance in the direction of the idea of a natural property right as conceived by John Locke. But it can be argued that the difference between doctrines of property as a convention and as a natural right has been exaggerated. Many thinkers who start with the proposition the world is originally a common *dominium* and is divided into private property by human convention or law nevertheless treat property as a sacred right, instituted by divine providence, whether to deal with the consequences of human sinfulness or to provide the conditions of social cooperation and the division of labour necessary to human survival, according to the principles of reason accessible to human beings, with all the force of natural law. It will be argued in a subsequent chapter that Locke's break with tradition has less to do with asserting property as a natural right than with making the right of property dependent on something more than occupation, use, or even labour, grounding the right of property in the production of exchange value.

was to lay out certain limits on what can be claimed as property. Since his main concern was to argue for the freedom of the seas, to challenge the right of commercial rivals like the Portuguese to claim ownership of the seas and monopolize trade routes, his principal objective here was to deny the possibility of any proprietary interest in the sea. We can have a proprietary right, he maintained, only to things we can individually consume or transform. The sea cannot be property, because, like air, it cannot be occupied or used in this way and is therefore a common possession. Furthermore, what cannot become private property, he argued (contrary to traditional conceptions of political jurisdiction), cannot, by the same token, be the public property of the state either, since both private and public ownership come about in the same way. No state jurisdiction is possible where the kind of control implied by property is even in principle impossible.

It is not difficult to see how military intervention might be justified on these grounds against those whose only wrong had been to assert a hitherto accepted right of state jurisdiction over neighbouring waters or the right to regulate certain fishing grounds and trade routes. Nor, of course, did this principle preclude the de facto monopolization of trade that the Dutch themselves were aiming for in certain places, where they simply coerced local populations into trade, establishing monopolies by forcing treaties on them (in a practice of treaties among 'unequals' that Grotius would endorse in *De Jure*), while aggressively repelling their European rivals.

Grotius has been called the father of natural law, or at least its first 'modern' exponent, because he elaborates a conception of natural law that does not depend on a theological grounding. It is a precept of reason accessible to every rational person and binding on every human being without reference to faith. His work has been claimed by some commentators as a, if not the, major advance in the theory of natural right, elaborating a 'modern' conception of rights as 'subjective', in contrast to 'objective' rights as conceived, most notably, by Thomas Aquinas. For Aquinas, as we have seen, *ius* denoted 'the just thing', what was 'right' or just in an action or a situation in accordance with natural law, while Grotius was vesting rights in the person, a moral power or entitlement inherent in the individual. Other commentators have contested these claims to Grotius's originality, arguing, for instance, that Suárez had already made the innovative move – or, indeed, that the conception of 'subjective' rights can be traced to twelfth- and thirteenth-century theology and canon law. But, whether Grotius's ideas were truly original or largely derivative, his arguments proceed in novel ways, in answer to specific theoretical requirements, in unique historical conditions.

In *De Jure Belli ac Pacis*, Grotius begins by defining law and laying out his conception of natural law. Human beings are social creatures, not only possessing a strong inclination to society but also, by virtue of reason, capable of determining what is required to create and sustain a social order.

These principles of social order accessible to reason and hence to all rational beings are natural laws, both in the sense that they represent the basic requirements of the social order needed to sustain human life and well-being and also in the larger sense that they are inherent in human nature. In a proposition that shocked some of his contemporaries, he suggests that these natural principles would apply even if there were no God or if human affairs were of no concern to him. But, he hastens to add, we cannot and should not assume that no God exists. There is ample evidence of his all-powerful existence and the divine rewards of obeying natural law, so we can and should assume that natural law derives from God and that obedience to him requires adherence to natural law.

Human beings create a social order to meet their natural needs, and they do so by mutual consent, which gives rise to an obligation that derives from natural law and applies to civic laws, which human beings promulgate to sustain their social arrangements. These laws are specific to particular communities, devised for their own needs; but there are also laws that apply beyond the borders of any particular civic community and regulate relations among communities. These may exist by agreement; but there are also unwritten laws, principles of reason, that derive from nature. War itself is not immune to laws of this kind; and, while the laws of particular states do not apply to the conduct of war, those common laws – the law of nations – remain in force. Just as individuals undertake an obligation to laws designed to maintain social order, which they need to satisfy requirements they cannot meet on their own, even the most powerful states will sometimes need the help of others, either for purposes of trade or merely in self-defence. In this sense, they belong to an international community, also governed by law. The argument that follows is informed by the principle that the law of nature entails rights – moral qualities inherent in the person, the observance of which is dictated by right reason. There are also rights created by civil power rather than by nature, and this includes the right of property; but once established by civil law, the obligation to respect them is a principle of natural justice and carries the obligation of natural law.

Having defined law in the *Prolegomena* and the general sense in which the law applies to war, Grotius goes on to consider what is right or lawful in war, or what constitutes a 'just war'. He first proceeds to demonstrate that war is not inconsistent with natural law or the law of the Gospel and then, distinguishing between public and private war, goes on to show that private war, that is, war conducted by someone not lawfully authorized, can still be lawful, in keeping with the law of nature, which permits aggressive action to ward off injury. To be sure, even to insist that natural law applies to the conduct of war may by itself imply limitations on the conduct of war; and it is not unreasonable to invoke Grotius as a theorist of restrictions on war. Yet the concept of just war has always been notoriously flexible, easily adapted to justify the most aggressive imperialist wars. The limitations Grotius imposes do not in any way preclude, and in many ways support, the most aggressive actions taken by the Dutch, and the East India Company in particular, with no other object than pursuit of private gain.

War, argues Grotius, is above all a defence against violations of rights against the self or property; and he constructs a whole political theory on the principle that self-preservation is the first and most fundamental law of nature. This means that individuals and states are permitted, perhaps even obliged, to acquire for themselves 'those things which are useful for life'. Although they may not, in the process, injure others who have not injured them, their own self-preservation comes first; and they are entitled to commit aggressive acts to ward off injury. Grotius's notion of injury turns out to be very broadly permissive, at least for states and private agents like the Dutch East India Company, while the moral limits to which private agents and sovereign states at war are both subject are minimal.

The notion that there exists some kind of international society bound together by certain common rules is regarded as one of Grotius's major contributions to international law and a peaceful world order. But his argument had far less to do with what private agents or states owe one another than with the right they have to punish each other in pursuit of self-interest, not only in defending themselves against attack but 'proactively', as it were, in purely commercial rivalries. 'Grotius', concludes Richard Tuck, 'endorsed for a state the most far-reaching set of rights to make war which were available in the contemporary repertoire.'[9] On the one hand, Grotius argues that states, which can have no powers that individuals do not already have in nature, must, like individuals, be governed by the same moral principles. On the other hand, this conception, with all its wide-ranging implications for political theory in general, was elaborated by Grotius to defend the East India Company, on the grounds that individuals, like and even before states, have the right to punish those who wrong them.

This implied not only a very wide-ranging international right of punishment but also, finally, a right to appropriate territory. To buttress that right, Grotius was obliged to develop his theory of property. In *Mare Liberum*, it had been enough to demonstrate that the sea could not be claimed as property. But now something more was required to justify the capture of territory. Having argued that something could become property only if it could be occupied, and individually consumed or transformed, which might be true of land but not the sea, he now elaborated the other side of that argument: if usable things were left unused, there was no property in them, and hence people could appropriate land left unused by others. Grotius argued that no local authority could legitimately prevent free passage or the occupation of

---

9 *Ibid.*, p. 108.

unused land, and any attempt to do so could legitimately be challenged by military means.

Nevertheless, since land, unlike the sea, was in principle capable of transformation into property, it was also susceptible to political jurisdiction. Grotius never denied that indigenous authorities retained their general jurisdiction over the land – something that Dutch trading companies in principle accepted by seeking the approval of these local authorities and even paying them for taking land out of their jurisdiction. But the basic principle remained: land left waste or barren was not property and could be occupied by those able and willing to cultivate it. Grotius's argument had clear affinities with the principle, in Roman law, of *res nullius*, which decreed that any 'empty thing', such as unoccupied land, was common property until it was put to use – in the case of land, especially agricultural use. This would become a common justification of European colonization.[10]

It soon becomes clear that Grotius, in defining the ultimate right of self-preservation, was far less interested in the rights of individual persons than in the actions of a 'private' agent like the Dutch East India Company. It is significant that, at the very outset of his argument, immediately after laying out his basic propositions about what constitutes a lawful war and explaining his distinction between public and private war, Grotius devotes a chapter to the question of the right of subjects to resist their superiors. It is here, and not in discussion of wars among states or the military acts of private companies, that the moral limits imposed on aggressive action are most unambiguously stringent. Applied to the rights of an individual in relation to the state, the right of self-defence is very narrowly defined; and Grotius mounts a fairly conventional argument against the right of resistance, not only effectively denying any such right to private individuals but even questioning the rights of 'lesser magistrates'.

For all these strict limits on the rights of individuals, Grotius's painstaking elaboration of the conditions for and against the conduct of war makes it possible to justify the Dutch East India Company's seizure of Portuguese ships or Spanish fortresses and trading posts, on the grounds that these commercial rivals had breached the laws of nature by claiming command of the seas and trade monopolies. It is no less possible, on Grotius's terms, to justify exclusive Dutch trading rights – that is, monopolies – on the grounds that they have been established by treaty or agreements, which, as

---

10 Pagden, in *Lords of All the World*, has a useful discussion of this principle and its employment particularly by the English and, to a lesser degree, the French, and the reasons for its absence in Spanish imperial ideology. See pp. 77 *passim*. The principle was obviously more useful in cases where imperialism took the form of settler colonies which displaced local populations, but of little use to the Spanish, with their empire of explicit conquest.

he makes unambiguously clear, are no less legitimate for having been imposed by a stronger party upon a weaker one, not only by means of just war but simply by bald intimidation. The Portuguese unlawfully asserted their rights of property over the sea, when no such property is possible. This gave the Dutch East India Company the right to intervene with military force, in defence of free commerce, which, since commerce is a condition of survival, are ultimately grounded in natural law and the right of self-preservation. The Dutch, on the other hand, legitimately claimed command of trade routes, by occupying territory and asserting property in it, even when it remained under sovereign jurisdiction, which could not interfere with the Company's property rights; or the Company could gain monopoly privileges, and even use of already occupied territory, by agreement with weaker powers whose sovereign jurisdiction they formally recognized, even while imposing their own superior will by nothing more nor less than tacit threats of force.

There are some significant theoretical manoeuvres in Grotius's argument, which mark a break in the history of political thought, even if not precisely the kind of 'modern' innovations sometimes claimed for Grotius. Much of Western political thought since Roman times, which had delineated two distinct modalities of power, *dominium* and *imperium*, had been concerned with the relation between property and sovereign power or jurisdiction.[11] In his account of how property originates and how individuals acquire a right of property in any given thing, Grotius's views in *De Jure Belli* do not depart in any significant way from those of a long line of theologians and jurists who maintained that in the beginning all the world was held as a common *dominium*, and that private property exists not by nature but by agreement – though it is no less consistent with natural law. Even if we interpret his argument, as some distinguished commentators do (see footnote 7 above), as leaning further in the direction of property as a natural right, it would not represent a significant departure from what went before. Where his argument takes an interesting turn is in his view of the relation between property and jurisdiction. Ownership and jurisdiction are not only separate – as others before Grotius had, for various reasons, emphasized – they also seem to be on equal terms as claims to territory. This means that unoccupied territory, even when it is already under sovereign jurisdiction, can be claimed as property by an occupier from outside that jurisdiction.

The real novelty here is not in the concept of property. We shall see in a

---

11 See my *Citizens to Lords* for a discussion of the a discussion of medieval debates on this subject, the ways in which the struggles between ecclesiastical and secular authority were played out as debates about property and jurisdiction, and the complexities arising from the 'parcellization of sovereignty', which made the line between property and jurisdiction more difficult to draw.

subsequent chapter how the needs of a distinctive social form, capitalism, and a new form of imperialism would generate a truly new conception of property, which departs from the tradition that occupation or use constitute proprietary right. For the purposes of Dutch commercial imperialism, something like these traditional theories was enough – provided that it allowed the Dutch East India Company to claim as its property territory that fell within the jurisdiction of a sovereign state other than the Dutch Republic. For that purpose, a variation in ideas of jurisdiction was more important that an innovation in the idea of property. Grotius would go on to dislodge the rights of jurisdiction even more radically from the core of political thought, with significant, if unintended, consequences.

Grotius's ideas on natural law and 'subjective' rights arise not primarily in connection with competing jurisdictions, nor even in considering the relation between citizen and state. It is the very particular questions arising from the actions of a trading company on the international stage that determine the direction of his argument. He was confronting wholly new conceptual problems posed by the Dutch East India Company. The first multinational joint stock company, formed by investors in search of commercial monopolies and profit, it also performed functions that in other imperial powers, in particular the Republic's main rivals, Portugal and Spain, belonged to sovereign states. There was, to be sure, nothing unusual in pre-capitalist Europe about the unity of public power and private appropriation. That was, after all, the common pattern in societies where the wealth of dominant classes so often depended on coercive force and where revenues derived from jurisdictional powers at various levels, from feudal lordship to state office. But in no other society, not even the Italian city-states, was public authority so intricately bound up with commercial dominance. While private wealth was still heavily reliant on extra-economic powers and coercion, those powers, when they did not derive directly from office, were aimed at dominance in trade – such as monopolies maintained by military force. In the Dutch Republic, ruled by urban elites who identified the public interest with commercial profit, there was a hazy line between the sovereign state and a commercial enterprise – as would be baldly demonstrated some years later when Dutch military action to place William of Orange on the English throne for purely commercial reasons would be subsidized by the Amsterdam stock exchange.

It was not Grotius's intention to weaken the sovereignty of the Dutch state (although he might have been tempted to weaken the States-General in favour of the province of Holland). It was not, in other words, his intention to question the state's claims to sovereign jurisdiction; and nor did he ever question the sovereignty of the Spanish or the Portuguese state. What he did was simply to claim for a non-jurisdictional agent certain rights normally associated with jurisdiction and state sovereignty. He was confronting the

challenge of justifying the quasi-state powers of the Company and particularly its right to undertake military actions in the pursuit of private gain.
The issue in this case, then, was not competing jurisdictions, as it typically
had been in the discourse on rights in relation to political authority. It was
not a question of the Company demanding its autonomy and jurisdictional
powers against intrusions from the state or other authorities, temporal or
ecclesiastical. Nor was it the protection of the one commonly acknowledged
private right, the right of property, against the claims of public jurisdiction.
The problem here was the state-like powers of a commercial company in
relation to rival states. In confronting this distinctive problem, Grotius
detached rights from jurisdiction in unprecedented ways.

The Dutch East India Company did not lay claim to public jurisdiction,
and nor did Grotius make such claims on its behalf. But he did have at his
disposal certain conceptions of rights, which might include the right of self-
defence, inherent in the private person – such as the idea, formulated by
Suárez, of a right as 'a certain moral power that every man has, either over
his property or with respect to that which is due to him'. Whatever Suárez's
purpose may have been in formulating the concept of rights in this way (and
we should, as we have seen, be careful not to make too much of the differences between his formulation and that of Aquinas), Grotius's intentions
are fairly transparent. The right of the Company to engage in military
ventures is assimilated to the rights of private individuals, who have no jurisdiction and no common status other than their humanity. He proceeds by
ascribing to the individual certain rights that can by extension be applied to
other private agents; and he accomplishes this by proclaiming the right of
self-preservation as the ultimate right, the one right that individuals and
states unquestionably have in common and that must apply to private agents
no less than to public authorities.

Grotius's concern, then, was not the rights of private individuals but the
state-like rights of trading companies against competing states. Yet, because
he claimed those rights not as public jurisdictions in competition with the
sovereign state but as the rights of private agents, the unintended consequence was to set the discourse of rights on what appears to be a 'modern'
course, vesting 'subjective' rights in individuals in a more elaborate and
systematic way than anyone had done before him. The conceptual consequence was to place rights residing in the private person, the sovereign
individual, on a par with the sovereign rights of the state.

Benedict Spinoza

Just a few years after Grotius died, the office of stadtholder fell vacant with
the death of William II. The province of Holland, to be followed by others,
chose to leave the office unfilled; and from 1650 to 1672, the so-called first

'stadtholderless' era, the urban patriciate enjoyed a period of undiminished power, under the leadership of the Grand Pensionary, Jan de Witt. It was during this period that Benedict Spinoza reached maturity. While his interventions in philosophical and theological debates were radical and profoundly controversial, he was above all a philosopher and not a political figure in the manner of Grotius. He was, nonetheless, politically engaged; and his political allegiances seem to have been with the republican elite. While he was critical of his friends and allies, those allegiances are clearly reflected in his political philosophy. De Witt himself was a friend and protector of Spinoza; and among the strongest influences on the philosopher's political ideas were members of the commercial elite and de Witt's supporters – such as Lambert van Velthuysen and the de la Court brothers – who elaborated republican ideas, especially those who, as paradoxical as it may seem, drew upon Hobbes as their principal authority.

Spinoza was born in Amsterdam in 1632, the son of a Portuguese Jewish merchant whose family had taken refuge in the Netherlands. Benedict was well schooled in Judaism and may even have been educated for the rabbinate. Yet he was soon excommunicated from the Jewish community, as well as denounced by the Catholic Church, no doubt for ideas that foreshadowed his great work, the *Ethics*. He would establish connections with freethinking Protestants, who had come under the philosophical influence of Descartes and included precisely the kinds of Cartesian republicans who brought Hobbesian ideas to the Netherlands. Although he would manage to shock even those like Velthuysen, who had begun by supporting Spinoza's philosophical ventures, there is no mistaking his affinities, political no less than philosophical, with those Cartesian circles. In 1672, the Germans and French invaded the Netherlands, de Witt was assassinated, and the Orangist faction restored the office of stadtholder, establishing a regime – with the support of popular forces – under which Spinoza would continue to feel threatened until his death in 1677.

Spinoza began in 1663 with reflections on Descartes' philosophy but soon went on to elaborate his own distinctive views. In the *Tractatus Theologico-Politicus* of 1670, he laid out a provocative attack on the kind of reactionary Protestantism that supported the House of Orange, at a time when religious and republican liberties were under threat. Like others among his Cartesian republican associates, he promoted religious toleration; and like them, he called for the freedom of philosophy, as distinct from theology, even in interpretation of the Bible – which, in Dutch confessional disputes, had clear political implications. But he followed these principles to their limits in ways his friends were not always willing to do. Ultimately it would be Velthuysen, at first a friend and collaborator on the question of religion and philosophy, who would denounce Spinoza as an outright atheist.

The guiding principle of Spinoza's philosophy, which is elaborated in his

Ethics, was the unity of God and nature. To speak of a transcendent creator who by his own will and for his own purposes forged the universe seemed meaningless to the philosopher. There is one single reality, which we can call nature; and if God is its cause, he is an immanent cause, not standing outside nature but acting as the principle of nature unfolding its immanent necessities. Arcane debates have raged about whether this makes Spinoza a pantheist or even an atheist; but one thing remains certain: Spinoza had gone further than anyone else in the Western philosophical canon in denying any form of transcendence beyond or alien to nature or any dualism of matter and spirit. Humanity belongs to nature too; and, just as all of nature is a unique and single substance, there is no meaningful way to speak of a division in humanity between mind or spirit and matter. At the same time, our participation in this unique and single reality allows for real human knowledge. The material complexities of the human body are expressed in a complex and uniquely human capacity for apprehending the single reality of which the human being is an integral part. While as natural beings we are driven by our passions, having a unique capacity to know and understand the forces that drive us, we need not be slaves to our passions, or indeed to uncritical and unreflective adherence to religion, and can live a free life in accordance with reason. We shall see how these principles are reflected in Spinoza's views on the ideal polity.

That Spinoza was a groundbreaking philosopher, whose philosophical ideas had radical implications beyond the boundaries of scholarly debate, is surely not in question. But, although he has long held his place in the canon of philosophy, his political ideas have in recent years enjoyed a resurgence. It is striking that the dominant theme in this revival has been the philosopher's political radicalism, celebrated not only by a mainstream historian like Jonathan Israel, who situates him at the heart of a 'Radical Enlightenment', but also by Marxist thinkers from Antonio Negri to Etienne Balibar.[12] Israel goes beyond those historians of political thought who regard Spinoza, with his conception of rational freedom, as a, if not the, founder of 'liberalism'. The Radical Enlightenment, with its source in Spinoza, can, according to Israel, be credited with modern ideas of 'democracy, racial and sexual equality; individual liberty of lifestyle; full freedom of thought, expression, and the press; eradication of religious authority from the legislative process and education; and full separation of church and state.'[13] Indeed, whether or not we attribute directly to his influence the revolutionary movements that

---

12   Michael Hardt and Antonio Negri, *Empire* (Cambridge, MA: Harvard University Press, 2000), and Etienne Balibar, *Spinoza and Politics* (London: Verso, 1998).

13   Jonathan Israel, *A Revolution of the Mind: Radical Enlightenment and the Intellectual Origins of Modern Democracy* (Princeton: Princeton University Press, 2010), pp. vii–viii.

followed in the eighteenth century in North America and France, Spinoza, suggests Israel, virtually invented modern democracy. Marxist commentaries may seem still more extravagant in their claims for him, if we understand them as ascribing to him even more radically democratic and egalitarian doctrines than the kind of liberal democracy Israel has in mind.

There is no great mystery about why Spinoza's metaphysics, his 'monism', 'naturalism' and repudiation of transcendence have had a strong appeal to thinkers of the left, ever since Marx himself. Such ideas undoubtedly represented a powerful challenge to all forms of established authority, political, ecclesiastical or cultural. Some Marxist advocates of a radical Spinoza are also drawn to him because of what they understand as a materialism denuded of the teleologism that has dominated Marxist conceptions of history, deeply influenced by conventional Enlightenment conceptions of progress and by Hegelian philosophy. Yet Spinoza's political theory is a different matter. His conception of democracy remains far more ambiguous and paradoxical than recent interpretations suggest.

When all is said and done, the polity that was in practice closest to his theoretical democracy was the Dutch Republic, and especially the province of Holland, a civic order unambiguously dominated by wealthy commercial elites. He would certainly have preferred a republic with more popular support from the lesser classes who tended to side with Orangists and stadtholders against the urban elites. But, while this would have required something different from the self-perpetuating, self–co-opting oligarchy preferred by the regents, it is not at all clear that Spinoza's definition of democracy is inconsistent with an urban republic like the one in which he lived, where high office remained a prerogative of wealth. In his ideal 'democracy', the government would not be self-recruited, but he is careful to avoid identifying the inclusiveness of the citizen body or access to office as a criterion of democracy.

In the *Tractatus Theologico-Politicus*, Spinoza describes democracy as the most 'natural' form of state, the one most consistent with natural liberty, and the one least likely to commit acts of folly endangering self-preservation. (*TT-P* XVI) He also tells us that the most 'absolute' form of sovereignty 'if any such thing exists, is really the sovereignty held by a whole people'. But it is in his later, unfinished *Tractatus Politicus* that he provides his most elaborate definition of democracy. The difference between democracy and aristocracy, he stresses, is that, while in the latter, 'the right to govern is entirely dependent on co-optation', in a democracy 'it depends mainly on a kind of innate right, or a right acquired by fortune'. (*TP* VIII.1) A stable and successful aristocracy should have a large patriciate, but even if the whole population is admitted to the patriciate it remains an aristocracy as long as the right of entry is determined by express choice and not by some general law or inherited right. At the same time, a state can be 'democratic' even if that general or hereditary right is limited to a minority. He goes on to explain:

> [I]n aristocracy the appointment of a particular individual to the patriciate depends entirely on the will and free choice of the supreme council, so that the right to vote and undertake offices of state is in no case an hereditary possession, and no one can demand that right for himself by law; but in the state I am now discussing [democracy] the opposite is true. For here all who are of citizen parentage, or who have been born within the fatherland, or who have done good service to the commonwealth, or who qualify on other grounds recognized by law as entitling a man to civic rights, all these, I say, can legally claim the right to vote in the supreme council and to undertake offices of state; and it cannot be denied them unless they are criminals or persons of ill repute.
>
> Thus if it is laid down in the constitution of a state that only older men who have reached a certain age, or eldest sons as soon as they attain majority, or those who contribute a certain sum of money to the exchequer, shall have the right to vote in the supreme council and to handle public affairs, then, although such provisions would make it possible for its supreme council to be smaller than that of the aristocracy I have dealt with above, the state will still have to be called a democracy, since those of its citizens who are appointed to govern the commonwealth are not selected by the supreme council as the best, but are assigned this function by law. (*TP* XI.1–2)

On Spinoza's criteria, then, there is nothing to prevent an oligarchic republic ruled by commercial elites, with a small and exclusive governing council and even a limited citizen body, from being called 'democratic'.[14] Yet he never repudiates what appears to be the approbation for 'democracy' in his earlier work; and it is not self-evident why it seemed so important to him to claim the title of democracy for what, by any conventional definition, might still look like an aristocracy or even an oligarchy. 'Democratic' was far from being the word of high praise it has in recent times become. In early modern Europe, where the understanding of 'democracy' was still rooted in its ancient, original meaning as rule by the (common) people or even the poor,

---

14   It should perhaps be emphasized that Spinoza's conception of democracy cannot be explained as simply involving the kind of distinction elaborated (as we shall see in the next chapter) by Jean Bodin, between the nature of sovereignty and the form of government. Bodin can, for example, speak of a sovereign monarchy which can be 'democratic' if state office is accessible not only to the nobility or to men of wealth or virtue, as in an 'aristocratic' form of government; but, as should be clear from the passage quoted here, this is not what Spinoza has in mind.

it was more likely to be a word of condemnation, conjuring up the spectre of mob rule and, among propertied classes, a threat to their very existence. Even those who argued in favour of 'mixed' constitutions, in which the powers of kings and aristocracies were leavened by a 'democratic' element, were generally arguing in favour of oligarchic rule. There was, then, no immediately obvious reason for going quite as far as Spinoza did to attach the merits of democracy to an essentially oligarchic republicanism. Who, after all, was likely to be moved by such a designation? Was there any conceivable audience that might have been persuaded by it?

It may be tempting to think that Spinoza's insistence on using the word 'democracy' as if it were indeed high praise reveals his true democratic faith. Might this mean that he was, indeed, a democrat at least in his earlier days, and that, once having asserted his allegiance to democracy, he was in his later work – inspired by the shock of defeat – compelled simply, and somewhat unconvincingly, to redefine democracy just for the sake of consistency, so that his earlier praise might still apply to a form of state not obviously democratic? The bloody victory of the Orangist faction and the restoration of the stadtholder, supported by popular forces, may have required a certain rethinking; and it is almost as if Spinoza, once having insisted that democracy was the 'natural' form of sovereign power, was now seeking a definition of democracy that would allow the inclusion of far less democratic forms.

It seems more likely, however, that another kind of logic was at work. We have already seen how the idea that political authority derives from the 'people' and is grounded in consent could be used in favour of anything but democratic power, invoked to support even monarchies against not only popes but popular resistance. There is an element of that in Spinoza too. In the course of his discussion of democracy in *Tractatus Theologico-Politicus*, he makes a striking move, which seems to suggest that what he says about democracy even in his earlier work represents not so much approval of the democratic state as a means of legitimating other, rather less democratic forms. He tells us that he has two reasons for deliberately concentrating on the democratic state: the first is that it seems to be the most natural form – a proposition that appears to be not a normative judgment but an empirical observation that democracy is closest to humanity's natural conditions; and the second reason is that

> it best serves my purpose of dealing with the benefits of freedom in a commonwealth. I therefore pass over the bases of other governments; indeed, it is no longer necessary for us to know how they have arisen – and often arise still – in order to discover their right, which is abundantly obvious from what I have just shown. For whoever has sovereign power, whether it be one man, or a few, or all, has undoubtedly a perfect right to command everything he wishes. (XVI)

This means that aristocracies or kings have the same right to supreme power in their own forms of state as do the people in a democracy, since they are ultimately rooted in the same foundation (XVI). These other forms, in other words, may derive their legitimacy from their democratic origin.

Yet there remains something distinctive about Spinoza's characterization of 'democracy', which still needs to be explained. The logic of his argument may be easier to follow if we situate it in the context of Dutch political debate in that specific historical moment, at a time when the main objective of political thinkers, such as Velthuysen and the de la Court brothers, who supported de Witt, was to exclude the stadtholder altogether from any share in state authority. At the same time, the de la Courts in particular, who were newcomers to Holland from the southern Netherlands and did not belong to the governing regents, argued in favour of a more open republic with a less restrictive patriciate, elected by citizens in an assembly; and this was clearly a position favoured by Spinoza. Here the influence of Machiavelli and the Italian city-republics was very clear – though the model of Venice, or a *governo stretto*, figured more prominently than Machiavelli's Florence, in its *governo largo* mode, as the ideal for Dutch commercial interests. To be sure, the right to rule should, according to the de la Courts (as, indeed, for Jan de Witt), be confined to wealthy classes, and even the citizen body would ideally not include the plebs; but the ruling oligarchy, while restricted to the wealthy, should not be self–co-opting, as the regents' patriciate had increasingly become, especially as the European economic crisis took hold in the Republic. Only if the possibility of office were more open would it serve to harness private greed to public good.

The main theoretical requirement for these oligarchic republicans was to rule out, at almost all costs, any notion of a mixed constitution. That classic idea had, since ancient Rome, often done service in support of oligarchic republicanism; and even Grotius had invoked it. But now it was being used by Orangists to defend the position of the stadtholder, claiming, among other things, that this office protected the people from the oligarchs' excessive power. If the politics of the day precluded any concession by republican elites to theories of 'mixed' sovereignty, some other means had to be found to describe Dutch oligarchic rule, which factored out the monarchical element. For the de la Courts as indeed for Spinoza, there was the added requirement of replacing the self–co-opting regents with a more open oligarchy and finding other ways of attracting popular sentiment away from the Orangists. This posed a wholly new conundrum: how to introduce a 'democratic' element into the oligarchic Republic without conceding a divided sovereignty.

It was in this spirit that the Dutch republicans eagerly adopted Hobbes and his theory of indivisible sovereignty. They were clearly impressed by his argument sustaining a single, undivided sovereign power, even though they mobilized it not in favour of an absolute monarch, as did Hobbes himself, but for a civic Republic against the stadtholder's claim to a share in state power. On Hobbesian principles, the Dutch were able to argue that neither the House of Orange nor those clerics who opposed the civic government had any legitimate claim to state power in the Republic.

Hobbes was not the first political thinker to argue for indivisible sovereign power, but he did so on distinctive grounds, which seemed to have a special appeal to the Dutch. Unlike Jean Bodin in France, he was (for reasons that will be discussed at greater length in a later chapter) not principally concerned with the need to combat various corporate powers contesting jurisdiction with the monarchy. Instead, he took as his central theme conflicts among self-interested individuals whose overriding motivation was not to gain a share of public authority but simply to ensure self-preservation.

This seemed to suit Dutch purposes. The issue for them, as for the English, was not a conflict among corporate jurisdictions. During the Dutch Revolt, opponents of the Spanish monarch had, to be sure, typically asserted various claims to particular jurisdictions, privileges, liberties, and the powers of 'lesser magistrates' against incursions by the monarchy. But, in the course of the Revolt, the nature of the conflict changed, with opponents of the monarchy increasingly claiming a free and sovereign republican government. As the Republic was established, there emerged new doctrines of sovereignty belonging to the 'people' as a whole. That sovereignty was embodied in the nobles and urban patricians conceived not as 'lesser magistrates' but, in principle, as delegates of the sovereign people.[15] When, in Spinoza's day, republican elites challenged the powers of the stadtholder, they were no longer contesting his power as claimants to competing jurisdictions or the powers of lesser magistrates. They challenged the very existence of the stadtholder's office in favour of a single, undivided sovereignty.

Reflecting on human nature and the purpose of the state in recognizably Hobbesian terms, they argued that human beings are creatures driven by their passions, in pursuit of their own selfish interests and their principal aim, self-preservation. A stable state, they maintained, requires that these passions be held in balance, something that can be achieved only by an indivisible sovereign power. In the Dutch context this had a particular meaning: the aim was to achieve not only peace among self-interested individuals but, more specifically, a form of polity that would encourage the pursuit of wealth, sustaining commercial dominance without creating instability among rival civic interests, while preserving the position of commercial elites.

The specifically Dutch element in these arguments is what we have called

---

15 See introduction to *The Dutch Revolt*, ed. Martin van Gelderen (Cambridge: Cambridge University Press, 1993).

the politically constituted commercial society. This implies not only that the Dutch Hobbesians assume a society in which commercial interests are inseparable from extra-economic power, political status and privilege, but also that, even in this profoundly commercialized society, the harmony of economic interests must, in their view, be achieved by political means. The critical instrument of harmony is not, as in the later Anglo-Scottish model of commercial society, the 'invisible hand' of the market. But neither is it, as in the French 'political economy', an absolutist monarchy. Political stability and harmony in this commercial society is best achieved by republican government, in which wealth is joined to public office.[16]

Although it would be a Dutchman, Bernard Mandeville, who, writing in early eighteenth-century England, would make famous the idea that 'public benefits' derive from 'private vices', something like that idea had already been proposed in France by Antoine de Montchrétien (as we have seen); even earlier, in sixteenth-century England, Sir Thomas Smith (about whom more in Chapter 7), had suggested that competing economic interests could be harmonized to forge a common good. For the Dutch, as for the French (and, indeed, for Thomas Smith), transformation of individual greed into communal well-being required active guidance by the state. Even Mandeville would continue to emphasize the role of political guidance, in an interesting contrast to Adam Smith, who, although he certainly assigns the state an important role in ensuring the conditions of a truly competitive market, looks to the market itself to discipline competing interests. Smith's idea was rooted in a capitalist market of a kind that existed only in England and nowhere else, not even in a thoroughly commercialized society like the Dutch Republic. What was distinctively Dutch was a conception of commercial harmony produced by carefully balanced republican institutions, which would guide the pursuit of selfish interests to promotion of the common good by joining wealth to public office.

If Hobbes's views on human nature, passions and the sovereign powers of the civil magistrate provided the essential building blocks for Dutch republicans, an argument originally designed to underwrite the sovereign power of an absolutist monarchy required substantial modification to fit republican requirements. Hobbes had, to be sure, allowed for a plural sovereign; but his argument was constructed to make it clear that an indivisible, truly sovereign, power resides most perfectly and absolutely in a single, undivided

16 Arguments like those of the 'Spinozan Marxists', who situate him – albeit abstractly – in the context of a 'market capitalism', tend to miss precisely what is distinctive about the Dutch commercial system. Spinoza's political philosophy seems more consistent and easier to comprehend in the context of what we are calling here a politically constituted commercial society, with all its assumptions about the unity of economic and 'extra-economic' power and about the political harmonization of interests.

mind or will, embodied in a monarchy. For the Dutch republicans, as for Hobbes, a 'mixed constitution' was not an option; but to make the strongest possible case for a sovereign power residing in a republican collective leadership, a republican power so indivisible that the stadtholder could have no place in it, required something more.

Whatever else Spinoza hoped to accomplish with his departures from Hobbes, he certainly sought to reverse the Hobbesian principle about the ideal location of indivisible power. A sovereign power must, it is true, express a common purpose; and Spinoza's theory faced the challenge of how such a common purpose could emerge from many minds and diverse passions. But there was no question of conceding to Hobbes that a monarchy was best, the surest way of translating a multiplicity of individual self-interests into a civil unity. An argument would have to be found that would give a plural sovereign the kind of primacy enjoyed in Hobbes's theory by a monarch.

Spinoza's argument, in simple terms, is that governments are generally stable to the degree that they enjoy the support of their subjects. Wide popular support, it would seem on the face of it, is more likely to exist if the people have a direct stake in government. The wider the scope of the sovereign power, the more 'absolute' it is, precisely because such a sovereignty is, by definition, more powerful, to the extent that it expresses the people's common purpose and is less inclined to stray from their common interests.

Yet the argument turns out to be more ambiguous than it seems at first sight. Does it, for example, mean that a democracy, as rule by an inclusive multitude, embracing a wider range of individuals and interests, must be more stable and secure than a less inclusive form, an aristocracy? Significantly, when Spinoza introduces the suggestion that sovereignty held by the whole people is more 'absolute', he does so not for the purpose of defending democracy but to demonstrate that an aristocracy with a council 'of sufficient size' is more 'absolute' than the rule of one man. A republic governed by a more open patriciate is, in other words, in this sense 'absolute'; and the passage even suggests that such an aristocracy is as close to 'absolute' as, in the real world, is conceivable. At the same time, even kings can garner popular support, if they govern for the common good (or even, possibly, if not?); and where they can maintain their power, the monarchy has no less right to rule than a democracy. Spinoza even suggests that monarchies have been historically more stable, while democracies have tended to degenerate into some other form like aristocracy.

Does this perhaps mean that democracy's claims to superiority have less to do with stability or security than with liberty? Even here, there are ambiguities. The philosopher does indeed claim that democracy is the form 'most consonant with individual liberty'; but he also tells us that freedom does not consist in acting simply in accordance with our own pleasures and passions, which may be contrary to our real advantage. True freedom means action in accordance with reason, which tends to be contrary to human inclinations. This means it requires strict obedience to a sovereign power, the sole legislative authority, acting in the common good, whether that sovereign power is a democracy or a monarchy. Indeed, a democracy that allows free rein to destructive or even simply useless passions is less free than a monarchy that governs for the people's benefit.

However radical Spinoza's philosophical system, his views on nature, reason or religion, may have been, it is virtually impossible to sustain an unambiguous case for his commitment to democracy in anything like its conventional meanings, ancient or modern, simply on the strength of what he explicitly says about the virtues and vices of specific political forms. Nor is it possible to brush aside the striking fact that his definition of democracy is carefully constructed to include an oligarchic republic, and that many of the observations seized upon by advocates of the philosopher's democratic radicalism are designed to underpin that kind of republican oligarchy. It is, nonetheless, fair to say that, whatever his intentions, his mode of argumentation opens certain democratic doors in strikingly unprecedented ways.

Here is how the case for Spinoza's democratic radicalism has been summed up by two of the principal advocates: while Hobbes, they say, 'plays a foundational role in the modern construction of a transcendent political apparatus', Spinoza is the philosopher of 'immanence', the philosopher who best expresses the idea that all power and authority are inherent in, and emanate from, the multitude. A similar, if rather more nuanced, argument has been made by Etienne Balibar. Spinoza, he suggests, asks a question never before raised by any political thinker, at least as an object of theoretical analysis: 'that of the basis of State power in the people, that is, in movements originating from within the "multitude" itself.'[17]

We can assess these claims by looking at how Spinoza's argument unfolds in relation to Hobbes's conception of the 'multitude'. Both philosophers start from the same premise: that, as Spinoza puts it in the *Tractatus Theologico-Politicus,* 'each has as much right as he has power' (II.8). Yet, if he identifies right with capacity or power in a manner similar to Hobbes, it is precisely here that, by his own account, he departs most significantly from the English philosopher: 'I always', he writes in Epistle 50 in response to a friend's enquiry about his differences with Hobbes, 'preserve the natural right in its entirety, and I hold that the sovereign power in a State has right over a subject only in proportion to the excess of its power over that of a subject'.

For Spinoza, in keeping with his philosophical 'naturalism', the emphasis here is on the 'natural', and the concept of right is defined in 'naturalist' terms, maintaining the identity of right and capacity or power, devoid of

---

17   Hardt and Negri, *Empire*, p. 83; Balibar, *Spinoza and Politics*, p. 56.

any normative significance. Hobbes, too, seemed to be arguing that anything individuals have the power or capacity to do in pursuit of self-preservation they have a natural right to do. Yet, because his conception of sovereignty allows for the unconditional transfer of rights to a sovereign power, which thereby acquires the right to decide for the subject what needs to be done to promote self-preservation, Hobbes has, in Spinoza's eyes, qualified the naturalist principle. If the sovereign power acquires an unconditional entitlement to rule by virtue of a voluntary transfer of rights from individuals, it would appear that right retains a normative element and is not entirely synonymous with power.[18]

On the face of it, Spinoza's unequivocal identification of right with power seems an even more unambiguous appeal to the prerogatives of power than Hobbes himself could contemplate. The English philosopher is reputed ruefully to have said to his friend John Aubrey that Spinoza had outdone him, having 'cut through him a barre's length, for he [Hobbes] durst not write so boldly.'[19] Yet Spinoza's daring formulation becomes not so much a statement of the principle that might makes right as a refusal of any idea that natural rights can be alienated and, arguably, an assertion of the multitude's political identity, in a way that contrasts sharply with Hobbes.

In his earlier work, Hobbes (who will be discussed at greater length in Chapter 7) had described democracy as the original form of sovereignty 'by institution' – that is, the first form of sovereignty created not by compulsion, nor by 'acquisition' or conquest, but as 'a creation out of nothing by human wit', by 'many men assembled together . . . which proceedeth from the assembly and consent of a multitude.' It is from this original form that the other forms – aristocracy and monarchy – derive (*Elements of Law* XX, XXI). In elaborating his idea of the contract in his later work, Hobbes abandoned this formulation. In *De Cive* and the *Leviathan*, he was not seeking to explain the historical origin of political authority but rather to emphasize that the voluntary transfer of rights to a sovereign power was absolute and unconditional, on the grounds that the multitude can never be more than a disparate collection of individuals, which can have no political identity.

Hobbes was confronting the problem of the 'multitude' in wholly new ways. The idea that sovereignty, of one kind or another, derives originally

18 In the *Leviathan*, a work Spinoza may not have known, Hobbes, as we shall see in the next chapter, seems to come closer to Spinoza by modifying his argument in a way that suggests the transfer of power is not as unconditional as it appears to be in *De Cive* and that the right to rule may indeed be conditional on the de facto power to maintain it – perhaps in order to justify Cromwell's accession to power and legitimate the Revolution that had overthrown a king.
19 'The Life of Thomas Hobbes of Malmesbury', in John Aubrey, *Brief Lives*, ed. John Buchanan-Brown (London: Penguin, 2000), p. 441.

from the people or a body of consenting individuals had, as we have seen, long been a convention in Western political thought; and it had no necessary implications for the people's political rights, within or against the state. It was typically invoked on behalf of one jurisdictional claim against another – for instance, by monarchies against the papacy, or by 'lesser magistrates' claiming to act as the people's corporate representatives in opposition to the king. But for Hobbes, as we shall see in Chapter 7, the 'multitude' presented a new kind of problem, which no political theorist had yet seriously confronted. Just as the language of individual rights took on a different meaning in the English context, where corporate powers were relatively weak and a new, less mediated political relation between private individual and state had displaced the old contest among jurisdictions, the question of the 'multitude' and its political identity took on a new significance.

In the English context Hobbes had felt compelled (as we shall see) to confront not only the conflict between Parliament and Crown but also the role of the people outside Parliament, the 'multitude', which had invaded the political arena in unprecedented ways. In his earlier work, it was enough to defend the crown against the claims of Parliament. By the time of *De Cive*, the work that established his reputation in the Dutch Republic, he was no longer simply defending the monarch against parliamentary forces or even against more radical claims to 'republican' liberty, but also seeking a way to deprive the multitude of any political identity.

In his earlier work, he had supported the Crown against Parliament by adopting an argument that, while certainly less grounded in corporatist assumptions, was not so different from that of his predecessors: that the people, as a collection of individuals, had created the sovereign by transferring their power. But in *De Cive*, he was confronting a different problem, the political role assumed by the people outside Parliament, who were taking to the streets in growing numbers and asserting a new kind of political identity. It was not here simply a question of tracing the sovereign power – whether of the monarch or of Parliament – to its original source in a multitude of consenting individuals. The problem Hobbes confronted was the multitude's assertion of its own direct political agency. His response was simply to say that the multitude had no political will or identity: 'When we say the People, or Multitude, wills, commands, or doth any thing', he insisted, it must be understood that it is the state itself 'which Commands, Wills and Acts by the will of one, or the concurring will of more, which cannot be done, but in an Assembly' (VI.1n). It is only once a multitude of individuals has given way to a united sovereign power that it is possible to speak of a political society.

Hobbes, then, was already grappling with the 'immanence' of the multitude's power in unprecedented ways. It could be said that, even if his objective was to demonstrate that the multitude's only political role was to relinquish and alienate its political agency, he went considerably further than Hardt and Negri or Balibar suggest in raising the question of the multitude as the direct and immediate, 'immanent' source of political power. He certainly went beyond anything proposed by medieval thinkers who had invoked the corporate 'people' or consent in the perennial contests over jurisdiction. *De Cive* may have set the terms of the debate for Dutch republicans; but any attempt to transform Hobbes's argument from a case for absolutist monarchy into a brief for an open republican oligarchy required a delicate balancing act, going one step further in establishing the 'immanent' power of the multitude, while retaining the dominance of the urban elite.

When Spinoza, in his earlier work, described democracy as the most 'natural' form of state, the one closest to the natural freedom of the individual, he was not so very far from Hobbes's early contention that democracy was the original form of state 'by institution'. Neither thinker was making a moral judgment so much as simply speculating on the most likely means by which a multitude of individuals might leave their natural state of freedom to institute political society. But both of them would later abandon this formulation, though for different reasons and in very different ways. Like Hobbes, Spinoza in his later work is no longer seeking the original, historical source of sovereignty. He no longer even mentions the idea of an original contract as the natural or primary source of sovereign power; but, unlike Hobbes, he seems to avoid any formulation, historical or normative, that may imply an original transfer of natural rights, however conditional, and takes for granted the political identity of the multitude. He allows for a kind of secondary contract, whereby the people, which already exists as a political entity, transfers powers to a king or aristocracy; and he even suggests that most aristocracies were originally democracies (*TP* VIII 12). This does imply that aristocracy and monarchy have a right to rule; and it may even suggest that democracies in reality have not typically been stable. Nevertheless, in Spinoza's formulation the political identity of the multitude remains at least in principle intact. Rights remain synonymous with powers – which means that sovereignty remains conditional on the maintenance of power and is likely to depend on a capacity to garner and to keep popular support.[20]

Yet, if this seems to lend some credence to those arguments that see a democratic essence in Spinoza's political theory, it remains entirely consistent with the view of the ideal polity espoused by prominent Dutch oligarchs: a commercial republic governed by an open urban aristocracy of wealth, in which republican institutions and the advantages derived from office help to channel private greed to the pursuit of common goods. Spinoza might prefer

---

20 Again, Hobbes would in the *Leviathan* come close to this, as we shall see in a subsequent chapter.

a more inclusive citizen electorate than did some of his compatriots, and the
TP leaves tantalizingly open the possibility of a more unambiguously democratic argument. The work is suddenly cut off just at the point when Spinoza
sets out to discuss the particular form of democracy in which, he says (for
reasons that must remain unclear), he is most interested: an inclusive democracy whose citizen body consists of all independent men, all those subject to
the laws of their government (as distinct from residents subject to other
governments) and leading decent lives. Nevertheless, his definition of
democracy itself, very painstakingly laid out, does not rule out exclusion of
the plebs (to say nothing of women, whose relative natural weakness appears
to justify their general exclusion from the citizenry[21]); and that definition
has the virtue of embracing a de la Court–style oligarchy without conceding
a divided sovereignty.

   Nowhere, indeed, is there a clearer statement of the Dutch Hobbesian
ideal than in Spinoza's observation that the state should be based

> on such laws as will cause the majority, not indeed to seek to live wisely –
> for that is impossible – but at any rate to be governed by those passions
> which are most useful to the commonwealth. Thus every attempt must be
> made to ensure that the rich, if they cannot be thrifty, are at any rate
> greedy for gain. For if this passion for gain, which is universal and
> constant, is reinforced by the desire for glory, most men will certainly
> make every effort to increase their wealth by honourable means so as to
> obtain office and avoid great disgrace. (*TP* X.6)

There is no mistaking the general principles Spinoza is outlining here: the
greed for gain is a, perhaps even the, human passion most useful to the
commonwealth; and it can be harnessed to the public good by making
wealth a means to achieve the honour of office. Whatever we may think of
the philosopher's observation that sovereignty is in principle most 'absolute'
when it resides in the whole people, in the real world a republic governed by
a commercial elite driven by greed seems best equipped to guide the passions
of self-interested individuals towards the common good – and this apparently applies no less to the philosopher's 'democracy' than to an aristocracy.
It is when greed is attached to republican office that governance by human
passions can be most readily translated into the rule of reason.

   We can gain some perspective on Spinoza's 'democracy' if we consider it

-----

   21 In his discussion of democracy, Spinoza considers at some length (*TP* XI.4)
whether the exclusion of women from the political domain and their subjection to the
authority of men exists by nature or merely by institution and concludes that the cause
– and the justification – is their natural weakness. Their power, and therefore their right,
is not equal to men's.

against the background of political developments elsewhere, which were accompanied by truly radical conceptions of the multitude and its claims to political agency. When the Dutch philosopher was still a boy, the political terrain was being redefined by the 'people' in England both in the streets and in the realm of ideas. We have already seen how Hobbes felt compelled to confront these popular intrusions into the political domain. But there were also far more radical expressions of the multitude's 'immanent' power. When, for example, Spinoza was fifteen years old, in the course of the English Civil War, a historically unique event took place in Cromwell's army, the so-called Putney Debates, in which fundamental questions concerning political rights and governance were discussed not by philosophers or theologians but by activists and soldiers who were truly speaking for the 'multitude', a 'rabble' of yeoman farmers, craftsmen, and the army rank and file. The extraordinary documentary record of those debates may not have achieved quite the canonical status of writings by a Hobbes or a Spinoza; and their theoretical influence, however significant, has been of a different kind. But the debates at Putney – to say nothing of even more radically democratic ideas that emerged out of the English Revolution – reveal a universe of democratic thinking that goes well beyond Spinoza's ideas on the 'multitude'.

6

FRENCH ABSOLUTISM

Between 1484 and 1560, successive French kings refused to summon the
Estates General, the national assembly of regional estates, depriving France's
representative bodies of their only significant function, the power of approving taxes. When they were finally recalled, it was a time of religious conflict
during which exactions for the maintenance of soldiers added to the burden
of taxation. The Estates General would meet again, without much effect,
several times from 1560 to 1614, when they finally dissolved in disarray, not
to be summoned again until 1789. France would have no national representative assembly, let alone a national legislative body, until the Revolution.
The centralizing project of the monarchy had, at least in this respect,
succeeded; and the 'absolutist' state prevailed.

Yet the failure of the Estates General was not a simple matter of monarchical success. If anything, the absence of a national assembly reflected the
fragmentation of the French state no less than it expressed the power of the
monarchy. The French monarchy, unlike the English, had emerged slowly, in
a prolonged contest among rival feudal families; and, while in England the
monarchy evolved as a cooperative project between feudal lords and kings,
French absolutism never quite overcame the legacy of dynastic rivalry or the
parcellization and particularisms of competing jurisdictions.

The royal state certainly succeeded in establishing its own apparatus of
power, with a bureaucracy unmatched in Western Europe; but this was not
simply a mark of its strength or of modern 'rationalization'. One of the
monarchy's principal devices for gaining the support of its opponents was
the distribution of patronage, especially in the form of state office; and the
growth of the bureaucracy was in large part a consequence of buying off
potential claimants to autonomous jurisdictions by offering the induce-
ments of lucrative state office, to say nothing of the opportunities for
plunder afforded by wars, foreign and domestic. The legacy of parcellized
sovereignty would continue to shape French political theory and practice
until the Revolution and even the Napoleonic state.

A System of Extortion and Embezzlement?

At the beginning of the sixteenth century, France was the most populous country in Europe. Of an estimated 18 million people, the vast majority, between 80 and 90 per cent, were peasants. Although in principle free and in secure possession of their land, they were still often subject to various seigneurial dues; and they also bore the brunt of growing state taxation. In the latter part of the sixteenth century the monarchy undertook a massive transformation of the state, expanding the bureaucracy and the tax burden with it, in a tax system that was evolving to finance not simply state projects but a 'massive spoils system', a 'semi-institutionalized system of extortion and embezzlement'.[1] Sections of the nobility, and a substantial part of the bourgeoisie, were co-opted by giving them access to the spoils of office as a means of private enrichment.

The distribution of offices no doubt increased support for royal power, but it also generated growing unrest among those who bore the burden; and even the beneficiaries of office proved unreliable. As the monarchy not only used the distribution of offices to consolidate its power base but also sold state offices to enhance its own fiscal solvency, this created a new dynastic class of venal officeholders, who would, in the seventeenth century, themselves become a source of opposition to monarchical power. Even when the 'absolutist' monarchy appeared to be firmly established, regional and corporate divisions persisted, as did the plethora of local legal systems.

Growing taxes and privileged exemptions from them were certainly enough to generate unrest, but the process of state centralization had produced increasingly complex social divisions. In a state where the monarchy had been the product of an inconclusive contest among rival noble families, dynastic rivalries continued to be fierce. At the same time, the centralizing monarchy was challenged not only by unprivileged classes that carried the burden of taxation but by nobles who had not been co-opted into the royal state and were defending their own jurisdictions. There were also conflicts not only between privileged and unprivileged estates but within the estates themselves. The Third Estate was divided in various ways, between rich and poor, bourgeois and peasant, urban and rural. Opposition to the monarchy was therefore never unambiguous. The bourgeoisie, while seeking to defend itself against excessive exactions, might also have reason to support the monarchy to strengthen its position against the aristocracy or to gain access to state office. Even peasants

---

1   Robin Briggs, *Early Modern France 1560–1715* (Oxford: Oxford University Press, 1977), p. 3; introduction to *Constitutionalism and Resistance in the Sixteenth Century: Three Treatises by Hotman, Beza, and Mornay*, ed. and transl. Julian Franklin (New York: Pegasus, 1969), p. 16. See also David Parker, *The Making of French Absolutism* (London: Edward Arnold, 1983), for an overview of the French state in the period.

might seek protection from the king against the aristocracy, while nobles co-opted into the state were pitted against those defending what remained of their seigneurial powers and local autonomy.

Nevertheless, as the royal state grew, so did opposition to it. Religious controversy sharpened the dividing lines, and there followed decades of conflict in which dynastic rivalries were compounded by confessional disputes and regional revolts of one kind or another. In France's fractured polity, religious dissent played a very particular role in unifying diverse oppositional forces and regions into a more or less united party of resistance. Ideas of resistance and popular sovereignty did cut across religious lines; but the Huguenots, though a minority movement, played a disproportionate role in generating what might be called the first organized resistance to royal power in Europe. While appealing to various classes for various reasons, Protestantism in France generated a forceful political movement when and because it was adopted by sections of the nobility, especially elements of the provincial aristocracy, for whom Catholicism, in the form of the Gallican Church, had become the creed of monarchy and the centralizing ambitions of the royal state. The most important political ideas bequeathed to the Western canon by the Wars of Religion in France were those that adapted Protestant doctrine to the interests of provincial nobles and municipal authorities asserting their local autonomy and particular jurisdictions.

The Reformation and religious division in France certainly crystallized political dissent, but the terms of religious conflict were politically defined from the start, shaped by the particular formation of the state. French Protestantism as an oppositional force, and the translation of its doctrines into theories of resistance and 'constitutionalism', belonged to a larger political struggle. In the series of bloody conflicts commonly described as the Wars of Religion, the battles between Catholics and Huguenots that erupted in 1562 and lasted for decades were inextricably bound up with rivalries among noble families for control of the monarchy, as well as conflicts between monarchy and aristocracy. At the same time, religious conflict aggravated already existing social unrest, not least by increasing the burden of taxation to finance the king's military forces. The development of the monarchical state as a means of private appropriation, always in tension with competing forms of 'extra-economic' power and 'politically constituted property'; its reliance on the proliferation and distribution of offices to sustain its power no less than its fiscal stability; the growth of the state not only as a means of maintaining order and protecting the private possessions of propertied classes but as itself a private resource – all this set the political agenda in specific ways and, with it, shaped religious controversy too.

There was, of course, nothing specifically French about the contest among competing jurisdictions; but the opposition between a centralizing monarchy and other claims to autonomous powers played a distinctive role. In the other major Western European monarchies the lines were drawn in different ways, and political discourse proceeded along different lines. In England, there was no fundamental challenge to a centralizing state, which served the interests of the aristocracy no less than of the monarchy; and, though the English Civil War would be ferocious, the contest between monarchy and Parliament – which jointly composed the centralized state – would not take the form of a battle between central state and other, partial jurisdictions. In Spain, the empire was, at least for systematic theorists of political theology, a more contentious issue than the royal state itself. In sixteenth-century France, the contest between monarchy and local jurisdictions played a central part in the formation of both 'absolutist' thought and theories of resistance.

The Reformation, the spread of Protestantism, the Wars of Religion, followed by the decline of the Huguenots and the rise of the Catholic League, brought to a head underlying social conflicts and provided ideological vehicles for conducting battles over taxation and tithes, privileges and exemptions, the powers of local patrician oligarchies, and royal absolutism itself. While the objects and intensity of struggle, as well as the nature and scope of social alliances, varied according to regional differences and variations in local privileges, parts of the country saw the outbreak of violent peasant protests and sometimes regional revolts in which peasants were allied with urban classes. Such outbreaks might begin as revolts against taxation and tithes and end as attacks on the whole system of power and privilege.

The period was rich in political ideas at every level of sophistication – the *cahiers de doléances*, which outlined the grievances of the three estates; the Huguenot resistance tracts; the political philosophy of Bodin – and all, in their various ways, reflected the distinctive configuration of the French state. The contrast between French and English political ideas is instructive. It was the English, not the French, who most readily adopted the idea of a 'mixed constitution', and they elaborated ideas of separated powers well before the French. This may seem paradoxical when we consider that it was the English, not the French, who possessed a more truly undivided sovereignty, and that even theorists of the 'mixed constitution' remained wedded to a centralized and indivisible sovereign power. But the 'mixed constitution' was, after all, perfectly consistent with a truly unitary state in which the sovereignty of the central state was shared by Parliament and Crown. In the English context the idea of a mixed constitution or divided power was not at all grounded in a fragmented sovereignty but, on the contrary, presupposed a unified sovereign state. The French were dealing with a different disposition of power and a more persistent contest among fragmented sovereignties, which called for different theoretical strategies.

English landed proprietors, who developed private and increasingly 'economic' means of appropriation, never came to rely so much on the state as a direct resource. Nor was the central state seriously challenged by corporate institutions, regional privileges, and politically autonomous urban communes. Royal taxation never played the same role for the English propertied classes that it did for the French; and the state never had the same reasons for either squeezing or protecting the peasantry as did the French state.

English property owners, when seeking to protect and augment their increasingly 'economic' means of appropriation, might struggle to defend their private rights of property against incursions by the Crown, to establish the supremacy of Parliament as an association of propertyholders, to thwart the consolidation of an absolutist monarchy by establishing 'limited government', while at the same time staving off threats from below. The propertied classes of France, who confronted the state both as a competitor for surplus labour and as a means of access to it, contended over taxation, the proliferation of offices and the means of distributing them, often struggling less to limit the state than to acquire property in it or prevent others from doing so. The English commoner, in defence against the landlord's efforts to augment his economic powers of appropriation, struggled against the enclosure of common and waste land. The French peasant, more oppressed by 'political' forms of exploitation, rebelled against royal taxation and seigneurial privilege. Englishmen asserted their individual rights; Frenchmen defended their corporate and regional privileges.

If the English were concerned with the relation between state and private property, the French were preoccupied with the state *as* private property. French anti-absolutism was not simply a matter of resistance to political tyranny but also an attack on the state as a means of private extortion. Popular resistance, too, often focused on exploitation by the state; and exploitation by means of direct seigneurial exactions might take second place to taxation (or the tax exemptions of others) as an object of grievance, just as the landlord might be less concerned about losing economic powers such as the right of enclosure than about relinquishing tax exemptions and political privileges.

French political discourse would long be preoccupied with the tax/office structure of the state and the fractured polity that underlay it. The principal issues typically had to do, as they so often did elsewhere in Europe, with contesting jurisdictions; but what distinguished French political debate was an emphasis on the role of the state as a proprietary interest, the monarchical state and its growing administrative and fiscal apparatus conceived as a means of private appropriation These questions were not, of course, specific to France; but they presented themselves to the French with particular force as the state became a major instrument of private appropriation for a growing class of office-holders, in ways and degrees unmatched elsewhere in Europe.

At the centre of French political thought in this period, then, stood a fragmented polity consisting of many particularisms whose unifying principle was yet another particularistic power, yet another proprietary interest. Advocates of monarchy were obliged to defend the monarch's right to rule, and especially his right to distribute office and impose taxation, by denying his particularity and claiming that he represented a public or general interest, transcending all the private and particular interests of his subjects or competing jurisdictions. His opponents might counter by insisting that the monarchy itself was nothing more than private and particular, just one proprietary interest against others, and that the various lesser jurisdictions truly represented 'public' interests.

Much of the debate surrounding the French monarchy concerned precisely this: the relation between public and private and who could claim to represent the public principle against the many private interests and jurisdictions that composed the polity of France. Arguments in favour of the centralizing monarchy, which claimed that the king embodied the public aspect of the state as against the private character of his subjects, suggested that a single superior will was required to bind together particular interests and produce a common good. A defender of the royal state like Bodin might claim that the will of the sovereign is law, on the grounds that the *res publica* or commonwealth – that which is common to all private individuals, families and corporate bodies – can only be constituted by a common subjection to the unifying will of the sovereign. Arguments against the centralizing mission of the monarchy voiced concern not only with the particularisms that divided the polity but also with the particularity of the state apparatus itself and the consequences of its use as private property – the proliferation and venalization of offices, the corruption of administration, the tax burden.

These conflicts did not necessarily pit monarchists against opponents of a monarchical state. Opposing sides were often embroiled in dynastic struggles in which one claim to royal power was contested by another. But even some adherents to an aspiring royal dynasty would often advocate the claims of lesser jurisdictions against a centralizing royal power. Even nobles or local magistrates who supported some kind of monarchy, or attached themselves to one dynasty against another, had reason to insist that royal power was rooted in, and created by, the nobility and other public officers, who therefore also had the right to depose kings. Against the monarch's claims to generality in contrast to their own particularity, these 'lesser magistrates', even while defending their particular jurisdictions, might claim to accept that the public interest or common good emanated from a unifying will or mind; but now, the unifying, generalizing will of the monarch, who was 'particular and single', was replaced by 'one mind compounded out of many', a collective will composed of nobles, 'lesser magistrates' or local authorities who acted as the people's public representatives.

From *Cahiers* to Constitutionalism

Jean de Bourg, arch-episcopal judge of Vienne, representative of the Third Estate to the provincial Estates and Estates General, from a province that experienced one of the country's bloodiest regional revolts in 1579–80, wrote the petition of grievances for the Dauphiné Third Estate to be presented at the Estates General at Blois in 1576.[2] He drew on philosophical principles and the classics of antiquity to support complaints and proposals for reform typical of his estate. The list of grievances he rehearsed focused on the privileges of the other two estates, especially their exemptions from taxation; the proliferation of useless offices with high salaries, secular and ecclesiastical; the tax burden imposed on the common people; and the inequitable political structure which gave the advantage of power to the privileged estates, so that they could manipulate the fiscal system for their own gain at the expense of the Third Estate. To these complaints – shared by bourgeois, craftsmen, and peasants – he added several of special concern to his own class, the bourgeoisie, and a few grievances of particular interest to the peasantry.

De Bourg's proposals for resolving these grievances included measures to strengthen the Third Estate, relieving its tax burden, augmenting its political powers in office and in the assemblies of Estates, and increasing the role of regional representative institutions. There were also suggestions in which the bourgeoisie's grievances against local oligarchies and seigneurial privilege converged with peasant complaints about rural administration. It is significant that these were met in part by proposals for restoring certain powers of local administration to the king in order to diminish the provincial powers of seigneurs, even though de Bourg pressed at the same time for reductions in the royal bureaucracy in order to reduce the burden of taxation.

De Bourg adduced philosophical arguments to support these proposals for reform. In particular, he developed the principle of corporate equality, drawing, for example, on Plato's concept of justice and Cicero's conception of a natural order based on a harmonious balance among the various social orders. It was this supposedly natural principle outlined by Cicero that, according to de Bourg, dictated the maintenance of social equality, not among individuals but among the three estates as corporate entities, and

---

2   I am relying for this account of de Bourg and the other lawyers on Le Roy Ladurie's *Carnival in Romans* (New York: George Braziller, 1980).

also (in particular, for purposes of tax assessment) among regions and cities. In this blend of philosophical speculation and political activism, de Bourg showed himself to be 'close to the great authors of Antiquity, and just as close to the aspirations of the common people of his own day, who had never read a word of Plato or Cicero'.[3]

De Bourg's main theme – the defence of a corporate balance among estates, especially with regard to taxation, based on the organic unity and harmony of the social order – remained the central focus of protest as voiced by his successors, the provincial lawyers who continued to do battle for the Third Estate in his region after the period of bloody revolt. Attacking the tax exemptions of the nobility, they invoked various organic metaphors – the mystical body of the state, or the musical metaphor of harmonious proportion so popular among the ancients from Pythagoras to Plato and Aristotle – in order to establish the fundamental unity of the state and the interdependence of its parts. By these means they sought to demonstrate the nobility's duty to the social whole and the essential function of the Third Estate in sustaining the body politic.

These protestors were not democrats. Men of substance, they represented essentially the interests of the urban bourgeoisie. The equality for which they strove was a corporate equality in which they would predominate over lesser members of their corporation, and a proportionate equality, an equality in difference, which acknowledged the hierarchical structure of the social whole. 'We . . . are not for government by the people, nor for equality, as the Nobles falsely claim', maintained Claude Delagrange in 1599. 'But our privileges are equal to [theirs].'[4] In other words, this was not so much an attack on the system of privilege, such as peasants or artisans might have wished, as it was a demand for access to it. 'The Third Estate needs the rules of harmonics, not arithmetic', wrote Antoine Rambaud. 'It does not want to make law of equality . . . It wants equal justice. But it does not want equal justice that follows arithmetic, with all things equal in weight and form. It wants the harmonic balance made up of different parts. Order and justice founded on proportional and harmonic equality, blending into one, are necessary to the survival of the State.'[5]

These conceptions of the state as a 'body', an organic unity, tended to be accompanied by a notion of a public or common good which was more than simply the sum of its parts, a principle of unity over and against the particularities comprising the body politic. Needless to say, the object of invoking this common good was to demonstrate that the nobility must subordinate its particular interests and privileges to the interests of the whole: 'The

3 *Ibid.*, p. 68.
4 *Ibid.*, p. 357.
5 *Ibid.*, p. 358.

Nobles use the privileges of the provinces as if they were theirs alone', complained Jean Vincent in 1598. 'The Nobles think they are born only for themselves. But according to Pericles as quoted by Thucydides, one should love the public good above all [and] consider oneself born not for the self but for the world.'[6]

For these bourgeois and far from radical protestors, the unity of the state, the 'One' to which the 'Multiple' must be subordinated, was embodied in the person of the king, the 'Father of the Common Welfare', as Vincent called him.[7] 'Aspiring to unity', explained Rambaud, 'does not mean making everything equal. Unity in music is nothing other than Monarchy in a State.'[8] It is not surprising that the lawyers should adopt this view, since the Third Estate might actually stand to gain from the appropriation of some (though not their own) corporate powers by the monarch. The corporate egalitarianism of these provincial lawyers was based on a view of society in which the unity of the state and the 'harmonious' balance of its constituent parts were expressed in and maintained by the sovereign power of the king. In this, they seem to have been true disciples of Bodin.

In contrast, Huguenot theorists advocated outright rebellion against the royal state. There is no reason to doubt that many Huguenots were motivated entirely by religious convictions (though similar ideas would later be adopted by the Catholic League); but it is equally certain that substantial numbers – especially among those social elements that transformed the movement into a powerful political force – were driven by other, less spiritual interests. The Huguenot resistance never had the support of more than 10 to 20 per cent of the French population, but it attracted disproportionate support among local notables, aristocrats and magistrates. For a time, Protestants controlled a great many towns, especially in the south of France; and in the 1560s, the Huguenot movement included close to half the nobility, at least in some regions of France, and especially the lesser, provincial nobility whose loss of feudal powers was not compensated by state office.

The Huguenots not only attacked the system of privilege and patronage, or fiscal and administrative corruption, but placed the blame squarely on the monarchy itself, with its bureaucratic apparatus in which royal office, including the office of king, was conceived as private property. This did not necessarily mean that they opposed the very idea of a monarchy. The most influential Huguenot resistance tract, the *Vindiciae Contra Tyrannos*, is attributed to a staunch supporter of Henry of Navarre, who would become Henry IV of France, the first Bourbon monarch – a king who would himself provoke opposition for his centralizing tendencies, which he would buy off (or threaten)

6   *Ibid.*, p. 353.
7   *Ibid.*
8   *Ibid.*, p. 359.

in the classic 'absolutist' manner. The fact that Henry was a Protestant (before converting again to Catholicism) is not, of course, insignificant; but to leave it at that, to explain Huguenot resisters' support for him simply on the grounds of their confessional allegiances, is perhaps to beg the question. It is surely worth considering the attractions that Protestantism, and especially Calvinism, held for various kinds of 'lesser magistrates', precisely because its doctrines offered support for their own power and autonomy when threatened by a centralizing monarchy.

The idea that no government is legitimate that is not in some sense based on the consent of the governed, that the king owes his authority to some kind of original compact with the 'people', was, as we have seen, not a new one. Nor was the idea that, while the king (as king, not as a person) was greater than any other individual, he was less than the community of the people taken together. It is certainly true that the French monarchomachs went further than some others in their elaboration of the principle that agreement to the king's rule is conditional, and that the king's legitimacy is contingent on fulfilling its terms. But for them, as for their medieval predecessors, the people remained a collective, corporate body, which is immortal, while individuals come and go.

The resistance tracts of the monarchomachs are often described as the beginnings of modern constitutionalism and modern ideas of 'popular sovereignty'. But, as we already know, much depends on what is meant by the 'people' – a flexible word that has had many meanings and served many different political purposes in Western political thought. The 'people' in this case was not simply a collection of private individuals. Individuals were not the basic constituents of the state, which was composed of corporate bodies, such as guilds, estates, provinces or towns; and the 'people' possessed political authority neither as individuals nor as a 'multitude' of individuals but as a collective, corporate body. The right, even the duty, to resist tyrannical power belonged not to individual citizens but to the body of the 'people' collectively, or, more precisely, to the officials who represented that collectivity. In fact, the authority – indeed, the duty – to resist tyrannical power was not strictly speaking an individual right at all but a function of office. Furthermore, the right that was being defended was not the right to give or withhold consent on a regular basis, as in periodic elections, but rather the right to resist in times of emergency, when the ruler failed to uphold his side of the bargain and was ruling tyrannically.

This undoubtedly helps to explain why in France, a largely Catholic country, the ideas of Protestants – at least for a time, when the centralizing monarchy was coming into conflict with the jurisdictions of local lords and magistrates – attracted large numbers of provincial nobles and municipal officials, in a war that was religious and political at once. Even if ideas like this were later appropriated by others and developed for more democratic purposes, and even if they established important principles of constitutional, limited and accountable government, there was nothing particularly democratic or 'modern' about them. These ideas were rooted in older, medieval principles, affirming the independent powers of lordship. The Huguenot doctrine of popular sovereignty had less to do with asserting the democratic rights of ordinary citizens than with defending older feudal powers, privileges and jurisdictions against encroachments by a centralizing state. The Huguenot solution to royal excesses was to augment the powers of other jurisdictions. While the case for the authority of magistrates or 'public councils' was formulated as a defence of the 'people's' inalienable right to resist, the insistence that this was not a private right of citizenship but a public function of officers or, in the Calvinist manner, of 'lesser magistrates', was intended both as an assertion of autonomous jurisdictions against the king, and, as in some other Protestant doctrines we have encountered, as a defence against popular rebellions and peasant revolts.

The Huguenot 'constitutionalists', then, were no more (and were in some respects less) democrats than were other sixteenth-century protestors who still looked to the monarchy for relief. It is not surprising that a substantial number of Huguenots and some of their leading spokesmen came from the ranks of the lesser, provincial nobility, precisely that section of the landed classes that had least to gain and most to lose from the growth of a strongly centralized appropriating monarchy. The most prominent Huguenot constitutionalists most commonly cited in histories of Western political thought, François Hotman, Theodore Beza and Philippe du Plessis-Mornay, all belonged to seigneurial families; and the social interests they represented are strikingly visible in the resistance tracts.

The first important text, Hotman's *Francogallia* (1573), formulated as a constitutional history of France rather than an overtly political tract, set out to demonstrate that, according to French tradition, the king was simply a magistrate, an office-holder; and even if he held his office in principle for life, he was subject to removal. The ultimate authority, which had been illegitimately seized in recent times by tyrannical kings, rightfully belongs to a 'public council' comprising the assembled estates, a council that has among its powers the power to create and depose kings. Beza, the spiritual leader of Protestants in France and Calvin's successor in Geneva, proceeded in his *Right of Magistrates* (1574) from a similar conception of French constitutional traditions but elaborated a more general doctrine of resistance, which unequivocally lodged the right to resist in 'lesser magistrates'.[9] While the

---

9   There were some attempts in Calvinist doctrine to defend a more inclusive right of resistance by extending the meaning of the 'lesser magistrate' to include private individuals, each acting as his own 'magistrate'; but this extension clearly – in fact, by definition – violates the meaning and intent of the original doctrine; and, in the case of the Huguenot

authority of magistrates derives from the people, resistance is, he insisted, a public function, not a private right, belonging not to private citizens but to public officers, 'among whom may be numbered dukes, marquesses, counts, viscount, barons, and chatelains', as well as 'the elected officers of towns'.[10]

The most influential Huguenot resistance tract, the *Vindiciae Contra Tyrannos* (published 1579, though perhaps written in 1574–5), attributed to du Plessis-Mornay, who was close to Henry of Navarre, developed Beza's doctrine into an outright call for revolt against the existing king. Starting from the premise that the king is no different from other men and that there is no natural division between ruler and ruled, this tract insists that kings are created by the people; but it becomes even clearer who the 'people' are and are not:

> When we speak of the people collectively, we mean those who receive authority from the people, that is, the magistrates below the king who have been elected by the people or established in some other way . . . And we also mean the assembly of the Estates, which are nothing less than the epitome of a kingdom to which all public matters are referred . . .
>
> In every properly constituted kingdom, this is the character of the officers of the crown, the peers, the lords, the patricians, the notables, and others chosen by the several estates who, in various combinations, make up the membership of the ordinary or the extra-ordinary council . . . For although these officers are severally below the king, they are collectively above him.[11]

Mornay does, very hesitantly and with exceedingly careful qualifications, suggest that there may be exceptional cases in which private individuals have been raised up by God to act as liberators; but, while his call to resistance may be more radical than that of other Huguenots, his argument in general is on the side of 'lesser magistrates', not in a metaphorical sense that includes private individuals, each acting as his own 'magistrate', but as public officials:

> [W]e are not speaking here of private individuals, who are not to be regarded as the basic parts of a community any more than planks, nails, and pegs are taken as the parts of a ship; or stones, beams, and mortar as the parts of a house. We are speaking rather of a province or a town, which is a part of the kingdom in the same way the prow, deck, and rudder

---

tracts, the intention is quite unambiguous.

10   Theodore Beza, *Right of Magistrates*, in ed. Franklin, *Constitutionalism and Resistance*, p. 110.

11   Philippe du Plessis-Mornay (?), *Vindiciae Contra Tyrannos*, in ed. Franklin, *Constitutionalism and Resistance*, p. 195. (The authorship of this tract remains in doubt.)

are the parts of a ship, or the roof, walls, and foundation are the parts of a house. And we are also speaking of the magistrate who is in charge of that province or town.

Huguenot ideas of resistance have been called a landmark in the development of modern constitutionalism largely on the grounds that they assume a sovereign community as the ultimate source of all political authority, which exercises its sovereignty by controlling the governing powers through institutions that represent the 'people'. Yet their conception of popular sovereignty was, if anything, more backward-looking than 'modern'. In defence of particular jurisdictions, the estates and 'lesser magistrates', they appropriated the principles that had long been used by monarchs to legitimate their own authority against, for example, emperors or popes, by claiming powers derived from the 'people' and even based on their notional consent. While such ideas could – and sometimes would – be adapted to more radical purpose, the contest between monarchy and 'lesser' authorities had more in common with medieval conflicts among jurisdictions than with modern democratic struggles for popular sovereignty or even just the limitation of state power.

Again, their arguments are based on a corporate and hierarchical conception of society. Since the right of resistance belongs to the 'people' not as private individuals but as properly constituted authorities, magistrates, and corporate bodies – the assemblies of estates, or towns and districts in the persons of their officials – rights are not individual but corporate. Indeed, in this argument – where the issue is not simply an appeal to the monarch to correct the imbalances among estates but a call to revolt against the monarch himself – the egalitarian aspect of the corporatist argument recedes; and its function as a limitation on popular rights comes to the fore at the very moment that the 'people's' rights are being so eloquently asserted.

To make the point that the right of resistance is based on the principle that it is the 'people' who constitute the king and not the reverse, the Huguenot resistance movement transforms the familiar idea of a unity in multiplicity, a common good emanating from a single unitary will, which others had used to justify the power of the king. Significantly, they do not abandon this idea of unity, nor do they propose a definition of the common good as a public interest whose substance consists merely of private interests and rights. Instead, they simply transfer the source of the unifying will from the monarch to the 'public councils' of the people. Much of their argument rests on contrasting the private, particular character of the king to the public, universal character of the 'people' embodied in their officers and councils, 'one mind compounded out of many'. The king as a person is 'particular and single';[12] the majesty of his office, its public character, derives

---

12 François Hotman, *Francogallia*, in *ibid.*, p. 78.

from the people – as represented by the notables who preside over them, the magistrates of towns, and (in keeping with the feudal interests of the nobility) the dukes, marquises, counts, and barons who 'constitute a part of the kingdom' and are established as 'guardians . . . for the several regions'.[13]

The Huguenot constitutionalists were in effect responding in kind to the advocates of royal power, adopting important aspects of their discourse; and they did so because this idiom was well-suited to deal with their grievances in a state conceived as private property. In particular, it provided useful language with which to assert the authority of the Estates to control the two major 'public' functions which lay at the heart of many grievances, the apportionment of taxes and the distribution of offices. While the 'particular and single' king, they argued, can dispose of his own private treasure at will and appoint his own personal counsellors, a careful distinction must be made between his private patrimony and that of the kingdom, the public treasury and public offices which are rightfully the province of the 'elders and experienced statesmen' who constitute the collective 'mind' of the kingdom.[14] While this theoretical strategy may be regarded as an important advance in 'modern' conceptions of public as against personal rule, it conceives the 'public' domain less as a modern impersonal state than as a composite of feudal jurisdictions.

The whole issue is summed up in the question: 'Is the King the Owner of the Kingdom?' More specifically, 'Does the king, then, have private property in the royal, or public, patrimony?'[15] The answer, of course, is no. And: 'Let me ask, furthermore, whether royal status is a possession or an office (*functio*). If it is a possession, then is it not at least a form of possession whereby the people, who conferred it, retain the proprietary right?'[16] As for the power of taxation, since taxes are intended for 'public purposes' – specifically the conduct of war – it cannot be the province of the king any more than the public domain is his private property. 'To guarantee that taxes will be used for public purposes', they must be authorized by the Estates, on the principle that the people 'taken collectively . . . are properly the owners of the kingdom' and their officers, as it were taken collectively, the only truly public being.

The Huguenot resistance movement may have failed in France; but monarchomach tracts were very soon taken up by resistance movements elsewhere, notably in the Netherlands and in England. Despite all the limitations of their resistance theories, the monarchomachs were articulating a relatively radical theory of consent. They certainly moved far beyond those

---

13   Mornay, in *ibid.*, p. 195.
14   Hotman, in *ibid.*, p. 79.
15   Mornay, p. 174.
16   *Ibid.*, pp. 175–7.

theories according to which the original agreement or contract that had founded political authority was an unconditional transfer of rights by the people to a ruler, and succeeding generations were bound by that original agreement. In medieval disputes between secular and ecclesiastical powers, for example, to defend royal power against the papacy, it had been argued that the emperor or king derived his power not from the pope but from God through the 'people'. This was something very different from the monarchomach idea that the authority of the king derived from the 'people', perhaps from a kind of compact between king and people, and that when the king exceeded his authority, violated the conditions of the compact and acted against the interests of the 'people', they had the right to rebel, even to the point of armed resistance. It may not, then, be unreasonable to claim for them a significant contribution to Western theories of popular sovereignty, the social contract, the supremacy of representative bodies, or at least 'constitutionalism'. But it is another testimony to the limits of the Western political tradition that ideas devised to reassert feudal rights against an encroaching monarchy, defending a hierarchical polity and the independence of corporate powers vested in nobles or municipal magistrates, as against a conception of active citizenship and popular power, can be treated as classics in the development of *democratic* ideas.

Jean Bodin

On a more abstractly philosophical plane, Jean Bodin addressed the same constellation of political problems. The theory of sovereignty, for which he is most famous, drew together several issues that were being contested in the struggles of the sixteenth century. The standpoint from which he sought to resolve these issues has much in common with that of the legal spokesmen for the Third Estate whom we have already encountered – and, indeed, Bodin was himself a lawyer and representative of the Third Estate for Vermandois at the Estates General of Blois in 1576. It is undoubtedly true that, when he wrote the *Six Books of the Commonwealth* in which his theory of sovereignty appeared, he was motivated in part by the desire to assert the sovereignty of the king against the dangers of rebellion and civil strife most dramatically embodied in the Huguenot resistance movement; but he also wanted to reform the structure of the state, the apparatus of office, the inequitable distribution of burdens created by the system of privilege and exemption.

Bodin was born in 1529 or 1530 in Angers, the son of a prosperous master tailor. Although his religious views in later life remain a subject of dispute, as a young man he joined the Carmelite order. He went on to study philosophy in Paris and law in Toulouse. His early work was humanist in inspiration, and he seems to have regarded humanism as a means of providing a unified education for all citizens, together with a single religion, to enhance political and religious harmony. The religious wars that ensued in France may, in his view, have been a necessity in the face of attacks against the 'true faith'; and religious unity was clearly for him a condition of civil peace. Yet, while religious diversity represented a threat to civil order, he would later make it clear that some kind of temporary accommodation with dissenters and a limited, and certainly not permanent, religious toleration would be a better means than violence to unify the commonwealth.

In 1560, Bodin became a member of the *parlement* of Paris. In the years that followed, he produced his most important political works: in 1566, the *Method for the Easy Comprehension of History* (the *Methodus*), spelling out the comprehensive historical and legal knowledge required to govern the state, and in 1576, the *Six Books of the Commonwealth* (*République*), on which his reputation as a theorist of sovereignty rests. The king began to consult him on matters of state; but, although as deputy for the Third Estate and then as president of the deputies, he took a very strong line against the privileged estates, he would also challenge the king on both financial and religious issues, opposing the monarch's rejection of accommodation with the Protestants and his efforts to appropriate the 'property of the people' as his own patrimony.

By the late 1580s, the country was in dynastic and religious crisis. With the assassination of the king and the ensuing rivalries, Bodin, by then a royalist magistrate in Laon, felt compelled – despite his own commitment to civil peace and at least a limited religious toleration – to join the Catholic League. It was, again, difficult to dissociate dynastic from confessional rivalries; and both were implicated in the classic jurisdictional battles: the major cities (and their magistrates) tended, for example, to side with the Duke of Guise and the League, while the nobility typically adhered to the Protestant King of Navarre. In that respect, the lines were drawn in ways that reflected the long-standing and complex relations among the estates and the monarchy; and Bodin came down on the side one might have predicted for a man of his estate and standing. When Henry of Navarre succeeded to the throne as Henry IV of France, the king remained under pressure from the powerful League; but, returning to the Catholic fold, he eventually brought about, in the Edict of Nantes of 1598, the kind of confessional accommodation Bodin might have wished for to maintain civil peace. By then, however, Bodin was dead, having succumbed to the plague in 1596.

There has been much debate about what to make of Bodin's theory of sovereignty and the changes it appears to undergo between his most important political works, the *Methodus* and the *République*. While the earlier work certainly outlines the idea of an indivisible sovereignty, it is not until the later work that this idea comes to be associated with the notion of 'absolute' power. To speak of Bodin as an advocate of 'absolutism' may be misleading if we take that to mean that he favoured monarchical power without limitation. There is no question that he was, from beginning to end, a believer in royal supremacy. Even in his earlier work, which contains no clear notion of 'absolute' power, the idea of indivisible sovereignty is already spelled out. Yet, while this certainly precludes a conception of the nobility or 'lesser magistrates' as joint or rival claimants to sovereignty, it does not rule out the limitations imposed on the ruler by natural or fundamental law nor the significant rights of office possessed by the estates or nobles according to the French juridical tradition. In his later work, Bodin combined the idea of indivisible sovereignty with a more unequivocal notion of 'absolute' power, that is, a comprehensive power including every legitimate state function; but even then, he never dismissed the political role of estates and corporations.

One eminent commentator on Bodin's political thought has suggested that the idea of sovereignty as 'absolute' represented an unfortunate resolution of a certain incoherence in Bodin's earlier work. To be sure, the idea of an indivisible sovereignty seemed to contradict the limitations on sovereign power implied by his concessions to the traditional authority of lesser magistrates and his conviction that certain actions of the king required the consent of the estates or *parlements*. But, this commentator argues, Bodin's resolution was a departure from conventional French discourse and not particularly well suited to French conditions. He might have done better 'to have defined the ruler's sovereignty as absolute (except with respect to the law of nature and fundamental law more narrowly defined), and conceded that its functions were divided among the king, the Parlements and the Estates'.[17] But having insisted on the notion of indivisibility, this argument goes, logic seemed to compel a kind of 'absolutism'; and what seemed to Bodin a logical compulsion became that much more powerful in the new historical circumstances, with the rise of the Huguenot movement and its doctrines of resistance.

Yet, whatever logical inconsistencies there may be in Bodin's notion of indivisible sovereignty, it does address the conditions of France, and, for all its innovations, in terms not at all foreign to his contemporaries. Although in response to armed resistance the *République* went further than the earlier work, both the *Methodus* and the *République* can be understood as seeking to limit the autonomous powers of the nobility and the 'parcellization of sovereignty' that continued to plague the monarchical state. At the same

---

17 Introduction to Jean Bodin, *On Sovereignty*, ed. Julian Franklin (Cambridge: Cambridge University Press, 1992), p. xxii. See also Franklin's *Jean Bodin and the Rise of Absolutist Theory* (Cambridge: Cambridge University Press, 1973); and his 'Sovereignty and the Mixed Constitution: Bodin and his critics', in the *Cambridge History of Political Thought 1450–1700* (Cambridge: Cambridge University Press, 1991), pp. 299–328.

time, both preserved important functions for lesser authorities and corporations. Even in his later masterpiece, despite his advocacy of an indivisible and absolute sovereign power vested in the king, Bodin clearly believed in enhancing the role of the Estates General, insisting, for example, that no tax could be levied without their consent. Indeed, his theory of sovereignty is not so distant from the views of those provincial lawyers who relied on the monarchy to maintain unity in a fragmented polity and to correct the social imbalance among its corporate constituents, in part by appropriating to itself the feudal prerogatives of the privileged estates.

Bodin's concern in constructing his theory of sovereignty was not simply to stave off rebellion of the Huguenot type but to deal with the underlying structural problems inherent in the French state and its political 'parcellization'. Whether he wanted to curtail the powers of the traditional nobility on behalf of the Third Estate or to strengthen the ruling class in spite of itself by bringing order to the anarchy of competing jurisdictions, he intended to transfer their particularistic, quasi-feudal powers to the monarchy, denying that noble prerogatives and offices belonged to their possessors by proprietary right (hereditary or otherwise) and rendering them dependent upon sovereign authority. The issue at stake was not simply the location of supreme and ultimate power but also the location of *unity,* the source of integration in a system of regional and corporate fragmentation: 'a commonwealth without a sovereign power to unite all its several members, whether families, colleges, or corporate bodies, is not a true commonwealth. It is neither the town nor its inhabitants that makes a city-state, but their union under a sovereign ruler.'[18]

Bodin's conception of sovereignty, then, represents in some respects an attack on feudal remnants, but it also presupposes a polity still organized on feudal, corporatist principles. It is in this light that his commitment to *indivisible* power must be understood. For representative institutions to share 'sovereignty' with the king would aggravate precisely the corporate fragmentation and political parcellization that Bodin's sovereign power was designed to overcome. But he did not envisage a society organized in a fundamentally different way, a society, like England, less divided into corporate fragments and integrated into a unitary state with a unitary representative body like the English Parliament. If anything, in some respects his argument was designed to strengthen certain corporate principles, and he regarded corporations as fundamental to the maintenance of social ties. It was the function of sovereign power to integrate and harmonize these necessary particularities.

Bodin nonetheless makes an important distinction between the form of state, based on the location of sovereignty, and the form of government, based

---

18   Jean Bodin, *Six Books of the Commonwealth*, ed. M.J. Tooley (Oxford: Basil Blackwell, 1967), p. 7.

on the principle by which lands, offices, and honours are distributed. A monarchy, for example, can be governed aristocratically or democratically, according to how the sovereign monarch chooses to grant honours and preferments. This distinction demonstrates that, however powers and offices may be distributed, these powers are ultimately vested in the sovereign and that it is in effect by the will of the sovereign that they are so distributed. The powers of office-holders or nobles are not held by proprietary right but by virtue of delegation from the sovereign – ideally, the sovereign in the person of a monarch. In this respect, the distinction between state and government, and the implied distinction between the sovereign legislative power and the subordinate power of execution, serves to reinforce Bodin's attack on feudal prerogatives and baronial anarchy, as well as on any other proprietary claims to political power apart from those of the sovereign. This feudal 'parcellization' of power, rather than 'divided sovereignty' in the English parliamentary sense, is, again, the main target of his insistence on the indivisibility of sovereignty. Whatever else he may have intended by distinguishing the form of government from the form of state, he clearly meant to sustain and enhance the authority of the monarchy against other particularistic claims to political power.

The notion of divided 'sovereignty' and limited government could, perhaps, more easily be elaborated in a polity that was not itself essentially divided and parcellized: a state which, like England, had achieved 'feudal centralization' with a relatively unified nobility, without territorial potentates like those of the Continent, with towns that lacked the political autonomy of Continental urban communes, and with unitary representative institutions for the ruling class, assemblies that were national in extent and represented a community of property holders not internally divided by region and estate. The unity of the English state, reflected in Parliament, made 'divided sovereignty' less threatening and more practicable; or perhaps the relative unity and strength of the ruling class made it inevitable. At any rate, Parliament quite early acquired legislative powers – at least the negative power to check the legislative activity of the king – in effect dividing between king and Parliament the very power which for Bodin constitutes sovereignty. In contrast, the French monarchy, whose power rested in part on the regional fragmentation of the state and the independent powers exercised by the nobility, remained largely free of limitation by representative bodies in this respect – if not in others, such as its fiscal powers. Bodin's concept of sovereignty, in short, speaks precisely to the historical conditions of France.

Political Economy

At the heart of Bodin's political theory, then, is a tension between a still feudal, corporatist, and fragmented social order and a centralized sovereign state, a tension characteristic of his time and place. The ruling class was still feudal to the extent that its mode of exploitation was a fusion of economic and political power, still rooted in the parcellization of the state. The tax/office structure of the monarchical state simply centralized this fusion of political and economic power, with a system of state taxation that has been described as a kind of 'centralized feudal rent'; and yet the state was at the same time anti-feudal in its attempts to unify the fragments of state power.

This tension is captured perfectly in the economic doctrines of the period, to which Bodin himself contributed. What is most characteristic of these economic theories is the unity of 'political' and 'economic' spheres, a view of the 'economy' as a politically constituted entity and an idea of the monarchy as the harmonizer of conflicting interests in a commercial order conceived as intrinsically divisive. Commerce certainly contributes to material prosperity and should be encouraged; but, in a commercial system based on 'buying cheap and selling dear' in transactions between separate markets, commercial activity is socially disruptive, and the function of the monarchical state is to integrate particular and conflicting economic interests, just as it unifies political particularisms. The economy was understood not as an integrated, self-sustaining mechanism but as subsumed under the political community. At the same time, the state itself, with its tax/office structure, was a form of politically constituted property, simultaneously a public, political institution and a private economic resource, quite different from the English economy, where purely economic modes of appropriation were far more developed.

The essential paradox that characterized both the French polity and its economy lies in the irreducible tension between their corporatist roots and an increasingly national economy, which required a more integrated market and the reduction of internal barriers to trade. Like the political theory of Bodin, contemporary economic doctrines depended both upon the maintenance of certain corporate powers, privileges and liberties, and on their transcendence by a powerful monarchy.

It is in this context that Bodin draws an analogy between the state and the household. The family, he suggests, is the origin of the state and its basic constituent unit; and household management is the model of good government. Taking issue with Aristotle and Xenophon for their separation of household management, *oikonomia,* and statecraft, he argues that the 'economic' art – knowledge of the acquisition of goods which Aristotle assigns to household management – is common also to 'colleges' and 'city-states'. Conversely, power, authority, and obedience, which apparently belong specifically to the political sphere, also belong to the family. In both cases the purpose of management is the acquisition of goods, the provision and prosperity of the household or state (as a condition, of course, for the good life in a higher sense). This object is best achieved under the supreme authority of a single head – the father in one case, the king in the other. The one fundamental difference between household and state is that the public character of the state exists in contrast to the private nature of the household, and this means that the former presupposes and must respect the private property of the latter.

The household/state analogy as formulated by Bodin represents a state dominated by an absolute ruler who, in promoting the acquisition of goods and increasing the prosperity of the state, guides and encourages the public 'economy', just as the father manages the household. Furthermore, since like the family the unity of the state should be grounded in concord and 'love', it is the task of state management to reconcile and bind together the constituent parts of the polity by creating a balance based on 'harmonic' justice. The presupposition of the analogy is an 'absolutist' monarchy which presides over a 'mercantilist' economy while it respects and protects the private property and (selectively?) the corporate liberties of its subjects.

Arguments in favour of the absolutist monarchy, then, were not confined to the political domain. The ideology of absolutism derived much of its force from the claims that were made for its role in promoting a prosperous economy; and it was not least on this basis that the notion of an 'enlightened despotism' would emerge. The idea that a successful commercial economy depended on an undivided sovereign power to harmonize conflicting interests, an idea which had already appeared in the work of Bodin, remained a recurring theme in French social thought. The state as an essential instrument of social integration would appear even in the work of the physiocrats, who, in the eighteenth century, articulated a groundbreaking theory of the economy as a systemic totality with its own internal operating principles, in the manner of modern 'economics'.

Even the term 'political economy' owes its origins to the kind of household/state analogy, together with its assumptions about the integrative role of the state in the economy, that underlay Bodin's theory of the monarchy. The analogy, together with language and logic strikingly reminiscent of Bodin, appeared in the work of Antoine de Montchrétien, as we have seen, who, if he did not actually invent the term, wrote what seems to have been the first book ever to contain the term 'political economy' in its title: *Traicté de l'oeconomie politique,* published in 1615. On the principle that the monarch should rule benevolently, like the father with an eye to the well-being, harmony, and prosperity of the household, he urged reforms that would encourage economic activity – especially measures to strengthen the Third Estate by protecting corporate liberties and equality, while integrating the polity into a national whole to encourage trade, presided over by a strong central state cleansed of its burdensome and corrupt system of office and taxation. Montchrétien eventually lost hope in the monarchy as the agent of reform and joined the opposition; but in the *Traicté*, he was writing in the tradition of those moderate reformers who looked to the king to protect them against the imbalance of power and privilege, and to integrate the body politic and the system of trade.

Montchrétien makes an interesting suggestion about the mechanism by which the desired effects of 'political economy' might be achieved. In a formulation that was to become very familiar in a different time and place, he suggests that selfish passions and the appetite for gain, far from threatening the common good, can be its foundation. In other words, Montchrétien proposes something very like the utility of selfish interests that was to be the basis of eighteenth-century, especially English (or, perhaps more accurately, Scottish). accounts of 'commercial society' and its capacity for promoting the common good without relying on the uncertainties of human virtue and benevolence.[19] But, in Montchrétien's argument, the social context for the operation of this principle was not English capitalism, with its integrated national market, driven by its own imperatives of competition. For Montchrétien, in French conditions, the mechanism for achieving the harmony of interest was not the 'invisible hand' sustained by a constitutional parliamentary state but rather the absolutist monarchy itself which was to serve as the agent of integration and harmonization. In this formulation, an active and forceful interventionist monarchy was the condition for transforming 'private vices' into 'public benefits'. This association of monarchy with the harmony of interests long persisted in French political thought.

The object of Montchrétien's proposal is especially to encourage economic activity and promote trade. His advocacy of selfish passions as the basis of public well-being is explicitly intended to defend the Third Estate, and in particular, the merchants who, he admits, are more commonly driven by selfishness and greed than by concern for the public good. These selfish passions ought not, he argues, be grounds for excluding such people (as, for example, Aristotle might do) from the citizen body as 'a kind of helot'.[20] It is these very appetites that motivate not only merchants but peasants, artisans, and lawyers to undertake and perform well the necessary and useful services on which the state depends.

The job of regulating these activities and establishing order among them belongs to the 'sovereign moderator of the State' and his officials, whose function is to protect the rights of the kingdom and 'particularly of each city'.[21] This regulation of the network of self-interest is to be achieved not only by ensuring just prices, stamping out corrupt commercial practices and frauds, and removing barriers to trade, but also by compensating for the

---

19 Antoine de Montchrétien, *Traicté de l'oeconomie politique*, ed. Th. Funck-Brentano (Paris: E. Plon-Nourrit & Cie, 1889), e.g., pp. 38–9, 140–4.
20 *Ibid.*, p. 141.
21 *Ibid.*

'inconsistency' of human 'inclinations' by introducing and managing (for example, through a system of royal manufactures) a division of labour and specialization now lacking in France – in contrast to the more commercially successful England and Germany.

The art of public management or 'political economy', then, consists, again, in maintaining a delicate balance between the preservation of corporate liberties and local privileges (in particular, the corporate liberties of the Third Estate and the urban communal privileges so vital to the bourgeoisie), and the unification of these particularisms into a 'harmonious' body politic and an integrated national economy. Again, the society presupposed by the notion of 'political economy' bears the traces of its feudal and corporatist lineage, while it takes for granted a strong monarchical state.

The Culture of Absolutism

By the end of the religious wars, France was effectively in social crisis and economic ruin. The 1590s were marked by famine, popular revolt and epidemics, as agriculture was fatally disrupted and many cultivators were forced off the land. The royal state began to seem the only viable solution to anarchy; and opposition to monarchical authority among its principal rivals receded, even while the monarchy introduced reforms that, among other things, redistributed the tax burden by excluding some privileged exemptions. Yet the seventeenth century would again be plagued by civil war. With the end of the Thirty Years' War and the Peace of Westphalia in 1648, the remnants of fragmented sovereignty reasserted themselves, aggravated not only by predatory bands of aristocratic soldiers returning from war but also by new dynasties of office-holders. In the time of the Fronde, the battles over jurisdiction, the burden of taxation, or access to state office and the profits of taxation, resurfaced in new forms. In a series of revolts from 1649 to 1652, there were successive waves of opposition to the king from the *parlement* of Paris defending its powers to limit the monarchy, from nobles asserting their autonomy, from popular forces resisting taxation, and finally from dynastic rivals.

The monarchy responded by consolidating central power. What followed is conventionally called the era of French 'absolutism': the revocation of the Edict of Nantes, which had granted significant rights to Protestants; reform of the fiscal and military apparatus to fortify the central state and weaken the aristocracy; a comprehensive programme by the state to promote commercial and industrial development; attempts to unify the legal system and to create a national French culture, from royal patronage of the arts to the standardization of the French language.

While the absolutist state survived the upheavals of the seventeenth century, the Fronde and peasant revolts, the grievances inseparable from the nature of that state – taxation, privileges and exemptions, administrative corruption, in a framework of regional and corporate fragmentation – continued to be the targets of social protest and proposals for reform. Absolutism would never overcome the fragmentation of the state; and the idea of a fragmented social order bound together by a single harmonizing will, a network of corporate entities integrated into an organic, hierarchical totality by a single sovereign power, would continue to shape French political thought. It also encouraged a conception of society in which the totality of social relations, including economic transactions, was subsumed in the *political* community. This constellation would continue to dominate French social thought up to the Revolution and beyond.

The 'parcellization' of political power in France, the survival of feudal prerogatives and privileges, their extension into new forms of patronage and proprietary offices, the persistence of regional and corporate particularisms, whether viewed from the perspective of the monarchy or the 'people', were often confronted theoretically by the notion of a single unifying mind or will which would bind them together. Defenders of the monarchy – whether motivated by the needs of a quarrelsome and self-defeating feudal nobility, the grievances of the Third Estate, or the proprietary interests of the monarchy itself – proposed that feudal prerogatives and proprietary rights in political office and power be appropriated by the monarchy, to constitute, as Bodin formulated it, a single, supreme and indivisible sovereign power. In moderate 'constitutionalist' doctrine, the royal will was to be rendered more truly public, cleansed of particularistic accretions in the form of a corrupt and venal administration, and tempered or informed by representative institutions, but not limited by sharing sovereignty with them.

Even in more radical attacks on royal absolutism, the public will of the state was not generally opposed, as in England, by asserting private interests or individual rights against it. Nor was the common good redefined as a public interest essentially constituted by private interests, in order to counter the public claims of a crown encroaching upon private rights. Instead, the public character of the absolutist state itself was questioned, and the location of the public will was shifted. The principle of generality in a system of particularisms was transferred in theory to representative institutions, the officers of the 'people', 'intermediate bodies'. Even where the common good was conceived as emerging from a harmony of private interests, the state – more specifically, the monarchy – tended to appear as the necessary agent of harmony, the unifying will that would integrate corporate particularities and partial interests. The threats posed by the state itself, its own particularistic and proprietary character, the growth of a burdensome administrative apparatus conceived as private property, were opposed not so much by attempts to defend the 'private' sphere from encroachment by the 'public', as by proposals for transforming the 'private' state into a truly public thing.

Under the Bourbon monarchy, the by now familiar argument that a unifying will in the person of the monarch was an inescapable necessity to maintain social order in an irreducibly fragmented state was taken to new extremes. In 1681 Bishop Bossuet, tutor to the son and heir of Louis XIV, had pushed the argument beyond all previous limits with the publications of his *Discourse on Universal History*. A staunch supporter of the king and the Gallican Church against both Protestants and papacy, he presented his pioneering work in 'philosophical' history as a lesson to the young dauphin. At the centre of the first volume, which covers a 'universal' history from the beginning of the world to the reign of Charlemagne, was the history of ancient Rome and the rise of Christianity. Bossuet's account of the later periods, up to 1661, would be reproduced from his notes after his death. The intention of this massive work was to demonstrate that the history of the world was providentially ordained in the interest of a unified Catholic Church; and one of its principal conclusions was that a single, indivisible sovereign monarch, as a repository of that single, unified Church, was required to fulfil God's purpose.

In the following century, the 'Age of Enlightenment', the culture of French absolutism would take a very different form; but the absolutist state remained at the core of the Enlightenment. However many national enlightenments there may have been, it was in France that the emblematic *philosophe* was born, a new kind of public intellectual whose mission to educate the modern reader was most vividly exemplified by the *Encyclopédie*, proposing to 'encompass not only the fields already covered by the academies, but each and every branch of human knowledge', and not only for the benefit of scholars but for the purpose of changing the 'common way of thinking'. This period is regarded as a distinctively cosmopolitan age in Europe and especially, perhaps, in France. Not unreasonably, the 'Enlightenment' is seen as a time when an 'Age of Discovery', three centuries of commercial and imperial expansion providing access to the material and cultural treasures of the world outside Europe, had driven European minds, and the 'republic of letters', beyond their narrow spatial boundaries. Encouraged by the intellectual legacy of humanism and a scientific revolution, this spatial expansion gave new life to universalistic visions of the world and human rights. Yet, for all their cosmopolitanism and inclusive ambitions, 'Enlightenment' reformers in France were still addressing specifically French questions about the proprietary state, patronage, taxation, and venal offices.

As the state long continued to be a major resource, even beyond the Revolution and Napoleon, complaints were often directed less at the inherent evils of the state as an instrument of appropriation than at the inequalities of opportunity blocking access to its fruits. If (as Jürgen Habermas has famously suggested) the Enlightenment created a new 'bourgeois public sphere', outside and independent of the state, allowing a new kind of critical distance, this had less to do with asserting 'bourgeois' interests against encroachments by the state, or marking out a new space outside the state for the development of capitalism, than with bourgeois demands for access to the state and to the fruits of office. It is not for nothing that, at a time when the traditional aristocracy was seeking to reassert its privileges, not least its privileged access to office, the slogan 'careers open to talent' had such resonance in the moments leading up to revolution.

The *philosophes* exposed the absolutist state and the Church to critical scrutiny, to say nothing of ridicule. They – though some more radically than others – espoused 'enlightened' principles of liberty and toleration with inimitable wit and eloquence. Their irreverence and their assaults on 'superstition' shocked many contemporaries and provoked established authorities, sometimes with dangerous consequences, including imprisonment. Even when their political views were far from democratic or displayed contempt for the common people, their educative mission was, by its very nature, liberating. For the most part the towering figures of the French Enlightenment – such as Voltaire, d'Alembert, Holbach, and Diderot – owe their intellectual force less to any systematic philosophical innovations than to that educative project.

Denis Diderot perhaps better than anyone else captures this specific quality and genius of the French Enlightenment. This is not to say that his views were typical of the *philosophes*. For all his flirtations with 'enlightened despotism' (he was invited to Russia to advise Catherine the Great), he was more democratic than, for example, Voltaire, and less inclined to display contempt for the 'common' people. He could be described as more progressive than was the norm on subjects like the rights of women or the wrongs of colonialism. But he has a special claim as representative of the French Enlightenment, because it was he, above all others, who sustained the *Encyclopédie*; and it was he who made most explicit the project of encompassing all knowledge in an inclusive, comprehensive educative mission, challenging both Church and state by changing 'the common way of thinking'. His own writings, which were wide-ranging and varied in style, would win the admiration of thinkers like Hegel and Marx. But the power of his vision, in a sense, depended on a conscious refusal of system. He can certainly be credited with a distinctive philosophical materialism, but its emphasis on change and uncertainty was perhaps best captured not by rigorous philosophy or political theory but by a characteristic work like *Rameau's Nephew*, a satirical dialogue ranging across a bewildering variety of subjects, full of confusions and contradictions, in which the standpoint of the author remains outside our grasp, yet which somehow succeeds in exposing enemies of enlightenment to ridicule.

Among the luminaries of the French Enlightenment, there were nonetheless at least two who could lay claim to systematic originality in social and political thought. Like the *philosophes* in general, Montesquieu and Rousseau, two of the most inventive and widely influential figures in the Western canon, belonged to a larger 'republic of letters', well schooled in cultural developments beyond the borders of France. Yet what is particularly striking about both these innovative thinkers is the degree to which their political ideas were deeply rooted in – and, in their very different ways, owed their distinctive character to – the specific discourse of French absolutism.

That the French Enlightenment's commitment to critical reason was, in one way or another, a response to royal absolutism is a commonplace. But to emphasize the cultural effects of absolutism is to say something more than simply that French arts and literature thrived under the extravagance of royal patronage and/or that the absolutist state provoked a culture of opposition, giving birth to an 'Age of Enlightenment' which celebrated reason, toleration, civil liberty and individual autonomy against oppression by an overbearing state supported by an intolerant Church and a culture of 'superstition'. Nor is it enough to acknowledge the continuity of grievances, from the sixteenth century to the Revolution. Throughout that period, the persistent tensions at the heart of the absolutist state remained at the core of French intellectual life in, so to speak, a more structural sense, presenting thinkers with specific questions and setting the terms of debate in particular ways. This is nowhere more visible than in Rousseau and Montesquieu.

Montesquieu

By the time Montesquieu published his *Considerations on the Causes of the Grandeur and Decadence of the Romans* in 1734, there was already a long tradition of debate on the origin and legitimacy of the French monarchy, as against competing jurisdictions. In the eighteenth century, old arguments like those of Hotman in the sixteenth century, which sought to challenge the monarchy's authority by invoking French historical traditions, were countered by alternative accounts of history – for instance, tracing the origins of monarchical authority to Roman imperial roots. Such arguments were challenged in turn by historical claims for the feudal powers of the nobility, which insisted that the absolute monarchy represented a historical corruption.

From this opposition would emerge the battle between the *thèse royale* and the *thèse nobiliaire*, the debate between those committed to an untrammelled, undivided sovereign monarchy and those who believed in a monarchical state limited by the autonomous powers of the nobility and corporate bodies. Whatever other ambiguities there are in Montesquieu's political philosophy, which have permitted commentators to describe him as everything from an apostle of reaction to a committed republican, his own contemporaries, including *philosophes*, had no difficulty situating him, for better or worse, on the side of the *thèse nobiliaire*.

In a letter to Montesquieu, for instance, Helvetius wrote:

> As to our aristocrats and our petty despots of all grades, if they understand you, they cannot praise you too much, and this is the fault I have ever found with the principles of your work . . . *L'esprit de corps* assails us on all sides; it is a power erected at the expense of the great mass of society. It is by these hereditary usurpations we are ruled.[22]

To be on the side of the *thèse nobiliaire* was not to oppose a monarchical state, as was clear to republican critics (not just in France but in America, for all the influence he is said to have had on the 'founding fathers') who denounced Montesquieu as a monarchist. Nor was there anything unusual or contradictory about asserting principles of liberty against the absolutist monarchy while remaining firmly wedded to the principles of aristocracy. But subscribing to the *thèse nobiliaire* did mean rejecting some of the most fundamental tenets of the absolutist state as embodied in the *thèse royale*; and the most efficient way of making sense of Montesquieu's apparent ambiguities is to place him in the context of that very French debate. At the same time, the conceptual innovations to which he owes his title as progenitor of modern sociology and/or the inventor of modern political science (or even political economy) are rooted in precisely his critical engagement with French absolutist ideology.

Montesquieu was born in 1689, the historical moment that in Britain produced the kind of 'balanced' government he would hold up as a model in his classic, *The Spirit of the Laws*. He came from an old and distinguished family of the *noblesse de robe*, an element in French society that would be at the very centre of his political ideas. Trained as a lawyer, he served in the *parlement* of Bordeaux and later became president; and this experience, as we shall see, would figure prominently in his theory of politics. A believer in venal office as a check on the central state, he sold his own office of president.

If the early movement of the *philosophes* began among courtly elites, it was Montesquieu who first moved significantly beyond the limits of salon conversation, with the publication of his *Persian Letters* in 1721. Like Voltaire's *Philosophical Letters*, published in 1734, Montesquieu's devastatingly witty epistolary novel, in which French society was viewed as through the alien eyes of a Persian visitor, advanced the Enlightenment,

---

22   Quoted by Franz Neumann in his introduction to Montesquieu, *The Spirit of the Laws* (New York: Hafner, 1962), p. xxvii.

as Robert Darnton puts it, 'from wit to wisdom', mixing 'libertine impieties with serious reflections on despotism and intolerance'.[23] But Montesquieu, unlike Voltaire, undertook a more ambitious intellectual project with his *Considerations on the Causes of the Grandeur and Decline of the Romans* in 1734, to be followed by *The Spirit of the Laws*; and it is here that the absolutist roots of French discourse in the 'Age of Enlightenment' are most visible.

Absolutist thought encouraged an idea of society as an interlocking whole, a systemic totality of social relations, constituted by political authority in the person of an 'absolute' monarch. The strategies adopted in defence of absolutism had the effect of encouraging totalizing visions of the social world and human history, which would have significant effects on the development of social theory. The 'philosophical history' of Montesquieu, as well as his theories of society and social change, belongs to that tradition. To say this may, on the face of it, run counter to interpretations of his work that treat him as a progenitor of modern sociology, whose discovery of 'society' as a self-subsistent entity, a network of relations with its own internal logic, had the effect of displacing the 'political' as the unifying force or organizing principle of human community. The 'laws' that Montesquieu has in mind are, according to such interpretations, not so much the products of human creativity and political agency as necessities arising from the nature of a given social system and its inherent systemic requirements. But, while it is certainly true that Montesquieu emphasizes the systemic interconnections among various factors – economic, ecological and cultural no less than political – his 'sociology' remains inescapably political and deeply rooted in the tradition of absolutist thought. Montesquieu's account of societies as systemic wholes, each with its own specific principle of coherence and change, represents an attempt to challenge absolutist arguments on their own ground, by offering a theory of social totalities – embracing everything from history and politics to economics – that did not inevitably point to absolutist monarchy. At the same time, if the absolutist monarchy is no longer the indispensable condition of social cohesion, political agency remains at the heart of his 'sociology'.

Bossuet's philosophical history, which sought to capture the totality of human history in a grand, all-embracing explanation, was the work that perhaps above all else inspired Montesquieu to embark on his own philosophical history of Rome, not simply a narrative of events and personalities but an account of a whole social order rising and declining according to its own intrinsic principles, as a counter to the bishop's 'absolutist' vision of the world. The *Considerations* introduced themes that would be developed

---

23 Robert Darnton, 'George Washington's False Teeth', *New York Review of Books*, 27 March 1997, p. 35.

in a different form in *The Spirit of the Laws*, on which his status in the canon of Western political thought mainly rests, published anonymously in 1748. In *Considerations*, Montesquieu's intent was not simply to present an alternative account of Roman history but to counteract justifications of royal absolutism by challenging the claims for Louis XIV as the divinely ordained agent of a universal history. He offers instead a 'natural' history of imperial Rome and the rise of Christianity, a 'philosophical' history but with only human agents, in sharp contrast to Bossuet's providential universal history.

Considerations is not an overtly theoretical work, but we can already detect the principles on which *The Spirit of the Laws* would proceed. In Montesquieu's history, there is no teleology or supra-human destiny of any kind. The history of Rome unfolds as a 'natural' process, and the rise of Christianity is nothing more than a part of that natural history. It has no more privileged historical status than any other Roman institution; and it is explicable in the same ways. But if history is a natural process, this is not to say that it proceeds in simple accordance with immutable natural laws. Human agency creates its own complexities. At the same time, history is not simply the product of great individuals. While the only historical agents are human, they act within specific contexts, specific institutions, common practices and the pervading culture, or the 'spirit' of the people, with their own intrinsic principles of change. It is in this sense that historical causes are general: the consequences of any particular cause – such as a military defeat – will be determined by a 'general' cause, the institutional framework of a specific society and the spirit of the people that pervades it. The early kings of Rome gave way to a republic not because of any great heroic acts by individuals but because the kings created an absolute monarchy, eliminating the intermediary powers of a nobility, and no such monarchy could be sustained for long. The republic achieved greatness, in power and size, not because of great individuals but because of the republican order and the particular public spirit that sustained it. Yet it was doomed to eventual decline because the nature and spirit of the republic encouraged, even required, constant conquests and expansion; and republics can survive only in a relatively small territory. Imperial expansion, while natural to the republic, was also the cause of its decline.

The Spirit of the Laws is a very different and more ambitious kind of work, but the amalgam of general and specific – the 'general' causes inherent in specific social forms – that appears in the *Considerations* is the guiding principle of Montesquieu's most influential classic. That sprawling work, with its huge temporal and geographical range, from France to China and beyond, while certainly acknowledged as a masterpiece, has also been accused of being contradictory, illogical and hard to follow, with ambitions that far exceed its accomplishments. But its weaknesses are at least to some extent the obverse of its strengths, the consequence of its author's innovative attempt to strike a theoretical balance between the general laws of social and political change and the distinctive operating principles or 'spirit' of specific political forms.

'I have,' he writes in his preface,

> first of all considered mankind, and the result of my thoughts has been, that amidst such an infinite diversity of laws and manners, they were not solely conducted by the caprice of fancy.
>
> I have laid down the first principles, and have found that the particular cases follow naturally from them; that the histories of all nations are only consequences of them; and that every particular law is connected with another law, or depends on some other of a more general extent. (*SL*)

One effect of treating all the many social forms and cultures on display in the world as equally 'natural' is to underwrite the toleration of diversity; and Montesquieu goes on to assure the reader that his purpose is not to censure the laws of any country whatsoever. His objective, he insists, is simply to illuminate the operating principles on which each type of government is based and the conditions conducive to its failures and successes, its rises and declines. 'Every nation will here find the reasons on which its maxims are founded.' The burden of proposing alterations 'belongs only to those who are so happy as to be born with a genius capable of penetrating the entire constitution of a state', and he himself would be happy simply to 'afford new reasons to every man to love his prince, his country, his laws' and 'to persuade those who command to increase their knowledge in what they ought to prescribe'. Yet, as Montesquieu proceeds, it becomes fairly clear that, however disinterested his scientific purpose, his exposure of the 'spirit' of all laws is, after all, also designed to promote the alteration of the existing French state. It is not too much to say that his grand scientific project is inevitably shaped by the particular requirements of a political programme.

Montesquieu starts from the premise that social and political change is intelligible, accessible to human reason; but to understand humanity's social and political practices requires something more than identifying certain fixed and invariable rules that are common to all nature. There are, to be sure, universal, immutable natural laws, which affect human beings as they do other natural bodies. 'Man, as a physical being, is like other bodies governed by invariable laws', but '[a]s an intelligent being, he incessantly transgresses the laws established by God, and changes those of his own instituting.' (I.1) These changes and transgressions are not unintelligible. The human 'laws' that are the subject of Montesquieu's study are no less susceptible to scientific knowledge than are the laws of nature as science understands them.[24] But the vast variety of social forms and customs, to say nothing of the vagaries of human passion, ignorance and error, means that it is not enough to discover the laws of nature in themselves – in the manner, for instance, of Hobbes, who tried to apply principles of physics and its laws of motion to human motivations. We must seek the internal coherence and logic of each specific social form.

We can certainly begin with certain common, fundamental human motivations, as does Hobbes when he describes the state of nature; and Montesquieu does briefly counter Hobbes's view: simple fear and the desire to dominate others can hardly explain how men live in society, and human motivations are far more complex. But the French philosopher is less interested in such primary motivations than in the complexities deriving from specific social forms. We can, he suggests, begin with the simple proposition that 'No society can subsist without a form of government'; and, in one way or another, all existing forms of government do conform to nature. But to say this is to tell us very little. 'Better is it to say', he goes on,

> that the government most conformable to nature is that which best agrees with the humor and disposition of the people in whose favor it is established . . . [and laws] should be adapted in such a manner to the people for whom they are framed that it should be a great chance if those of one nation suit another . . . They should be in relation to the climate of each country, to the quality of its soil, to its situation and extent, to the principal occupation of the natives, whether husbandmen, huntsmen or shepherds: they should have relation to the degree of liberty which the constitution will bear; to the religion of the inhabitants, to their inclinations, riches, numbers, commerce, manners, and customs. In fine, they have relations to each other, as also their origin, to the intent of the legislator, and to the order of things on which they

---

24 Louis Althusser, in *Politics and History: Montesquieu, Rousseau, Hegel and Marx* (London: New Left Books, 1972), makes an important argument about the 'revolution' of method accomplished by Montesquieu, in particular his redefinition of 'law'. While other thinkers had already secularized the concept of natural law, they had, argues Althusser, 'retained from the old version its teleological structure, its character as an ideal masked by the immediate appearances of *nature*. For them natural law was as much a *norm* (devoir) as a necessity. All their demands found refuge and support in a definition of law which was still foreign to the new one.' But Montesquieu 'proposes quite simply to expel the old version of the word law from the domains which it still held. And to consecrate the reign of the modern definition – law as a relation – over the whole extent of beings, from God to stones. "In this sense, all beings have their laws; the Deity his laws, the material world its laws, the intelligences superior to man their laws, the beasts their laws, man his laws" (I.1)' (p. 35).

are established; in all of which different lights they ought to be considered. (I.3)

Montesquieu proceeds to canvass a vast array of factors that set the terms of government and law, famously including long discussions of non-social determinants like climate and topography. But he still constructs his analysis on a familiar organizing principle, a formal typology of governments. He identifies three species of government: republican, monarchical, and despotic, each characterized by its own particular structure and the particular passions, or spirit, that ensure its survival. This classification is, of course, a departure from the ancient distinction among democracy, aristocracy, and monarchy (together with their corrupted forms); but, like much else in Montesquieu's work, it has roots in Machiavelli: instead of democracy and aristocracy, he proposes, as does Machiavelli, the republican form, in which the 'people' or some part of it possess supreme power and which therefore can be either democratic or aristocratic. But Montesquieu adds his own particular departure both from ancient classifications and from Machiavelli by proposing a distinction between monarchy and despotism: the distinctive characteristic of despotism is that 'a single person directs everything by his own will and caprice', in contrast to monarchy, 'in which a single person governs by fixed and established laws' (II.1).

The ancients did, to be sure, have a concept of 'despotic' rule. The word *despotes* in its original meaning simply described the head of a household or a master of slaves, a meaning that the Greeks by extension began to apply to their understanding of Asiatic forms of imperial rule, in contrast to Greek constitutions. In the sixteenth and seventeenth centuries, various thinkers – such as Bodin, Grotius, Hobbes and Locke – applied the term to denote regimes that effectively enslaved a subject people, or at least deprived them of rights, which these regimes could do legitimately on the grounds of just war. By the time Montesquieu elaborated his classification of political forms, which systematically included 'despotism' as one of the three major forms, the term had already become part of anti-absolutist discourse in France, to censure not an Asiatic 'despotism' or imperial rule over a subject population but a specifically European monarchy and its rule over its own people. In *The Spirit of the Laws*, Montesquieu makes the despotic form a central organizing principle of the whole work.

Montesquieu, then, proposes two types of formal criteria for distinguishing the principal forms of government: whether the state is governed by one person or more – which distinguishes republics from monarchies and despotisms; and whether the state is governed by 'fixed and established laws' – which distinguishes republics and monarchies from despotisms (although, as we shall see in a moment, this criterion is less straightforward than it may appear at first sight). It may be significant that whether the state is governed by a few or by many, a question so central to ancient classifications, does not have the same status as do those principal criteria: both aristocracies and democracies are republican forms. But this was true for Machiavelli, too, for whom the political universe was governed by a contest between principalities and city-republics, and the distinction between a *governo stretto* or a *governo largo*, his preference for the latter notwithstanding, was rather less important. For Montesquieu, the stakes, of course, are different. His classification of political forms seems designed to advance a particular agenda: the promotion of a monarchy, in which a government by 'fixed and established laws' is guaranteed by the autonomous powers of the nobility and other intermediate bodies.

How, then, is that purpose served by Montesquieu's distinctions among the forms of government, together with the very particular 'spirit of the laws' that sustains each one of them? Although he elaborates the differences between democratic and aristocratic republics, the most important message that emerges from his analysis of republican forms, whether democratic or aristocratic, is that they are very difficult – if not ultimately impossible – to sustain, requiring an onerous degree of probity or virtue not required by either despotic or monarchical states. The principle or 'spirit' that sustains the laws and institutions of democracy is a kind of civic virtue, a love of the laws and the country, that goes against the grain of other, simpler human passions. It can easily give way to 'the spirit of inequality', which drives people to put their own private interests and status above those of their fellow citizens, or, on the contrary, a spirit of excessive equality, which inclines people to disobey their governors in order to manage everything themselves. Aristocracies depend on a kind of 'moderation' that requires aristocrats to act in opposition to their inclinations and ambitions, which would naturally tend towards increasing the distance and the inequality between them and the common people, inevitably with corrupting and destabilizing effects. Republics, in other words, make unusually, even unnaturally, heavy demands on civic institutions, communal cohesion and devotion to the public good. To the extent that such demands can be met at all for any length of time, it is only in small and exceptionally homogeneous or integrated societies.

Montesquieu's discussion of republics, then, effectively rules out the republican form as a viable option for a country like France, or, indeed, for any other rising European power; but it does lay down certain ground rules of political survival, which can serve in analyzing other forms. We can, for example, analyze the monarchical form by discovering the principle that sustains it in a way analogous to civic virtue but without making the same demands on the people as republics do:

In a monarchy policy effects great things with as little virtue as possible. Thus in the nicest machines, art has reduced the number of movements, springs, and wheels.

The state subsists independently of the love of our country, of the thirst of true glory, of self-denial, of the sacrifice of our dearest interests, and of all those heroic virtues which we admire in the ancients, and to us are known only in tradition. (III.5)

The basic principle of monarchy is honour, 'that is, the prejudice of every person and rank', which takes the place of political virtue and, when joined with the force of laws, can serve the purpose of government as well as virtue itself can do (III.6).

But there are very particular conditions that alone enable monarchy to sustain itself without demands on civic virtue, conditions without which rule by one man would simply be despotic. Governance by law means something very specific in the case of monarchy. Describing 'the relation of the laws to the nature of monarchical government', Montesquieu makes it clear that what finally distinguishes a lawful monarchy from a despotic form is the existence of 'intermediate, subordinate, and dependent powers' that stand between the people and the single ruler who governs by fundamental laws. Indeed, the very existence of 'fixed and established' fundamental laws presupposes such intermediate powers:

These fundamental laws necessarily suppose the intermediate channels through which the power flows, for if there be only the momentary and capricious will of a single person to govern the state, nothing can be fixed, and, of course, there is no fundamental law.' (II.4)

In the despotic form there are no such mediations, which means that, even if a despotism gives the appearance of governance by fixed and established law, it is really governed by the will and caprice of the ruler. Its operating principle is neither virtue nor honour but simply fear. Despotism is, in its way, certainly natural, driven by passions that come all too easily to human beings; but, while other forms of state are susceptible to corruption when their sustaining principles are compromised, despotic states are by nature corrupt from the start.

This brings us to another, more fundamental distinction among the types of state, the difference between 'moderate' and immoderate forms. The real danger of corruption comes not when 'the state passes from one moderate to another moderate government, as from a republic to a monarchy, or from a monarchy to a republic; but when it is precipitated from a moderate to a despotic government' (VIII.8). It is surely not insignificant that the principle specifically attached to aristocracy – the principle of 'moderation' – becomes the virtue of good government in general; and, indeed, Montesquieu goes on to make clear that a monarchy, as distinct from a despotism, is 'moderate' precisely because it is sustained by preserving autonomous aristocratic powers. What Montesquieu means by 'moderation' is revealed less by an explicit definition of this virtue than by the consequences he attributes to it and the means he prescribes to sustain it: a 'moderate government may, whenever it pleases, and without the least danger, relax its springs', unlike a despotism, in which the only guarantee of public order is blind obedience, driven by fear; and what ultimately makes this 'moderation' possible is a particular kind of balance among the powers of government:

> To form a moderate government, it is necessary to combine the several powers; to regulate, temper, and set them in motion; to give, as it were, ballast to one, in order to enable it to counterpoise the other. This is a masterpiece of legislation, rarely produced by hazard and seldom attained by prudence. (V.14)

This rare effect was achieved in republican Rome; and in Montesquieu's own time, he suggests, it exists particularly in England – although the English form as he describes it was, in reality, rather different from the monarchy he had in mind for France.

Here we come to one of the most disputed points in Montesquieu's work: whether what he was proposing was a 'separation of powers' in the sense that term is now conventionally understood. Debate surrounds his influence, or lack of it, on the American 'founding fathers' and the 'separation of powers' as encoded (though never specifically mentioned in those terms) in the US Constitution. It is certainly true that the 'founders' invoked Montesquieu and may even take credit for establishing his reputation as the inventor of the idea; but, however much the authority of Montesquieu was cited, the US doctrine of 'separate' powers, together with the 'checks and balances' it was meant to promote, produced something quite distinct from Montesquieu's intentions.

He tells us that '[i]n every government there are three sorts of power: the legislative; the executive in respect to things dependent on the law of nations; and the executive in regard to matters that depend on the civil law', the last of which can be called the judiciary power. (XI.6) But his account of 'moderate' government seems to suggest from the start that what he has in mind is not the separation of powers of a kind the US Constitution would produce. The most viable form of balanced and moderate government is monarchy; and he goes on to tell us that most kingdoms in Europe are 'moderate' because the prince, while possessing legislative and executive powers, leaves judiciary power to his subjects.[25] Yet it soon becomes clear that powers are

---

25   Althusser is right to suggest that the notion that Montesquieu proposed a 'separation of powers' is largely a historical illusion, a 'myth' (*Politics and History*, Ch. 5). But it should be added that, while there is debate about Montesquieu's meaning, there is

'separated' not in the sense that the three main governmental functions belong to different institutions. If anything, these functions are ideally combined but invested in more than one repository of power.

The ideal 'separation of powers' for Montesquieu clearly entails a monarchical state, in which the monarchy is checked and balanced by another source of power. In the English case, which he describes as the existing constitution most conducive to liberty, legislative power is embodied in the classic combination of 'the Crown in Parliament'. But there seems to be, for him, a different, perhaps even better, option, which has more to do with French conditions. Having told us that the 'intermediate, subordinate, and dependent powers constitute the nature of monarchical government', in which the 'fundamental laws necessarily suppose the intermediate channels through which the power flows', he goes on to explain that '[t]he most natural, intermediate, and subordinate power is that of the nobility. This in some measure seems to be essential to a monarchy, whose fundamental maxim is, no monarch, no nobility; no nobility, no monarch' (II.4, 15-16.).

This characterization of 'intermediate' powers suggests that there are two distinct issues at stake. It is one thing to distinguish among the various functions of the state and to insist that one or the other should not be placed entirely in the same hands. But to speak of the nobility in the way Montesquieu does is to raise a different set of questions.[26] The issue is not only the relation among legislative, executive and juridical powers but the survival of autonomous jurisdictions in relation to the central state.

Here, we can look back to the *Persian Letters* for some guidance about Montesquieu's preoccupations. The letters are set between 1711 and 1720. They span a period of crisis in the French state, with its climactic moment in 1715, the year of Louis XIV's death, followed by a regency which seemed at first to hold the promise of substantial change. 'The monarch who reigned for so long is no more', writes Usbek to Rhedi in 1715 (Letter XCIII). Usbek goes on to reflect on the possibilities that seem to have been opened, and it

---

nothing particularly novel or shocking about the contention that he never had in mind the 'separation of powers' in the now conventional sense. It is probably more common than otherwise among historians to point out that Montesquieu never meant what some Americans claimed for him.

26   The difference between these issues is perhaps more easily rendered in French. See Althusser, *Politics and History*, on the distinction between power as *puissance* and power as *pouvoir*: 'We then confront *two powers*: the executive and the legislature. Two *pouvoirs* but three *puissances*, to use Montesquieu's own words. These three *puissances* are the king, the upper chamber and the lower chamber, i.e. the king, the nobility and the "people" . . . The famous *separation of powers* is thus no more than the calculated division of *pouvoir* between determinate *puissances*: the king, the nobility and the "people"' (pp. 90–1). Yet even this formulation may not quite capture what Montesquieu has in mind.

is striking that his principal concern is with the *parlements*. These old institutions

> resemble those ruins which are trampled underfoot but are reminiscent always of some temple famed in the antique religion of the people. They now interest themselves only in judicial questions, and their authority will continue to weaken unless something unforeseen rejuvenates them. These great bodies have followed the destiny of all things human: they have yielded to time, which destroys all, to moral corruption, which enfeebles, and to supreme authority, which overthrows everything.

Yet there is hope:

> [T]he regent, who wishes to make himself agreeable to the people, has so far appeared to respect this shadow of public liberty. As if he intended to rebuild the temple and the idol, he has decreed that they may be regarded as the support of the monarch and the base of all legitimate authority.

In *The Spirit of the Laws,* Montesquieu appears to be reviving the hope that these 'great bodies', these embodiments of 'public liberty', might renew the monarchy of France. The *parlements* fit his account of 'intermediate bodies', the essence of 'moderate' government, more aptly than does any other institution; and this distinctive feature of the French political tradition makes sense of Montesquieu's obscure account of 'balance' among powers in a way the English 'Crown in Parliament' does not.

The *parlements* embodied all the characteristic tensions of the complex relation between the French monarchy and other jurisdictions. They had played a critical part in extending royal authority, acting as a conduit for royal administration in the provinces; yet, as venal offices, they had become the hereditary property of office-holders, the *noblesse de robe*, with autonomous claims against the king; and they came to represent opposition to the monarchy in the name of the people and French constitutional liberties. They had become above all courts of law, as distinct from representative legislative assemblies in the manner of the English Parliament; yet they combined judicial powers with other state functions, administrative or executive – at least, they did so, as Montesquieu suggests in *Persian Letters*, before they were weakened under Louis XIV. They enjoyed police powers across a wide spectrum, from religion and morality to trade and industry; but their most important political function was to register royal decrees, or to object to them by invoking the *droit de remonstrance*, the right to protest royal edicts, which was revoked by Louis and restored by the regency. This right may not have been particularly efficacious and could be circumvented by the king; but, in the eyes of the French public, the *parlements* succeeded to a remarkable degree in identifying the interests of a venal, quasi-feudal oligarchy with the protection of French liberties.

Montesquieu, whose own political experience was rooted in the *parlement* of Bordeaux, had no illusions about the benevolence and rectitude of this institution and had, indeed, subjected his colleagues to harsh criticism. But there is no doubt that, with a certain amount of idealization, the *parlement* represented for him the model 'intermediate power'. It is the quintessential institution of the *noblesse de robe*, a group that can perform its essential and distinctive function because of its location between the great nobility and the people (*SL* XX.22). Combining aspects of all three 'separate' powers, the *parlement* 'balances' the powers of the monarchy by acting as the channel through which royal authority flows, retaining a degree of aristocratic and regional autonomy, protected by the rights of venal office (which Montesquieu supports), without fatally compromising the political and legal unity ideally conferred by the monarchy on a fundamentally fragmented state. What emerges is a model of 'moderate' government in which a strong and stable centralized power is balanced and checked by preserving a degree of fragmentation and regional particularity, together with the autonomy of noble powers in *every* function of the state, executive, legislative and judiciary – a model that remains far closer to the realities of French absolutism than to the English pattern even in idealized form.

The political balance that Montesquieu attempts to strike is distinctively French. He clearly approves of a strong central power and would even advocate a kind of unified national system of law, which England then had but France, for all the absolutist pretensions of the king, had yet to achieve. Nevertheless, he still identifies liberty with the preservation of autonomous powers vested in the nobility and corporate bodies, in a manner very different from the English state.

Montesquieu's discussion of judiciary power is at once both ambiguous and revealing. He tells us that, of the three powers, 'the judiciary is in some measure next to nothing; they remain, therefore, only two' (XI.6). At the same time, the judiciary power is the one whose possession by the 'people' seems the most critical in defining moderate government; and since moderate government is the minimal condition of liberty, it is reasonable to assume that a properly constituted judiciary power is the ultimate guarantee of liberty. It is, perhaps, possible to reconcile these two apparently conflicting propositions about the importance of judiciary power simply by pointing out that Montesquieu was relatively sparing in his demands on the judiciary. It has been argued, for example, that his principal claim to be 'one of the greatest of liberal thinkers . . . rests not on his famous homage to the English constitution, but on his theory of the criminal law and punishment', because for him '[t]he single most important requirement for the realization of liberty is that only a very few misdeeds should be criminalized at all.'[27]

Yet if this seems to reduce the powers of the *parlement* as a judicial body, its role as an 'intermediate power' rests not simply on its function as a court but on a degree of aristocratic autonomy in *all* functions of the state, not only the judiciary. Montesquieu can advocate a national system of law that challenges France's legal fragmentation, while at the same time calling for the preservation of the *parlements* as both less and more than courts of law. His views on crime and punishment are certainly significant, but the all-too-capacious concept of 'liberalism' should be applied here with caution. If it is taken to imply a 'modern' turn of mind, it may obscure the ways in which his conception of judicial power remains rooted in French absolutism, while 'liberty' is still identified with the remnants of parcellized sovereignty and aristocratic autonomy.

Commerce

The French *parlements* resolve the ambiguities in Montesquieu's 'separation of powers' in a way the English model does not. But there is another feature of the English model that Montesquieu admires with, on the face of it, less ambiguity. *The Spirit of the Laws* devotes a great deal of attention to commerce, remarkably so for a work ostensibly on politics and law – or, to put it more precisely, commerce as he conceives it plays a role no less political than 'economic'. Not only is England, for instance, a prime example of commercial success, but it represents a distinctive blend of liberty with commerce. 'Other nations', he says, 'have made the interests of commerce yield to those of politics; the English, on the contrary, have ever made their political interests give way to those of commerce' (XX.7). It is exceptional, too, in the ways and degrees that the commercial spirit permeates the whole society, as even the nobility engage in commerce. And lest that seem intended as a criticism, Montesquieu assures us that '[t]hey know better than any other people upon earth how to value, at the same time, these three great advantages – religion, commerce, and liberty'.

The English are unique in another way, which is clearly related to the nexus of commerce and liberty: they alone have successfully combined monarchy and 'economic' commerce, as distinct from the commerce of luxury. While monarchies typically devote themselves to procuring 'everything that can contribute to the pride, the pleasure, and the capricious whims of the nation', it is more common in republics to encourage trade that has 'an eye to all the nations of the earth, [bringing] from one what is wanted by another' (XX.4). Monarchies also tend to distrust merchant

---

27   Judith Shklar, *Montesquieu* (Oxford: Oxford University Press, 1987), p. 89.

classes, while republics are inclined to preserve their safety and their security of property. 'Great enterprises, therefore, in commerce are not for monarchical, but for republican, governments.' In all these respects, England represents a notable exception, combining, it seems, monarchical and republican elements in both politics and commerce.

Montesquieu's elaborate discussion of commerce is said to have sparked an interest in political economy among the French; and it would indeed be French thinkers who, not long after, produced groundbreaking work in economic theory, giving new life and meaning to the term 'political economy'. François Quesnay and his physiocratic school, even before the Anglo-Scottish 'classical' political economists, have been credited with a major breakthrough in the evolution of modern economics, on the grounds that they were the first to treat the economy as a systemic totality, in which the processes of production, exchange and consumption were united in an interdependent 'circular flow'; and for them, too, if for somewhat different reasons, England was the model.

Montesquieu was never a 'political economist' in that technical sense, but he did give some credence to the idea that the economy – or the network of commerce – was a self-sustaining mechanism, which, left free to follow its own principles, could promote not only liberty within the state but peace among nations. While he had no illusions about the connections between commerce and war or colonial conquest, he went some distance in questioning the common assumption that trade among nations is a zero-sum game. At least for nations with adequate movable resources to trade, commerce with others possessing more or less equal endowments serves to unite and enrich all parties to the exchange. Those who have little tradeable wealth should stay away from commerce even to obtain the things they do not have: 'it is not those nations who have need of nothing that must lose by trade; it is those who have need of everything' (XX.23).

At the same time, Montesquieu tells us, 'if the spirit of commerce unites nations, it does not in the same manner unite individuals' (XX.2). The commercial spirit displaces all humane and moral virtues, reducing everything to money. Commerce may in some respects do the work of civic virtue, but it cannot by itself serve as the social bond or economic mechanism that automatically converts private vices into public benefits. Yet again, it appears that what is required to harmonize interests and guarantee the common good, or even simple equity, is political authority. The question then may be what form of state can serve this function while maintaining liberty. The English state appears to be the model here; but, in a section disarmingly entitled 'A singular reflection', Montesquieu interjects some comments on France that suggest another option, which resonates with what we already know about his political preferences:

Persons struck with the practice of some states imagine that in France they ought to make laws to engage the nobility to enter into commerce. But these laws would be the means of destroying the nobility, without being of any advantage to trade. The practice of this country is extremely wise; merchants are not nobles, though they may become so. They have hope of obtaining a degree of nobility, unattended with its actual inconveniences. There is no surer way of being advanced above their profession than to manage it well, or with success; the consequence of which is generally an affluent fortune . . .

The possibility of purchasing honor with gold encourages many merchants to put themselves in circumstances by which they may attain it. I do not take it upon me to examine the justice of this bartering for money the price of virtue. There are governments where this may be very useful. (XX.22)

As with Spinoza, then, commerce can work to the public advantage when the lust for money is harnessed to the public good by making wealth a means to achieve the honour of office. But, in accordance with French conditions, the principal agents of the public good for Montesquieu are not republican oligarchs, as in the Dutch Republic, but venal office-holders and specifically those of 'the long robe, which places those who wear it between the great nobility and the people', the *noblesse de robe* that serves as 'the depository of the laws' (XX.22). The wealth derived from commerce can, it would seem, most directly serve the public good when used to purchase office.

A few years later, the physiocrats would invoke the model of English agrarian capitalism to construct their science of political economy. Montesquieu may indeed have been in some respects their forerunner; but the physiocrats systematically developed, in a way that he never did, the principle that the 'economy' has an internal and self-propelling logic of its own. On the strength of that principle, and the slogan *laissez faire, laissez passer,* which they helped to promote, they are commonly regarded as founders not only of political economy but of 'liberal' economics, who influenced the likes of Adam Smith and other classical political economists.

Yet the physiocrats, in a distinctively French context, assigned to the state a role very different from anything envisaged by their Anglo-Scottish equivalents. While they looked to the example of England and its productive agrarian sector in support of their argument that agriculture was the driving force of a 'modern' economy, they acknowledged the fundamental differences between French conditions and the English model – above all, the absence in France of what we have been calling a capitalist landed class. It was, for the physiocrats, up to the state to transform French society, to act in effect as the agent of what Adam Smith would call the 'original accumulation'; and the monarchy still appeared – in the French manner – as the principle of universality in a constellation of particularisms, the principal means of overcoming corporate interests, the fragmentation of both state and economy. In this respect, too, they had something important in common with Montesquieu. But, unlike Montesquieu, for whom 'intermediate bodies' were the guardians of liberty, the physiocrats had their eyes more firmly fixed on economic progress; and this, in their view, required the suppression of fragmented powers by a form of 'legal despotism'. The purpose of the monarchical state was certainly not to impose its own arbitrary will. It was meant to ensure the operation of the 'natural' laws of society and economic mechanisms; but those natural laws had as their condition a strong central state. [28]

Jean-Jacques Rousseau

In the few years between the appearance of Montesquieu's *Spirit of the Laws* and Quesnay's *Tableau économique*, Rousseau produced three of his most important works: the *Discours sur les sciences et les arts* (1750), which first established his reputation as a social thinker; *Discours sur l'origine et les fondements de l'inégalité parmi les hommes)* (1754); and *Discours sur l'économie politique* (1755). His ideas would undergo significant development from one work to the next; but the three discourses have at least one common theme, which would remain at the foundation of all his political thought: a challenge to social doctrines – such as those espoused, Rousseau suggests, by Hobbes and Mandeville – according to which society is bound together above all by the force of personal interest.

It is tempting to avoid any mention of Rousseau's biography. His notoriously difficult personality is certainly important in accounting for the vagaries of his career, his broken friendships with other *philosophes* like Diderot, and his unmistakable vantage point as an 'outsider', which goes beyond his identity as a Genevan in an alien Paris; and, of course, his private life is on dramatic display in his *Confessions* and his *Reveries of a Solitary Walker*, in a way unmatched by almost any other thinker. But his psychological weaknesses have too often permitted a lazy and tendentious dismissal of his political ideas as the neurotic outpourings of a disordered psyche, perhaps an 'authoritarian personality' with a penchant for 'totalitarian democracy'; and we may, as will be argued in what follows, learn less about his work from his personal life than we do from the French historical context which inspired his political ideas.

---

28   On the physiocrats and their conception of the relation between the state and the economy, see David McNally, *Political Economy and the Rise of Capitalism* (Berkeley: University of Californian Press, 1994), Ch. 3.

About his life, it is probably enough to know that he was born the son of a well-educated watchmaker in 1712 in Geneva, which would remain an idealized model for his political reflections; that he fled Geneva at the age of fifteen; that, largely self-educated, he was introduced to French society and intellectual life while under the protection and influence of Mme de Warens, a Catholic lay proselytizer (though he would later return to Calvinism to regain his Genevan citizenship); and that, when he moved to Paris in 1742, he established a close friendship with Diderot and other *philosophes*. His work embraced an astonishingly wide range of subjects, from the philosophy of education in *Émile* to musical theory (which he seems to have regarded as his most important contribution); and his novel, *Julie, or the New Héloise*, is often cited as a founding work of the 'romantic' movement. By the time of his death in 1778, he had established a formidable reputation and also succeeded in breaking with his friends among the *philosophes*, on both personal and intellectual grounds.

Rousseau first made his reputation with the *Discourse on the Arts and Sciences* (which already set him at odds with the 'Enlightenment'). Responding to critics of the *Discourse,* he begins to explain his objections to conceptions of society as held together by the bonds of personal interest, which laid the foundation for his political ideas:

> Our writers like to regard absolutely everything as 'the political masterpiece of the century': the sciences, the arts, luxury, commerce, laws – and all other bonds which, in tightening the social knot with the force of personal interest, make men mutually dependent, give them reciprocal needs and common interests, and require that all pursue the happiness of others in order to be able to pursue their own. These ideas are, to be sure, quite attractive, and can be presented in a most favorable light. But . . . [i]s it really such a wonderful thing to have made it impossible for men to live together without mutual bigotry, mutual competition, mutual deceit, mutual treason and mutual destruction? . . . After all, for every two men whose interests converge, there are perhaps one hundred thousand who are adversaries.[29]

Society in Rousseau's time, then, is, in his view, essentially and unavoidably adversarial. The commonality of private interests, whether sustained by force of law or by commercial networks, is largely a sham. In his replies to critics of the first *Discourse* (and there are hints in the *Discourse* itself), he already moves in the direction of singling out private property, with the inequalities that inevitably spring from it, as the principal cause of these

---

29 Jean-Jacques Rousseau, *Narcisse,* Preface, in *Political Theory,* Vol. 6, No. 4, November 1978, p. 549.

adversarial relations. In the second *Discourse* he develops this conception of society, in which men are divided between the rich few and the many who serve them, while the only social ties among them are the deceitful conventions that bind the many to obey and labour for the few, and the networks of commerce that make men rivals to each in the guise of mutual benefit. There can, in such conditions, be no genuine convergence of private interests and a public good; and any invocation of the public welfare or the common good can only be deception in the interests of a few, enforced by state coercion. In circumstances such as these, in other words, there can be no such thing as freedom.

Rousseau was thus from the start at odds with a wide range of thinkers who relied on commerce or the absolutist state, or both together, to sustain the social bond and convert private interests into public goods. At the same time, whatever his nostalgia for some ancient golden age of civic virtue, he denied the possibility of its return, if it ever existed at all. The problem he set himself, which would drive his political ideas from beginning to end, was to find a mechanism for attaining common goods that emanated freely from the individuals who shared them, rather than from some external power of coercion, but did not make unreasonable demands on civic virtue or depend on mutual deception.

In the first *Discourse*, written by Rousseau for a competition staged by the Academy of Dijon, he was replying to a question posed by the Academy: 'Has the restoration of the sciences and arts tended to purify morals?' Rousseau's reply in the negative was not as unusual or provocative as we might think or, indeed, as he himself liked to pretend. There were other contestants who denied the moral benefits of scientific and cultural progress as understood in eighteenth-century Europe; and, for that matter, there existed an important tradition, in the 'quarrel between the ancients and moderns', that questioned the value of modern cultural developments by associating them with Athenian aestheticism as against the civic virtue of ancient Rome or Sparta. Rousseau's departures from this tradition would become far more evident in the second *Discourse*, where his social and political radicalism comes to the fore; but the foundations are laid in the first *Discourse*.

In his reply to critics, Rousseau contemptuously dismisses a conventional reading of his attack on modern culture, which he sums up as follows:

'Knowledge is good for absolutely nothing, bad by nature, it does only ill. It can no more be separated from vice than ignorance from virtue. All literate peoples have been corrupt, all ignorant peoples virtuous. In a word, there is vice only among the learned, while a virtuous man is he alone who knows nothing. There can then be but one way for us to regain honesty; we must move with dispatch to proscribe both learning and the learned, to burn our libraries, to close our Academies, our colleges and our universities, and to plunge back into the barbarism of earliest times.'

There it is – all of what my adversaries have so effectively refuted.

Except that I never thought, never uttered one single word of any of it.

Nor could anything more contrary to my system be conceived than this absurd doctrine they have had the goodness to attribute to me.[30]

He goes on to say that morals have not, to be sure, been purified by cultural developments as we know them; but there remains the question of causal connections, and here Rousseau appears to suggest that the causes may lie not in learning itself but in its social context:

> What a strange and fatal condition – where accumulated riches facilitate still greater riches, but where men with none can acquire none; where the good man knows no way out of his misery; where the most roguish are the most honored and where virtue must be renounced for men to remain honest . . . And so, in the end, my vision is both consoling and useful, for it demonstrates that all these vices belong less to man than to man badly governed.[31]

This passage is significant enough in its attribution of 'vices' not to some universal human nature but to specific modes of organizing social life, but precisely what its author meant by 'man badly governed' would become clearer only in his later works. The first *Discourse*, nonetheless, already gives us some idea of where Rousseau is going. 'Luxury', he tells us,

> rarely develops without the sciences and arts, and they never develop without it . . . Granted that luxury is a sure sign of wealth, that it even serves, if you like, to increase wealth. What conclusion must be drawn from this paradox so worthy of our time; and what will become of virtue when one must get rich at any price? Ancient politicians incessantly talked about morals and virtue, those of our time talk only of business and money . . . They evaluate men like herds of cattle. According to them a man is worth no more to the State than the value of his domestic consumption.[32]

It is in the second *Discourse* that Rousseau lays out more precisely what he means when he attributes 'vices' not to human nature but to the social

---

30 *Ibid.*, p. 546.
31 *Ibid.*, p. 550.
32 Rousseau, *First Discourse*, in *The First and Second Discourses,* ed. Roger Masters (New York: St Martin's Press, 1964), p. 51.

contexts in which it manifests itself. At the very heart of the *Discourse on Inequality* is the principle that human beings have a *history* and not an abstract 'human nature'. Rousseau begins by dissociating himself from concepts of the 'state of nature' such as those proposed by Hobbes or Locke. 'The philosophers who have examined the foundations of society', he writes, 'have all felt the necessity of going back to the state of nature, but none of them has reached it.'[33] They have attributed to human beings in the state of nature ideas and practices – conceptions of justice, property and government – that derive from specific social conditions, which have a long history. The philosophers have ascribed to human nature characteristics that could arise only in specific social conditions. Rousseau would later reinforce this social definition of human nature in *Émile*, which, while ostensibly devoted to the development of a uniquely isolated individual, starts from the premise that even the sense of self is produced by relations with others, so that the development of individuality and the direction it takes depend on the nature of relations with others.[34]

What, then, can we say about the original 'nature' of humanity? There are two principles anterior to reason, Rousseau tells us. The first natural instinct is a love of self (*amour de soi*) or, more precisely, an instinct for self-preservation. But we should not, he immediately explains, make Hobbes's fundamental error in defining this natural instinct, which is to assume that the drive for self-preservation necessarily puts us in conflict with others and that 'by virtue of the right [man] claims to the things he needs, he foolishly imagines himself to be the sole proprietor of the whole universe.'[35] Hobbes was right to question all modern definitions of natural right, but he drew conclusions that were no less false. What he should have concluded from his own premises was that, since the state of nature – before the advent of property and government – is the condition in which our own self-preservation is least prejudicial to the self-preservation of others, it was more, not less, conducive to peace. Instead, Hobbes came to the opposite conclusion, because he ascribed to the natural instinct of self-preservation 'the need to satisfy a multitude of passions which are the product of society and which have made laws necessary'. This is not to say that 'savage' human beings are naturally 'good'. It is simply to acknowledge the social conditions that compel self-preservation to take one form rather than another.

The second original instinct is compassion (*pitié*), an 'innate repugnance' in human beings to see their fellows suffer. This instinct is, for example,

33   Rousseau, *Second Discourse,* in *ibid.,* p. 102.

34   For a detailed discussion of this point, see Ellen Meiksins Wood, *Mind and Politics: An Approach to the Meaning of Liberal and Socialist Individualism* (Berkeley: University of California Press, 1972).

35   Rousseau, *Second Discourse,* in *ibid.,* pp. 128–9.

recognized by Mandeville; but he fails to see, Rousseau insists, that this is the source of precisely those social virtues Mandeville seeks to deny, those very qualities that make it possible for human beings, in the right conditions, to promote the mutual preservation of the species. If this natural instinct is suppressed or overshadowed in contemporary society, that is, again, a function of social conditions that compel human beings to perceive their interests as mutually antagonistic.

There are, of course, natural differences among human beings, but these cannot by themselves account for the divisions of servitude and domination, or the capacity of some to live on the labour of others. The watershed in the development of humanity was the invention of private property. Rousseau may not be unambiguous about how this revolution came about; but one thing is clear: whatever the first cause of private property, or the social division of labour that seems to have brought it about, the invention of property was decisive in making inequality the principal determinant of social life. Whatever other inequalities there may be among human beings, whether rooted in psychology or innate talent, it is the invention of property that accounts for the divisions between masters and servants, those who labour and those who appropriate the labour of others, and finally the division between rulers and ruled. This also produces the transformation of *amour de soi* into *amour propre*, the conversion of an instinct for self-preservation into active egotism and the antagonisms of self-interest, which other philosophers have mistaken for the natural condition of humanity:

> in a word, competition and rivalry on one hand, opposition of interest on the other; and always the hidden desire to profit at the expense of others. All these evils are the first effect of property and the inseparable consequence of nascent inequality. [36]

It is this account of private property and its consequences that would from then on determine Rousseau's political philosophy. He would in his later work go on to oscillate between the stance of *Émile* (1762), which purports to portray the education of an isolated individual, divorced from a world in which civil society can never be anything but an instrument of the rich against the poor, and, in the same year, the apparently contrary impulse of the *Social Contract*, in which the civic bond is powerful and just. But – and here we should take seriously Rousseau's own contention that all these major works formed a unity – both these classics start from the same premise: that there can be no freedom in society as it now exists, grounded as it is in the inequalities of property and power.

The eponymous hero of *Émile* is educated to withstand all the inevitable

---

36   *Ibid.*, p. 156.

corruptions of a polity like France, with its inequalities of wealth and power, where the few exploit the labour of the many and society is bound together simply by commercial networks or the impositions of the absolutist state. He is, Rousseau seems to suggest, to be educated as a man and not as a citizen. Once Émile's private persona has been shaped, his political education will consist in being sheltered for some time from the real political world while he learns the principles of Rousseau's *Social Contract*, which will, presumably, help to inure him to corruption and maintain his autonomy when once he ventures into civic life.

Émile's arena as a man, before he is a citizen, is the household, not the state. It is in this context that Rousseau elaborates his controversial ideas about the role and education of women. Sometimes dismissed as pure misogyny for emphasizing the differences between women and men and reducing women to mere objects of men's pleasure, his arguments have also been interpreted as in some respects progressive, perhaps a reaction to the culture of the *salon*, which was then regarded as the province of elites guided by the tastes of leisured ladies. In interpretations such as these, Sophie represents a counter to aristocratic sensibilities or the pretensions of the bourgeoisie. What is clear is that, with the specific powers and intelligence Rousseau unquestionably ascribes to women (all great revolutions began with the women, he tells us, and an age when women lose their ascendancy and fail to make men respect their judgment will be the 'last stage of degradation'), Sophie will be the guiding spirit of the household and act as Émile's principal protector from the perversions of corrupt society.[37]

Whatever we make of Rousseau's views on women, with all his characteristic paradoxes, *Émile* must be understood less as a treatise on education – of men or of women – than as a deliberately stark antithesis to the social realities of his time and place. Rousseau denied that *Émile* was ever intended as a blueprint for an ideal education. His presentation of an isolated individual brought up in an artificial environment is an exercise of the imagination that presents a dramatic antithesis to the world as it is. It also amounts to a statement of despair: no good can come of a society constructed on the foundations of property and inequality. The *Social*

---

37   In Chapter 5, in his discussion of Sophie's education, Rousseau makes a significant observation about the difficulties that confront the institution of marriage in the world as it is: 'while social life develops character it differentiates classes, and these two classifications do not correspond, so that the greater the social distinctions, the greater the difficulty of finding the corresponding character. Hence we have ill-assorted marriages and all their accompanying evils; and we find that it follows logically that the further we get from equality, the greater the change in our natural feelings; the wider the distance between great and small, the looser the marriage tie; the deeper the gulf between rich and poor the fewer husbands and fathers. Neither master nor slave belongs to a family, but only to a class.'

Contract makes the leap from that counsel of despair to the portrayal of a civic order in which the social conditions from which *Émile* has withdrawn have somehow been transcended, and civil society can be constructed on a wholly new foundation.

The transition from the first two *Discourses* to the *Social Contract* is impossible to understand without the intervening step of the *Discourse on Political Economy*, where the core of his political thought and many of the key concepts developed in the *Social Contract* – the 'general will', the distinction between 'government' and 'sovereignty' – received their first elaboration. This is a fact of no small significance, and it is a pity that this work is so often neglected. Since the article was written for the *Encyclopédie*, there is every reason to suppose that its primary purpose, like that of many other contributions, was not simply to muse in abstraction about perennial questions but to subject contemporary French institutions to trenchant, if oblique, criticism. The article has a more immediate relation to the urgent issues of his time and place and to the conventional currents of debate than do his other works, and it helps to provide a means of tracing the central ideas of his political theory to their foundations in his specific historical context and in the social struggles of his time.

Rousseau was writing in a tradition of social criticism that decried the corruption of the court, an inflated royal bureaucracy, and an exploitative system of taxation which served not only public purposes but private gain. In these grievances and proposals for reform, the state generally took centre stage, both as the object of complaint and as the proposed agent of reform, often in the same breath. Reformers often presented their cases in the form of claims for the *public* sphere against the essentially *private* character of the feudal principles still embodied in the state and the system of privilege.

It is against this background that Rousseau's political theory must be understood. It has, for example, been said that he was the thinker who 'reduced the *thèse nobiliaire* and the *thèse royale* to insignificance' and who 'put the political problem on an entirely new basis, that of pure democracy.'[38] This may seem an odd and objectionable proposition to those who regard Rousseau's concept of the 'general will' and his provocative formula 'forced to be free' as supremely undemocratic, even 'totalitarian'. But such interpretations seem less plausible when Rousseau's political ideas are grounded in the context of absolutist France. The *Discourse on Political Economy* reveals how his theory of popular sovereignty was shaped by a criticism of specifically French conditions, the French absolutist state and its attendant evils, and how traditional debates surrounding these conditions served to fix the terms in which his argument was cast.

Like Bodin and Montchrétien, Rousseau approaches the issue of the

---

38   Ed. Neumann, introduction to Montesquieu, *Spirit of the Laws*, p. xxix.

French state by first considering the household/state analogy; and he effectively declares his opposition to the prevailing principles of that state by
immediately attacking the analogy. In its original French usage, political
economy – referring to the management of national resources to increase
the nation's prosperity – implied an analogy between the household or
family and the state. While the state economy is designated 'political' to
distinguish its generality and its public character from the particularity and
the private nature of the domestic economy, the distinction presupposes a
significant similarity between the art of state management and *oikonomia*,
the art of household management. It is this similarity that Rousseau questions in the article on political economy; and, by rejecting the analogy as a
basis for redefining the concept of 'political economy', he is making a statement about the set of historical conditions for which that analogy stands.

It is in this context that the 'general will' appears. The concept of the
general will is usually treated by commentators – whether hostile or sympathetic to Rousseau – as simply a principle governing the conduct of citizens;
but in the *Political Economy*, Rousseau's general will has a different object.
Here, his argument is, in the first instance, directed not at the individual
citizen but at the 'magistrate' or rulers. His purpose in attacking the house-
hold/state analogy is to demonstrate that the magistrate cannot legitimately
act in accordance with principles appropriate to the head of a household.
'The principal object of the efforts of the whole house', argues Rousseau, 'is
to conserve and increase the patrimony of the father.'[39] This principle of
private, domestic 'economy' if applied to the state – treating the state as a
means of increasing the 'patrimony' of the magistrate – is fatal to the public
interest. The magistrate, therefore, unlike the father who governs the household, cannot rely on his personal, natural inclinations and passions as a
standard for governing the state but must follow 'no other rule but public
reason, which is the law'.[40] The concept of the general will is introduced to
express the uniquely public principle that should regulate the governance of
the 'political economy', the management of the state. It is the principle to be
followed by the magistrate, the government, whose function is simply to
execute the public 'will' which expresses the interests of the community.

At this stage in Rousseau's argument, then, the concept of the general
will represents an attempt to define the state as a truly public thing, not a
form of private property, and to locate the legitimacy of government in its
adherence to the public will and interests of the people, not the private will
and interests of the magistrate. Rousseau would later extend the principle of
the general will to the community of citizens, especially in the *Social*

---

39   Rousseau, *A Discourse on Political Economy*, in *The Social Contract and Discourses*, ed. G.D.H. Cole (New York: Dutton, 1950), p. 286.
   40   *Ibid.*, p. 288.

Contract. In the Political Economy Rousseau introduces the concepts around which the *Social Contract* is built: sovereignty, the distinction between sovereignty and government, the general will. At least parts of the article seem to have been drawn from the work Rousseau had already done for his projected major study of political institutions, a project he never completed as planned except in the abbreviated form of the *Social Contract,* which he described as an extract from it. The essential unity of the *Discourse on Political Economy* and the *Social Contract* is evident in the first version of the latter work, the so-called Geneva manuscript, where some of the major points of the *Political Economy* – notably some remarks on the household/state analogy – appear almost verbatim. The *Political Economy* and the *Social Contract* belong to the same structure of argumentation, and the logic of the latter work remains incomplete in the absence of ideas contained in the former.

In the *Discourse on Political Economy*, Rousseau first draws a distinction between government and sovereignty and proceeds to outline a theory of *government*, which he treats as synonymous with 'political economy'. In the *Social Contract*, Rousseau develops the theory of *sovereignty*, which is the other side of the coin, only touched upon in the earlier article. In the interim, his interest may actually have shifted from the problem of government to the problem of sovereignty, with a growing conviction that only true popular sovereignty and radical democracy, not simply a reformed and enlightened government, could correct the social ills outlined in his earlier works. In the *Political Economy* the 'general will' is introduced as 'the first principle of public economy and the fundamental rule of government'.[41] The point of this formulation is to identify legitimate government as government in which 'the magistrates belong to the people' and not the reverse, so that the interests it serves are not simply those of the rulers. The *Social Contract* proceeds from here.

Both Bodin and even the less 'absolutist' Montchrétien had constructed the analogy between household and state on the assumption that the king, with the help of his officers, is the appropriate agent of the common good, the representative of universality and the general or public interest, as against the particular and partial interests that comprise the body politic. It is precisely this assumption that Rousseau rejects when he attacks the analogy. His own argument is based on the contrary assumption that rulers are just as likely as are their subjects – indeed, even more likely – to represent a particular or partial interest. For Rousseau, the household/state analogy – in which the state is treated, in effect, as a private estate – simply confirms the reality of the French state and the use of public office, including the office of king, as private property. He insists that a completely different principle – opposed to the private motivations of household management,

---

41   *Ibid.*, p. 292.

with its goal of increasing the patrimony of the master – must guide the management of the state.

Having criticized the analogy on which the notion of political economy is based, he must then go on to redefine 'political economy' itself accordingly, in keeping with the uniquely public purpose of the state. It is here that he introduces the distinction between sovereignty, the supreme legislative power, and government or 'public economy', which merely executes the will of the sovereign.[42] Rousseau was, as we have seen, not the first to draw a distinction between sovereignty and government. Bodin had elaborated that distinction long before. But the differences between Bodin and Rousseau on this score are even more striking than the similarities.

Rousseau's purpose in adopting a similar conceptual device is precisely the opposite of Bodin's. Although, like Bodin, he identifies sovereignty with the power of legislation and maintains the indivisibility of sovereign power, his object in doing so is quite different. Where Bodin's argument is a defence of royal absolutism, Rousseau's is an attack upon it. Rousseau's distinction – again in a sense like Bodin's – is intended to relegate the functions of the magistrate or government to a subordinate position, subject to and dependent upon a higher principle or 'general will'. Yet his intention is not to consolidate but to undermine the power of rulers. The 'Magistrate' stands not only for lesser officials but for all rulers, including kings; and the general will becomes not the will of the ruler, not a manifestation of his supremacy, but an expression of his subordination to the community.

Where Bodin subordinates the particularity of the people to the universality of the ruler, Rousseau subordinates the particularity of the ruler to the universality of the people. For Rousseau, the sovereign will is not something that creates a community out of particular and partial interests by imposing itself from without through royal legislation and the art of public management or 'political economy'. Instead, it is something that emanates from the community itself, expressing its actual common interests, and is imposed on those – the magistrate, the government, the agents of 'public economy' – whose function is merely to execute that will. The logic of this argument demands that it culminate in a radical theory of popular sovereignty, giving full effect to the principle that the sovereign will emanates from the community by actually vesting the sovereign legislative power in a popular assembly. In the *Discourse on Political Economy* Rousseau did not pursue that logic to its conclusion, but he certainly did in the *Social Contract*.

If Rousseau's argument owes a great deal in its form to the idiom of absolutism and to the language of a single, supreme and indivisible public will, he turns that idiom against itself. As many theorists have done, he adopts the form of his adversary's argument to attack its substance. There may be

---

42   *Ibid.*, p. 289.

an element of truth in the proposition that the only French 'tradition of discourse' to which Rousseau was 'not much indebted' was constitutionalism and that, while 'he was one of the great proponents of the rule of law . . . his dedication to that principle was distinct from that of French constitutionalists such as Domat or Montesquieu.' In particular:

> In Rousseau's theory, law is identified with the sovereign will, as it was in the absolutist tradition, rather than an external bridle on that will, as it was in the constitutive laws of the French polity. His hostility to intermediate bodies in the state and scorn for representative assemblies, set him off clearly from the constitutionalist tradition.[43]

Yet if Rousseau departed from the constitutionalist tradition, it is in part because the mainstream of French constitutionalism (and arguably even its radical Huguenot form) did not imply a transfer of sovereign legislative power to the 'people' even as embodied in representative institutions. Rousseau's concern is not merely to 'bridle' the absolutist monarchy but to overturn it, not simply to guide sovereign power but to transfer it. But there is another sense in which Rousseau's argument is, after all, best understood in relation to French constitutionalism, at least in its more radical form as exemplified by the Huguenot resistance movement.

The ideological strategy adopted by the Huguenot constitutionalists in their assault on absolutism was, as we have seen, to confront absolutism on its own ground by stressing the particularity of the monarch, attacking his treatment of the state as private property. They insisted instead on the 'people's' proprietary right in the state, asserting that the 'people' constitute the 'majesty' of the king, and transferred the public 'mind' from the king to the 'people', embodied in their officers and representative institutions – 'one mind compounded out of many'. Rousseau's strategy is strikingly similar, except in one decisive respect. He also proceeds by attacking the proprietary character of the absolutist state and the particularity of the ruler, and counterposes to them a common public will residing in the community; and he also maintains that the ruler is constituted by the people. At the same time, he perceives a threat not only in the particularity of the monarch but in that of the 'Magistrate' in general. He therefore locates the public will not in the 'public council', in officials and 'intermediate bodies', or in assemblies of estates, but in the people themselves.

Rousseau's attitude towards 'intermediate bodies' is often regarded as one of the more alarming aspects of his thought, an attack on the most cherished principles of liberalism, checks on state power, the freedom of

---

43   Nannerl Keohane, *Philosophy and the State in France: The Renaissance to the Enlightenment* (Princeton: Princeton University Press, 1980), p. 442.

association and opinion, of individual dissent and minority rights, and so on. This is, again, to misread Rousseau's meaning by extracting his argument from its historical setting. Rousseau's refusal to lodge the public will in intermediate institutions does indeed cut him off from the French constitutionalist tradition even in its most radical forms. Yet his rejection of these institutions should not be understood as a ('totalitarian') violation of constitutionalist principles but rather as an attempt to extend and democratize them. Rousseau shares with the radical constitutionalists their concern for transforming the state into a truly 'public' thing which derives its public or general character from the people. That is precisely the message of the *Discourse on Political Economy*.

In the *Social Contract*, if not unequivocally in the earlier article, Rousseau advances from the creation of a truly public magistrate – a magistrate answerable in some unspecified way to the demands of the common good, the 'general will' – to the actual embodiment of that common good and the general will in a functioning popular sovereign. If, in the process, he resumes the language of absolutism in order to vest in the people the powers hitherto lodged in the absolute monarchy, he travels that route not past but through the concerns of constitutionalism and the tradition of popular resistance.

Chapter 1 begins with his famous proposition that 'Man is born free; and everywhere he is in chains.' The 'social contract' as hitherto imagined by philosophers simply represents, in one form or another, a contract of subjection. Rousseau offers an alternative formulation of the principles on which a just and free civic order should be founded. Stripped of inessentials, it comes down to this: 'Each of us puts his person and all his power in common under the supreme direction of the general will, and, in corporate capacity, we receive each member as an indivisible part of the whole.'[44] But to make this undertaking more than just an empty formula, it must be understood to mean that anyone who refuses to obey the general will shall be compelled to do so; and this means nothing less than that 'he will be forced to be free'.[45]

Rousseau might simply have said that civil society, which replaces our liberty in the state of nature with a new kind of civil liberty, including secure proprietorship of our possessions, requires obedience to law; but, instead of making the point that we relinquish certain freedoms in exchange for, and to gain the protection of, others, he chooses to formulate the meaning of his 'social contract' in a deliberately paradoxical and provocative way. We can, up to a point, discount his penchant for paradox and provocation; but there is clearly something more to be said to allay the suspicion that Rousseau is advocating something like 'totalitarian democracy'.

---

44 Rousseau, *Social Contract*, in ed. Cole, *The Social Contract and Discourses*, p. 15.
45 *Ibid.*, p. 18.

Let us first be clear what Rousseau is *not* saying. In invoking the general will, Rousseau is not suggesting that it exists as an abstract 'common good' that can be imposed from without whatever the will of the individuals who constitute the sovereign power. It is, above all, a rule of thumb, the question citizens must ask themselves when they exercise their sovereign power. So, for example, 'the law of public order in assemblies is not so much to maintain in them the general will as to secure that the question be put to it, and the answer always given by it.'[46] A legislative assembly, in other words, should ask itself what decision would promote not this or that private interest but the public good. The general will is not, to be sure, synonymous with the 'will of all'. A majority may choose, and choose knowingly, a course that does not express the general will because it is not conducive to the common good; but no one can claim (as a Robespierre might do) to represent the general will against the will of the majority. When the social bond is broken and there is no common sense of what constitutes the public good, the general will is mute. The principle that the liberty of citizens requires the realization of the general will 'presupposes, indeed, that all the qualities of the general will still reside in the majority: when they cease to do so, whatever side a man may take, liberty is no longer possible.'[47]

Whatever else we can say about Rousseau's general will, it is clear that it can only reside in a sovereign people and can only be effected by at least a majority. It cannot be imposed by a governor who claims to know better. The point is reinforced by Rousseau's account of the distinction between sovereignty and government. While the act of association that establishes the sovereign power can be treated as a contract, the executive power of government cannot be conceived in this way: it is clear, says Rousseau, 'that the institution of government is not a contract, but a law; that the depositories of the executive power are not the people's masters, but its officers; that it can set them up and pull them down when it likes; that for them there is no question of contract, but of obedience'.[48]

But if the people, and not the prince or other magistrates, are truly sovereign, in a way not envisaged by any of Rousseau's Enlightenment compatriots, what checks are there on the sovereign people themselves? It is certainly true to say that Rousseau did not devote his attention to the rights of the minority or to constitutional checks on sovereign power; and it may not be enough to say that, in his time and place, he was preoccupied less by how the sovereign people should conduct themselves than by how their sovereignty could be defended against all other claimants. But the very least that we can say is that his views on 'intermediate bodies', which are commonly regarded as the

---

46   *Ibid.*, p. 104.
47   *Ibid.*, p. 107.
48   *Ibid.*, pp. 99–100.

most telling evidence of a distinctively 'illiberal' turn of mind, have a rather different meaning if we read them in context.

It is again a question of historical perspective. The 'intermediate bodies' that concern the French constitutionalists are not the 'voluntary associations' so important to English liberals, organizations in the private sphere as distinct from – and, at least potentially, against – organs of the state.[49] The French 'intermediate bodies' are the corporate and representative institutions – estates, *parlements,* municipalities, and colleges – which constituted part of *la police*, organs of the polity. It is these institutions whose role in the state constitutionalists proposed to increase, in varying degrees and with varying preferences for some over others. But neither are these bodies legislative assemblies on the model of the English Parliament. These were, in effect, feudal remnants, fragments of the feudal 'parcellized' state. They were recognized, and defended, as such by constitutionalists even as late as Montesquieu, who regarded these elements of 'Gothic' government as essential to the 'moderation' and legitimacy of the French monarchy. This implied, too, that the notion of intermediate bodies was, in the eighteenth century as before, often closely associated with the defence of aristocratic power and might be not only undemocratic but anti-democratic in spirit.

In the eighteenth century, even more explicitly than before, the principle of 'particular' or intermediate powers interposed between king and people was invoked to support the enlargement of power for the nobility, as in the *thèse nobiliaire*. In these formulations the claims of the nobility against the absolutist monarchy were likely to be equally claims against the Third Estate. The notion of constitutional checks and balances thus assumed a clearly aristocratic cast. The theory of intermediate powers was opposed to popular power more unequivocally than were English theories of representation, however undemocratic the intentions of the latter might be. Those who, like Montesquieu, preferred the *parlements* as the model of intermediate powers only partly modified the aristocratic character of the principle by extending it to include the *noblesse de robe*; and their principal claim to autonomy was the venality of office. Even in more radical and anti-absolutist or constitutionalist formulations, as we have seen in the case of the Huguenots, the insistence on intermediate bodies had the deliberate effect

---

49 As for Rousseau's views on voluntary associations, it is worth considering his remarks on the *cercles* of Geneva in the *Lettre à d'Alembert* and his answers to criticisms of these remarks voiced by his friends among the burghers of Geneva who felt that the *cercles* corrupted the republic's artisans and gave them an excessive taste for independence. Rousseau suggests in reply that these *cercles* provide the appropriate education for free citizens, midway between the public education of Greece and the domestic education of monarchies 'where all subjects must remain isolated and must have nothing in common but obedience'. Letter to Theodore Tronchin, 26 November 1758, *Correspondance Complète,* ed. R.A. Leigh (Geneva: Institut et Musée Voltaire, 1965), Vol. V, p. 743.

of limiting not only monarchical but also popular power – for example, by stressing that the right of resistance belonged to the 'people' only as embodied in their officers and corporate representatives. Given the historical meaning and ideological function of these institutions in French political experience, the defence of intermediate bodies did not lend itself so easily to democratic extrapolation and extension, not even to the extent permitted by English theories of parliamentary representation. A democratic argument such as Rousseau's would, in that context, almost inevitably be formulated as an attack on intermediate institutions.

The 'General Will' Redefined

In the end, the question comes down to the particular social interests at stake. For those who felt aggrieved at their inadequate access to the means of extra-economic appropriation provided by the state, for those who, even when they were subject to the state's appropriation through taxation, themselves appropriated the labour of others, constitutional reforms designed to give them a piece of the state might serve very well. But these were not the interests represented by Rousseau. His concern, clearly expressed in the *Discourse on Political Economy*, was for those on whose labour the whole structure of privilege, office, and taxation rested: small producers and notably peasants. Much of the *Political Economy* is devoted to the problem of taxation, and Rousseau's proposals for reforming the fiscal system are explicitly designed to relieve the peasants who bear its brunt. It is here that he provides the clearest insight into his view of the existing state as a system of private appropriation and exploitation; and this is the specific target of his proposals for reform:

> Are not all advantages of society for the powerful and rich? Do they not fill all lucrative posts? Are not all privileges and exemptions reserved for them? . . . [W]hatever the poor pay is lost to them forever, and remains in or returns to the hands of the rich; and, as it is precisely to those men who take part in government, or to their connections, that the proceeds of taxation sooner or later pass, even when they pay their share they have a keen interest in increasing taxes.[50]

The terms of the social contract as it actually exists between the two conditions of men can, Rousseau suggests, be summed up as follows: 'You need me, because I am rich and you are poor; let us therefore make an agreement: I will permit you the honour of serving me, on the condition that you give

---

50 Rousseau, *Political Economy*, in ed. Cole, *The Social Contract and Discourses*, pp. 322–3.

me the little that remains to you for the pains I shall take to command you.'[51]
This is the principle on which taxation is now based. Rousseau proposes a
system of taxation based on opposing principles, by reforming the state to
eliminate the use of taxation as a means of private appropriation and by
transferring the tax burden for clearly public purposes to those more able to
bear it, in a system of progressive taxation. He dismisses with contempt the
idea that the peasant will lapse into idleness if not compelled to work by the
demands of taxation: 'Because for him who loses the fruits of his labour, to
do nothing is to gain something; and to impose a fine on labour is a very odd
way of banishing idleness.'[52]

Rousseau was not, of course, alone in proposing to reform the system of
taxation, privilege, and exemption, corrupt administration and venal
offices. Similar reforms were part of the Enlightenment agenda in general,
with its demands for rationalization of the state and the fiscal apparatus,
the unification of law and administration, and a system of office open to
merit. All these proposals for reform were in one way or another, directly or
indirectly, conditioned by the function of the state as an instrument of
appropriation, a private resource, even if some reformers wanted only to
extend access to its fruits. And many reformers were convinced of the need
to redistribute the burden of taxation in order to stop the drain on the countryside which fed the luxuries of city and court.

Yet Rousseau was alone among the great Enlightenment thinkers to focus
on the political structure specifically as a system of exploitation, and to do
so not simply from the paternalistic vantage point of enlightened elites but
from the perspective of the petty producers whose labour was exploited. He
could not be content with reforms that would merely rationalize the apparatus of office that appropriated the fruits of peasant labour. To the extent
that his political reforms were intended to attack the state not simply as an
inefficient, unequal, or illiberal system of administration and representation
but as a system of exploitation, he had eventually to conclude that only
absolute popular sovereignty, as the sole means of displacing altogether the
proprietary state, would suffice.

Once Rousseau had decided on the necessity of true popular sovereignty
if the state and its officers were indeed to be subject to 'public reason', he
was obliged to consider how the 'general will' could actually operate, not
merely as a notional standard for the behaviour of rulers and citizens but as
a practical and active principle of political organization, a 'will' actually
emanating from the people and expressed in practice as law. His answer was
again shaped by the particular conditions of the existing French state and by
the particular ways in which his adopted countrymen had formulated their

---

51 *Ibid.*, pp. 323–4.
52 *Ibid.*, pp. 324–5.

own responses to questions about the common good, how it is to be deter-mined and implemented. The typical French solution, as we have seen, conjured up a single public will, usually embodied in the monarch, or a collection of partial and selfish interests woven together by the king and the officers of the state. None of these solutions, not even those which replaced the monarchical will with 'one mind compounded out of many', simply redefined the common good as a public interest constituted by private inter-ests which would magically coalesce by the workings of an invisible hand, or aggregate themselves in the process of deliberation and legislation by a Parliament representing private interests. That may have been the English model, but it did not conform to French conditions.

When Montesquieu argued that republican government required special virtue, and that monarchy had the advantage of allowing the implementa-tion of the common good with minimal virtue or self-sacrifice on the part of its subjects, he was expressing an assumption common to all these formulations: that while self-interest could serve as the basis of society, perhaps through the networks of commerce, the common good would not naturally emerge out of the interplay of private interests but required either the virtuous suppression of natural self-love or the active interven-tion of a 'harmonizing' state – not, it must be emphasized, through the medium of representative bodies that assembled all competing interests but as a single unifying will most likely embodied in the absolutist monarch or at least a 'legal despotism'. If the English (and their Scottish spokes-men) in contrast thought – or purported to think – otherwise, especially in the eighteenth century, their optimism did not reflect a greater faith in human nature or an absence of deep divisions in English society. It had more to do with the particular conditions of their economy, a rising capi-talism, especially during that brief period when England's commercial empire reigned supreme. It also presupposed the traditionally unitary character of English representative institutions and the relatively secure and united propertied classes whose triumph over both king and people was expressed in the supremacy of Parliament.

French pessimism on this score did not prevent political thinkers from proposing self-love and self-interest as the proper motivating forces of the body politic. Indeed, as we have seen, it became a common theme to suggest that selfish passions translated into interest could be the basis of public well-being, and even that society could fruitfully be conceived as a commer-cial transaction. Yet this view of society, far from disputing the need for strong monarchical power, generally served to emphasize its necessity. The disruptive and divisive character of commercial transactions, in which all parties pursue their own selfish gain, was as essential to this imagery as were the benefits of commerce. Arguments that, in England, might serve to support a doctrine of limited government might, in France, appear in defence of royal absolutism or even, as in physiocratic doctrine, *laissez faire, laissez passer* enforced by 'legal despotism'. In any case, whether such arguments were marshalled in support of absolutism or 'moderate' constitutional monarchy, the notion of a polity based on the harmony of selfish interests tended to postulate as its necessary condition an alien integrating will.

This is the context in which Rousseau formulated his conception of the general will as an expression of the common good emanating from the sovereign people. Much of his work, even before the *Social Contract,* had been devoted, directly or indirectly, to attacking the conception of society as a commercial transaction in which everyone sought his own gain in the other's loss or enlisted the aid of others only by persuading (or, more likely, deceiving) them to see their own profit in granting it. It is the consequence of property and inequality, he wrote, that each man

> must therefore incessantly seek to interest them in his fate, and to make them find their own profit, in fact or in appearance, in working for his. This makes him deceitful and sly with some, imperious and harsh with others, and makes it necessary for him to abuse all those whom he needs when he cannot make them fear him and not find his interest in serving them usefully.[53]

For Rousseau, such mutual deception was not a cure but a symptom. It was nonsense to suppose that the social bond and the common good could be based on the antagonisms of interest that divided people. Rousseau was bound to be especially hostile to this self-contradictory notion in view of its association with the idea of an external mediating will in the person of a powerful ruler. It clearly seemed to him especially absurd to imagine that a single, monarchical will, or even the will of a plural magistrate, which itself represented a very particular interest, could weld together a common good out of these antagonistic particularisms. At the same time, it was entirely in keeping with his conception of personal autonomy to adopt the view that self-love ought to act as the source of the public good. He therefore set himself the task of discovering how self-love and self-interest could produce a common good without the mediation of 'commercial' transactions or mutual deception and without the intervention of an alien will. His object was to find a form of social organization in which the social bond was based not on what divided people but on what united them, a common interest composed of interests that people really had in common.

It is, then, a mistake to think that in his concept of the general will Rousseau is proposing the suppression of natural instincts and the

---

53 Rousseau, *Discourse on Inequality,* in ed. Masters, *First and Second Discourses,* p. 156.

submergence of self-interest in an abstract 'general will', the individual in
the collectivity; nor is it helpful to suggest some kind of antithesis between
the 'individualism' of a Diderot and the 'collectivism' of Rousseau.[54]
Individual interests are not, for Rousseau, in principle opposed to the general
will, any more than *amour de soi* is synonymous with *amour propre*.
Interests are 'partial' as opposed to 'general' only when circumstances put
them necessarily and essentially in opposition to the interests of others, in
the sense that one person's gain is another's loss. Society as it is now constituted forces interests into such mutual antagonism. Rousseau simply
acknowledges that no amount of reason or enlightenment will induce these
divisive impulses to serve as the basis of social cohesion, at least not without
mass delusion or autocratic imposition, both of which are not only undesir-
able but unreliable. The point is precisely that people cannot be made to will
what is against their self-interest. Summarizing the argument of his
Discourse on the Origin of Inequality, Rousseau writes elsewhere:

> When finally all particular interests conflict with one another, when self-
> love [*amour de soi*] in ferment becomes egotism [*amour propre*], so that
> opinion, making the whole universe necessary to each man, makes men
> born enemies to one another and compels each man to find his advantage
> only in the other's loss, then conscience, weaker than inflamed passions, is
> extinguished by them, and remains in the mouths of men only as a word
> designed for mutual deception. Each one then pretends to wish to sacrifice
> his own interests to those of the public, and all of them are lying. No one
> wants the public good unless it accords with his own; thus this accord is
> the object of true politics which seeks to make people happy and good.[55]

This is far from saying that self-interest is in principle opposed to the
common good; indeed, it is to assert that it *must* be the source of the
common good. If the 'general will' has any meaning, it is only on the understanding that people actually do have individual self-interests in common,
interests that are common not only when mediated by commerce or an
external will, but intrinsically; and politics must be built on this common
foundation.

The *Social Contract* outlines the political principles appropriate to a
society so organized. Though Rousseau is never unequivocally clear about
the social pre-conditions for such a political order, his social criticism,

---

54   See Philipp Blom, *A Wicked Company: Freethinkers and Friendship in pre-
Revolutionary Paris* (London: Weidenfeld & Nicholson, 2011), where the quarrel between Diderot and Rousseau is characterized in this way.
55   Lettre à Christophe de Beaumont, *Oeuvres Complètes* (Paris: Gallimard, 1964),
Vol. IV, p. 937.

especially in the first and second *Discourses*, suggests very strongly that a complete transformation of society would be required. He never tells us how this transformation might be brought about. In the *Social Contract* the best he can do is introduce a kind of *deus ex machina*, the Legislator who lays the foundation for the new society and then withdraws himself. But elsewhere – for example, in his letter to d'Alembert – Rousseau gives indications of how his ideal society might be constituted: a small community of independent petty producers, more or less self-sufficient peasants and artisans. However utopian this picture may be, and however naïve in its understanding of modern economics, it expresses clearly the principle which for Rousseau is the basis of a free society: that no one should be able to appropriate the labour of others or be forced to alienate his own. In the *Social Contract*, he suggests that the fundamental principles of the common good are liberty, the absence of individual dependence, and equality, which is the condition of liberty. These require a distribution of power and wealth in which no citizen can do violence to another and 'no citizen is rich enough to buy another, and none poor enough to be forced to sell himself'.[56]

It is, at the very least, clear that there are conditions without which the social contract cannot exist. For the general will to represent an expression – not an unnaturally (and impossibly) virtuous or forcible violation – of their own self-interest, people must actually, objectively, have interests in common. The common ground shared by interests in society as it is actually constituted is simply too narrow. To widen the scope of commonality requires the removal of those social relations and institutions, most especially inequality, that render people in reality and necessarily enemies by interest. Democratic sovereignty, it appears, is the necessary condition for a state based on 'public reason', rather than on the private interest of the magistrate; and social equality, the breakdown of the division between appropriators and producers, is the condition of democracy.

Rousseau's controversial concept of the 'general will' should, then, be treated not as an idiosyncracy but as an innovation on an old French theme, not as a disturbingly illiberal answer to English questions about the relation between private rights and public interests but as a radically democratic answer to French questions about the source of universality and the public will.

---

56 Rousseau, *Social Contract*, in ed. Cole, *Social Contract and Discourses*, p. 50.

7

THE ENGLISH REVOLUTION

Between late October and early November of 1647, in the midst of civil war,
something extraordinary happed at Putney, south of London. Certainly one
of the most remarkable episodes in English history, it was and remains a
unique historical event. In the course of civil war, the New Model Army, the
distinctively well-organized and disciplined military force constructed by
Oliver Cromwell and his supporters in their conflict with the royalists, was
proving to be not just an effective military machine but a militant political
force. Yet deep divisions had emerged between the army 'grandees' and radicals within the rank and file. Against the oligarchic leanings of Cromwell
and his allies, and even in fear of a restored monarchy, radicals had drafted
a constitution, the first ever in history, intended to establish something like
a democratic form of government based on a conception of inalienable
rights: 'An Agreement of the People for a Firm and Present Peace, upon
Grounds of Common-Right and Freedom; as it was Proposed by the Agents
of the Five Regiments of Horse; and Since by the General Approbation of
the Army, Offered to the Joint Concurrence of All Free COMMONS of
ENGLAND'. This draft constitution was the subject of a thorough debate,
which began in St Mary's Church, Putney and continued at the lodgings of
the Army's quartermaster general.

   That there exists a documentary record in the form of a transcript taken
down at the time is a truly astonishing piece of historical luck. It allows us
to follow, in the colourful and moving words of the participants themselves,
a debate conducted not only in the cool light of reason but also in the heat
of passion, about some of the most fundamental questions of social organization and political governance. These debates are being conducted not by
philosophers or theologians but by activists and soldiers, speaking in their
own language, often the language of the Levellers, political militants and
theorists accustomed to addressing not scholars, priests or lawyers but
craftsmen, yeoman farmers and the Army rank and file.

The Tudor Era

The remarkable events at Putney no doubt have much to do with personalities and the unpredictable contingencies of civil war; but the issues at stake and the terms in which the ideological battle was joined are inexplicable without reference to a larger historical context, the specific patterns of English economic and political development. In Chapter 1, we considered briefly how the social and political organization of England – in particular, the process of state-formation and the development of agrarian capitalism – differed from that of its neighbours and specifically from what may have appeared, in the seventeenth century, to be the most advanced and powerful kingdom, France. The 'absolutist' state in France was built on a foundation of corporate institutions and competing jurisdictions, while England already had a more strongly unitary state. The French ruling class still depended to a significant extent on 'extra-economic' powers, or 'politically constituted property', which now included office in the monarchical state, giving them access to the fruits of peasant labour in the form of taxes instead of only rents. English landlords, relying more and more on purely 'economic' forms of appropriation, depended on their tenants' profitable production. A vast proportion of land in France remained in the possession of peasants. In England, land was more concentrated in the hands of large proprietors and worked by tenant farmers, increasingly on economic leases, which made them unusually subject to the pressures of economic competition. While French agriculture in the seventeenth century was still largely tied to traditional methods of peasant farming, English landlords and their tenants were already becoming increasingly interested in agricultural 'improvement', finding means to enhance the productivity of labour in response to competitive pressures, especially by innovative use of land, which required redefinition of property rights. This would produce a unique historical dynamic of self-sustaining growth that sharply distinguished England from its neighbours – a difference that would be clearly visible when the English economy alone escaped the general European crisis of the late seventeenth century.

Between the sixteenth and eighteenth centuries, in response to the imperatives of competition and 'improvement', there were mounting assaults on customary rights, assertions of exclusive private ownership against communal rights to common land, challenges to customary tenures and an assortment of use rights to private land, together with various oppressive practices and extortionate rents, accompanied by legal and theoretical efforts to redefine the meaning of property, all of them fiercely contested. These distinctively English patterns in the development of the state and property, not surprisingly, gave rise to specific kinds of conflict, and they defined the major political issues in particular ways. So, for example, where taxation was the major grievance for French peasants, English smallholders were more concerned with protecting their customary rights and warding off expropriation.

The developments that produced these specifically English conditions stand out in sharp relief during the sixteenth century. The Tudor monarchy, while continuing the process of state-centralization that had begun long before, consolidated it in particularly visible ways, not least in the establishment of a state Church. At the same time, the realignment of property relations caused major social disruptions. Historians may still disagree about the condition of the English economy in the sixteenth century, whether it was marked by economic growth or declining living standards (or, indeed, both); but, while it may be safe to say that, in the seventeenth century and even perhaps in the latter part of the previous one, living standards for sections of the population were relatively high by European standards (and by the eighteenth century would be more unambiguously so), there is little doubt that many paid a heavy price for it. The sixteenth century was marked by widespread dispossession and distress, causing social upheavals, riots and rebellions of various kinds – as well as the first compulsory system of poor relief, which says much about both England's wealth, the newly consolidated powers of the central state, and the social disruptions it was compelled to confront.

Some historians dispute the extent of eviction by enclosure in the sixteenth century – in particular, enclosure to replace arable with pasture – and there were certainly other economic causes of dispossession and poverty. But there is no mistaking where contemporary observers, not least the Tudor monarchy and its officials, sought to place the blame: a growing propertyless class, which they attributed mainly to enclosure for highly profitable sheep-farming at a time when the economy was not yet ready to absorb a host of dispossessed labourers, was producing a plague of vagrancy and vagabondage. This rabble of 'masterless' men aroused deep trepidation among the ruling classes and spawned a distinctive literature of social criticism, intended not to justify rebellion by disadvantaged classes, nor even necessarily to voice a protest on their behalf, but to articulate the anxieties of their superiors, indeed the Tudor monarchy itself, with a view to bringing the ruling classes to their senses in the face of growing lawlessness, theft, and the danger of civil disorder.[1]

Under the Tudors, one act after another was passed – without much effect – to limit enclosure. It is certainly true that the monarchy had reasons to exaggerate the threat, if only to challenge the power of the landed aristocracy; but there were also critics of enclosure who were more inclined to promote aristocratic power against an overweening monarchy. One such

---

1   On this literature, see Neal Wood, *Foundations of Political Economy: Some Early Tudor Views on State and Society* (Berkeley: University of California Press, 1994).

LIBERTY AND PROPERTY

critic was Thomas Starkey. His *Dialogue Between Pole and Lupset*, apparently written in the 1530s but undiscovered till the nineteenth century, lays out a programme of reform which (though he served as chaplain to Henry VIII) seems intended to balance the powers of the centralizing monarchy with a stronger aristocracy, creating an educated and enlightened ruling class capable of maintaining civil order by improving the conditions of the people. There was also a group of highly placed clerics of Lutheran inclinations in the Church of England – the so-called Commonwealthmen – who, though never openly attacking government or calling for political reform, presented a devastating picture of England's social conditions, spiralling prices, dispossession, poverty, homelessness and growing vagrancy. The blame, it seems, lay largely with 'ungentle gentlemen', those greedy enclosers, landlords and graziers, who, like their sheep, were 'caterpillars of the commonwealth'.[2]

This is the context in which Thomas More's classic, *Utopia*, was composed. It begins with observations on the social consequences of war, which are general to all European powers, and then comments pointedly on a social evil peculiar to England, which can be taken as the underlying theme of the whole book:

The increase of pasture . . . by which your sheep, which are naturally mild, and easily kept in order, may be said now to devour men, and unpeople, not only villages, but towns; for wherever it is found that the sheep of any soil yield a softer and richer wool than ordinary, there the nobility and gentry, and even those holy men the abbots, not contented with the old rents which their farms yielded, nor thinking it enough that they, living at their ease, do no good to the public, resolve to do it hurt instead of good. They stop the course of agriculture, destroying houses and towns, reserving only the churches, and enclose grounds that they may lodge their sheep in them. As if forests and parks had swallowed up too little of the land, those worthy countrymen turn the best inhabited places into solitudes, for when an insatiable wretch, who is a plague to his country, resolves to enclose many thousand acres of ground, the owners as well as tenants are turned out of their possessions, by tricks, or by main force, or being wearied out with ill-usage, they are forced to sell them. By which means those miserable people, both men and women, married and unmarried, old and young, with their poor but numerous families (since country business requires many hands), are all forced to change their seats, not knowing whither to go; and they must sell almost for nothing their household stuff, which could not bring them much money, even though they might stay for a buyer. When that little money

2 Cited in Neal Wood, *Foundations*, p. 176.

is at an end, for it will be soon spent, what is left for them to do, but either to steal and so to be hanged (God knows how justly), or to go about and beg? And if they do this, they are put in prison as idle vaga-bonds; while they would willingly work, but can find none that will hire them; for there is no more occasion for country labor, to which they have been bred, when there is no arable ground left.

More's response to this catastrophe is not an elaborate analysis of England's ills, nor a programme of reform, nor a systematic political theory, but a fantastical fiction portraying 'Utopia' or 'Not-Place', a supremely well-ordered and happy republic without private property. This masterpiece has been interpreted as everything from pure fantasy, with no political intent, to a founding text of modern socialism. There is, of course, no decisive way of adjudicating these differences of interpretation – though it seems, on the face of it, implausible that More truly believed in a community of property. A man of substantial property, he was himself an encloser; and he showed no sign in his active political life of subscribing to egalitarian, let alone collectivist, principles, nor, for that matter, did he evince much compassion for the lower classes.[3] Even his zealous, not to say bloodthirsty, opposition to the Lutheran heresy – as lord chancellor he took an active part in the persecution of 'heretics' – was inspired in part by his conviction that it was to blame for the peasant revolt in Germany, which aroused the fears of English men of property like More himself. Even in his radical *Utopia*, he outlines a justification of colonization based on a principle that would later serve the English well: that people can be deprived of their land by just war if they fail to make productive use of it. Had More embarked on a programme of practical reform, he might have found himself – at most – not very far from Thomas Starkey (who was influenced by him) in seeking ways to civi-lize the ruling classes. But whatever his conception of the ideal society, it seems likely that his immediate objective, if indeed he had one, was to hold up a mirror to 'ungentle gentlemen', challenging their excesses with a 'utopian' image of their opposite.

For all the turmoil of the sixteenth century, there was, nonetheless, a fundamental unity of purpose and practice between monarchy and landed classes, as partners in a distinctively centralized state. The English aristoc-racy was no longer a militarized feudal nobility, but neither did the Tudor state possess a standing army; and both depended on their partnership to maintain social order. To be sure, the most effective popular rebellions were those supported by local elites; and, in the following century, the landlords would mobilize popular forces in their own conflict with the monarchy. Yet, when in the Civil War the English ruling class came into fatal conflict with

---

3   On More's 'enlightened conservatism', see Wood, *Foundations*, Ch. 6.

the king, it was a battle for control of an already unified English state, and not, as in the French Wars of Religion in the sixteenth century, a struggle between competing jurisdictions or a war between a centralizing monarchy, on the one hand, and, on the other, nobles or municipal authorities protecting their independent powers and privileges, their own little fragments of the state, their 'parcellized sovereignties'.

These historical conditions were reflected in the distinctive patterns of English political thought. In the sixteenth century, for example, the specific development of English society and the English state produced a tradition of political thought in which individuals, without mediation by corporate entities, were conceived as the basic constituents of the state – nicely summed up by Sir Thomas Smith, then Queen Elizabeth's ambassador to France. In a treatise on the English body politic, at least in part intended for the edification of a French audience and therefore assuming no knowledge of English conditions among his readers, he defined a 'commonwealth' or 'societie civill' as 'a societie or common doing of a multitude of free men collected together and united by common accord and covenauntes among themselves, for the conservation of themselves aswell [sic] in peace as in warre.'[4] This represents a telling contrast to the definition of a commonwealth by his contemporary, Jean Bodin, who, reflecting on French conditions, defined it as composed not of free individuals but of 'families, colleges or corporate bodies'.

Smith did not draw any radical conclusions from this definition of the body politic. He took for granted a limited parliamentary franchise, and his conception of representation in Parliament simply assumed that the propertied classes would govern, while other classes would be 'present' in Parliament (as all men, of whatever station, had a right to be), not as members or even as electors but by virtue of the men of property who represent the interests of the commonwealth. The 'sort of men which doe not rule', those who do not enjoy the parliamentary franchise, include

day labourers, poore husbandmen, yea marchantes or retailers which have no free lande, copiholders, all artificers, as Taylers, Shoomakers, Carpenters,

---

4 Thomas Smith, *De Republica Anglorum*, Ch. 10. It is worth mentioning, too, that Smith already identified the particularities of England's social property relations in his account of the yeomanry: 'these be (for the most part) fermors [i.e., tenants] to gentlemen, and with grasing, frequenting of markettes, and keeping servauntes, not idle servants as the gentleman doth, but such as get both their owne living and parte of their maisters: by these meanes doe come to such wealth, that they are able and daily doe buy the landes of unthriftie gentlemen' (Ch. 23). Smith is here describing what would come to be known as the triadic structure of English agrarian capitalism, the relations among landowners, their capitalist tenants, and the wage labourers employed by capitalist tenant farmers.

Brickemakers, Bricklayers, Masons, &c. These have no voice nor authoritie in our common wealth, and no account is made of them but onelie to be ruled, not to rule other. (Ch. 24)

The 'consent' of Parliament, he adds, 'is taken to be everie mans consent'.

It would be a pupil of Sir Thomas Smith, Bishop John Ponet, often associated with the Commonwealthmen, who would elaborate a justification of violent resistance by private individuals. He produced, in other words, a theory of resistance based on Smith's conception of political society as constituted by a multitude of individuals. In this respect, the contrast between Smith and Bodin is replicated in the difference between Ponet's ideas of resistance and those of the French 'constitutionalists', whose point of departure remained the contest among corporate jurisdictions and a right of resistance as a function of office – precisely the view of resistance that Bodin was seeking to counter.

In Ponet's *Shorte Treatise of Politike Power* (1556), he adopts a conception of the state that might be called 'modern' in its application to an impersonal institutional entity and not simply the personal rule of a monarch; and, for all his religious preoccupations, he emphasizes the secular nature and purpose of the state. The state's objective is the 'wealthe and benefit' of the people; and government is a trust, in which the office-holder acts as a 'proxy', 'attorney' or 'proctor' to the people, who can withdraw the mandate granted to their governors if the government ceases to act in the common interest as defined by the people themselves. While, as we have seen, Protestant doctrine had been used to justify more radical resistance than its canonical founders, Luther and Calvin, had ever been ready to contemplate, Ponet goes beyond existing doctrines in spelling out the right of 'private men' forcibly to resist unlawful or unjust officers and rulers. The difference between Ponet and his 'constitutionalist' counterparts in France or elsewhere on the Continent is sometimes put down to the relative security of Protestants in England (or, indeed, Scotland), which allowed them to risk more radical ideas of individual or 'private' resistance; but Ponet's conception of individual rights surely has structural roots in a distinctively English conception of the polity as constituted not by corporate entities or even a single mystical body, the 'people' as a corporate entity, but in 'a multitude of free men collected together' – an idea that is rooted in a distinct historical reality.

The case of Smith and Ponet illustrates that the idea of a commonwealth constituted by a 'multitude' of individuals, like the conception of the body politic as grounded in corporate entities, could accommodate a fairly wide range of political opinion. The idea of a corporate community did not, to be sure, disappear from English political thought. But, while on the Continent it could operate across a spectrum of opinion from the most unforgiving doctrines of obedience to fairly wide-ranging justifications of resistance, in English conditions it no longer served a useful purpose in resistance theories. Some thinkers would still find it helpful to invoke a mystical corporate community not to justify resistance but to sustain a theory of political obligation and the duty to obey political authority in England. Yet even the most notable defender of royal absolutism, Thomas Hobbes, would feel compelled to counter doctrines of resistance by constructing his argument on a foundation of individual rights and a political society created by a multitude of individuals.

In the sixteenth century, the most noteworthy English exponent of a mystical corporate body as a source of obligation was Richard Hooker. His *Of the Laws of Ecclesiastical Polity,* the first five books of which were published in the 1590s (the last three appeared posthumously in the early seventeenth century), is a classic of Anglican orthodoxy. Aimed against a challenge from Puritan clerics, it was intended to affirm the royal supremacy over the Church. But in the course of his argument, he raises more general political questions and lays out a theory of obligation based on a kind of mystical community to which every individual belongs and whose prior act of submission is binding on future generations. Proceeding from what first appears to be an unambiguous theory of government by consent ('For any prince or potentate to exercise [the power of making laws] not by commission from God or else by authority derived at the first from their consent upon whose persons they impose laws is no better than tyranny.'), he goes on to say that 'to be commanded we do consent when that Society, whereof we be a part, hath at any time before consented, without revoking the same after by the like universal agreement' (I. x). To make the point clearer still, he tells us:

> Wherefore as any man's deed past is good as long as himself continueth; so the act of a public society of men done five hundred years sithence standeth as theirs who presently are of the same societies, because corporations are immortal; we were then alive in our predecessors, and they in their successors do live still.

This means, among other things, that 'In many things assent is given, they that give it not imagining they do so, because the manner of their assenting is not apparent' – an idea of *tacit* consent that would, as we shall see, be taken up by Locke, to somewhat different purposes (though perhaps not as different as some interpreters insist).

Hooker was, it seems, opposed to rule by the arbitrary will of one man, without known laws; but his notion of consent is perfectly compatible with absolute monarchy – as he makes clear when he offers this as his first example of cases in which men give consent not imagining they do: 'when an absolute monarch commandeth his subjects that which seemeth good in his own discretion, hath not his edict the force of law whether they approve or dislike it?' But, however we choose to interpret his theory of consent and the limits it does or does not place on arbitrary power, his notion of the corporate community is striking not only in the ways it differs from Thomas Smith's idea of a commonwealth created by a multitude of individuals but also in the ways it shares with Smith certain common assumptions about the nature of the English body politic.

Hooker takes for granted the absence or weakness of 'intermediary' corporate entities and jurisdictions standing between individual and state. Like Thomas Smith, he assumes the existence of an unusually unified state, a fairly homogeneous and united ruling class and a unitary representative body, which can be said to represent the whole community – in sharp contrast to the French estates, which lie at the heart of Bodin's commonwealth. Hooker's corporate community, in other words, begins to look more like a *national* community, embodied in an English nation state. If the unity of national state and national Church seems less than 'modern', this very particular English unity is possible only because, and to the extent that, the English state – in contrast to 'parcellized sovereignties' and competing jurisdictions elsewhere in Europe – represents a truly sovereign power.

The reality of sovereign power, then, is certainly reflected in English political theory; but the reflection in this period – with the notable exception of Thomas Hobbes – is and remains largely indirect. It is not expressed in a clear idea of indivisible sovereignty. Since in England there was no fundamental conflict of jurisdiction between the monarchy and ruling classes, there was no need to assert the power of one over the other with a conception of indivisible sovereignty. On the contrary, the ancient idea of the 'mixed constitution' was widely held in English political thought, at a time when a French thinker like Bodin was very keen to repudiate such notions and to replace them with one clear and undisputed centre of political authority, a single, indivisible and absolute 'sovereign' power. The English attachment to the idea of the 'mixed constitution', as against the French invention of a clear and systematic idea of sovereignty, did not, as we have seen, mean that France enjoyed a more unified 'sovereign' state. The English 'mixed constitution' expressed the reality of a unitary state, in which monarchy and aristocracy were fundamentally united in joint control of state power. The idea of the 'mixed constitution' was another way of describing, in theoretical terms, the joint control of the state more conventionally expressed in the formula 'the Crown in Parliament', which to this day is used to describe the essence of constitutional power in Britain. Although this state was jointly controlled, it possessed the features of 'sovereignty' far more than did the French state at the time.

The same paradox appears in English and French conceptions of law and the 'sovereign' power of legislation. While Bodin was insisting that the essence of sovereignty was the power to make law and that law was simply the will of the sovereign, the English remained attached to their conception of the common law as the embodiment of age-old custom. They tended to talk about Parliament not so much as making law but as 'discovering' some pre-existing law, perhaps some custom or unwritten constitutional principle that had existed 'time out of mind'. Yet, in reality, the English legal system was already in the sixteenth century far more unified than the French, and Parliament (or the Crown in Parliament) really did have legislative functions more like Bodin's sovereign power. Again, the English conception of law took for granted some long-unchallenged practices, while the conceptual innovations of a thinker like Bodin reflected critical attempts to resolve at least in theory real conflicts over state power, which in practice would remain unresolved until the Revolution.

Crown, Parliament and Multitude

When the Stuarts embarked on their absolutist project, England's ruling classes were still committed to the long-standing partnership between Parliament and Crown, which, despite some moments of tension, had served them very well; but there was neither an inclination nor a social base for a Continental-style absolutism. The propertied classes in general were not in principle opposed to the monarchy. Indeed, they regarded it as a necessary bulwark against social disorder. Both monarchy and aristocracy were strengthened by the bargain in which the demilitarization of the aristocracy, which ceded its traditional coercive powers to the state, was compensated by the state's defence of landed property, underwriting and protecting the aristocracy's purely economic powers of exploitation.

At the same time, the more the propertied classes came to depend on economic exploitation, the less they could tolerate a state that continued to act in the traditional ways of a feudal monarchy. What members of the ruling class wanted was a state that maintained order and sustained their own absolute property rights. They certainly did not want monarchs who themselves behaved like feudal magnates, with their own personal followings, their own economic interests and resources in competition with the landed class. The English ruling class had little to gain from a state which served as just another kind of property, instead of simply serving to protect private property outside the state. So, to the extent that the political development of the monarchical state lagged behind the economic development of the ruling class, conflicts were bound to arise (quite apart from other sources of conflict, such as religious controversies, the complexities and instabilities of Britain's multiple kingdoms, or problems generated by particular royal personalities, which in the case of the stubborn Stuart kings are hard to ignore).

We should not, nonetheless, underestimate the tenacity of the partnership between Parliament and Crown – which was, if anything, strengthened by the long history of social disorder, riots and regional uprisings, religious and political, that preceded the Civil War. However varied the causes, certain social issues were never far from the surface, issues having to do with the realignment and redefinition of property. All this was accompanied by a proliferation of religious sects and open challenges to the authority of the established Church – the national Church which had contributed so much to the centralizing project of the state and which, since the English Reformation, had played an indispensable role in maintaining the state's institutional and ideological authority. On the eve of the Civil War, then, religious and political authority were already in a precarious state; and this certainly predisposed the ruling class to cling to its partnership with the monarchy, in defence of social order.

It is clear from the events leading up to the breach between Parliament and Crown that the propertied classes were willing to go some distance with the king. Still, there were limits, and the Stuarts repeatedly exceeded them – not least, of course, when Charles I ruled for eleven years without convoking Parliament. The imposition of taxes without parliamentary approval, especially in order to support the king's military adventures, was, needless to say, especially unpopular. At any rate, whatever the causes, long-term and immediate, national and local, relations finally broke down and war ensued.

If the landed class had long been united in supporting the partnership between Crown and Parliament, it was no less united in its opposition to the Stuart absolutist project. By far the majority of ruling opinion, inside Parliament no less than in the country outside, fell within the range of opposition to absolute and arbitrary government – at least, monarchical government unaccountable to Parliament. Until late in 1641, parliamentary classes in general remained opposed to what the king was doing; and a substantial majority in Parliament supported the radically anti-absolutist legislative program, including attacks on the Laudian Church, introduced in the preceding months.

Nevertheless, while in 1641 Parliament was all but unanimous in its anti-absolutist programme, historians now repeatedly emphasize that many, indeed most, MPs had no real wish to dispense with monarchy as such. They were generally not, in other words, republicans. We cannot dismiss as mere rhetoric their claims, when they went to war in 1642, to be fighting 'for king and Parliament'. Still, they were equally certain that they could not tolerate – that their own class interests could not sustain – a Continental-style absolutism. There was, besides, no clear division between an old feudal aristocracy defending the king, and a new bourgeoisie, or a capitalist aristocracy, trying to throw off the fetters that impeded its pursuit of progressive economic interests. The landed class was far

more homogeneous than that old formula suggests, and little remained of
the old-style feudal aristocracy.

Yet by now there were other forces in play that would disrupt this unanim-
ity. The 1620s had marked a turning-point in the political role of the English
'multitude'. Before the king suspended Parliament for eleven years in 1629,
his financial problems, among other things, had led to repeated calls for new
parliaments to raise the necessary revenues. At the same time, a growing
gentry meant that there were more aspirants to membership in Parliament,
and elections were more contested than ever before. The electorate was also
changing. Inflation alone had the effect of making basic property qualifications less exclusive, widening the social base of the electorate; but expansion
of the franchise was also a matter of policy. The gentry were becoming more
aware of the political advantages to be gained from mobilizing the people,
both in pursuit of their internal rivalries and in disagreements with the
Crown. In subsequent decades, there would be retreats (not least by Oliver
Cromwell) from this opportunistic commitment to a wider franchise; but
between 1621 and 1628, the Commons voted repeatedly to extend the franchise. By 1640, writes one eminent historian of the period, 'the situation in
the counties as well as the boroughs had changed out of all recognition from
Elizabethan times, and we witness the birth of a political nation, small,
partially controlled, but no longer coextensive with the will of the gentry'.[5]

Popular mobilization was not confined to voting. By 1640, the people
were taking to the streets with growing regularity. The first acts of the Long
Parliament in the autumn of that year were greeted with joyful demonstra-
tions by large crowds in the streets of London. In December, 15,000 people
signed the Root and Branch Petition demanding the abolition of episcopacy,
and hundreds of them carried the petition to the House of Commons.
Archbishop Laud was impeached for treason a week later. The people took
to the streets regularly thereafter; from January 1641, there were almost
daily popular riots in London. When the Earl of Strafford was executed in
May of that year, it was largely under pressure from the 'mob', for whom he
had become the chief representative of the absolutist monarchy. At the end
of that year, Parliament issued the Grand Remonstrance, listing its grievances – more than two hundred of them – against the king in particularly
provocative terms. What made the list especially provocative was that it was
clearly intended as an appeal directly to the people outside Parliament, with
the objective of mobilizing popular sentiment against the Crown.

This was a new mode of politics, which put the wind up some parliamentarians and suddenly transformed them into royalists. At first, the
mobilization of popular forces, especially in London – the hub of the nation

5   J.H. Plumb, 'The Growth of the Electorate in England from 1600-1715', *Past and
Present* 45 (1969), p. 107.

and disproportionately huge both in its population and in its economic importance – had been the opposition's trump card. But, if riots and popular agitation had been useful instruments of war against the king, they always threatened to exceed the bounds of ruling-class objectives. As the parliamentary debate about the Grand Remonstrance makes clear, it was the calculated appeal to the people, as much as the substance of the document, that some found so alarming and caused them to change sides. We can get a taste of the growing unease from Sir Edward Dering, who had been on the side of the people in the execution of Strafford but was driven into the royalist camp by the Grand Remonstrance. 'Mr. Speaker,' he said,

> when I first heard of a Remonstrance, I presently imagined that like faithful councillors, we should hold up a glass unto his Majesty: I thought to represent unto the King the wicked counsels of pernicious councillors; the restless turbulency of practical Papists . . . I did not dream that we should remonstrate downward, tell stories to the people and talk of the King as of a third person.

The Grand Remonstrance proved to be a major turning-point in the creation of a significant royalist faction. But it was not the first time, nor the last, that anxious members of Parliament expressed their fears of popular mobilization. Before Dering, Sir George Digby, still an active opponent of the king in 1640, had changed sides. Not the least of his worries was the role of the 'multitude' in carrying the Root and Branch Petition to Parliament. He warned the house against the mobilization of

> irregular and tumultuous assemblies of people, be it for never so good an end . . . [T]here is no man of the least insight into nature, or history, but knows the danger, when either true or pretended stimulation, of conscience, hath once given a multitude agitation . . . [W]hat can there be of greater presumption, than for . . . a multitude to teach a parliament, what is, and what is not, the government according to God's word.

The defection of nervous parliamentarians made it possible for the king to rally a substantial force well beyond his personal followers and the relatively small sections of the propertied classes whose interests were inextricably bound up with his – such as the old company merchants who benefited from royal monopolies. At the same time, it meant that the parliamentary cause was now led by those more inclined to popular mobilization. The process of defection, which had begun when some parliamentarians took fright at the impeachment and execution of the Earl of Strafford and at the Grand Remonstrance, would be repeated several times in the following years of civil war, as increasingly radical dangers drove more sections of the opposition away from the parliamentary cause. Even the victorious parliamentarians of the Long Parliament were prepared to negotiate with the king as late as 1648, as, indeed, the leaders of the New Model Army had been in 1647. The next-to-last stage of that peeling-away was the conflict between Cromwell and the Levellers, and the final stage came in the Restoration.

Political Ideas in the English Civil War

The Civil War was not only a time of military conflict but a period of unique intellectual ferment. The breakdown of authority encouraged an unprece-dented outpouring of political debate. The population was unusually literate by the standards of the day; and people were regularly exposed not only to the ruling ideologies but to subversive ideas, typically in sermons from their often sectarian parish preachers. A wide range of issues and conflicts were canvassed in a vast profusion of pamphlet literature, addressed not just to the usual elites but to the common man and woman. Yet the breakdown of authority is not enough to account for the airing of griev-ances and aspirations that might otherwise have remained submerged beneath ruling-class hegemony. The very structure of English society and politics, the specific need of the ruling classes for alliances and popular mobilization, placed radical ideas on the agenda in unprecedented ways.

Let us consider, as it were from the top down, some of the many political ideas that were circulating at this turbulent moment. Before the reign of James I, it was widely accepted that England had a mixed constitution, and this idea continued to play an important part in English political thought across a wide political spectrum. It could be used to defend the rights of Parliament against the Crown; but it certainly did not preclude a major, and in some versions even a dominant, role for the king, as long as it was under-stood that all rule was ultimately subject to the law as promulgated by the 'Crown in Parliament', which meant the monarch together with the two houses of Parliament.

The erudite King James I himself challenged that idea by claiming, in his book *The Trew Law of Free Monarchies* (1598) and elsewhere, that kings ruled by divine right and were not accountable to any earthly authority. He also famously commissioned a translation of the Bible – the 'Authorized Version' or 'King James Bible', which was intended to displace the English-language Calvinist 'Geneva Bible', not least because of what he took to be its seditious marginal commentaries sanctioning resistance to monarchical authority. Yet even James, while admitting no constitutional limits on his rule, conceded, at least in theory, that the king should rule according to existing law.

Few Englishmen were willing to take a very strong and unambiguous position on the 'absolute' powers of the king, and there was only a short period in the seventeenth century when a small number of royalist thinkers made more absolute claims for royal sovereignty. The most famous of these is Thomas Hobbes, whom we shall discuss in what follows. Another was Sir Robert Filmer, whose major defence of royal absolutism, *Patriarcha*, though written in the 1640s, remained unpublished until long after his death. It was resurrected and, for the first time, printed in 1680 during the renewed conflicts between the king and Parliament, only to be famously and fatally attacked by John Locke, who, as we shall see, singled it out as the main target of his own assault on absolutism.

For the moment, we need only keep in mind that strong absolutist arguments were very unpopular in England. Both Filmer and Hobbes, in their different ways, remained untypical, even among royalists. For that matter, the English never seemed to be much bothered about locating a single, absolute and indivisible sovereign power, residing in the king or in Parliament. They had long grown accustomed to their 'mixed constitution', the joint rule of king and propertied classes in Parliament.

When the time finally came, then, how did the ruling class defend its right to rebel against the king? There were, of course, well-established doctrines of resistance available to them, not least the constitutionalist doctrines of the monarchomachs that had emerged from the French Wars of Religion. In France, the idea of popular sovereignty could readily be invoked to sustain the autonomous jurisdictions of aristocrats and 'lesser magistrates'; but this was not in the first instance the preferred ideological strategy of English parliamentarians. In fact, at least in the early years of the Civil War, the principal theorists of the parliamentary cause actually repudiated doctrines of popular sovereignty. They seemed very reluctant even to claim the sovereignty of Parliament and to replace the Crown in Parliament with an unambiguous parliamentary supremacy.

The battle the English were fighting was different from that of the French. It was not, again, a war of competing jurisdictions and fragmented sovereignties. It was not a matter of particular corporate bodies and privileges defending their autonomy against a monarchical drive to unify the state and replace corporate fragments with one overarching sovereign power. In an already unified sovereign state, which was constituted by king and Parliament together, Parliament was not asserting its own, 'popular' sovereignty against the king's competing claims so much as accusing him of violating their partnership, of breaching their composite sovereignty.

In the period leading up to the Civil War, when tensions between king and ruling class were mounting, Parliament in 1628 produced the Petition of Right, which has come to be regarded as a cornerstone of the English constitution. The distinctive tone of English conflicts between Crown and ruling classes is nicely captured in this document and in the debate surrounding it in Parliament. The petition undoubtedly claimed certain powers for

Parliament, yet it represented itself not as an assertion of parliamentary
sovereignty but as a statement about the 'rights and liberties of the subject'.
In other words, it is not about competing jurisdictions or sovereignties so
much as about the rights of the citizen (or subject) against a state whose
unified jurisdiction is taken for granted. It represents a different kind of
constitutionalism, which does not concern the rights of one kind of lordship
against another, or the claims of lesser lords against greater ones, or 'lesser
magistrates' against princes and kings. It has more to do with the relations
between individual and state (even if the individuals most immediately
concerned are members of the propertied classes).

The debate in Parliament is also telling. When the Commons had
accepted the Petition of Right and it went to the Lords, there was a
proposal to add a clause 'to leave entire that sovereign power wherewith
your Majesty is trusted'. It is perhaps significant enough that those who
proposed this amendment saw no incompatibility between the demands of
the petition and this assertion of royal power. But even more interesting is
the argument advanced by one MP against the proposed clause, in a confer-
ence between the two houses of Parliament. In a climate of discontent and
anger, argued Sir Henry Marten, the 'vulgar' multitude may not be very
friendly to the sacred sovereign power. 'This petition will run through
many hands', he said,

> and men will fall to arguing and descanting what sovereign power is . . .
> what is the latitude? whence the original? where the bounds? etc., with
> many such curious and captious questions . . . Sovereign power is then best
> worth when it is held in tacit veneration, not when it is profaned by vulgar
> hearings or examinations.

For Marten, this may have been a rhetorical ploy, but he understood the
mind-set of the ruling class very well: the less said about sovereignty the
better. Why raise the issue at all? Why let the 'vulgar' start asking awkward
questions about the sources, scope and limits of sovereign power? Let sleep-
ing dogs lie. And so their lordships did, as the Petition of Right was passed
without the embarrassing clause.

This whole episode is richly revealing. It tells us much about the disposition of the ruling classes and their relations with the Crown. Grievances
they certainly had, but they were apparently confident enough of their partnership with the Crown and their joint role in the state not to feel a strong
need to clarify the issue of sovereignty. Besides, whatever issues divided
Parliament and Crown, they were united in their common front against the
'vulgar' multitude.

This brings us to another factor that may help to explain the reluctance
of parliamentary leaders and thinkers to invoke the doctrine of popular

sovereignty. When the French articulated the right of resistance, they had the option of reserving it to 'lesser magistrates' or corporations. But what would happen if the basic constituents of the state were conceived not as 'colleges and corporations' but as a 'multitude of free men'? What implications would it have where corporate powers had largely given way to a centralized state, where the intermediate institutions between the individual and the state had been weakened, and where individuals and their private property had been detached from 'extra-economic' powers and identities? One possibility, of course, was to attach political significance to property, as distinct from prescriptive corporate status or privilege; and this was, of course, done. But the purely quantitative measure of property was more dangerously elastic than qualitative differences of privilege and rank. Would a right of resistance then be claimed by the popular multitude?

The mainstream parliamentary justification of opposition to the king in 1642 tended to be somewhat equivocal. Parliamentarians were inclined to say not so much that the people had a right of rebellion but that the king was the one who was rebelling, so that Parliament had the duty to restore the constitution and the traditional balance between Crown and Parliament. Any true republicans – certainly in today's conventional sense, as genuine opponents of monarchy in principle – stayed largely under cover until 1648, when the conflict had apparently reached a point of no return.

There were, however, a few early attempts to establish a theory of parliamentary sovereignty, the most notable being Henry Parker's *Observations upon some of his Majesties late Answers and Expresses* (1642). Parker claimed that 'power is originally inherent in the people' and that royal authority is derived from that original power through the medium of contracts and agreements. But like French theorists of resistance, Parker still had in mind the 'people' as a corporate entity, on the grounds that it is only as a collectivity that the people were superior to the king, so the people could exercise their powers only through their constitutional representatives. More particularly, he argued that, once having established a Parliament to represent them, the people could not reclaim their original power. It was up to Parliament to guard the interests of the people and to resist the king when he violated their liberties. Parker certainly did not call for the abolition of the monarchy and continued to speak in the language of a mixed constitution, or the King in Parliament; but he did give Parliament, as the people's representative, the last word. Parliament, he argued,

> may not desert the king, but being deserted by the king, when the kingdom is in distress, they may judge of that distress, and relieve it, and are to be accounted, by the virtue of representation, as the whole body of the state.

This argument may have appeared more risky in England than it had in France, because the notion of the people as a corporate entity had already been weakened both in theory and in practice, giving way to the idea of the people as a multitude of individuals. This may help to explain why royalists could counter Parker's argument by claiming that, if Parliament can rebel against the king, there was nothing to prevent the people's similarly rebelling against Parliament.

Parker's defence of parliamentary sovereignty was too extreme even for some prominent parliamentarians. In what appears to be a reply to Parker, the distinguished lawyer, John Selden (1584–1654), long known as a defender of the 'subject's liberties' and the rights of Parliament, argued against Parker's first premise. In his *Table Talk*, written in the early 1640s but unpublished until 1689, Selden, in the entry on 'Contracts', explores the implications of contracts between the people and their rulers. Contracts would mean nothing, he insists, if we could just withdraw from them whenever they cease to be convenient. 'If once we grant we may recede from contracts upon any inconveniency that may afterwards happen, we shall have no bargain kept. If I sell you a horse and do not like my bargain, I will have my horse again.' By the same rules of contract, the principle that the people as a collectivity are greater than the king simply cannot stand up. Just because the people made the king, they are not therefore greater than he, any more than I am greater or richer than you after I have given you my whole fortune and left myself destitute. If I made you greater, greater you remain. Selden's friend Thomas Hobbes was to use related arguments, but in outright defence of royal absolutism.

As for genuine republicanism in the Civil War, some prominent historians insist that republicans never represented more than a small minority against the mainstream of parliamentary thinking. Others point to an important body of 'republican' thought – including political works by the poet John Milton – that had emerged by the late 1640s, which was to have substantial influence in the eighteenth century, not least in the American Revolution. Yet it is not always clear what is meant by 'republicanism'; and the concept is especially ill-suited to capturing the English political experience. The Roman idea of a civic community, to which 'republicanism' is commonly traced, in its original form presupposed a ruling aristocracy that governed itself collectively and in amateur style, with a minimal state. The English context was very different. England had long had an effective central administration; and this political form, the product of distinctive social developments, was unlike any other in Europe or anywhere else. The partnership of monarchy and Parliament was recognized even by so-called republicans, who might argue against absolutism and for a 'mixed constitution' without necessarily advocating abolition of the monarchy.

The term 'republicanism' is often used by historians of political thought in reference not so much to anti-monarchism as to political theories that place strong emphasis on a community of citizens, the importance of 'civic virtue', and the accountability of any political authority to the civic community. But in the English context, a 'republican' emphasis on the civic community, a community of citizens, is often hard to distinguish from other forms of anti-absolutism. The civic community was likely to be identified with Parliament no less by 'republicans' than by more moderate defenders of Parliament against the Crown. This could mean specifically the accountability of any government to a representative institution like Parliament – at which point this 'classical republicanism' shades into less radical forms of mainstream parliamentarism.

In specifically English conditions, what does stand out in sharper relief, as we shall see in a moment, is the division between those for whom the ruling class in Parliament was the rightful embodiment of the civic community or popular power and those for whom the people outside Parliament were truly sovereign. The idea of 'republican liberty' is not very helpful in identifying this division, not least because the Roman Republic was an oligarchy and the original Roman idea of liberty was never democratic. In the concept of 'republicanism', even the distinction between oligarchy and democracy may disappear from view, making it hard to distinguish, for instance, between oligarchic republicans and more radical defenders of the people's liberty against the crown, such as the Levellers. More particularly, the 'people outside Parliament' is a category without meaning in any other context but the English. It has no bearing on the Roman civic community where the 'republican' idea was born, nor on the Italian city-state where it was revived, nor indeed in the Dutch Republic; while in absolutist France, the relevant players in the contest between absolutist kings and those who opposed them were, as we have seen, necessarily different.

It is certainly true that, by the end of the 1640s, there were prominent radicals who favoured an unambiguous parliamentary supremacy and severe restrictions on the power of the Crown and the House of Lords. There were those who even supported the abolition of the monarchy. But some so-called republicanism is not unambiguously opposed to monarchy as such. Republicans in this sense could be advocates of the mixed constitution and could even accept some kind of constitutional monarchy. Even the great republican Algernon Sidney (1622–83), who was to be condemned for treason in 1683 after the failure of the Exclusion programme, continued to speak of a mixed constitution even while calling for revolution in the manuscript that led to his death, the *Discourses Concerning Government*, finally published in 1698.

One thing, at any rate, is clear: even those MPs who were willing to go the whole distance and abolish the monarchy, and to assert some kind of 'popular sovereignty', were likely to take away with one hand what they had given with the other. They generally situated 'popular sovereignty' in Parliament, and not in the 'people' outside – to say nothing of the restrictions they would have placed on the right to elect Parliament. This was true even if they allowed power to revert to the multitude in moments of extreme crisis, as when Cromwell mobilized a popular army whose rank and file he would allow to fight but not to vote. Henry Ireton, Cromwell's son-in-law and the chief spokesman of the 'grandees' in the Putney Debates, was himself a republican of this radical but undemocratic variety. This is exactly the point at which more democratic forces like the Levellers parted company with these oligarchic republicans, claiming sovereignty not just for Parliament but for the multitude, and not just in extreme emergencies but in normal political life.

The body of literature that has come to be known as classical republicanism, of which the most important exponent was James Harrington (1611–77), did produce a distinctive conception of citizenship and civic liberty, which can be said to distinguish it from the traditions of 'liberalism' associated with thinkers like John Locke. The republican conceptions of citizenship and liberty imply something more than the passive enjoyment of individual rights or the 'negative' freedom from external impediments to action. Republican liberty, as Quentin Skinner has argued, is the absence of dependence in any form. The very existence of arbitrary power, however permissively or even benignly it may be exercised, reduces men to servitude, so that free individuals can exist only in free states, governed by a civic community of active citizens. But republicans of this kind seem to have been no less wedded than were less 'republican' parliamentarians to an exclusive political nation. At the very least, their conception of citizenship did not preclude a division between propertied elite and labouring multitude.

Harrington, in the years following the publication of his *Commonwealth of Oceana* (dedicated to Cromwell) in 1656, wrote in opposition to the restoration of the monarchy and was imprisoned in 1661. But even a genuinely radical republican like this was not necessarily a democrat in the sense that we, or even the Levellers, would understand the term. In *Oceana*, Harrington makes some significant observations about the connections between political and economic power. Political power, insofar as it rests on control of the food supply, is grounded in landed property. In some respects, this observation was a double-edged sword. On the one hand, it was the basis of Harrington's claims for the supremacy of representative bodies – at least in places where, as in England, land was no longer in the hands of a feudal nobility but was widely distributed among commoners. This principle could also be taken to mean that property should be more widely and equitably distributed, so that the body of men who are fit to be citizens might be enlarged; or at least landownership should be stabilized by means of the kind of agrarian law he proposed, regulating the acquisition and inheritance of land in order to maintain a relatively wide distribution of political power. This kind of regulation might even be understood as opposing the increasing concentration of landed property that was continuing in England.

On the other hand, on the basis of the same principle, Harrington was very emphatic that citizenship could belong *only* to those who had the 'wherewithal to live of themselves' – that is, it would exclude a substantial number of people without property or dependent for their livelihood on labouring for others. Even in his more or less utopian commonwealth, he never imagined the disappearance of people such as these, though their numbers might be limited. In the real world of his own contemporary England, many people would have been excluded from full rights of citizenship on the basis of such Harringtonian principles.

The Levellers and the Putney Debates

If the main parliamentary leaders were reluctant to invoke the notion of popular sovereignty because they feared its subversive possibilities, their fears were soon to be justified. The war and popular mobilization inevitably opened that Pandora's box. During the revolutionary period, the world was indeed 'turned upside down'. Radical religious sects defied some of the most basic principles of ecclesiastical hierarchy and even conventional social morality. Various groups in which religious and political ideas were inseparable challenged political authority and the dominant system of property, their ideas ranging across a broad spectrum up to and including the most radically democratic doctrines and even the repudiation of private property itself.

By 1647, a wide-ranging programme of political reform was taking root in the New Model Army. Many in the Army rank and file were driven by anger, often generated by Parliament's refusal to pay the soldiers; but many were also motivated by democratic opposition to the parliamentary oligarchy, and even those officers of a less radical disposition were forced to adopt a more militant stance, if only to maintain Army unity and discipline.

The Army itself became a major political issue, its very existence a bone of contention among parliamentarians. When fear of military radicalism and of the 'rabble' of ordinary soldiers drove some parliamentarians to call for the New Model Army to be disbanded, the Army stood firm, refused to accept Parliament's order to disband, and retaliated with a coherent and radical political programme. Largely the work of Henry Ireton, it called for constitutional and religious reforms that went well beyond what Parliament had hitherto demanded, not to mention a purge of Parliament itself to rid it of corrupt MPs and the Army's chief opponents.

The Army was united in defying Parliament's orders to disband, but that unity disguised the divisions within its own ranks and the tenuous control now exercised by Cromwell's officers over the rank and file. There is even debate among historians about whether the Army's seizure of the king in June of 1647 really had the approval of Cromwell or was simply an action by radicals, accepted by Cromwell and Ireton after the fact. These internal divisions had taken shape in the election of regimental Agitators, whose function was to represent the interests and grievances of the rank and file. It was these Agitators who established links with radicals especially in London, and specifically the Levellers. Soon they became the conduits for more wide-ranging discussions, in which not only the nature of the new regime in England but also the most fundamental issues of religion and politics were openly debated in the most democratic way, by officers and ordinary soldiers. The division between the Army grandees and the Levellers represented a substantial divergence between what has been called an 'oligarchic republicanism' and a more democratic radicalism.

The thinkers and activists who have been called 'Levellers' represented a fairly wide range of views. The name itself seems to have appeared earlier in the century to describe people who rose up against practices such as enclosure, 'levelling' hedges, fences or walls; but increasingly the term was used pejoratively to accuse certain radicals of wanting to equalize or 'level', indeed even to abolish, private property.

The man who is commonly regarded as the most important Leveller writer, John Lilburne (1615–57), never showed any inclination to do away with private property. This is perhaps not surprising in a man destined to be a 'middling' merchant himself, apprenticed to a wholesale cloth merchant from 1630 to 1636, though later impeded by monopolies in his attempts to carry on in the same trade. In approximately eighty pamphlets, he consistently defended the rights of the people, generally under the heading of 'life, liberty or estate'. His radicalism consisted above all in his insistence on the power of the people, as against either king or Parliament. One of the leaders of the London crowd when it took to the streets to call for the impeachment of Strafford, he spent the rest of his career defending the 'ancient' rights and liberties of England, the freedom of the people against tyranny and arbitrary rule, the freedom of conscience, the right to due processes of law, and so on. In 1638 he was punished for printing and circulating unlicensed books, and aggravated his situation by denouncing episcopacy. Thereafter, he was to be tried three times for treason, and between 1645 and 1652 imprisoned seven times. In 1652 he was banished for life because of his opposition to corruption and his consistent defence of political and religious liberty, which were evidently no more welcome to Cromwell than they had been to the king and his supporters. Lilburne returned to England in defiance of the banishment order and was tried for treason, acquitted but again imprisoned. He died a few years later, having become a Quaker like many other disappointed radicals. Yet throughout this long and courageous history of struggle in defence of liberty, Lilburne was never a Leveller in the sense intended by those enemies who accused people like him of seeking to abolish all distinctions between rich and poor and promoting common ownership.

Nor was Lilburne exceptional in taking for granted the right of private property. This was typical of the people we now know as Levellers, who were active during the Civil War. In fact, as we shall see, their views on property provoked some even more radical activists – the Diggers – to describe themselves as *True* Levellers, to distinguish themselves from those less inclined really to 'level' property. Still, despite explicit denials, the Levellers continued to be accused – for example, by Ireton in the Putney Debates – of endangering the whole institution of property; and these accusations were not simply tactical. They testify to a real threat posed to ruling-class interests by the Leveller programme.

Even if the mainstream Levellers fell short of advocating communal property, they nonetheless espoused some very radical political ideas which threatened to undermine the rule of the dominant propertied class. At the root of these radical ideas is the notion that the people were sovereign – not Parliament, not some other representatives of the people, not the 'people' in mythical corporate form, but the people as popular 'multitude'. This idea may have made its first explicit appearance in 1645, in *England's Miserie and Remedie*, an anonymous pamphlet in defence of Lilburne attributed at one time or another to various Levellers, including Lilburne himself.

Although in general the Levellers represented small and 'middling' proprietors, craftsmen, traders and yeoman farmers, many of them, including some of their most influential spokesmen, were not only well educated but also fairly prosperous. Even the Putney Debates display a range of views, some more radical than others; but on the whole, we cannot go far wrong if we assume that the Levellers were principally spokesmen for smaller independent proprietors as against large landowners and wealthy merchants, especially the old monopolists. At a time when small proprietors were an increasingly endangered species, as property was becoming increasingly concentrated, they opposed practices such as enclosure and other attacks on customary rights, which accelerated the concentration of property; and they defended the right of the craftsman or farmer to the fruits of his labour.

They were especially opposed to the association of privilege and political rights with large properties. Their programme included reform of taxation, in order to shift the burden to larger proprietors; they strongly opposed taxes that hit the small man hardest, like the excise, and other forms of indirect exploitation of small producers, like the costs of litigation, the laws on debt, church tithes, and so on; they attacked trade monopolies (here they had something in common with many richer parliamentarians) in defence of free trade; they defended customary rights and sought security for customary tenures, which were increasingly being challenged by larger land-owners; and they called for various political reforms such as annual or biennial Parliaments, reform of the legal system (they despised lawyers) and the extension of the franchise. Always bound up with their political programme was an overriding commitment to religious toleration. Perhaps the most radical aspect of their political programme was their emphasis on local self-government, and Levellers not only challenged executive government but also called for a weaker Parliament, in the interests of stronger local government.

The *Agreement of the People*, which provoked the Putney Debates, ranged over a broad spectrum of constitutional, political and religious issues: regular and frequent election of Parliament but with increasing devolution of government to local control (the agreement makes no mention of executive prowess), an extension of the franchise, religious toleration, democratic control of the military, the abolition of tithes and certain other taxes. In the debates, the chief spokesman for the grandees was the outstandingly clever and articulate Commissary-General Henry Ireton, certainly a revolutionary if not a democrat, son of the lesser gentry and married to Cromwell's daughter. The most eloquent spokesman for the other side was Colonel Thomas Rainsborough (1610?–48). The issues in dispute drew a sharp line not only between different constitutional positions but divergent class interests.

That part of the Debates that raised the most fundamental political questions turned on the reform of the franchise. The discussion went beyond matters of policy to more fundamental underlying issues, indeed to the very foundations of political order and the system of property. To sustain their political claims, the radicals invoked some revolutionary ideas about the fundamental rights of men (they did indeed mean *men*) and the basis of legitimate government. They argued that every man in England, even the poorest, had a right not to be governed except by his own consent, and that this right was attached to the person and not to property. These ideas were sharply challenged by Ireton and Cromwell, who saw the dangers – not only to government but to property itself – that would follow from taking such arguments to their logical conclusion.

Leveller views on the franchise have been a subject of fierce debate among historians. Part of the problem lies in the tactical retreats of the Levellers in their negotiations with the Army grandees, evidence of which can be found in the Putney Debates and in the various revisions in the *Agreement of the People*. Some historians have argued that the Levellers would have excluded not only 'dependent' people like women, beggars and alms-takers, but also all hired labourers. But the dominant view now is that, while none of the

Levellers ever questioned the exclusion of women (even women, however radically militant they often were in other respects, failed to demand the suffrage for themselves), the starting position of the Leveller leaders – from which they retreated in order to get the agreement of Cromwell and Ireton – was universal adult male suffrage. At the very least, they supported a household suffrage, in which every head of household represented his dependents: women, children and live-in servants. The more radical position was certainly very prominent in the Putney Debates, eloquently articulated by the leading Leveller spokesman, Colonel Rainsborough.

The debate on the franchise revolved especially around the clause in the *Agreement of the People* which demanded: 'That the people of England, being at this day very unequally distributed by counties, cities, and boroughs for the election of their deputies in Parliament, ought to be more indifferently proportioned, according to the number of inhabitants.' There are, to be sure, certain ambiguities in this formulation, and the clever Henry Ireton was very quick to seize on them. The clause could be read as calling simply for correction of anomalies in the current voting system. Not only were there places with a very wide franchise and others with a very limited electorate, but a large town might have no representative at all (because it had not been incorporated prior to some specific date in the past), while some practically depopulated rural areas did. Perhaps, then, the demand for representation apportioned according to population went no further than sorting out these inequities.

Cromwell and Ireton would not have objected to a change of this kind – and they actually did institute such electoral reforms; but Ireton immediately saw in the clause something more. He notes the reference to distribution according to the number of inhabitants, 'the people of England, etc.' and remarks that

> this does make me think, that the meaning is that every man that is an inhabitant is to be equally considered, and to have an equal voice in the election of those representers . . . and if that be the meaning then I have something to say against it.

Rainsborough makes no effort to disguise that the more democratic construction of this clause is exactly what he has in mind. And here he states, in the most eloquent and moving speech, the principle on which he stakes his claim:

> [F]or really I think that the poorest he that is in England has a life to live as the greatest he; and therefore truly, sir, I think it's clear that every man that is to live under a government ought first by his own consent to put himself under that government; and I do think that the poorest man in

England is not at all bound in a strict sense to that government that he has
not had a voice to put himself under.

Ireton immediately sees the implications of this argument. Rainsborough's
claim that the poorest man in England has the same rights as the greatest
implies that certain rights inhere in men as men (and it is, unfortunately,
always men), just by virtue of their living and breathing: because 'the poorest
he has a life to live', he also possesses the right not to be governed except by
his own consent. 'Give me leave to tell you', Ireton replies, 'that if you make
this the rule, I think you must fly for refuge to an absolute natural right, and
you must deny all civil right.' It can perhaps be argued that, while the Levellers
themselves were still clinging to the rights of 'free-born Englishmen', Ireton
on their behalf constructed a conception of natural right.

At any rate, Ireton's distinction between 'natural' and 'civil' right is a critical one, around which much of the debate revolves. Englishmen, says Ireton,
do have certain rights, but they are rights historically established by English
constitutional traditions and practices. These traditions do not include an
equal franchise, any more than they include equality of property. To establish
the kind of right that Rainsborough demands means circumventing the
English constitution and appealing to some more universal, absolute right,
not based on historical precedents but on the laws of nature itself.

This may be more than some Levellers intended to claim. After all, they
repeatedly talk about the birthrights or 'native rights' of 'free-born
Englishmen', not of mankind in general. In fact, their argument often rests
not so much on an appeal to natural right as on an alternative account of
English history. In answer to Ireton's claim about England's ancient constitution, for example, John Wildman insists that

> Our very laws were made by our conquerors; and whereas it's spoken
> much of chronicles, I conceive there is no credit to be given to any of them;
> and the reason is because those that were our lords, and make us their
> vassals, would suffer nothing else to be chronicled.

So the historical record to which Ireton is appealing records history as the
ruling class has dictated. There is another, suppressed story to be told – and
here Wildman is alluding to a theme widespread among radicals: that the
present constitution of government and property is the legacy of conquest,
the Norman Conquest, and can therefore enjoy no legitimacy.

But if the argument often turns on the popular radical theme of the infamous 'Norman Yoke', there is no doubt that something like a more universal
conception of natural rights keeps emerging from beneath that historical
argument. In fact, the Norman Yoke is illegitimate not just because it has
destroyed a more ancient order in England but apparently also because it

violates certain more basic principles. Those principles may not be system-atically laid out in the Putney Debates, but they did get full expression elsewhere, most notably in Richard Overton's *An Arrow Against All Tyrants*, which begins:

> To every individual in nature, is given an individual property by nature, not to be invaded or usurped by any: for every one as he is himselfe, so he hath a selfe propriety, else he could not be himselfe, and on this no second may presume to deprive any of, without manifest violation and affront to the very principles of nature and of the Rules of equity and justice between man and man.

It is on this notion of 'self-propriety', the inviolable property that every man has in his own person, that the Levellers base their claims not only to the franchise and other political rights but to freedom of conscience and reli-gion. This idea was later to be put to different uses by John Locke; but in the hands of the Levellers its radical implications are unmistakable, and Ireton spells them out thus: once you claim this kind of natural right, he argues, 'then I think you must deny all property too'.

Ireton's argument here needs to be looked at more closely. The view that private property itself is a natural right may seem familiar and even commonplace; and John Locke, the political theorist who did most to provide a systematic defence of this view, based it, as we shall see, on something like the Leveller idea of 'self-propriety'. To argue that private property is a natural right may seem the most powerful defence of proper-tied interests, yet in the Putney Debates we find a defender of the propertied classes like Ireton arguing instead that property is not a natural right but merely a human convention, established by human constitution, grounded in history rather than in nature. But Ireton's view was not at all unusual. It had, as we have seen, long been common in the Western tradition to argue that property is a convention – or, at least, that even if the institution itself is divinely ordained, as Ireton himself concedes, its specific form and distribution are merely conventional.

The idea that property is a right by convention rather than by nature had never in the Western tradition seemed threatening to propertied interests and, in the English context, may even have seemed far less dangerous. Ireton sees that, far from weakening the defence of property, this may indeed be a safer ideological strategy for the propertied classes, because it is not so easy to explain and justify gross inequalities of property on the basis of a natural right vested in the individual. His own argument is simply that the present system has existed as long as anyone can remember, that it belongs to the English constitution, and that any attack on the constitution is a threat to any social order and peace, and hence finally to property itself.

If rights inhere in the person, he argues, why would a man not then also have, by the same right of nature, the right to anything he needs to sustain his person – 'the same right in any goods he sees: meat, drink, clothes, to take and use them for his sustenance' – and indeed a right to make use of land itself in any way he liked? How could any ownership of property, even the most modest, be secure with such an unrestricted and disruptive conception of rights (never mind the more obvious consideration that a majority of poor voters are likely to play havoc with the rights of the rich)? What limits are there to such natural rights? 'I would fain have any man show me their bounds, where you will end, and take away all property.'

Rainsborough, like other Levellers, denies any intention to destroy the institution of property. Many of the people he represents, after all, are proprietors themselves. At the same time, if forced to make a choice, these radicals – or some of them – seem prepared to put aside the sanctity of property. As Major William Rainsborough says, 'the chief end of this government is to preserve persons as well as estates, and if any law shall take hold of my person, it is more dear than my estate'. So the rights of persons prevail over the rights of property – which is precisely what disturbs Henry Ireton.

The position advocated by Ireton is that the franchise should not belong to anyone whose stake or 'interest' in society is only what 'he may carry about with him', who has only – to use Colonel Rainsborough's words – a 'life to live', only the 'interest' of living and breathing, a man who is merely, as Ireton puts it, 'here today and gone tomorrow'. Only those who have a 'fixed' and 'permanent interest' in society, in the form of landed property or the so-called 'freedom' of a corporation, an officially licensed right to conduct trade – only men such as these have a real stake in the state; and so the fate of the community should be in their hands.

When asked directly whether any man can be bound to obey laws to which he has not himself consented (by electing those who make the laws), Ireton says unequivocally, yes – with one proviso: that he can freely leave if he is dissatisfied. A man with a 'permanent interest', one with property 'that does locally fix him in this country', cannot freely leave, while the propertyless, or even those who possess only money, can come and go as they please. In that respect, they are no different from foreigners who visit our shores. We all expect foreign visitors to obey our laws while they are in our country, and to respect those who make the laws, even though they have no right to vote for the legislators.

The Levellers keep insisting on their native rights and ask what the soldiers have fought for in the war, if they are now to be denied those rights. They fought, Edward Sexby declares, 'to recover our birthrights and privileges as Englishmen . . . There are many thousands of us soldiers that have ventured our lives; we have had little property in the kingdom as to our estates, yet we have had a birthright.' To this, Ireton's reply is straightforward: what the Army fought for was the right to be governed by a representative body and a known law rather than by the arbitrary rule of one man. And they fought for the freedom to do business and acquire property. Their true birthright is the English constitution itself, principles of property and government that have stood the test of time, and the security they derive from this constitutional order. To put it another way, the Levellers demanded something closer to democracy in its literal meaning as 'rule by the (common) people'; Ireton offered them constitutional or limited government instead.

The radicals did try to compromise on some of their proposals, in order to reach an accommodation with the grandees; but events were soon to overtake them. The king escaped, a Leveller mutiny was suppressed and army discipline re-established. In December of 1648 came Pride's Purge, when, with or without direct orders from Cromwell, Colonel Thomas Pride drove all opposition to the Army grandees out of Parliament. The king would soon be executed, and Cromwell's commonwealth would truly be in power. Later, Cromwell repudiated his most radical allies and arrested their leaders. Thereafter, the Levellers more or less disappeared from the political scene. But whatever the fate of Leveller thinkers or the availability of their writings, the ideas they represented were already too much a part of the revolutionary culture to disappear with them; and radical ideas such as theirs, to say nothing of the multitude's intrusion into politics, set the agenda for political debate thereafter – not least in the ideas of more 'canonical' theorists like Thomas Hobbes and John Locke.

The Levellers were not the most radical group to emerge during the Civil War.[6] There were others who found their proposed political reforms inadequate and their doctrine of natural right insufficient. There were those, in particular the 'Digger' Gerrard Winstanley, who were willing to acknowledge and accept the dire consequences that Ireton perceived in the concept of natural right, consequences that Levellers like Rainsborough denied, and to insist that there could be no true liberty without destroying the system of property. Yet even the Levellers had proved too radical, and they lost the political battle. Their ideas nonetheless remained a potent force and had a lasting effect on the ideological front. The revolution and their part in it had irrevocably changed the terms of political debate.

One measure of their influence is what happened to the notion of government by consent. The idea of government founded on a contract or the consent of the 'people' had long existed, as we have seen, in various versions,

---

6   For an illuminating contextual discussion of radical ideas in the period, see Geoff Kennedy, *Diggers, Levellers and Agrarian Capitalism: Radical Political Thought in Seventeenth-Century England* (Lanham: Lexington Books, 2008).

from defences of secular authority to justifications of resistance. But not till the Levellers introduced their innovations did the idea of government by consent become the basis of a democratic theory. A definition of the 'people' as consisting of a multitude of individuals may already have established itself; and, in the case of someone like John Ponet, this idea may even have produced a theory of individual resistance. But the Levellers took these ideas much further, while also redefining consent. Here, it was not corporate communities but individuals who would do the consenting, and more than that: the consent would have to be constantly renewed. It is worth noting, too, that the emphasis here is on the original, natural and inviolable rights of the people, not on any sort of mutual agreement or contract which stresses the obligations of subjects as much as their rights. The 'people', furthermore, though it would still leave out at least half the population (women), would come much closer to comprising the popular, labouring multitude, rather than an exclusive political community of propertyholders. And these people would exert their 'popular sovereignty' not just by reclaiming their rights in tyrannical emergencies but regularly and repeatedly, in the normal exercise of their everyday political rights as citizens.

After this theoretical innovation, and after the historic events that brought it into being, English political theory was never the same again. Theorists of a far less radical disposition, including even a defender of royal absolutism like Hobbes, felt obliged to meet the radical argument on its own ground, even to show that their preferred, and less democratic, forms of government met this new test of political legitimacy. In John Locke's time, when the threat from below seemed, to propertied classes, less immediate than the threat from above, Leveller ideas could be selectively mobilized by far less democratic forces in their battles with the Crown (about which more in what follows). The Whig aristocracy, led by Locke's mentor, the first Earl of Shaftesbury, could even associate themselves with the Green Ribbon Club, whose eponymous symbol had been the insignia of the Levellers, worn by mourners in remembrance of the murdered Rainsborough. So the influence of Leveller ideas can be found not only in later radical traditions, in the American Revolution or in the philosophy of the modern British Labour Party and even socialist movements, but in more conservative political ideas which have attempted to appropriate, domesticate and neutralize the radically democratic ideas that emerged in the English Revolution.

Thomas Hobbes

The mobilization of the 'multitude' in Parliament's conflict with the Crown created radicals and royalists together. The English ruling class had a particular need for popular support in pursuit of its struggle against monarchical power; but that need itself divided the propertied classes between those who were willing to take the risk and those who found the king, even with his absolutist aspirations, a safer bet. Just as some MPs were from the beginning more anxious than others about the dangers of popular mobilization, some observers very quickly saw its theoretical as well as its practical implications. No one saw them more clearly than Thomas Hobbes, the man who, despite the almost universal unpopularity of his ideas in his own time and place, is regarded by many as England's greatest political philosopher – if not always for the substance of his arguments, then at least for their rigour, ingenuity and style. Fear of the multitude was very much on his mind.

Already in 1628, in the year of the Petition of Right, he had revealed his political inclinations, translating the *History of the Pelopponesian War* by Thucydides, whose main attraction for Hobbes was that he regarded democracy as, to use Hobbes's own words, 'a foolish thing'. In 1640, Hobbes wrote his first major political work, *The Elements of Law: Natural and Politic* (privately circulated until its publication in 1650), in which he defended absolute sovereignty, in response to the claims of the Short Parliament. A few months later, Hobbes was, as he would later claim, 'the first of all that fled', escaping to France when the Long Parliament convened in November 1640 and began its proceedings against Strafford and Laud. Hobbes evidently feared that Parliament would prosecute him, too, for the subversive (absolutist) ideas expressed in *The Elements of Law*. In self-imposed exile in France, he wrote *De Cive*, at a time when mobs at home were demanding the abolition of episcopacy, and when the House of Commons was giving formal expression to its appeal for popular support in the Grand Remonstrance.

In *De Cive*, Hobbes developed the principles outlined in *The Elements of Law*, elaborating an argument that effectively denied the political legitimacy of the multitude and those who claimed its support. This work, written in Latin and published a decade later in English as *Philosophical Rudiments Concerning Government and Society*, would also form (with some significant and telling variations in response to intervening events) the basis of his great classic, *Leviathan*, written at the end of his exile and published in 1651, after which he returned from France.

Hobbes was a remarkable and in many ways contradictory figure. In an autobiographical poem he describes himself as born a twin with fear in 1588, the year of the Spanish Armada, and fear was certainly to figure prominently in his life and his work. Yet there is nothing cautious about his provocative ideas. The son of a lowly cleric, he was not a wealthy man himself; but throughout his life, after his education at Oxford, he associated with and faithfully served aristocracy, especially as tutor and secretary to William, second Earl of Cavendish, and later to William Cavendish, third Earl of Devonshire. Yet his work displays a consistent, if paradoxical, egalitarianism which seems genuine and deeply rooted despite the reactionary political purposes to which it is applied. There can be no doubt of his commitment to royal absolutism; and while in France, he even served as mathematics tutor to the exiled Prince of Wales. Yet his arguments in favour of absolutism were so unorthodox, indeed so clearly inspired by radical ideas, that even royalists found him dangerous. Some even accused him of being democratic, to say nothing of those who attacked his views on religion as little short of atheism. In 1666, after the Restoration, the House of Commons cited Hobbes's atheism as a cause of the fire and plague of London, and only intervention by influential friends (including, possibly, the king, his former pupil) saved him from being punished for heresy.

Not only did Hobbes's defence of absolutism start from what looked like dangerously radical premises, but it also treated with contempt all more traditional justifications of monarchical rule. Not for him the divine right of kings or reliance on biblical precedent. Hobbes chose to found his argument on the latest and most advanced principles of science and mathematics – as might be expected from someone who was acquainted with Galileo and who even (apparently) served as secretary for a short time to Francis Bacon, besides carrying on a scientific correspondence with Descartes. Nor was his defence of absolutism incompatible with the execution of the king and his replacement by the 'Protectorate'. Hobbes's argument in *Leviathan* could, as we shall see, just as well legitimize an Oliver Cromwell as a Charles or James Stuart – and, in fact, it has been suggested that his classic work was written as part of the so-called Engagement controversy of 1649–52, in which people debated the propriety of taking an oath acknowledging the legitimacy of the existing Cromwellian regime. Finally, this purveyor of some very unappealing and misanthropic political ideas seems to have been a rather attractive, humorous and lively personality, a brilliant conversationalist, and a generous man (charitable to the poor, for instance, in a way that his famous successor John Locke – ostensibly more democratic, more kindly disposed to human nature, and certainly richer – never was). And whatever else we may say about him, he is without doubt one of the greatest prose stylists among English philosophers.

In the early 1640s Hobbes put his genius, and his taste for paradox, to work on the new ideological and theoretical problems thrown up by the politics of this turbulent moment in English history. The most obvious problem he confronted was how to defend absolute monarchy in the face of powerful and almost universal opposition to it. *The Elements of Law*, composed when Parliament was assembled for the first time in eleven years and the tensions leading to civil war were coming to a head, already laid out his defence of absolute sovereignty. Here, his main objective was to defend the king against the claims of Parliament. The role of the 'multitude' in this work was simply to transfer its powers unconditionally to an absolute sovereign. In *De Cive*, Hobbes elaborates this argument in a way that indicates a preoccupation with another, more far-reaching problem than the rights of Parliament against the Crown. Among the most difficult questions for a man of his persuasion had to do not just with Parliament but with the political role of the 'multitude' outside Parliament. This is an aspect of Hobbes's thought that commentators have neglected. Yet it was Hobbes who translated into theoretical terms the opposition, from both royalist and parliamentarian camps, to the multitude's invasion of the political domain.

Parliament's reliance on popular support gave a new political function to people who up to now had lacked an acknowledged presence in the political arena, a recognized role as active citizens. Not only did the parliamentary opponents of the king claim legitimacy for their cause on the basis of the multitude's support, they also seemed to be moving in the direction of empowering the multitude itself. The gentry had shown itself at times willing to expand the franchise; and in moments of crisis, parliamentary leaders were ready to include in the political nation, at least temporarily, an even wider body of people, if not as electors then as agents of resistance to tyrannical rule. Eventually, the political personality of the 'multitude' as revolutionary agents would be given dramatic expression by the mobilization of the New Model Army; and finally, their spokesmen would demand full rights of normal citizenship.

In *The Elements of Law*, Hobbes confronted this process of political inclusion in its earlier stages. In his later work, he would face its more extreme and radical manifestations. We need to remember, too, that any political rights claimed by the multitude in England would belong not to Jean Bodin's 'colleges and corporate bodies' but to Sir Thomas Smith's 'multitude of free men collected together'. This could be taken to mean – as the Levellers insisted it did mean – that political rights belonged not just to some corporate entity or its official representatives but to each and every man just by virtue of being alive. Hobbes took on this challenge, too, and met these claims on their own terms.

The Elements of Law and *De Cive*

Both *The Elements of Law* and *De Cive* have the effect of denying the political role of the multitude – or, to put it more accurately, in these texts Hobbes finds a way of redefining and neutralizing that role. Where there had been other defenders of obedience to secular authorities who had relied on ascribing consent to a corporate body of the 'people', Hobbes adopts a more difficult solution, ascribing consent to a multitude of free and equal individuals, each endowed with natural rights unmediated by any corporate body or representative. He then sets out to demonstrate that the political task of the multitude is to create an absolute sovereign power; and it does this by handing over its own powers, wholly and unconditionally. The multitude expresses its political personality not by resisting tyrannical rule but by giving up its right to resist.

Hobbes's argument, especially in *De Cive*, is ingeniously constructed. He

starts with certain propositions about what human life would be like without government, in the so-called state of nature, depicting human nature in
the starkest and most dismal terms and bringing into sharp relief just those
qualities in human nature that make 'civil society', society with government,
necessary and desirable. Since all men seek glory and profit in comparison
with others, they would normally be inclined to strive for domination over
others more than simply for their company. So the principal feeling they
have for one another is not goodwill but fear. The main reason for this
mutual fear is that men are naturally equal (the great inequalities among
human beings are not natural but 'civil', that is, created in and by civil society and its laws). More specifically, they are equal enough to be able to kill
one another. Driven by the natural desire to avoid evil, their chief motivation
is the fear of death, the greatest evil in nature. This inclination to avoid evil
in general and death in particular is as natural and inevitable as the motion
by which a stone is impelled to roll downward.

Hobbes here introduces the idea of natural rights, but in his own
distinctive way. If self-preservation, or the avoidance of death, is a natural
impulse, it is reasonable for human beings to do everything necessary to
preserve themselves. When we speak of 'rights', we mean nothing more
than 'that liberty which every man hath to make use of his naturall facul-
ties according to right reason' (I.7). So the foundation of natural right is
that every man must do his utmost 'to protect his life and members'. But,
of course, since every other man has the same right, the end result is that
no one is secure, and the state of nature is a state of war 'of all men
against all men'. The exercise of natural right proves to be self-defeating,
and some way must be found out of this impasse. Natural law dictates that
a way must be found to provide the security lacking in the state of nature.
The answer is civil society, where every person is protected against every
other by the coercive force of government.

There are, argues Hobbes, two ways for men to join together in civil society: either by coercion or by consent, that is, by conquest or by agreeing to
help one another. Government by conquest is perfectly legitimate and even
in a sense consensual (so much for the illegitimacy of the 'Norman Yoke'),
and those subjected to it are bound to obey their masters, unless they choose
to die. As for government established by direct consent, people may agree to
pursue the same goals and the common good; but there will inevitably be
constant disagreement and conflict among them, and constant dissent when
their private interests seem to diverge from the common good.

Human beings, in other words, have many and divergent individual or
particular wills; so the secret of civil society is to unite their wills into one
single will, to submit their own individual wills voluntarily to some single
person or council. The object is to create a kind of civil person, an artificial entity with a will of its own, apart from the individual people who

compose it. This entity, to which 'each particular man hath subjected his will' – whether that entity is embodied in a single person (as Hobbes clearly prefers, since a single person can more easily embody a single will) or in an assembly – 'is said to have the Supreme Power, or Chiefe Command, or Dominion; which power, and Right of commanding, consists in this, that each Citizen has conveyed all his strength and power to that man, or Counsell; which to have done . . . is nothing else than to have parted with his Right of resisting' (V.11).

Hobbes stresses that this supreme or sovereign power is absolute, unlimited by laws or constitutional restrictions. For power to be limited, it would have to be limited by some other power, which would then become sovereign. So in every state, whatever illusions people may have about it, there exists some ultimate authority which is sovereign and absolute. There is no 'mixed constitution' for Hobbes.

Here is a carefully elaborated defence of absolute rule, which provides a persuasive case for the kind of absolute power sought by Charles I, and against Parliament's demands for its rightful place in the mixed constitution. Yet, on the face of it, an absolute parliamentary sovereignty would do just well as an absolute monarchy. It would, at any rate, satisfy Hobbes's definition of sovereign power, if not his real preferences. But there is more to his argument than this; and its significance, in his historical context, is clear enough. At least as interesting and significant as Hobbes's definition of sovereignty is what he has to say about the multitude.

Hobbes has painstakingly constructed a theory of government by consent, created by a multitude of individual men voluntarily, in pursuit of their own self-interest. This much is consistent with the distinctive English idea of a commonwealth constituted by the 'people' as individuals rather than as a corporate body or a collection of corporate entities. So far, what he says might even be consistent with the views of the Levellers. Yet, for Hobbes, this multitude of individuals can and must establish an absolute sovereign power in order to constitute a political society, and this same multitude cannot by its own volition simply dissolve the sovereign power it has itself created.

Hobbes is very insistent about what a 'multitude of men' is and is not, what it can and cannot do. The multitude is many individuals, not one. As a single collectivity, it does not exist, except insofar as the individual wills and powers of which it is composed are transferred to some single artificial entity: 'a multitude of men (gathering themselves of their owne free wills into society) . . . is not any one body, but many men, whereof each one has his owne will, and his peculiar judgment' (VI.1). The multitude as a collection of individuals has no collective identity, no legal status. It 'cannot promise, contract, acquire Right, conveigh Right, act, have, possesse, and the like, unlesse it be every one apart, and Man by Man; so as there must be as many promises, compacts, rights, and actions as Men' (VI.1 note). Nor can anyone claim legitimacy for an act of rebellion on the grounds of support by the multitude. Since only individuals can act or consent, no one can claim the support of the 'multitude', nor can the 'multitude' claim any status apart from those – and only those – individuals who compose it.

In *The Elements of Law*, Hobbes showed that the rights claimed by Parliament belonged to the sovereign, in this case the king, by arguing that civil society and the sovereign power had been created by a transfer of power from the people to the sovereign. In *De Cive*, he finds it necessary to emphasize that, once civil society and the sovereign power have been established, the people or 'multitude' has no further political role. Where there is a sovereign monarch, that monarch acts for the 'people'. Where the sovereign power consists of more than one person, the 'people' can act only in the form of an assembly, such as Parliament. There are clearly no circumstances in which the people outside Parliament, in the streets or anywhere else, can act as a political body:

> When we say the People, or Multitude, wills, commands, or doth any thing, it is understood that the City [i.e., the state] which Commands, Wills and acts by the will of one, or the concurring will of more, which cannot be done, but in an Assembly. (VI.1 note)

If in *Elements* Hobbes was challenging the claims of Parliament against the Crown, in *De Cive* he is forced to turn his attention not only to a recalcitrant Parliament but, even worse, to the mob in the streets.

In *De Cive*, Hobbes is clearly preoccupied with 'sedition' and the prospects of civil war:

> Neither must we ascribe any action to the multitude, as it's one, but (if all or more of them doe agree) it will not be an Action, but as many actions, as Men. For although in some great Sedition, it's commonly said, That the People of that City have taken up Armes; yet is it true of those onely who are in Armes, or who consent to them. For the City [the state], which is one Person, cannot take up Armes against itselfe. (VI.1)

But why, then, cannot each individual withdraw his consent and overthrow the sovereign by means of many such individual acts combined (or perhaps, *in extremis*, an individual act of tyrannicide)? Even if, answers Hobbes, it were true that the sovereign power is merely the product of each man's agreement with every other to join in mutual self-help, the dissolution of that agreement would require every single individual to withdraw his consent – something that seems very unlikely. Furthermore, even if a rebellion were supported by a majority, that majority itself would have no standing. No such majority can claim to be acting on behalf of the whole multitude, because the principle of majority rule – the principle that everyone is bound by the majority's decision – is itself a product of civil society and cannot apply outside it or against an established government.

The contract that establishes civil society is not just an agreement among individuals in a compact of mutual self-help. The sovereign power is certainly established by their mutual agreement, but it is an agreement to transfer their powers to someone else. So they are obligated not only to each other but to the sovereign power to whom they conveyed their powers and rights. 'Wherefore no subjects, how many soever they be, can with any Right despoyle him who bears the chiefe Rule, of his authority, even [i.e., especially] without his own consent' (VI.20).

It is hard not to admire the skill with which Hobbes has gone about his task. He not only accepts that the English state is a 'multitude of free men collected together' but even insists on giving that proposition its most radical construction: the commonwealth is a multitude of free and equal individuals, each possessing the same natural rights as all others – rights inherent in the individual person, not in his corporate status or in his property. Hobbes then constructs an absolutist argument on premises of which no Leveller would be ashamed.

Hobbes makes use of the proposition that the multitude is a collection of individuals rather than a corporate entity not in order to stress the political rights of the multitude but, on the contrary, to deprive the multitude of its political personality. To put it more precisely, in his theory the political function of the multitude is to cancel itself. The very act that establishes the multitude as a political entity is the act by which people give up their right of resistance. And he has turned the idea of individual rights on its head: yes indeed, every man possesses certain rights by nature, but he cannot enjoy his natural rights without effectively giving them up to a sovereign power.

It is worth pausing here to summarize again the ways in which Hobbes's argument is conditioned by the specific historical circumstances he is confronting. The immediate context is clear: Parliament, in its challenge to the absolutist aspirations of the king, has not only claimed its rightful share of the 'Crown in Parliament'. It has also mobilized the multitude outside Parliament and justified its own resistance by claiming the support of the many. Hobbes has undermined Parliament's case by repudiating both the mixed constitution and the political status of the multitude.

But there are also more fundamental, so to speak structural, reasons for this concerted attack on the rights of the multitude, rooted in specifically English conditions. In France, as we have seen, Bodin's groundbreaking theory of sovereignty had countered doctrines of resistance that vested the right to resist in corporate bodies and their representatives, by claiming that such bodies had no autonomous powers. All such lesser powers derived from the higher, ultimate, absolute and sovereign power. Bodin makes no attempt to argue that these corporate bodies somehow consented to an absolute monarch. Taking for granted that the state is a patchwork of fragmented jurisdictions, he simply argues that, among all the apparently independent powers and entities which represent merely particular or regional interests, there must be some superior power that unites them into one and represents the interests of the whole.

Hobbes, too, invokes such a sovereign power, but he does so in a different context. He is not dealing with a French state in which a growing absolute monarchy both supports and competes with a ruling class that claims its own autonomous powers and privileges. Hobbes's context is a unified English state, in which the ruling class has forfeited its independent powers to the state, accepting and even sharing in that unified state. This ruling class depends on private property and economic exploitation more than on the independent powers of jurisdiction or corporate privilege. This much is obviously clear to Hobbes, even if we do not accept the arguments of commentators who call him a 'bourgeois' thinker or attribute to him a precocious understanding of England's growing capitalism. It is also clear that the English ruling class, economically strong as it is in its control of land, and politically powerful as it is in its control of Parliament, does not enjoy the kind of independent jurisdictional and military power that would permit a successful challenge to the Crown without the support of the popular multitude.

So Hobbes has to cope not with Bodin's 'colleges and corporate bodies' but with Sir Thomas Smith's 'multitude of free men collected together'. If that multitude is, as Smith suggests, 'united by common accord and convenauntes among themselves, for the conservation of themselves aswell in peace as in warre', if individuals are united in a commonwealth by 'common and mutual consent for their conservation', Hobbes now has to show that their conservation requires an absolute sovereign power and that such a power is itself established by their 'common and mutual consent'. And now, in the midst of civil war, he has to confront the 'multitude' not only as a theoretical abstraction or as a passive mass but as a real political agent, a multitude of common folk whose political role is growing every day. His task is to acknowledge this reality while removing its sting.

Leviathan

When Hobbes was writing *De Cive*, the Civil War was just beginning. By the time he wrote *Leviathan*, events had moved far and fast. The New Model Army had been mobilized, the king had been executed, Parliament had passed acts to abolish the monarchy and the House of Lords, and Cromwell had established the Commonwealth. These events were accompanied by fierce debates, at every level, inside and outside Parliament, in broadsides, pamphlets and philosophical treatises – debates about the legitimacy of regicide, about the authority of Cromwell's regime and whether it was right to take the oath of 'engagement' to be faithful to it, about the extent and limits of political reform. And, of course, a wide range of radical ideas and movements had emerged, forcing onto the agenda much more far-reaching political programmes than even Cromwell had in mind.

In this new context, Hobbes revived, elaborated and modified the arguments of *De Cive*. By this time, he not only had to come to terms with the intervening dramatic events but with significant changes in his own circumstances. His earlier work had provoked violent reactions, especially among theologians, and he apparently lost his position in the exiled royal household thanks to their interventions. The hostility felt by Hobbes for critics of this kind is vividly evident in the ideas on religion outlined in *Leviathan*. That hostility, together with his willingness, or need, now to reconcile himself to Cromwell, gives that work much of its distinctive flavour.

Leviathan is, to be sure, a self-conscious effort to elaborate a science of politics with the same kind of certainty enjoyed by physics and mathematics. Its philosophical foundations are carefully and systematically constructed, in explicit or implicit debate with other philosophers as far back as Aristotle, with the most ostentatious applications of the latest scientific principles. Yet if all this makes *Leviathan* seem less like a political tract written for a specific occasion than a treatise designed for all times and all seasons, there can be little doubt of its political and personal urgency, to say nothing of its burning anger.

The argument of *Leviathan* is generally the same as that of *De Cive*, and much of the text is little more than repetition or paraphrase of the earlier work. But the few substantive divergences between the two books are significant. One of the most striking features of *Leviathan* is the space Hobbes devotes to religion. Something like half the book deals with the 'Christian Commonwealth'. This preoccupation reflects not only his anger at his theological critics but, above all, his conviction that religion has been a major cause of civil war. In his history of the Civil War, *Behemoth*, written after the Restoration, the corruption of the people by ministers, papists, and sectarians would head his list of reasons for that great disorder. There can be no doubt that religious liberty had been a principal objective in the revolutionary programme, and more particularly, religion had played a central role in legitimating rebellion against the king.

In *Leviathan*, Hobbes's main objective in the discussion of religion was to demonstrate that true Christianity requires obedience to secular authority. There can be no conflict between Church and state. A man cannot serve two masters, and there is no universal Church that can claim precedence over every particular secular power. The Church in every commonwealth is subject to its own civil sovereign. In this respect, Hobbes's views on religion merely sustain his absolutist political argument. Yet it is one of the many paradoxes in Hobbes's thought that the theological arguments he mobilized to make this absolutist case – materialist and secularist arguments inimical to orthodox brands of Christianity, whether Catholic, Anglican or Presbyterian – seemed to his critics to have more in common with the religion of radicals like Winstanley than with the theology of royalists like Archbishop Laud.

As for the main political argument, *Leviathan*, like *De Cive*, starts with the natural condition of humanity. This time, Hobbes spells out in greater detail the characteristics of human nature which make civil society necessary. Applying the principles of physics and its laws of motion, he tries to reduce human motivations to their most basic, as it were atomic, components, treating human passions – notably, of course, the impulse to avoid pain, the instinct of self-preservation, and the fear of death – as instances of matter in motion, the principles of attraction and repulsion. The result of this exploration is an account of the state of nature much the same as that depicted in *De Cive*: a state of war, 'of all against all'. This might not mean constant fighting, but it would generate a state of fear and uncertainty during which there would be no assurance that open war would not break out. Life would be, in Hobbes's most famous phrase, 'solitary, poore, nasty, brutish, and short'. And again he spells out the laws and rights of nature that must lead to the establishment of civil society. Without it, there can be no security of the person or property, let alone comfort and 'commodious living'. In the state of nature, there is no proper distinction between *mine* and *thine*, since every man gets what he can; so the right of property is a civil right which depends on the sovereign power.

Here, too, all men are naturally free and equal, all endowed with the same rights of nature, yet those natural rights are self-defeating without a sovereign power; and here, too, the state of war is ended by mutual agreement among individuals to transfer their powers to an absolute sovereign. Starting with the most extreme premises about natural equality, he ends with an equally extreme absolutism. His starting premises about natural equality, which imply that there is no systematic and universal inequality among human beings that could account for domination and subjection, even extends to the relations between men and women. Hobbes goes further than most political theorists in acknowledging the equality of women; but just as his convictions about the equality among men does not prevent him from justifying absolute rule by some over others, he can find reasons for the almost universal dominion of men over women. It is men who generally found commonwealths, probably because they are generally stronger and monopolize coercive force; and so civil law almost universally gives men dominion over their families. But the subjection of women to men, like the subjection of men to a sovereign power, is in principle consensual. In both cases, the basic reason for consent appears to be fear, either fear of the conqueror himself or fear of others from whom the subject person is seeking protection.

In *Leviathan*, as in *De Cive*, Hobbes is fighting his battle on several fronts. He is, at least implicitly, challenging various available anti-absolutist arguments, such as those of the monarchomachs in France; but he is also taking issue with existing absolutist theories, if only to fill loopholes in them and to make them more airtight against new and unprecedented challenges. A conception of sovereignty such as that of Bodin would certainly serve some of Hobbes's purposes. For example, it challenges the notion of a mixed constitution, and Hobbes is able to use something like Bodin's conception to argue against the claims of Parliament by demonstrating that power must be absolute and indivisible. Bodin's definition of law as simply the will of the sovereign is also useful to Hobbes. In the English context, it can be used against the common law tradition and against Parliament's claim to be the paramount interpreter of common law. But if the French doctrine of sovereignty is capable of serving many of Hobbes's purposes, there is one major thing it cannot do: it cannot cope with a multitude of free individuals who claim the right of resistance and even more active and continuous political rights.

Some commentators have argued that the individualism of Hobbes's argument was forced on him by monarchomach theories of resistance (as well as by his scientific aspirations, the thought experiment of breaking down the civil order into its atomic particles). These French theories of resistance were based on the idea that the royal power ultimately derived from the people as a collective entity. The people, though individually inferior to the king, were collectively superior to him. Therefore, as a corporate community they had a collective right to resist through the medium of their representatives. So Hobbes, it has been argued, set out to deny that such a corporate community existed in the first place. Outside civil society, he maintained, there exists only a multitude of individuals. Only a sovereign power can transform such a motley collection of individuals into a community. So the sovereign power is not created by or answerable to some pre-existing community. On the contrary, the sovereign power creates the community itself.

Now Hobbes was certainly thinking of the monarchomachs in some of his arguments. But it still remains unclear why it would not have sufficed simply to take over Bodin's argument against the monarchomachs. Why was it not enough just to say, as Bodin did, that the unity of the commonwealth can be created only by a sovereign power, without which there exists only a collection of disunited, fragmented and particular interests which cannot represent a single overarching common good? Why was Hobbes compelled to think in terms of individuals endowed with natural rights, and to defend absolutism by starting with a multitude of free and equal individuals?

Hobbes's argument about the multitude, as we have already observed, addressed some very specific conditions in England, conditions which French thinkers like Bodin were not compelled to confront. The monarchomachs, for example, asserted not the rights of individual citizens but the autonomous powers of nobles and various corporate bodies. The issue, in other words, was not so much the rights of persons as the rights of office, or, to put it another way, it was not so much a question of rights at all so much as a question of powers and privileges. If anything, resistance was a duty attached to public office, not an individual right inherent in humanity.

These French doctrines of resistance assigned no political role to the multitude; and in countering them, an absolutist thinker like Bodin did not have to deal with either a theory of individual rights or with the multitude's claims to political agency. The problem he faced was not so much popular activism as the pretensions of lesser nobles and municipal officials and their claims to own a fragment of the state. His task, then, was to challenge the autonomy of these corporate powers and privileges, which continued to play such an important part in the French polity. He simply had to deny their independence and to demonstrate that they ultimately derived from the sovereign power. In the fragmented polity of France, he was also able to counter their claims by invoking a larger, more comprehensive corporate entity, the kingdom as a whole, represented by the sovereign power.

Hobbes, as we have seen, faced a wholly different set of problems when he wrote *De Cive*. The structure of the English state and English property relations in general, as well as the immediate conditions of England in 1640 in particular, meant that the monarch, faced not with a host of fragmented jurisdictions but with a unitary representative and legislative body, had no greater claim than did Parliament to represent the body politic in its entirety, in the way the French king could claim to represent a larger corporate entity than did the estates or 'lesser magistrates'. English conditions also compelled Hobbes to deal with the 'multitude', and with the rights of citizens, in completely new ways. The intervening developments between *De Cive* and *Leviathan* obliged him to take the argument one step further.

In *De Cive*, Hobbes imagines a multitude of free individuals who contract with one another to transfer their powers, once and for all, to an absolute sovereign. From then on, the sovereign represents them and they have no right to call back the powers they have given away. Even in the unlikely case that every individual were to agree with every other to withdraw the powers they have granted to the sovereign, they still could not dissolve the sovereign power, because their mutual agreement to transfer their powers to someone else means that they have an obligation not only to each other but to the sovereign power they created and which they cannot remove without its consent.

In *Leviathan*, the argument undergoes some subtle but significant changes. One of them, emphasized by Quentin Skinner, is a modified definition of liberty. In *Elements*, Skinner points out, Hobbes never clearly defined freedom or liberty, while in *De Cive*, in order to counter 'republican' arguments that the very existence of absolute or arbitrary government reduces men to servitude, he offers a clear and simple definition of liberty as 'nothing other than *the absence of impediments to motion*'. However absolute the sovereign power may be, our subjection to it cannot be equated with servitude. Finally, in *Leviathan*, Hobbes defines liberty not simply as the absence of impediments to motion but the absence of *external* impediments. This is, for Skinner, 'a moment of great historical significance'.[7] Hobbes can now distinguish between liberty and power, the absence of impediments to action, on the one hand, and, on the other, the capacity to act. Intrinsic limitations or constraints – such as the fear that leads to submission – may take away our power, but only external obstacles can take away our liberty. This represents a landmark in the modern theory of liberty because Hobbes is here 'the first to answer the republican theorists by proferring an alternative definition in which the presence of freedom is construed entirely as absence of impediments rather than absence of dependence'.[8] In this way, Skinner argues, Hobbes sets in train the divergence between republican and liberal conceptions of liberty.

Hobbes also modifies his account of the agreement that creates the sovereign power. In *De Cive*, the agreement to establish a sovereign power was formulated like this: 'I conveigh my Right on this Party, upon condition that you passe yours to the same' (VI.20). In *Leviathan*, the wording is different: 'I Authorise and give up my Right of Governing my selfe, to this Man, or to this assembly of men, on this condition, that thou give up thy Right to him, and Authorise all his Actions in like manner' (XVII). The new element here is the idea of authorization: people create a sovereign to represent them not simply by transferring their powers to him but by authorizing him to act on their behalf, making themselves the authors of the sovereign's every action.

What is the effect of this apparently minor change of wording, and why did Hobbes feel obliged to introduce it? On the one hand, the new formulation appears to make the powers of the sovereign even more absolute or unlimited. In the earlier version, although there is no agreement between people and sovereign but only an agreement among the people to transfer their powers, Hobbes may have felt that there was still some hint of a compact with the sovereign when he suggested that the original agreement creates a 'double obligation', a bond not only between each subject and

7 Quentin Skinner, *Hobbes and Republican Liberty* (Cambridge: Cambridge University Press, 2008), p. 131.

8 *Ibid.*, p. 157.

every other but also between each subject and the sovereign. In the new formulation, Hobbes emphatically denies any suggestion of a mutual bond or obligation between subject and sovereign. He insists that the sovereign is party to no compact or covenant, has no contractual obligation to his subjects, is subject to no contractual conditions and therefore can be guilty of no breach of any covenant. The argument is strengthened by the claim that the sovereign's every act is not only his own but that of its 'authors', the subjects who 'authorized' him and whom he represents. So having been authorized to maintain peace and preserve the lives of his subjects, he has an unlimited right to determine the means to achieve those ends, without conditions and without interference from his subjects. He can, indeed must, even control the public expression of opinion. And he can do all these things as tyrannically as he likes without breaking any rules of justice. Hobbes expects his sovereign to rule by means of law that is known to his subjects, but there is no real check against the ruler's tyrannical behaviour except his own rationality. If every act of the sovereign is 'authorized', to accuse him of injustice would be to accuse the 'author' of committing an injustice against himself.

On the other hand, the very same formulation has another, apparently contrary meaning. The transfer of powers in *De Cive* is performed once and for all. The people have permanently alienated their powers and cannot under any circumstances take them back or bestow them elsewhere. In *Leviathan*, by contrast, subjects do not simply give away the power to act but always remain the 'authors' of the sovereign's acts. So the act of authorization may imply some limiting conditions after all. If subjects simply give away their powers, what the sovereign does with those powers is, in a sense, no longer their business. But if every subject remains the author of the sovereign's actions, those actions must, in the end, be consistent with the authors' purposes. If the authors authorized a sovereign power to preserve their lives and their security, the sovereign may have unlimited rights to decide how to do this; but the one thing the authors cannot have authorized him to do is to fail at this task.

And so, Hobbes tells us:

> The Obligation of Subjects to the Soveraign, is understood to last as long, and no longer, than the power lasteth, by which he is able to protect them. For the right men have by Nature to protect themselves, when none else can protect them, can by no Covenant be relinquished . . . The end [goal] of Obedience is Protection; which, wheresoever a man seeth it, either in his own, or in anothers sword, Nature applyeth his obedience to it, and his endeavour to maintaine it. (XXI)

And clearly, any sovereign power – with its capacity to keep the peace – is subject to violent death, in foreign wars or in 'Intestine Discord'. When the sovereign power can no longer keep the peace or protect its subjects it no longer exists, and obligation ends (which may bring Hobbes closer to Spinoza).

In the face of Hobbes's insistence on the unlimited and absolute nature of sovereign power, this concession may seem empty. It certainly does not mean that he is imposing 'liberal' standards of legitimacy upon the sovereign power, entitling subjects to resist a ruler that exceeds the limits of legitimate authority. At best, it means that rulers who fail to maintain their power have, *ipso facto*, lost their authority to rule. Yet in its historical context, this principle is significant enough; for one of its main consequences – and perhaps its main purpose – is to legitimate the power of Oliver Cromwell. In the earlier formulation, the sovereign authority no longer belongs to the people after the original agreement. Even a defeated Stuart king would continue to possess that authority once it had been granted and passed on to him by its original recipient. But now, in *Leviathan*, since the people's authority has never been truly alienated, it does not belong to the fallen king or his successors but still to the people. At least, authority passes, if not directly to the people themselves, then to whoever can preserve the peace, whoever can fulfil the purpose for which they created the sovereign power. By definition, it belongs to the victorious man or men whose sword can guarantee the 'protection' which compels obedience, in this case Cromwell, who would become the 'Lord Protector'.

With his concept of authorization, then, Hobbes has perfected his defence of absolutism built on radical premises. On the face of it, his conclusion is deeply anti-democratic: any de facto government, any government capable of maintaining order, no matter how tyrannical, must be regarded as legitimate. It must even be regarded as based on consent, authorized by its subjects. Yet Hobbes's absolutist theory of authorization has the effect of legitimating a revolutionary regime. As one intepreter of Hobbes's work has argued, 'The first modern revolution had taken place, and Hobbes believed it would be wrong to seek to reverse it.'[9]

While his conclusions were anything but democratic, Hobbes reached them by appropriating some of the most radically democratic ideas of his day. The Levellers had accomplished a revolution in political thought by insisting that consent to government must be given by a multitude of individuals rather than by some corporate body that claims to represent them, and that such consent must be given continuously – not just by reserving the right of resistance *in extremis* but in the form of the vote – and not in one act of submission that binds them indefinitely. Hobbes met the Leveller challenge with his theory of authorization, a theory of continuing consent

---

9 Introduction to *Divine Right and Democracy: An Anthology of Political Writing in Stuart England*, ed. David Wooton (Harmondsworth: Penguin, 1986), p. 58.

without voting. With that theory, he put the finishing touches on a justification of absolutism built on the premise that men are free and equal in the state of nature, that they are endowed with certain natural rights, and that they cannot be bound to obey any government to which they have not, as a multitude of individuals, given their continuous consent.

John Locke

Although radicals like the Levellers effected a revolution in political theory and set the agenda of political debate in England from then on, in practice they were roundly defeated, as Cromwell turned against the radical alliance which had brought him to power while frightening away the bulk of the parliamentary classes. With that betrayal, the Commonwealth lost the wider social base that might have sustained the republican revolution; but the irony is that even this was not enough to reassure less radical parliamentarians. The experience of the Civil War, with the revolutionary forces it had unleashed, ended by reuniting the propertied class, not behind the parliamentary project that had driven them to conflict with the king but, on the contrary, behind the restoration of the Stuart monarchy. Anything, even a renewal of the absolutist threat, was evidently better than a 'world turned upside down'.

The Restoration was not, of course, the end of the matter. It simply postponed until 1688 the realization of the parliamentary project begun in 1641. The years between 1660 and 1688 saw renewed and growing conflicts not so very different from the ones that had brought about the Civil War. By the late 1670s, there had emerged parliamentary opposition ready to take on the king yet again, and another decade of crisis finally ended in success. The so-called Glorious Revolution ended Stuart rule, bringing William and Mary of Orange to the throne, and with them, or so historical convention informs us, the kind of constitutional monarchy and parliamentary supremacy that remains in place today – the kind of political order, in other words, that the ruling class in Parliament had sought in 1641.

In the renewed conflicts between Parliament and Crown, there was yet another recurring theme. Among the aristocrats who led the parliamentary opposition in the 1670s and early 1680s, there were, again, some who were prepared to further their cause by forging alliances with radical forces, especially in London. Between 1679 and 1681, there was what amounted to a revolutionary crisis – the Exclusion Crisis – sparked by (ultimately failed) attempts to exclude from the royal succession Charles I's presumptive heir, his brother James, on the grounds that he was a Roman Catholic and, it was feared, likely to revive the Stuart's absolutist project. The most important leader of these radical Whigs, as they came to be called, was Anthony Ashley Cooper (1622–83), first Earl of Shaftesbury, a wealthy and 'improving' landowner who was also deeply involved in colonial trade, employer, patron and friend of the philosopher John Locke. The association between the two men was very close, and Locke appears to have been actively involved in Shaftesbury's political activities. Their dealings with radicals have persuaded some commentators that Locke's true sympathies lay with the radicals; and they have interpreted his political writings, specifically his famous *Two Treatises of Government*, on that assumption. But Locke's relationship with radical ideas is more complicated than that and requires closer scrutiny.

Locke, born in 1632 the son of a country attorney and small landowner on the fringes of the lesser gentry, began his career as an Oxford don. Although he started as a lecturer in Greek, rhetoric and moral philosophy, he began to study medicine informally. In 1666 he met Shaftesbury and soon joined his household as secretary, family tutor and physician – in which capacity he saved his employer's life by removing an abscess of the liver. Before and after his mentor's death in 1683, Locke held various government posts having to do with the colonies, plantations and trade, matters in which Shaftesbury, Lord Chancellor for a time in the 1670s, was keenly interested. Locke managed to amass a tidy, if moderate, fortune from his inheritance, his government salaries and various investments in lucrative commercial ventures. Because of his – or at least his patron's – involvement in subversive activities, he cautiously removed himself to Holland for a time in the 1680s, returning after the 'Glorious Revolution' and serving the new government.

Locke's intellectual interests were many and varied. He published significant works on economics and theology; an influential work on education, *Some Thoughts Concerning Education* (1693); and the ground-breaking *Letter on Toleration* (1689), a powerful plea for religious toleration. He was keenly interested in agriculture; and this interest, as we shall see, is reflected in his theory of property. Probably his most famous work, which became one of the most widely read books of the eighteenth century and a major influence in the Enlightenment, was *An Essay Concerning Human Understanding* (1690), a treatise on the origins and nature of human knowledge.

The *Essay* was addressed in part to the rejuvenation of the gentry which Locke believed was in decline: self-indulgent, extravagant and slothful. Among his aims was to show how ordinary literate people might become more 'industrious and rational' – in the words of his *Second Treatise of Government*. Locke was writing a kind of 'natural history' of the human psyche, in the tradition of Francis Bacon's 'natural histories' of plants, animals and various human practices and institutions. Like Bacon, Locke urges his readers to purify their minds by freeing themselves from the yoke of custom, fashion and received opinion. Then, as autonomous, self-directed individuals, they should reason about their own ideas and those of others.

Gentlemen are warned that without self-improvement, they will eventually be replaced by those of lower condition who surpass them in knowledge.[10]

Locke's argument is based on the by now familiar concept of the mind as a *tabula rasa*, a blank slate, at birth, on which sensations from the natural and social environment are imprinted. His view that knowledge derives from sense experience is the basis of 'empiricist' theories of knowledge, but it also implies that most human differences are due not to heredity but to different circumstances and education. At the same time, throughout his works, though cherishing the self-made man, he is convinced that the rich and poor will always be with us and that the former will always dominate the latter. Not only does he take for granted the relations between 'master' and 'servant', he even justifies slavery. Still, the ruling class, if only out of prudent self-interest, must govern in an enlightened and rational way, resisting tyranny while upholding political institutions limited by law and accountable to some kind of electorate, in a pluralistic society enjoying freedom of speech, association and religion. He stresses the value of labour, industry, thrift, sobriety and moderation, in sharp contrast, for example, to Hobbes's fondness for the classic heroic (and aristocratic?) virtues of courage, nobility, magnanimity, honour and glory.

Locke's most important intervention in political debate, the *Two Treatises*, was published anonymously in 1690; and he always denied authorship throughout his life, acknowledging it only in a codicil to his will. There has even been much debate about exactly when the *Treatises* (which, for all practical purposes, represent a single work) was written. It used to be thought that it was written not long before its publication, and thus represented a justification of the Glorious Revolution after the fact. It is now more generally accepted that the *Treatises* was written a decade earlier, probably in 1679–81 – that is, around the time of the Exclusion Crisis. This makes it not a retrospective justification of a revolution already safely completed but a subversive call to revolutionary action. If this is so, it certainly explains Locke's reluctance to admit authorship, especially since the Revolution never looked absolutely secure to its participants. Whatever Locke's motivations in writing this work, it was to have great influence in later centuries, across a wide political spectrum, not least in the American Revolution and in other revolutions thereafter.

One thing – and perhaps only one – is clear and uncontroversial about Locke's *Two Treatises of Government*. It is a powerful attack on absolute monarchy, a call for 'limited', constitutional, parliamentary government and the rule of law. These are the qualities that people have in mind when they

---

10   For a comprehensive discussion of these points, see Neal Wood, *The Politics of Locke's Philosophy: A Social Study of 'An Essay Concerning Human Understanding'* (Berkeley: University of California Press, 1983).

describe it as a founding text of 'liberalism'. Beyond that, the interpretation of Locke's political ideas remains a subject of fierce controversy. In particular, commentators are divided about how radically democratic Locke was – whether, for example, his political ideas came close to those of the Levellers or, on the contrary, represented the interests of the Whig aristocracy. Another major subject of debate has to do with Locke's position in relation to the 'rise of capitalism' – whether 'capitalism' is a meaningful category at all in discussions of the seventeenth century and, if it is, whether Locke can be considered a commentator on, or even an advocate of, those social and political changes we associate with capitalism in its early stages.

It will by now to be clear to readers of this book that its author regards the 'rise of capitalism' as a useful idea, for reasons laid out especially in Chapter 1 and earlier in this chapter.[11] It should also be blindingly obvious that to speak of the 'rise of capitalism', or to situate Locke in that historical context, in no way suggests that he or his contemporaries had any notion of 'capitalism' or any prescience about future historical developments. It simply means, as we have seen, that he lived at a time of significant changes in relations and conceptions of property, which were always fiercely contested, and that Locke was very conscious of the issues at stake in both practice and theory. He was, as will be argued in what follows, on the side of the 'improving' landlords; and his argument was ideally suited to the interests of a progressive landed aristocracy engaged in capitalist agriculture and colonial trade: in short, to the interests of men like Shaftesbury.

This is not to deny that Locke was, in the context of his time and place, some kind of 'radical'; but his radicalism, as we shall see, had more politically in common with Cromwell or Ireton than with the Levellers. What makes his political theory especially complex and interesting is that he arrives at Ireton's conclusions (though without any hint of repudiating monarchy) while starting from Leveller premises. He adopts radical ideas to make the strongest possible case against absolutism but is always careful to limit their most democratic implications.

The *Two Treatises of Government*

The *First Treatise*, less commonly read than the *Second*, is a detailed refutation of the case for royal absolutism in *Patriarcha*, written by Robert Filmer decades earlier but resurrected and published by supporters of the

---

11   For more detailed arguments on this score, and on Locke's political theory in general, see my articles 'Locke Against Democracy: Representation, Consent and Suffrage in the *Two Treatises*', *History of Political Thought* XIII.4, Winter 1992, pp. 657–89; and 'Radicalism, Capitalism and Historical Contexts: Not Only a Reply to Richard Ashcraft on John Locke', *History of Political Thought* XV.3, Autumn 1994, pp. 323–72.

king in the monarchy's new conflicts with Parliament. In painstaking detail, in language dripping with irony and ill-disguised contempt, Locke takes apart Filmer's ingenious and idiosyncratic argument that royal power descends from Adam and the patriarchal power bestowed on him by God. Locke's efforts here are devoted less to laying out a coherent political theory of his own than to challenging Filmer's logic, as well as his biblical scholarship, by demonstrating (sometimes unfairly) the absurdities and inconsistencies in *Patriarcha*; but the fundamental premises of the *First Treatise*, though spelled out more systematically in the *Second*, are clear: men are naturally free and equal, and no free man can be bound to obey a government without his own consent, so that no absolute government can be regarded as legitimate.

In the *Second Treatise* Locke is no longer just debating with one specific author, and he constructs a systematic and more or less coherent political theory. Like Hobbes, he begins with a 'state of nature' and outlines the conditions that make civil society necessary and desirable. But where Hobbes concludes that any government capable of maintaining order – and, more particularly, an absolute government – is better than the 'state of war' which would exist in its absence, Locke's purpose is precisely to deny the legitimacy of the kind of government Hobbes advocates. For Locke, a government's capacity to keep the peace is not enough to compel obedience to it, and something more is required to explain how men, born free and equal, acquire an obligation to obey.

Locke's argument is not always easy to follow. His concept of the state of nature is especially ambiguous. He is, to begin with, very keen to dissociate his conception of the state of nature from Hobbes's state of war. The state of nature, he insists, is a condition governed by certain laws of nature, certain divinely ordained moral precepts, which human reason can discover. Locke's account of human nature also seems far less grim than that of Hobbes. Human beings, it seems, are capable of living together without government, and they even take pleasure in each other's company. If Hobbes bases civil society on the worst in human nature, Locke founds it on the best of human qualities, reason and the capacity to live by moral rules. Yet this version of the state of nature appears to be less an account of some historical reality than a kind of moral ideal. Its main purpose is to serve as a standard against which to judge what counts as a legitimate government, a true civil society. Just as Hobbes's worst case scenario was designed to emphasize the necessity of absolute government, Locke's optimistic portrait is meant to rule out all absolutist forms as contrary to natural liberty, equality and reason.

At the same time, there seems to be another state of nature in Locke's theory, not just a moral ideal but something like a historical condition – if not an actual historical stage in human development then at least what the world would really be like without government. Here, the emphasis seems to be on human selfishness, perhaps based on a belief in original sin. If men really could live together governed only by their own reason and by the laws of nature, Locke now makes clear, civil society would be unnecessary.

In the end, Locke's 'real' state of nature is not a million miles away from the condition of uncertainty that is Hobbes's state of war. Society without government is fraught with uncertainties and 'inconveniencies'. In particular, in the state of nature, where the only laws are natural laws, and where every man must execute the laws himself, there is no impartial judge to whom people can appeal in case of conflict, so each man must be judge in his own case. Such conditions are inevitably unstable, and no one can be certain that the smallest conflict will not end in war. Since Locke, as we shall see, imagines the (historical) state of nature as a form of social organization in which private property already exists, the likelihood of conflict is, of course, that much greater. So men (and it is indeed men) have found it useful, even necessary, to establish civil society.

Locke's account of the state of nature may not be as clear and consistent as it could be, but his message here is reasonably unambiguous: free, equal and rational men agree to establish civil society in order to avoid the inconveniences of the natural state, as they do in Hobbes's version of the story. But since rational men can never be understood as having agreed to something that would worsen their condition, much depends on how their 'natural' condition is presented. For Hobbes, any form of government capable of maintaining peace and order is better than the state of war. In Locke's case, what men are trying to avoid is not – or not simply – a state of war but a condition in which their obedience to natural law is made too uncertain and unsafe by the absence of a common and impartial judge.

This has important implications in establishing the criteria of legitimate government. Against the background of Locke's state of nature, free men can never be understood as having agreed to absolute government, a government not subject to the rule of law. In relation to a ruler who is above the law, people would still be in the state of nature, comparable to their relations with other men at a time when there was no impartial judge to settle conflicts between them. The ruler would here be judge in his own case. In fact, in such circumstances the government's use of its coercive powers on its own subjects – the use of its official powers of enforcement and punishment – would be 'force without right', and therefore nothing better than a state of war.

Locke's civil society, too, is established by agreement among free individuals, but unlike Hobbes's government founded by consent, the agreement to establish civil society is not simultaneously a transfer of power. Men, according to Locke, first agree to form a society and then, in a separate act, establish some form of government, not by unconditionally handing over their powers but as a kind of trust. Government, in other words, is entrusted, but only on certain conditions, with the powers each man enjoyed in the state of nature. If those conditions are violated, power returns to the people. They do not, however, thereby return to the state of nature. The dissolution of government does not, as seems to be the case for Hobbes, mean the disintegration of society. This account of the state of nature and the formation of civil society for Locke means, among other things, that men do have a right of revolution, a right to resist and overthrow a tyrannical or unlawful government; and they can do so without fear of dissolving society itself.

In the end, the differences between Hobbes and Locke have less to do with fundamental disagreements about human nature, or about what the world would be like without government, than with very immediate political considerations. Hobbes's objective is to legitimize absolute government, whether in the hands of a Stuart king or a Cromwellian 'Protector'. Locke is seeking to justify resistance to a Stuart king and the establishment of parliamentary supremacy. Both men make use of radical ideas and arguments, Hobbes to turn them on their head in defence of absolutism, Locke to strengthen his anti-absolutist case. But if Locke's anti-absolutist argument is more consistent with radical principles than is Hobbes's absolutism – more consistent, for example, with the Leveller view of 'self-propriety' and rights – his use of radical ideas is, in its own way, no less complex and ambiguous than Hobbes's.

Locke's political theory as outlined in the *Second Treatise* might be understood as a theoretical expression of the alliance between the Whig aristocracy and London radicals, a mobilization of radical ideas in order to advance the interests of the propertied classes. It is also useful to keep in mind that when Locke was writing, England was no longer in the throes of civil war, popular radicalism had been effectively suppressed and the threat from below was less immediate than the threat from above. This may have given him the confidence to appropriate revolutionary ideas which radical parliamentarians in the 1640s – men like Cromwell and Ireton – had rejected and feared. But the fact that Locke adopts the very Leveller concepts that Ireton, in the Putney Debates, so forcefully refuted does not by itself make Locke a Leveller. A major part of Locke's theoretical strategy is to adapt such radical ideas for the sole purpose of making the strongest case for Parliament against the king, and for the right of revolution, while at the same time depriving those ideas of their most democratic implications.

Readers will remember that, during the Putney Debates, Ireton warned against the consequences of adopting a conception of natural right. Followed to its logical conclusion, he insisted, it would end by endangering all property. Yet Locke adopts precisely such an idea of natural right. He even bases it on the Leveller principle that every man has a property in his own person, from which follow certain inalienable rights. Locke cannot have been familiar with the transcript of the Putney Debates, even if he knew about Leveller ideas; but such ideas were in the air, and his argument proceeds uncannily as if his object were to demonstrate that Ireton's fears (like Filmer's warnings) were unfounded. He seems to be saying that a doctrine of natural right, based on the Leveller concept of 'self-propriety', can be construed in such a way as to argue for a right of revolution against an absolute monarch but without any 'levelling' consequences, any danger to property, or any threat of popular democracy.

Ireton (like Hobbes and many others) took it for granted that the surest way to sustain the interests of the propertied classes was to insist that property, or at least its existing form and distribution, was simply a human convention, not derived from natural right but upheld by constitution and tradition. Locke, by contrast, sets out to demonstrate that property itself does indeed exist by right of nature, and he not only denies that the notion of natural right represents a threat to the existing social order but even finds a way of turning the concept of natural right to the defence of property and inequality.

We shall return to Locke's theory of property in a moment. But there are also other ways in which he adapts something like Leveller ideas to something like Ireton's politics. At the heart of Locke's political theory is his doctrine of consent. Again, no free man can be obliged to obey a government to which he has not consented. Much, then, depends on what is meant by consent – and, as we have seen, it could, in seventeenth-century England, mean almost anything. For the Levellers it meant that free men must have the right to vote. For Hobbes it meant that men have effectively consented to absolute monarchy or at least any existing government capable of staying in power and keeping the peace. What, then, does it mean for Locke?

Locke cites with approval Hooker's notion of consent which, though it meant something less extreme than it did for Hobbes, implied that men were bound by agreements made in the distant past. But Locke is far more concerned than Hooker to rule out absolute government, so there is obviously more to be said about his doctrine of consent.[12] We can probably learn more about Locke, again, by reading the *Second Treatise* against the background of the Putney Debates.

In response to the Leveller question of whether any free man can be obligated to a government to which he has not given his individual consent – a consent requiring constant renewal in the form of the franchise – Ireton replied that of course there are cases in which people are obliged to obey without consenting by means of the vote: foreigners, who certainly do not enjoy the right to vote, are expected to obey the law. They are free to leave the country if they choose not to obey. By contrast, men with a 'fixed,

---

12   For more on Locke's relation to Hooker, see my 'Locke Against Democracy', pp. 664–7; and 'Radicalism, Capitalism and Historical Contexts', pp. 331–3.

permanent' interest in the form of property cannot easily depart and leave everything behind; so their political obligation must be based on consent. Those without property, who merely have the 'interest of breathing', are more like foreigners in this respect. They are 'here today and gone tomorrow' and require no special rights apart from the right to depart.

Locke, at first glance, appears to be on the Levellers' side, with his insistence on the universal right of all free men to be governed by their own consent. Yet he finds an ingenious way of making universal consent consistent with Ireton's less democratic conclusion. Locke, like Ireton, cites the example of the foreigner who visits our shores. Locke, like Ireton, points out that such a person, indeed anyone who uses our highways and breathes our air, is expected to obey our laws. But there is one significant difference between Ireton and Locke: while Ireton cites this as a case of obligation without consent, Locke suggests that, even in such cases, consent has actually been given after all. The point is simply that there are two kinds of consent, 'express' and 'tacit', the latter probably derived from Hooker's notion of a 'secret' consent and the idea that people can give their consent even without knowing that they do so. Anyone who lives and breathes within our borders has given tacit consent to our government and has thus accepted the obligation to obey.

Locke has shown how, even with Leveller premises, we need not arrive at Leveller conclusions or suffer the consequences feared by Ireton. Ireton and the Levellers both argued on the basis that consent meant the franchise, so Ireton was compelled to demonstrate that obligation did not require consent. Locke adopts a different strategy: obligation does require consent but consent does not require the franchise. For that matter, Locke's argument is not inconsistent with the view that an individual can be 'represented' in Parliament without the right to vote, just as propertyless men could, according to Thomas Smith or Richard Hooker, be 'present' in Parliament or (as later thinkers would describe it) 'virtually' represented.

Locke never tells us in so many words what he thinks about the franchise, except for one passage (§158) that appears to propose nothing more than the correction of the notorious anomalies in the voting system, in much the same way that Ireton himself had suggested. We need to remember, too, that throughout the seventeenth century, regulations on the franchise fluctuated constantly, as the ruling class shamelessly manipulated the right to vote, its generosity growing whenever it needed popular support against the Crown, as was the case during the Exclusion Crisis. It is possible that Locke would have advocated this tactical expansion of the franchise at such a critical moment. But it remains significant that, with the doctrine of tacit consent, he neatly severed the connection between consent and the franchise, which both Ireton and the Levellers had taken for granted.

Locke seems to have a more elastic idea of consent than does Ireton. Had he not already laid a foundation for excluding absolutism as a legitimate form of government, his 'tacit' consent might come dangerously close to Hobbes's view that the mere existence of a functioning government implies consent. But however easily, even unconsciously, people may give their consent, according to Locke, there are, again, only certain kinds of government to which free men can be understood as having consented, and these do not include absolute monarchy, because such a government defeats the very purpose for which civil society was established in the first place.

When a ruler acts not according to the law but by his own arbitrary will, or when he interferes with a properly constituted legislative body or tries to change the means of electing it, when government subjects the state to a foreign power (all of which Stuart kings could be accused of doing), or when government, including legislative bodies, violates the trust reposed in it by invading the liberties and properties of the subjects, government is dissolved and the people have a right to constitute a new one. In general, as long as a properly constituted legislative power – Parliament in England – exists and is allowed to go about its business without undue interference, it can be assumed that no right of revolution exists, though there may be times when even legislators act contrary to their trust. In any case, if the normal processes of changing government have been denied to the people, they have a right to rebel and set up a new one by extra-parliamentary means.

It should be emphasized here again that granting people the right of 'revolution' need not entail granting them more normal, everyday political rights, as we already know from Cromwell and Ireton, who granted some people the right to take up arms against a government but not the right to vote for one. We also know that even the most radical convictions about *natural* equality need not be expressed in equally radical views of *political* equality. The view that men are naturally free and equal was, in the seventeenth century, consistent with everything from radical democracy to royal absolutism, everything from Winstanley to Hobbes – and Locke seems to stand somewhere between these extremes.

The disconnection between natural and political equality is even more vividly demonstrated in what Locke has to say about women. He may not go as far as Hobbes in explicitly granting the equality of women; but in his argument against Filmer's patriarchal defence of royal absolutism, Locke goes quite far in asserting joint parental or even maternal powers in the family against the kind of absolute paternal right on which Filmer bases his case for the absolute power of kings. Locke does not deny the superiority of fathers, or the 'foundation in nature' of the husband's authority over his wife. But he goes some distance in denying a divine command that subjected Eve to Adam, or women to men, and accuses Filmer of substituting his own 'fancies' for divine truths. Yet none of this has implications for the political rights of women. So much does Locke, like virtually all his contemporaries

– including, apparently, women themselves – take for granted the exclusion
of women from the political sphere, that in giving them a more exalted role
in the household he senses no political danger, no possibility of being misun-
derstood as proposing to admit women into the realm of politics.

Locke, beginning with the Leveller idea of 'self-propriety' and natural
right, ends in a political position perfectly consistent with Ireton's more
oligarchic stance. He does, to be sure, seem to hold a fairly radical view on
the right of revolution in extreme emergencies, a right he is prepared to
grant to the 'people' in general (that is, perhaps, to all free male heads of
households), and not just to their representatives in Parliament. This was a
view shared only by the most radical Whigs. But, as the examples of
Cromwell and Ireton dramatically demonstrate, even a more radical view of
revolution did not, in seventeenth-century England, necessarily rule out the
exclusion of many free men from more normal political rights. After all, the
rank and file of the New Model Army had been accorded a right of revolution in no uncertain terms, but the very same Army grandees who had
mobilized them insisted on denying them the simple right to vote for their
representatives in Parliament. When asked why the Army had fought, if they
were to be denied political rights, Ireton replied that they had won enough
by gaining the right to be governed by a representative body and a known
law rather than by the arbitrary rule of one man, and the freedom to do
business and acquire property. This, too, is what it means to be a member of
political society; but to be an 'elector', endowed with the franchise, is
another matter altogether.[13]

Locke's Theory of Property

Although the chapter on property seems to have been added to the *Second
Treatise* after its original completion, it certainly plays a significant part in
Locke's political theory. It is here that he fleshes out the theory of natural
right which forms the basis of his anti-absolutist argument. He does so by
elaborating the principle that every man has a property in his own person
from which other rights follow. But if, for Locke as for the Levellers, the
property that men have in their persons entails certain inalienable natural
rights, it does not, as we have seen, necessarily entail all those political rights
envisaged by the Levellers. A closer look at Locke's distinctive elaboration of
'self-propriety' and how it differs from that of the Levellers reveals a great
deal about both his theory of property and his politics.

God, says Locke, 'hath given the World to Men in common' (§26). Yet
the view that the world began as a common *dominium* was, as we have
seen, fairly conventional in the Western tradition and could accommodate

---

13   For more on this point, see 'Locke Against Democracy', pp. 688–9.

everything from a strong defence of private property to Winstanley's radical repudiation of property. Locke sets out to demonstrate not only that men's common ownership of the earth is compatible with private property but that such property is grounded in natural right. Here he puts to brilliant use the idea of 'self-propriety'. 'Though the Earth, and all inferior Creatures be common to all Men', Locke begins, 'yet every Man has a Property in his own Person. This no Body has any Right to but himself. The Labour of his Body and the Work of his Hands, we may say, are properly his' (§27). Self-ownership, and the property that every man has in his own labour, then becomes the source of property in things and land. Anything in which a man 'mixes his labour', anything which, through his labour, he removes or changes from its natural state, anything to which he has added something by his labour, becomes his property and excludes the rights of other men. This is how private property grows out of common ownership, not by common consent but by natural right – as an extension of a man's person and his labour, in which he has an exclusive right by nature. In any case, although God did give the earth to men in common, he did not give it to them in order to waste it. He gave it to the 'industrious and rational' for the sake of 'improvement', to add to its value, usefulness and productivity by means of labour.

Locke does, to be sure, maintain that there are certain limits on accumulation established by natural law. The most obvious – apart from the physical limits of the capacity to labour – is that no man should accumulate so much that he cannot consume it and lets it go to waste or spoil. Nor should he accumulate so much that he damages the interests of his fellows. He must leave enough, and good enough, to respect everyone else's right to subsistence. These 'spoilage' and 'sufficiency' limitations seem to mean that a man's own capacity for labour together with that of his family, and his own capacity for consumption together with that of his household, set strict natural – and moral – limits on what he can accumulate. So it is hard to imagine how large accumulations and vast inequalities of wealth can be consistent with natural law.

Locke has a simple answer. There is one development in human society that changes everything: the invention of money. Money makes it possible for people to accumulate more than they themselves can consume without violating the natural law of prohibition against spoilage. The decision to attach some kind of value to gold or silver as a medium of exchange means that wealth can be accumulated in a form that keeps indefinitely. It also permits exchange and profitable commerce, which in turn create an incentive for increasing productivity and wealth. Without money and commerce, there would be neither possibility nor motivation for 'improvement' and accumulation.

The improvement of land encouraged by money and commerce also means that less land can support more people. On the one hand, this might be taken to mean that, although people now can accumulate more without violating the spoilage limitation, they have no need to do so in order to live well. They can produce more wealth, and they can therefore leave more for others. Locke has indeed been interpreted as opposing large concentrations of property in this way. On the other hand, Locke suggests that money, commerce and 'improvement', by making land more productive and giving it more value, actually add to the 'common stock' of humanity. This means that people can accumulate more without depriving others and without violating the 'sufficiency' limitation. A man who accumulates and improves large holdings, far from violating the rights of others, actually enhances their well-being.

In such conditions, furthermore, many people can even live without any property at all, because they can exchange their labour for a wage. It turns out that the labour which gives a man a right to property may be someone else's labour. Locke clearly takes for granted that some will have large properties and others none at all. Indeed some will create the wealth of others by working for them. 'Master and Servant', he writes, 'are Names as old as History' (§85), and servants (a term that, in the seventeenth century, included many wage labourers) can sell their labour without losing their natural liberty, as long as the relation between master and servant is a contractual one, not an unconditional and permanent alienation but a sale of labour for a certain time. (Locke also justifies slavery, but on different grounds: a man who loses his liberty by conquest in a lawful war may be spared his life in exchange for his permanent servitude.) And where land is 'improved' and profitably utilized, even the servant may be better off than the owners of unimproved land.

Nor does Locke stop there, for the invention of money has yet another implication. Since money has value only because men have consented to it, this also implies that they have consented to its consequences: 'it is plain, that Men have agreed to disproportionate and unequal Possession of the Earth, they having by a tacit and voluntary consent found out a way, how a man may fairly possess more land than he himself can use the product of' (§50). Although specific laws and constitutions regulate specific systems of property, the inequality to which men have consented is not dependent on any such specific laws. It applies wherever money exists. This appears to mean that no government can override that agreement by seeking to alter the conditions of inequality to which men have agreed. The invention of money and everything that follows from it changes conditions so radically that natural law, together with man's natural freedom, equality and common possession of the earth, become consistent not only with private property but also with gross inequalities. And all of this has the legitimacy that comes from free consent.

Locke was not the only, or even the first, to suggest that property originates in labour; but he was certainly the first to elaborate this principle so systematically, both as a theory of property and as a theory of natural right. He also, as we shall see, gives a very specific twist to the idea that property originates in labour, which sets him decisively apart from his predecessors. Locke's conception of natural right is central to his argument against absolutism; but the implications of his theory of property go well beyond his anti-absolutist politics. Here, again, we can learn a great deal about Locke by considering his theory against the background of the Putney Debates.

Readers may recall Major William Rainsborough's remark at Putney that 'the chief end of this government is to preserve persons as well as estates, and if any law shall take hold of my person, it is more dear than my estate'. The Levellers certainly believed in the right of private property, but Major Rainsborough was here giving the *person* priority over property, and this was precisely the principle Ireton most feared. Here, as elsewhere, Locke finds a way of circumventing this consequence of Leveller doctrine.

Locke states unequivocally that the 'chief end' of civil society 'is the preservation of Property' (§85). This seems unambiguous enough, and at first glance appears to leave no room for rights that inhere in the person as distinct from property. Yet when, in his controversial chapter on property, he defines property itself, Locke often uses a broad definition which includes 'life, liberty and estates'. Formulae such as 'life, liberty and property', or 'persons, liberties and estates' had become conventional in asserting the rights of the subject since the Petition of Right, appearing, for example, in the Grand Remonstrance; and Lilburne had asserted the 'ancient' fundamental right of every Englishman to be protected from arbitrary and illegal intrusions on his 'life, liberty or estate'. Locke's inclusion of all these rights in the single category 'property' certainly implies that the purpose of government is, as Major Rainsborough insists, 'to preserve persons as well as estates', that every man, even one without 'estates', possesses something that government is obliged to preserve, and that therefore such a person has certain basic rights. It is on the basis that rights inhere in the person, with or without a 'fixed interest' in the form of property, that Colonel Thomas Rainsborough demands an extension of the franchise even to the 'poorest he'. Ireton sees the danger of invoking rights that inhere in the person just by virtue of living and breathing, which implies that such rights exist by nature and not by convention or the English constitution. But Locke has found a way of ascribing natural rights to the person while avoiding the hazard foreseen by Ireton and has, yet again, made Leveller principles consistent with Ireton's politics. His doctrine of consent, for instance, makes it possible to speak of such natural rights without requiring anything more than what Ireton is willing to concede: that the rights of every person are adequately protected by the existence of a representative body and a known law rather than by the arbitrary rule of one man.

As for property, when Locke describes it as a natural right, he seems to mean something rather different from what the Levellers intended, or more particularly, he is answering a different question. In the debate between Rainsborough and Ireton, both parties seem to agree that the institution of private property is divinely ordained (though this does not preclude the belief that in the beginning the earth was given to men in common). For example, in response to the accusation that the doctrine of natural right endangers all property, Rainsborough insists that he has no such intention and that the demand for a voice in government certainly does not imply the destruction of property. Property, in fact, exists by divine law: 'The law of God says it, else why God made that law, thou shalt not steal?' Although Ireton repudiates the idea of natural right as the basis of property, he does not deny this divine commandment, nor does he suggest that property as such has no divine authority. But this, for him, is not the main issue. The question is whether the existing distribution of property and, more particularly, the distribution of political rights that goes with it are legitimate.

Ireton argues that the institution of property in general may exist by divine law, but the particular right of any individual to any particular property is no more divinely ordained than is the right to elect Parliament. 'Divine law', he says, 'extends not to particular things.' It 'does not determine particulars but generals, in relation to man and man, and to property, and all things else'. Any connection between divine law and a particular man's property is very remote, and 'our property descends from other things'. Particular rights to property, no less than political rights, derive from convention and historical precedent. If we challenge those conventions and precedents by appealing to some transhistorical natural right, we shall endanger all property. After all, if every man has a natural right to whatever he needs for his subsistence, then surely no private property can be secure.

Colonel Rainsborough does indeed invoke some kind of natural right, though he denies any intention of endangering private property. But the significant point is that neither he nor the other Levellers invoke natural right as a way of explaining how people come to have a property in some particular thing. Certainly, the Levellers dispute the legitimacy of the historical and constitutional precedents invoked by Ireton to support the existing distribution of property and political rights. The Levellers offer different historical precedents, and they claim certain 'native' rights which have been violated by the Norman Conquest. They do call on a notion of natural right or self-propriety to support their historical claims; but the main object of that notion is liberty, not private property.

The Leveller argument was most clearly laid out by Richard Overton in his pamphlet *An Arrow Against All Tyrants*, whose eloquent and frequently cited definition of 'self-propriety' was quoted earlier. Overton certainly insists that 'mine and thine' could not exist if men had no inviolable property in their own selves, but he simply means that no man can securely enjoy what he possesses if his natural freedom is subject to usurpation and his person to arbitrary violation. As to the origin of material property itself, Overton says nothing; but we can get some sense of what he thinks from his reference to the principles of Magna Carta, repeated in the Petition of Right, and his quotation from Sir Edward Coke's commentaries:

> No man shall be disseised, that is, put out of seisin [have taken from him], or dispossessed of his free-hold, that is, lands or livelyhood, or of his liberties or free customes, that is, of such franchises and freedomes, and free customes, as belong to him by his free birth-right; unlesse it be by the lawfull judgements, that is verdict of his equals (that is of men of his own condition) or by the Law of the land . . . by the due course and processes of law.

The relevant property rights here are various civil and customary rights, recognized by statute or customary law (freehold tenures, the 'freedom' of corporations, 'franchises' or licences to conduct business, and so on). Overton says nothing about the natural origin of property. He only insists that a man's natural freedom gives him an inalienable right to 'the due course and processes of law' and that no interference with his property is legitimate without such processes. The emphasis, again, is not on property as such but on liberty and the illegitimacy of arbitrary power.

The Leveller argument seems to be something like this: every man has a property in his own person. From this follow certain liberties: the liberty not to be subject to anyone else's authority without consent, the liberty to follow one's own religious beliefs, and, indeed, the liberty to enjoy one's possessions without unlawful interference, that is, without interference by any power not properly constituted, accountable and acting according to the due processes of law.

Certainly, the Levellers undoubtedly dispute the legitimacy of the historical and constitutional precedents invoked by Ireton, and they do so by claiming 'native' rights which have been violated by the Norman Conquest. The argument based on self-propriety makes clear what the Levellers think about legitimate power, but it does not explain how some people come to have legitimate possessions. It does mean that political rights cannot be based on property in the sense of 'estates'. These rights belong to the person. And it also means that the existing distribution of property represents little more than theft, acquired by conquest and preserved by illegitimate power. The Levellers want to dissociate political power from wealth and privilege, and they want to protect small property from unjust and oppressive interference.

But there is nothing in their arguments that would be inconsistent with Ireton's principle that particular properties exist by convention. The point is simply that some conventions are legitimate and others not, depending on whether they respect or violate natural liberty.

If demonstrating the natural origin of particular properties was not the objective of radicals like the Levellers, John Locke's purpose is rather more complicated, though the issue has been somewhat confused by commentators who emphasize the continuity between Leveller ideas of self-propriety and the Lockean theory of property. Locke sets out precisely to answer the difficult question of particulars: 'how any one should ever come to have a Property in any thing' (§25). His reasons are complex, but one clear objective is to strengthen the inviolability of property by making it independent of, and prior to, civil society: if men have a right to property before and apart from civil society, which belongs to them by nature and not by grant from government or the community, that simply reinforces the principle that no government can interfere with property unlawfully.

Locke is also undoubtedly trying to meet, yet again, a challenge from Filmer. In support of his claim that political power and property descended by grant from God to Adam, Filmer takes issue with all those who claim – and this, in one way or another, includes thinkers as diverse as Hobbes and Ireton, and perhaps even the Levellers – that property exists by the consent of men, because this implies that possession of the earth was originally common. Filmer simply argues that, if this were so, private property would be an unimaginable sin against God's will; and, at the very least, it would have required the universal consent of mankind, of which there is absolutely no evidence. Locke, in his refutation of absolutist theory in general and Filmer in particular, takes on this argument too. He demonstrates how it is possible for private property to be consistent with God's grant of the earth to men in common, 'how Men might come to have a property in several parts of that which God gave to Mankind in common, and that without any express Compact of all the commoners' (§25).

But there is more to Locke's conception of natural right than its role in his case against absolutism, as becomes evident when we compare him, again, to the Levellers. We may begin to understand the differences between Locke and the Levellers by considering one simple fact: the Levellers had no strong incentive to accept Ireton's argument that natural right was an enemy to custom and convention. They certainly wanted to repudiate some conventions and customs, those that established the current system of power and privilege. But one of their main objectives was to *protect* certain customs, the customary rights and tenures of ordinary 'free-born' Englishmen, which were being attacked by the dominant classes. So the Levellers were not really interested in demonstrating that natural right took precedence over custom in general. What they wanted to show was that certain customary rights had the support of more universal, even natural, principles, and that the extinction of these rights without due processes of law and by an illegitimate government was a violation of natural liberty.

Locke appears to have no comparable attachment to customary rights. His theory of natural right does indeed endanger custom and convention, but not in the sense feared by Ireton. Locke's theory of natural right threatens not the properties of landlords like Shaftesbury but the customary rights of commoners. At any rate, Locke adapted and modified the Leveller idea of 'self-propriety' in an ingenious way, again preserving the delicate balance which is characteristic of his political theory in general: on the one hand, a radical anti-absolutism, and on the other, a careful limitation of its democratic implications.

Locke's theory of property gives substance to the notion of natural right which he deploys so powerfully in his attack on absolutism. To invoke a natural and inalienable right to 'life, liberty and estate', which no government is entitled to violate, certainly adds strength to the case against absolutism. The argument that property is rooted in an individual right which belongs to every man was also designed, again, to counter Filmer's claim that all political power and property are derived from God's grant to Adam and not from some universal (male) human right.

There may be other political reasons for Locke's argument too. It has, for instance, been suggested that the chapter on property, and the importance Locke attaches to labour as the source of property, represents a gesture to the 'industrious' classes whom Shaftesbury's party was courting in its attempts to forge an oppositional alliance during the Exclusion Crisis (though we shall see in a moment that 'labour' has a rather flexible meaning in Locke's theory of property, which fits the 'improving' landlord no less than the 'industrious' classes who work with their own hands). At the same time, the chapter on property also helps to neutralize some of the more democratic possibilities inherent in the radical conception of natural right. The theory of property includes a neat justification of gross inequality, which makes Locke's revolutionary theory compatible with the existing distribution of property in England.

In all these ways, the chapter on property has an important political meaning for Locke, but it also has implications that go far beyond its consequences for his theory of politics. The chapter represents a major rethinking of property in principle, which has to do with distinctively English historical developments.

Improvement

Locke's argument on property turns on the notion of 'improvement'. The theme running throughout the chapter is that the earth is there to be made productive and that this is why private property, which emanates from labour, trumps common possession. The very word 'improve', it is worth noting, in its original sense (derived from the Anglo-French *emprouwer*) means to 'turn to profit' or to 'manage for profit'; and this is clearly the sense in which Locke and his contemporaries used it. Locke repeatedly insists that most of the value inherent in land comes not from nature but from labour and improvement: 'tis *Labour* indeed that *puts the difference of value* on everything' (§40). It is clear, too, that the 'value' he has in mind is exchange or commercial value. He even offers specific calculations of value contributed by labour as against nature. 'I think', he suggests, 'it will be but a very modest Computation to say, that of the *Products* of the Earth useful to the Life of Man, $9/10$ are the *effects of labour*', and then immediately corrects himself: it would be more accurate to say that 99/100 should be attributed to labour rather than to nature (§40). An acre of land in unimproved America, which may be as naturally fertile as an acre in England, is not worth 1/1000 of the English acre, 'if all the Profit an *Indian* received from it were to be valued and sold here' (§43). Unimproved land is waste, so that a man who takes it out of common ownership and appropriates it to himself – he who removes land from the common and encloses it – in order to improve it has given something to humanity, not taken it away.

We already know that, for Locke, there is no direct correspondence between labour and property, because one man can appropriate the labour of another. It now appears that the issue for Locke has less to do with the activity of labour as such than with its profitable use. In calculating the value of the acre in America, for instance, he refers not to the Indian's labour, his expenditure of effort, but to the (lack of) profit he receives, in the absence of a well-developed commerce. The issue, in other words, is not the labour of a human being but the productivity of property and its application to commercial profit.

In a famous and much-debated passage, Locke writes that 'the Grass my Horse has bit; the Turfs my Servant has cut; and the Ore I have digg'd in any place where I have a right to them in common with others, become my *Property*' (§28). Much ink has been spilled on this passage and what it tells us, for example, about Locke's views on wage labour (the labour of the servant who cuts the turfs). But what is truly striking about this 'turfs' passage is that Locke treats 'the Turfs my Servant has cut' as equivalent to 'the Ore I have digg'd'. This means not only that I, the master, have appropriated the labour of my servant, but that this appropriation is in principle no different from the servant's labouring activity itself. My own digging and my appropriating the fruits of my servant's cutting are, for all intents and purposes, the same. But Locke is not interested in simply passive appropriation. The point is rather that the landlord who puts his land to productive use, who improves it, even if it is by means of someone else's labour, is being industrious, no less – perhaps more – than the labouring servant.

We have become so accustomed to the identification of 'producers' with the employers of labour (as in 'automobile producers' in conflict with trade unions) that we fail to see its implications, but it is important to keep in mind that certain very specific historical conditions were required to make it possible. Traditional ruling classes in pre-capitalist societies, passively appropriating rents from dependent peasants, would never think of themselves as 'producers'. The kind of appropriation that can be called 'productive' is distinctively capitalist. It implies that property is used actively, not for 'conspicuous consumption', nor simply to obtain the means of 'extra-economic' coercion, but for investment and increasing profit. Wealth is acquired not simply by using coercive force to extract more surplus labour from direct producers, in the manner of rentier aristocrats, but nor is it acquired by 'buying cheap and selling dear' in the manner of pre-capitalist merchants. Wealth is created by increasing labour productivity (output per unit of work), to produce profits that are realized in market transactions.

By conflating 'labour' with the production of profit, Locke becomes perhaps the first thinker to construct a systematic theory of property based on something like these capitalist principles. He is certainly not a theorist of a mature, industrial capitalism; but his view of property, with its emphasis on productivity for profit, already sets him apart from his predecessors. His idea that value is actively created in production is already vastly different from traditional views which focus simply on the process of exchange, the 'sphere of circulation'. (Only William Petty, often called the founder of political economy, had suggested anything like this 'labour theory of value' in the seventeenth century.) Locke in his economic works is critical of those landed aristocrats who passively collect rents without improving their land, and he is equally critical of merchants who simply act as middlemen, buying cheap in one market and selling at a higher price in another, or hoarding goods to raise their price, or cornering a market to increase the profits of sale. Both types of proprietor are, in his view, parasitic. They are anything but 'producers'. Yet his attack on proprietors of this kind should not be misread as a defence of working people against the dominant classes. He certainly praises industrious artisans and tradesmen, but his ideal seems to be the great improving landlord, whom he regards as the ultimate source of wealth in the community, what he calls the 'first producer' – a man like Shaftesbury, capitalist landlord and investor in colonial trade, a man who is not only 'industrious' but whose vast property contributes greatly to the wealth of the community.

Locke's view of property is very well suited to the conditions of England in the early days of agrarian capitalism. It clearly reflects a condition in which highly concentrated landownership and large holdings were associated with a uniquely productive agriculture (productive not just in the sense of total output but output per unit of work). He also, like Sir Thomas Smith, takes for granted the triadic structure of English agriculture, the triad of landlord, tenant, and 'servant' or wage labourer, which, though not widespread throughout the country was well established in the southern and south-western parts of England that Locke knew best. His language of 'improvement' echoes the scientific literature devoted to the techniques of agriculture which flourished in England at this time, especially emanating from the Royal Society and the groups of learned men with whom Locke and Shaftesbury were closely connected. More particularly, his constant references to common land as waste, his praise for the removal of land from the common, and indeed for enclosure, had very powerful resonances in that time and place.[14]

We need to be reminded that the definition of property was, in Locke's day, a very immediate practical issue. A new definition of property was in the process of establishing itself, challenging traditional forms not just in theory but in practice. It was constantly arising, for example, in disputes over common and customary rights. Increasingly, the principle of 'improvement' for profitable exchange was taking precedence over other principles and other claims to property, whether those claims were based on custom or on some fundamental right of subsistence. Enhancing productivity itself became a reason for excluding other rights.[15]

There are in the seventeenth century already examples of legal decisions, in conflicts over land, where judges invoke principles very much like those outlined by Locke, in order to give exclusive property precedence over common and customary rights. Such arguments were used to support the landlord seeking to extinguish the customary rights of commoners, to

---

14   At one point in his argument, Locke acknowledges that there may be, as in England, common land recognized by law, and in such circumstances, it cannot be enclosed without consent (§35). But this qualification is not as restrictive as it may seem at first sight. As I argue in 'Locke Against Democracy': 'Even if we leave aside the kinds of coercion that were available to larger landowners in relation to vulnerable poor men, which could compel the latter to consent . . . [t]here were, of course, already massive concentrations of land outside the reach of communal rights, and there were also many cases in which common rights on land already legally owned, often by a large landlord, existed by custom but without unambiguous legal standing. The extinction of such customary rights was, above all, what enclosure was about and the reason for the conflicts it generated. There is nothing in the *Second Treatise* that would tend towards the protection of these customary rights, and a great deal, having to do with the benefits of enclosure and its contribution to the wealth of the community, that would argue in favour of their extinction, in the interests of the commonwealth. In fact, as we have seen, it was precisely the kind of argument from improvement employed by Locke that was increasingly being used as a legal challenge to customary rights' (pp. 681–2).

15   E.P. Thompson charts the transformation in the idea of property rights as it manifested itself in practice in 'Custom, Law and Common Right', in his *Customs in Common* (London: Merlin, 1991).

exclude them from common land, to turn common land into exclusive private property by means of enclosure. Enclosure, exclusion and improvement, as Locke had said, enhanced the wealth of the community and added more to the 'common stock' than it subtracted. In the eighteenth century, when enclosure would rapidly accelerate with the active involvement of Parliament, reasons of 'improvement' would be cited systematically as the basis of title to property and as grounds for extinguishing traditional rights.

This is not the only way in which Locke's theory of property supported the interests of landlords like Shaftesbury. We have already alluded to Locke's justification of slavery. His views on improvement could also be easily mobilized in defence of colonial expansion and the expropriation of indigenous peoples, as his remarks on America and its native peoples make painfully obvious. If the unimproved lands of the Americas represented nothing but 'waste', it was a divinely ordained duty for Europeans to enclose and improve them, just as 'industrious' and 'rational' men had done in the original state of nature. 'In the beginning all the World was *America*' (§49), with no money, no commerce, no improvement. If the world – or some of it – had been removed from that natural state at the behest of God, anything that remained in such a primitive condition must surely go the same way. Locke may not have been alone in devising a justification of empire that had less to do with jurisdiction than with property, but he went far beyond the simple principle of *res nullius* invoked by other defenders of colonial appropriation. The issue for him was not simply vacant or unused land but rather land left unimproved for profitable commerce. Nor was he simply arguing, as Grotius had done, that things become property when and because they are used and transformed. The right of property – and that includes colonial appropriation – for Locke derived from the creation of value.[16]

John Locke constructed a powerful defence of parliamentary, 'limited' government, but without embracing democracy. It would take a very long time, and a great deal of struggle, before parliamentary government was democratized even to the point of universal male suffrage of a kind approaching what the Levellers had demanded, to say nothing of the vote for women. When these victories were won at last, they were certainly worth winning; but by that time, the franchise could no longer make the kind of difference that the Levellers had hoped it would. The issue had by then been settled in favour of capitalist property. The old political struggles over common and customary rights had been lost, and many spheres of social life were subject

16 Something like Locke's argument was used decades earlier to justify the English colonization of Irish lands. Sir John Davies, one of the architects of English policy in Ireland, justifies expropriation and settlement in strikingly Lockean terms, precisely by measuring the value created by improvement. I discuss these points at greater length in my *Empire of Capital*, chs 4 and 5.

not to the requirements of democratic accountability but to the imperatives of capitalist competition and profit-maximization.

The Lockean Paradigm in Eighteenth-Century England

Much of the scholarly debate about eighteenth-century Western political thought, and Anglo-American thought in particular, has for some time now revolved around the relation between virtue and commerce, a debate in which John Pocock is the major reference point.[17] Pocock's narrative as it concerns eighteenth-century England goes something like this:

In the mid-1690s there was a financial revolution that produced a 'sudden and traumatic discovery of capital', in the form of public credit and with it the growth of government patronage. The critical and emblematic moment was the establishment of the Bank of England. This represented nothing less than a revolution in the nature and idea of property. The essential shifts in the structure and ideology of English property which some people see earlier in the seventeenth century, or even in the sixteenth, were, it would seem, of little consequence. The *real* transformation of property, the transformation of its structure and morality, occurred with 'spectacular abruptness' in the mid-1690s and was accompanied by sudden changes in the psychology of politics. This revolutionary shift marked the beginning of commercial society. It was the moment when relations among citizens, and between them and government, began to take the form of capitalist relations – which, in Pocock's terms, means relations between creditors and debtors.[18]

Political discourse, says Pocock, had to find ways of dealing with this transformation, to contest or justify a new commercial, oligarchic and imperial Britain. The vocabulary of classical republicanism was mobilized to deal with a revitalized conflict between landed and 'monied interests', preceded and shaped by a conflict between real property and government

---

17 See Pocock's collection of essays, *Virtue, Commerce and History: Essays on Political Thought and History, Chiefly in the Eighteenth Century* (Cambridge: Cambridge University Press, 1985).

18 Pocock has suggested that his approach to history is more 'diachronic' than 'synchronic' in the manner of Skinner. Skinner's 'historical intelligence', says Pocock, is focused on 'the synchronic, the detailed reconstruction of language situations as they exist at a given time', in contrast to Pocock's own approach, which, he says, 'leans to the diachronic, the study of what happens when languages change or texts migrate from one historical situation to another' (*Rethinking the Foundations of Modern Political Thought*, eds A. Brett and J. Tully, Cambridge: Cambridge University Press, 2006, p. 45). But it cannot be said that historical *process* figures very prominently in Pocock's account of eighteenth-century England. His revolutionary moment does indeed occur with 'spectacular abruptness', with no apparent grounding in the social transformations of the previous centuries.

patronage; and here we can find the origins of commercial ideology, in the controversy between 'virtue' and 'corruption'. One of the main ideological requirements for the new commercial ideology in its defence against opposition was to finesse the antithesis of virtue and commerce. It had to challenge the counterposition of an independent landed interest and a more or less corrupt – or at any rate corrupting – monied interest. The answers provided by ideologues of commercial society generally had to do with the civilizing effects of commerce, which eliminates the need for civic virtue by taming the passions or harnessing them to the public good. So the main axis of controversy in eighteenth-century political discourse concerns the opposition between a conception of property which stresses possession and civic virtue, and one that stresses exchange and its civilizing of the passions.

This narrative also has the effect of displacing Locke from the centre of the modern revolution in property and the theorization of an emergent capitalism. Locke is, according to this argument, irrelevant to the ways in which capitalist or commercial society was reflected on, criticized or legitimated. He is irrelevant both in the sense that commercial society did not yet exist and was not yet an issue in his period, and in the sense that the categories, the vocabularies, used to conceptualize commercial society in the eighteenth century were different from and often opposed to Locke's.

There is, to be sure, considerable controversy about Pocock's narrative and his assumptions about the relations between virtue and commerce in early modern European discourse. There are those who object not only to his analysis of Britain but to his analytic categories in general. After all, civic humanism in Italian city-states linked commerce, liberty and virtue; and commerce was readily embraced by Dutch republicans. Others insist that the importance of republican discourse in eighteenth-century England has been grossly exaggerated, and still others that American thinkers, building on both English and other European traditions of discourse, were perfectly capable of combining liberal and republican discourses, or, indeed, civic virtue and commerce. But, even when questions are raised about the nature and extent of civic humanism or republicanism, or about the relation between virtue and commerce in political discourse, the fundamental terms of the debate remain unchallenged.

It has already been suggested here that the idea of 'republicanism' is a rather blunt instrument, which is particularly ill adapted to the specificities of English politics. Much the same can be said about 'commerce', whether or not it is conceived as antithetical to, or as a substitute for, virtue. The very idea of 'commerce', to say nothing of 'commercial society', conceals as much as it reveals. The distinctive development of capitalism set England apart from other commercial societies. The commercial, oligarchic and imperial order of the eighteenth century was grounded in agrarian capitalism and its very specific property regime; and any opposition between landed and monied interests presupposed a more fundamental commonality among the propertied classes. Both country gentlemen and merchants, whether Tories or Whigs, belonged to the capitalist property regime.

The so-called commercial revolution did not just materialize from nowhere, nor was it simply a linguistic transformation. It was the end of a long process of development – the development of what we are calling agrarian capitalism. This was a process that created a powerful capitalist landed class, which, having defeated absolutism, came out of the revolution of 1688–9 effectively in command of England and in strong position to consolidate the property regime they had been establishing throughout the previous century. The foundation of the Bank of England – Pocock's revolutionary moment – was a result of their victory, particularly the greatest among them, the Whigs who had led the Revolution of 1688 and were its main beneficiaries.

The fact that the Bank of England emerged in response to the needs of an emergent landlord capitalist class made it different from any other public bank in Europe and tells us much about the specificities of English history. The Bank was a uniquely English institution; and this difference has a history, because banking in England had already developed in distinctively English ways. The Bank of England was the culmination of developments that had been in process since at least the sixteenth century. Banking on the Continent had developed largely to finance and facilitate long-distance trade or arbitrage among separate markets. The English system was fairly weak in those respects in the early days, but it developed ways to meet its own specific needs. In particular, it developed forms of banking which catered to investment by the landed class; this was something completely new, with no parallels on the Continent, and clearly an expression of England's agrarian capitalism.

Long before the Bank of England, the English agrarian economy had already developed in distinctive ways. The particular relations between large landowners and tenants who were capital farmers meant that English agriculture was responding to new requirements of competition and profit-maximization with no historical precedent. This created new needs for investment capital in ways unknown to capital-starved Continental peasants or even rentier landlords; and English banks developed as providers of investment capital to facilitate production in unique and historically unprecedented ways.

The English banking system, more than any other, dealt with transactions among producers – not just among commercial agents, or even producers and consumers, but among producers themselves in an increasingly specialized network of production. This was not a function of some late commercial or industrial economy. It was born in the English countryside, in particular with the specialization of English farming countries, which meant producers were obliged to deal with each other in distinctive ways very different from, say, the peasant economy and local peasant markets in France. English banking developed to meet the needs of an increasingly integrated domestic market, and a metropolitan market centred on London. This was not just a matter of geographic scope, the difference between short- and long-distance trade. It had to do with fundamental features of English society and the English economy which set England apart from its European neighbours.

The immediate forerunners of the Bank of England were the goldsmith bankers. Their object was not just to facilitate old forms of trade, profit on alienation or buying cheap and selling dear, but to encourage investment in profitable production. What distinguished the Bank of England was not that it was a public bank but almost the opposite: that the public bank in England was an extension of private banking in its specific English form. It is true that it acquired the right to conduct its private business by offering to provide public credit, especially to finance war, but its principles and its general banking functions continued already existing English private banking practices.

The Bank of England did not, then, represent the sudden emergence of a thoroughly novel commercial regime. It was an extension of long-developing social property relations, the property relations of agrarian capitalism. These developments had set in motion a new and unprecedented historical dynamic, one major feature of which was an unprecedented self-sustaining economic growth – unlike anything anywhere else in Europe, including the highly commercialized Dutch Republic. The commercial capitalism of the eighteenth century in England was firmly rooted in these distinctive developments and would have been impossible without them. Whatever novelties emerged in eighteenth-century England, the revolutionary transformation in the property regime preceded them and was their precondition.

What, then, of the growth of government patronage enabled by the emergence of public credit? The apparatus of patronage, which would in the eighteenth century grow into what William Cobbett famously called 'Old Corruption', was a parasitic growth that fed on wealth created as much by capitalist agriculture as by mercantile activity. If landed wealth, in other words, was, by definition, 'real' rather than 'mobile', it was no less 'commercial' for that. If anything, the agrarian interest conformed to the capitalist logic more than did the monopolistic trading companies which survived as a pre-capitalist relic. The Tory country squire engaged in productive and improving agriculture was more capitalist than the old East India Company merchant; and the squire's wealth was more capitalist than the fortunes of the privileged few who grew rich on state patronage and public corruption.

There was, of course, nothing new about the use of state office, privilege or patronage in pursuit of personal wealth. This was, as we have seen, as much the rule as the exception throughout Europe. What distinguished the English mode of 'extra-economic' appropriation from, for example, the French, was that in eighteenth-century England it was a secondary, parasitic growth. French office-holders lined their pockets above all by directly taxing the productive classes, in particular the peasants. When the Land Tax was instituted in England in the 1690s, at the very moment that Parliament firmly established its control of taxation, the English propertied classes in Parliament were taxing themselves, transferring to the state wealth they had already appropriated from producers in the form of rent or profit. Old Corruption was a bone of contention not only among radicals like Cobbett but also among propertied elites, not because it represented a new commercial or capitalist order pitted against an antagonistic landed interest but, on the contrary, because it was parasitic on capitalist wealth that was at least as much landed as mercantile. The problem was not capitalist property. It was that a few corrupt and parasitic types were creaming off the profits of productive capital.

There certainly existed a strand of criticism that counterposed the moral qualities of landed property to the values of commercial profit; but even the most uncompromising critics testify to the realities of agrarian capitalism. The target of criticism was likely to be precisely a capitalist landlord who put profit above duty and responsibility, the obligations of hierarchy, rank and deference. Such critics might scorn the fruits of 'improvement' or imperial expansion; but, for the most part, if there was an opposition between virtue and commerce in eighteenth-century political discourse, it was a conflict within a ruling class generally agreed on England's novel property regime, even if some were more opposed than others to its excesses. If there was, for such critics, an opposition between the values of commerce and the virtues of landed property, it was not about an antithesis between agriculture and profit. It was about commerce unrestrained by moral values or class duties, about the excesses of Whig expansionism, about the abdication of traditional responsibilities by landowners who subordinated all their duties, the obligations of rank, to their commercial profits, about the ostentation of country parks and landscape gardens as against the productivity of agricultural improvement.

What divided critics like this from defenders of 'commercial society' like Joseph Addison or Daniel Defoe (Pocock's examples) was not a conflict over capitalist property. It had to do with the uses to which capitalist wealth was being put. Addison, for instance, was all in favour of large landed estates combining pleasure with profit, agricultural improvement with luxurious landscape gardens. Defoe's admiration for England's distinctive planted gardens lay along the same lines, a tribute to profit and rural aesthetics at the same time. But to critics, agricultural improvement and profitable production were one thing, ostentatious display and luxurious excess quite another.[19]

---

19 I discuss the very specifically English rural aesthetic that joined beauty with productivity and profit, in the manner of Addison and Defoe, in Ellen Meiksins Wood, *The Pristine Culture of Capitalism: A Historical Essay on Old Regimes and Modern States* (London: Verso, 1991), pp. 109–113.

Even when the virtues of the landed classes were held up against the vices of merchants, that opposition was likely to be deployed not against but in favour of the capitalist property regime. The fear that commerce could endanger virtue was an important theme even in the classics of political economy – nowhere more than in the work of Adam Smith. But it surely tells us something about the specificities of British capitalism that Smith, in the *Wealth of Nations*, sought a solution to the moral conundrum of commerce and virtue, which had troubled him throughout his career, by turning more, not less, to the commercial disciplines of competition and looking to the state not to impose a civic virtue alien to commercial transactions but rather to ensure that commercial disciplines would truly operate, against the inclinations of merchants and manufacturers. Even his friend Adam Ferguson, who continued to be plagued by the tensions between commerce and virtue (and even if we ascribe to him some kind of 'republicanism'), nonetheless regarded market mechanisms as the engine of progress (about which a little more in the next chapter). More particularly, neither one of them, whatever they may have thought about the corrupting effects of commerce or the vices of merchants, advocated a form of landed property that was not subject to the economic imperatives of 'improvement'; and nor did many other less equivocal critics of 'commercial society'.

Both advocates and critics took for granted agrarian capitalism, the product of transformations that had happened long before; and their discourse was accordingly distinctive. England certainly was not the only European state to have a powerful interest in commerce; and nor, as we have seen, did English thinkers first make commerce do the work of civic virtue. What was unique to England was that commerce itself was conceived in new ways in both theory and practice, a capitalist commerce with a dynamic of its own and, indeed, a new morality.

It seems perverse to define political discourse in eighteenth-century England in the terms of a dispute among propertied classes whose agreements on the existing property regime far outweighed their disagreements, or to magnify ill-tempered disputes among gentlemen into conflicts of revolutionary moment. Debate there certainly was; but, seen against the background of the turbulence and violence of other, truly fundamental oppositions in the history of England, the eighteenth century seems more remarkable for its settled consensus among men of property. The property regime that governed England during that century resulted from a long history of conflicts, all of them involving a great deal of force. It was established in struggles against threats from above and below – ranging from the defeat of rebellions by small proprietors in the sixteenth and early seventeenth centuries, to the destruction of unparliamentary taxation; from the suppression of popular threats which had emerged so dramatically during the Civil War, to the final suppression of the threats to property posed by royal absolutism, decisively defeated in

1688–9. In the eighteenth century, there were significant developments that followed from that history: for instance, parliamentary enclosures and a forceful redefinition of property rights by means of what has been called judicial terror, the criminalization of customary rights and introduction of the death penalty for many new offences against property.

There would, of course, be major changes in British society with the advance of industrial capitalism; but the transformative moments in the history of England's distinctive 'commercial society' belong more to the seventeenth, and even the sixteenth, century than to the eighteenth. These transformations laid the foundations of capitalist industrialization, generating an economic system that not only made agricultural producers uniquely subject to market imperatives and the requirements of competitive production but also propelled the mass dispossession that created both a labour force and a new kind of consumer market for wholly new forms of industrial production.[20] It is certainly true that seventeenth-century thinkers could hardly have imagined a market mechanism in the eighteenth-century manner, but they could and did conceptualize the property regime that was its essential condition. Whatever innovations occurred in eighteenth-century 'discourse', they did not represent an abrupt transformation but the consolidation of already established principles. Parliament and the courts, for instance, could increasingly be relied on to put into practice the conception of property which had come to the fore in the seventeenth century; and resistance to those principles did not come from propertied classes but from below. Nothing reveals more effectively the connection between the earlier transformation and what followed than the fact that after the settlement of 1688, which consolidated the property regime in Parliament, the state no longer opposed landed interests by interfering with enclosure in the way it often had before. Parliament itself became the enclosers' principal agent.

Locke did not, of course, invent this property regime; nor did he invent a wholly new discourse to capture it. In less systematic form, the idea of claims to property deriving from 'improvement' and the creation of value had been at work for some time, both in domestic property disputes and in justifications of empire. It was certainly visible in seventeenth-century improvement literature, as well as in disputes between landlords or capitalist tenants and those whose use rights impeded improvement and capital accumulation. The same idea appears early in the seventeenth century, as we have seen, in defence of English imperial policy, particularly the colonial settlement of Ireland. But Locke gave the conception its first systematic elaboration, and in that sense his theory gave conceptual expression to the revolution in the English property regime. What we observe in the eighteenth century are the consequences of that regime still playing themselves out.

---

20 For more on this, see my 'Question of Market-Dependence', esp. pp. 80–84.

The Lockean paradigm was, in this sense, very much still present – indeed, came fully into its own – in eighteenth-century England. What, then, should we make of the fact that the greatest British philosopher of the century (considered by many the greatest philosopher ever to have written in the English language) was a thinker whose principal contribution to philosophy had the effect of denying the very possibility of political theory in the manner of Locke? David Hume was not a political theorist; but he had much to say about what kind of theorizing about politics is *not* possible, and that included Locke's political ideas. Starting from an 'empiricist' premise apparently akin to Locke's, that all knowledge ultimately derives from sense experience, Hume ends with a philosophical scepticism that challenges precisely the pretensions of human reason that are central to traditional ideas of natural law, natural right and social contract.

Reason, Hume tells us, can do no more than establish connections among ideas, which themselves are feeble derivations from original sense impressions. It cannot reach beyond original perceptions to any kind of ultimate truth. We can trace connections between premises and conclusions, but we can never be certain about the truth of the premises themselves. This means that our beliefs, even about such basic principles as cause and effect, to say nothing of our moral and political judgments, cannot claim to be grounded in necessary truths or universal, immutable natural laws. There is, to be sure, a human nature, which, among other things, inclines human beings to recognize that their interests require political communities, property and the security of agreements needed to maintain them, which we can call the principles of justice. But there is no basis for judging forms of government on the grounds of abstract 'rational' principles or natural law.

Hume, somewhat paradoxically, attributes to human nature a propensity to 'sympathy', which, on the face of it, seems very like Rousseau's *pitié*, a projection of our sense of self to others, which is the basis of human sociality and even morality. A natural benevolence or a feeling for humanity even form the basis of justice, although that emerges through the mediations of convention, particularly in circumstances of scarcity that require the security of property. But Hume finds himself unable consistently to sustain the idea of sympathy without challenging his own philosophy, which allows for no conception of the self beyond the simple awareness that accompanies each of our sense impressions. Yet rather than relinquish the idea of sympathy, he eventually ends by putting in question his own philosophical system and embraces a scepticism even more profound than before, no longer seeking to explain sympathy as a projection of the self.[21]

---

21   For a discussion of this point, see my *Mind and Politics* (Berkeley and Los Angeles: University of California, 1972), esp. pp. 66–73.

Hume's philosophy seems to represent a striking challenge to Locke's political theory, but his work in the end confirms the depth of the settled consensus and the persistence of what we are calling the Lockean paradigm. If his epistemology puts in question the very possibility of Locke's political philosophy, his classic *History of England,* which during his lifetime remained his greatest success, tells us something more about his views on politics and property. It is true that, in Hume's account of English history since Roman times, he makes no unambiguous claims for the superiority of England's 'mixed constitution' and remains true to his philosophical scepticism: it seems that any form of government that operates according to some kind of regular and settled laws should probably be supported. But what may tell us more about the Lockean consensus is that Hume appears to take for granted the distinctly English property regime of agrarian capitalism. When he associates commercial society with progress, as do the classical political economists, he does not oppose the virtues of real property to commerce. It is not just that, for him, commerce promotes prosperity, liberty and even politeness. He also sings the praises of the 'rising gentry', a dynamic agrarian class quite unlike the 'ancient barons'. This new landed class, instead of dissipating its fortunes, 'endeavoured to turn their lands to best account with regard to profit'; and in the process, they increased the cities and enhanced the wealth and power of 'the middle rank of men'.[22]

Hume's friend Adam Smith was no less committed to the idea of 'sympathy', though his convictions about 'moral sentiments' and a natural 'feeling of humanity' may seem to run counter to the *Wealth of Nations,* where the pursuit of self-interest appears to overtake benevolence as the driving force of social interaction. Despite his distrust of mercantile classes and their selfish inclinations, Smith is able to advocate the advancement of 'commercial society' and to reconcile the moral demands of sympathy and justice with self-interest; but he can do so because, and perhaps only because, he is convinced (however mistakenly) that market disciplines will enhance equity, indeed equality, as well as 'opulence'. This conviction may have come more easily to him because of specifically English conditions. England not only

---

22 David Hume, *History of England,* Vol. 3, Appendix 3 (London: T. Cadell, 1773), pp. 488–9. Much the same could be said about another major figure of the eighteenth century, Edmund Burke. A discussion of his political thought will have to await another volume that encompasses the American and French revolutions, which, for better or worse, inspired so much of his political thinking. For now, it is worth simply noting that when he launched the attack on the empire in India which was perhaps his most notable political act, his chief complaint, as head of a parliamentary committee, was that the empire had become 'completely corrupted by turning it into a vehicle for tribute', when it should instead 'fix its commerce upon a commercial basis'; 'Ninth Report of the Select Committee', in ed. Peter Marshall, *The Writings and Speeches of Edmund Burke* (Oxford: Oxford University Press, 1985), p. 241.

had an unusually integrated market and an unusually integrated state. It also came closer than other trading nations to his model of 'the natural progress of opulence', in which commercial success is driven less by mercantile interests than by a productive agriculture. Adapting physiocratic ideas to English conditions may have encouraged Smith to be more sanguine about the self-sustaining integrative power of the market and its spontaneous capacity to forge a common good.

'Commercial society', then, was rooted in the transformations of the previous century; and in the eighteenth century the property regime captured by Locke's theory of property was very much alive. Locke's political discourse may not have been the language of Addison or Defoe – though they certainly shared the ethic of improvement. It may not have been the philosophical language of David Hume. Locke's language of contract and natural right may not have been the language of eighteenth-century political or economic theory. But the discourse of this property regime was more than ever the language of Parliament in defining crimes against property, in property disputes and in deliberations on enclosure. If the Lockean paradigm was more or less invisible, it was because it represented a settled consensus within the ruling elites. They may have had less use in the eighteenth century for arguments based on natural rights or on contracts than did their seventeenth-century forebears defending Parliament against the Crown. They also increasingly had reason, in an age of revolution, to avoid any language that could be turned against them from below. But on certain very basic principles they were agreed, and these were principles that Locke had spelled out more systematically than had any other political thinker.

These principles constituted a very particular conception of property, including a commitment to its productive and profitable use, especially in the form of agricultural improvement, and the primacy of its purely economic value over common and customary rights. This was a conception of property that favoured capitalist production and appropriation as against non-capitalist forms, including the kind of political appropriation still favoured by the French and other Continental elites. Disputes within the English ruling elements, about virtue and commerce or real and mobile property, could be conducted in the secure knowledge that, when all was said and done, the antagonists stood together on the same solid ground. There was no longer any need to talk about it, at least not in polite company.

8

ENLIGHTENMENT OR CAPITALISM?

Their goal was not mainly to gain a greater understanding of the physical world, but to bring reason to bear on man's place within it – that is, among other things, to bring morality and politics wholly within the scope of rational inquiry. On the face of it, these ambitions were realised. The ideas of the Enlightenment changed the world. Their legacy was western modernity . . . The West's inheritance from the intellectual battles of the 18th century was liberalism and capitalism. These have made the West, for good or ill, what it is.

This characterization of the Enlightenment assumes that, whatever national variations there may have been in Western history, 'the West' came together in the Enlightenment to form a common liberal and capitalist 'modernity'. That account comes not from a scholarly source but from an article in *The Economist* published in the 1990s.[1] Yet its portrayal of 'western modernity' – in which liberalism, capitalism and the intellectual project of the Enlightenment together represent a single cultural formation whose first principle is rationalism – could have been written, with this or that stylistic adjustment, by a wide range of historians and social thinkers, supporters or critics of the Enlightenment (or both together), from Max Weber, or indeed Hegel long before him, to anti-Enlightenment postmodernists today. From passionate advocates to unrelenting critics, commentators have portrayed modernity, for evil or for good, in much the same way. This has been so whether the Enlightenment is regarded as the pinnacle of human emancipation or as an abject failure that at best has been unable to forestall the tragedies of modern times (the 'dialectic of Enlightenment') and at worst has been their source, the cause of genocide and threats of nuclear annihilation. If there is today a conventional idea of 'modernity', it remains a composite of the capitalist market, formal democracy, and technological progress, rooted in the 'rationalism' of the Enlightenment.

---

1   'Crimes of Reason', *The Economist*, 16 March 1996, p. 97.

There have, of course, been various refinements in historical accounts of 'the Enlightenment'. We now have not just one Enlightenment but many, produced by many national cultures; and we have a 'Radical Enlightenment', with roots in the seventeenth century and especially Spinoza, which preceded the more moderate variety typically acknowledged by historical convention and would continue to influence more radical and democratic forces. The proliferation of 'Enlightenments' may even put in question whether there was ever any definable moment or movement deserving of the name 'the Enlightenment' or any other special designation of its own. 'The Enlightenment is beginning to be everything', writes one distinguished scholar, 'and therefore nothing.'[2] But none of this has displaced the portrait of modernity in which the various threads of 'rationalization', cultural, political and economic, are inextricably connected, even if they have reached their full realization in some places more than in others.

The argument that follows here is intended to disentangle some of these disparate threads. More particularly, it is intended to disentangle the 'Enlightenment project' from the culture of capitalism. It is not here simply a question of the many differences among national and local cultures that mark the particular Enlightenments of, say, France, the Netherlands, or Germany. What is at issue here is the connection – or the lack of it – between the intellectual and political themes most commonly associated with the 'Enlightenment(s)' and the distinctive culture of capitalism.

Modernity and the 'Bourgeois Paradigm'

'Neither the historian nor the philosopher', Jonathan Israel tells us, 'is likely to get very far with discussing "modernity" unless he or she starts by differentiating Radical Enlightenment from conservative [or] moderate mainstream Enlightenment.' Anyone seeking to investigate the rise of modernity 'as a system of democratic values and individual liberties', he continues, must pay closer attention than is normally given to 'the crucible in which those values originated and developed – the Radical Enlightenment'.[3]

Since our objective here is precisely to investigate 'modernity', and especially its values of democracy and liberty, let us start with Israel's distinction between the two competing strands of the Enlightenment. The critical distinction is 'the difference between reason alone and reason combined with faith and tradition [which] was a ubiquitous and absolute difference.' On the one hand, the 'moderate mainstream' associated with Newton and Locke

---

2   Darnton, 'Washington's False Teeth', 27 March 1997.
3   Jonathan Israel, *Radical Enlightenment: Philosophy and the Making of Modernity 1650–1750* (Oxford: Oxford University Press, 2002), pp. 11, 13.

aspired to conquer ignorance and superstition, establish toleration, and revolutionize ideas, education, and attitudes by means of philosophy but in such a way as to preserve and safeguard what were judged essential elements of the older structures, effecting a viable synthesis of old and new, and of reason and faith.

On the other hand, the Radical Enlightenment, with its most important roots in Spinoza,

> whether on an atheistic or deistic basis, rejected all compromise with the past and sought to sweep away existing structures entirely, rejecting the Creation as traditionally understood in Judaeo-Christian civilization, and the intervention of a providential God in human affairs, denying the possibility of miracles, and reward and punishment in an afterlife, scorning all forms of ecclesiastical authority, and refusing to accept that there is any God-ordained social hierarchy, concentration of privilege or land-ownership in noble hands, or religious sanction for monarchy. From its origins in the 1650s and 1660s the philosophical radicalism of the European Early Enlightenment characteristically combined immense reverence for science, and for mathematical logic, with some form of non-providential deism, if not outright materialism and atheism along with unmistakably republican, even democratic tendencies.[4]

It would be reasonable to ask how far Israel's distinction between the two 'Enlightenments' can take us in understanding modern ideas of democracy and liberty. This distinction, whatever its other strengths (and weaknesses), considerably overstates the gulf between the conservatism of the 'moderate mainstream' and the 'democratic tendencies' of the 'Radical' Enlightenment. Spinoza himself was certainly more radical than Locke in his approach to religion and ecclesiastical authority; but, on the political spectrum from Locke to, say, the Levellers (to say nothing of other, more radical forces), the Dutch philosopher's oligarchic republic may seem closer in spirit to Locke's parliamentary government (even while the two philosophers seem closer to each other in their philosophical radicalism, or, for that matter, in their attitudes to religion, than either one would be to radically democratic religious sects in the English Revolution).

But even if we set aside all the complexities in the relations among philosophical, religious and political radicalisms (and even if we pass over a conception of 'democratic tendencies' so restricted that it places a 'radical' Spinoza in diametric opposition to a 'conservative' Locke), it is still worth asking how much we can learn about 'modernity' and 'democratic values'

---

4   *Ibid.*, pp. 11–12.

by concentrating on the 'Radical Enlightenment'. The problem is not only that, when placed along such a limited spectrum, the differences between 'radical' and 'moderate' may seem greater than they are. The point is that even when there seems to be substantial philosophical agreement on the subject of equality or liberty, there are limits to what that can tell us about modern democratic values if we ignore contextual divergences that may give very diverse meanings to conceptions of democracy, equality and liberty. It is not, again, simply a question of national differences. We may speak, with caution, of a 'European Enlightenment' ranging 'from Portugal to Russia and from Ireland to Sicily', all of them 'preoccupied not only with the same intellectual problems but often even the very same books'.[5] But even if we do allow for an inclusive 'European' culture of Enlightenment, this cannot dispose of major contextual differences, such as those between (French) absolutism and (English) capitalism, which engendered different concep- tions of equality and liberty and left very different political legacies.

It may after all be useful to begin, as Robert Darnton has suggested, by 'deflating' the Enlightenment – not belittling its importance, nor even under- estimating the commonalities of European culture, but considering at least one 'Enlightenment' as a concrete historical phenomenon, a 'movement, a cause, a campaign to change minds and reform institutions', in a specific time and place. This movement, which began in early eighteenth-century France, Darnton tells us, certainly had origins that can be traced to intel- lectual developments in other parts of Europe, in the previous century or even before; and it certainly had affinities with cultural trends elsewhere. But the educative and reforming mission of the French Enlightenment remains distinct.

In eighteenth-century France, and specifically in Paris, there was an explosion of activity among intellectuals and men of letters, who, whatever their other similarities and differences, self-consciously identified them- selves with

> a new spirit, the sense of participation in a secular crusade. It began with derision, as an attempt to laugh bigots out of polite society, and it ended with the occupation of the moral high ground, as a campaign for the liberation of mankind, including the enserfed and enslaved, Protestants, Jews, blacks, and (in the case of Condorcet) women . . . [It] grew out of a crisis during the last years of the reign of Louis XIV [and] came to a head while France suffered through a series of demographic, economic, and

---

5 *Ibid.*, p. v. Israel is rather too insistent on dismissing national differences – even when, for example, he acknowledges that the interests of the English landed gentry produced 'appreciably different' cultural effects than those of 'urban and commercial' classes in the Dutch Republic (p. 22).

military disasters [during which, with the state] on the verge of collapse, men of letters attached to the court . . . questioned the basis of Bourbon absolutism and the religious orthodoxy it enforced.[6]

This 'secular crusade' soon moved well beyond a conversation among courtly men of letters. The *philosophes*, as we have seen, took on a mission far more ambitious and inclusive than the subjection of bigots in polite society to ridicule; and this mission would have influences far beyond French borders. The writings of the *philosophes* would plant their seeds in everything from Kantian philosophy to revolutionary doctrines in America. But Darnton's judicious account of a 'movement' with clear geographic and temporal boundaries and a more or less explicit practical objective places it in perspective in a way that more grandiose and capacious conceptions of 'Enlightenment', even those that distinguish between 'moderate' and 'radical' Enlightenments, do not.

There may be a difference between speaking, on the one hand, of *the* Enlightenment as a trans-European, even global, phenomenon without a specific historical referent, or, on the other, of many particular Enlightenments with very specific locations and times. But both presuppose a common denominator, a culture of 'reason'; and, even when they acknowledge the many different ways and degrees in which that culture challenged superstition or faith in, say, England, France, Germany, Italy, Russia or Romania, they are likely – when not explicitly, then often by default – to leave intact a model of modernity that lumps together scientific, political and economic 'rationality', or liberal democracy and the capitalist market.

In this model, the Enlightenment, for many the pivotal moment in the onset of modernity, is typically bound up with capitalism. This is so not only in the most simplistic forms of Marxism, in which the Enlightenment is a bourgeois – and hence, in common usage, capitalist – class ideology. The Enlightenment and capitalism are also intertwined in the Weberian notion of 'rationalization', in which the rise of the 'rational' (bureaucratic) state and the 'rational' (capitalist) organization of production belong, for better or worse, to the same historical process as the Enlightenment elevation of reason over ignorance and superstition. Whether that process is a cause for celebration or lament, whether it constitutes the liberation of the individual or the 'iron cage' or both together in the ambiguities of 'disenchantment', these economic, political and cultural manifestations represent the many facets of a single historical tendency. The bourgeois here too is the principal agent, the undifferentiated bearer of economic, political and cultural rationalization.

Conventional ways of thinking about capitalism and its history tend to

---

6   *Ibid.*, p. 35.

obscure its specificity, taking it for granted and naturalizing it, as if its principles and laws of motion were universal, natural laws.[7] Either capitalism has always existed in one form or another, at least in embryo or in the depths of human nature, or it is the natural destination of history. Even if it is the final outcome of a long historical process, that destination seems to have been reached by historical movements that were themselves already driven by essentially capitalist laws of motion, like the need for constant technological progress to increase labour productivity. The implication is that there really is no need to explain the origin of capitalism. Since historians first started writing about the emergence of capitalism, with very rare exceptions, there has scarcely existed an explanation that did not begin by assuming the very thing that needed to be explained. Accounts of the origin of capitalism have been fundamentally circular: they have assumed the prior existence of capitalism in order to explain its coming into being. Capitalism comes about by means of already capitalist processes, an already existing capitalist rationality. It is just a maturation of age-old commercial practices and their liberation from political and cultural constraints. All that historians are obliged to do in explaining the development of capitalism is to account for the removal of obstacles to the free development of an age-old, eternal historical dynamic, not the emergence of a radically new one.

This conception of capitalism is deeply embedded in Western culture. It is manifest in the conventional conflation of 'bourgeois' and 'capitalist', together with conceptions of modernity – and now postmodernity – that are based, explicitly or implicitly, on that conflation. Underlying the identification of bourgeois and capitalist is a model of Western historical development – which I call the 'bourgeois paradigm'[8] – that represents capitalism as a natural product of commercialization, the growth of cities and the expansion of trade. The same model underlies some familiar dichotomies, which tend to be closely linked: rural v. urban, agriculture v. commerce and industry, status v. contract, aristocracy v. bourgeoisie, feudalism v. capitalism, and, of course, superstition (or magic, or religion) v. reason. In these accounts the burgher or bourgeois – by definition a town-dweller – is the principal agent of progress, whether he achieves his ends by means of bourgeois revolution or by some less cataclysmic means.

The argument here proceeds from a different conception of capitalism and the historical process that brought it about. It also departs, of course, from accounts of 'commercial society' that evade the historical issue by

---

7   The work of Robert Brenner represents the most important departure from this tendency, especially in his contributions to *The Brenner Debate*. I discuss the historiography of capitalism and its origin at greater length in *The Origin of Capitalism: A Longer View* (London: Verso, 2002), chs 1–3.

8   I first suggested this phrase in my *Pristine Culture*, pp. 2–11.

treating the emergence of capitalism not as a social transformation but as a sudden shift of language. The argument here insists on the specificity of capitalism as a system with unique imperatives, a system distinctively driven to improve the productivity of labour by technical means, in order to meet the requirements of competition and profit-maximization. It has nothing to do with the distinction between urban and rural, or agriculture and commerce or industry. Just as agriculture and landlords can be capitalist (and the presupposition of the present argument is that capitalism was born in the English countryside), so too can cities, commerce, industry and the bourgeoisie be non-capitalist. This means that bourgeois modernity and the Enlightenment are one thing, while capitalism is something else altogether.

To make the distinction between English capitalism and the historical context of the French Enlightenment is not to deny that they shared certain common historical preconditions nor that the culture of capitalism displayed certain traits that we associate with the Enlightenment – such as an interest in science and technology. The point is rather that capitalism's distinctive economic logic has been accompanied by its own very specific cultural and ideological formations which set it apart from others, which depart in significant ways from the cultural pattern associated with the Enlightenment, and which are even sometimes diametrically opposed to Enlightenment principles.

Bourgeois but Not Capitalist

If there is a kernel of truth in the crude proposition that the ideas of the French Enlightenment were somehow 'bourgeois', it is certainly not in the sense that they were capitalist. The relevant context here is not capitalism but absolutism. The absolutist state, as we have seen in earlier chapters, constituted both a political and an economic system in the sense that the state was a primary economic resource, a form of 'politically constituted property'. Office in the state was a form of private property, not only in the sense that many offices were venal but more generally in the sense that it gave its possessors access to peasant-produced surpluses through the medium of taxation, which was a source of private wealth no less than of public revenues. There also were other, decentralized forms of politically constituted property, not only the remnants of feudal lordship but various other corporate powers and privileges. The role of corporate autonomy, rights and privileges as means of appropriation helps to account for the strength of corporate principles in France, in theory and practice.

The eighteenth-century French bourgeoisie was not a capitalist class, or even, in large part, a commercial class of any kind. A typical French bourgeois, the kind of person who would, for example, constitute the revolutionary bourgeoisie of 1789, was likely to be an office-holder, a professional, even an intellectual (about which more in a moment). The material interests of the French bourgeois were likely to be bound up with the state. This could be either directly through office or stipends from the state, or indirectly, negatively, through opposition to exclusion from privilege, to exclusion from higher offices reserved for birth or wealth, and to the aristocracy's most precious privilege, exemption from the taxes that so burdened the Third Estate.

How did these material interests find expression in Enlightenment principles? The interests of such non-capitalist bourgeois were typically expressed in the commitment to civil equality, for example, in principles that would be embodied in the slogan 'careers open to talent' – which meant, in particular, access to state office. The same interests were also expressed in the assertion of universalism against particularism, specifically the universalism of the *nation* or *citizenship*, and ultimately humanity itself, against the structure of corporate privilege, against special status, private law, exclusive rights, and so on – in other words, inclusive against exclusive principles, universality against privilege.

This is not to say that bourgeois class interests by themselves created the preoccupation with equality, or even that Enlightenment ideas belonged exclusively to the bourgeoisie. After all, enlightened aristocrats played a prominent role. But bourgeois class interests, in a society structured by corporate hierarchy, help to explain the salience of equality and universalism in Enlightenment culture.

There is, nonetheless, something more specific to be said about the relevant bourgeois culture. The culture of the Enlightenment is not some undifferentiated bourgeois ideology but a much more particular expression of one specific section of the bourgeoisie, the intellectuals. The particular character of the French Enlightenment in many ways derives from the mentality, the corporate consciousness, the *esprit de corps*, even the caste-consciousness, and indeed the material interests, of a new type of professional intellectual. But it also needs to be emphasized that the professionalization of the intellectual in France was less a symptom of 'modernity' than a feature of the ancien régime and the corporate structure of the absolutist state. It was very much a part of a system in which the state and office were primary economic resources. What is at issue here, then, is the professionalization of the intellectual as a kind of office-holder in a society where office was a form of appropriation. It was also a society organized on corporatist principles, and that too has a great deal to do with the mentality of Enlightenment intellectuals in France. In the context of France's corporatist organization, the intellectual profession assumed some of the character of the 'intermediary bodies' that were so much a part of the French polity and French political thought, with its own corporate solidarity and consciousness, and even a certain corporate autonomy, or at least an aspiration to that kind of autonomy.

The clearest and most important illustration of this formation is the Paris Academy. Here, first, is how Voltaire, in his *Lettres philosophiques,* compares the *académies* in France with the Royal Society in England. We can discount the heavy irony with which these little essays are written because, on the main point, Voltaire's account is accurate and goes right to the heart of the matter:

> The English have had an Academy of Sciences much longer than we, but it is not as well organized as ours . . . The Royal Society of London lacks the two things most necessary to men, payment and rules. A place in the [French] Académie is a small but certain fortune for a geometrist, or a chemist. In London, on the contrary, it costs them to belong to the Royal Society.[9]

Voltaire goes on to make a distinction between the amateurs who belong to the Royal Society, and the experts who belong to the Académie in Paris; and he draws an analogy between well-disciplined and well-paid soldiers, on the one hand, and volunteers on the other. This epigrammatic comparison points to some real and significant differences between English and French intellectuals, and also to more fundamental social, economic and political divergences between England and France. It should be emphasized that the difference between the two academies is not that one was more interested in applied and the other more in pure or theoretical science. Both engaged in 'pure' science, and both are also notable for the degree to which their conception of science was utilitarian; but their utilitarian objectives were different and, more particularly, they were responding to different needs.

The members of the Paris Académie before the Revolution were agents of the absolutist state, and the Académie itself was part of the absolutist project to centralize culture around the king. It performed essential functions for the state, and its research projects were often directly dictated by the needs of the state – such as, in its early days, long-term projects having to do with navigation, mapping French territory, military mechanics, and (this is exquisitely emblematic) developing a hydraulic theory for the construction of fountains. The Académie also increasingly became the official arbiter of technological matters, judging inventions presented to the king. By contrast, the Royal Society, effectively founded in 1660 (though it received its first charter in 1662), deliberately set itself apart from the state. Instead of choosing another contemporary model, Samuel Hartlib's 'Agency of Universal Learning', which would have been supported by the state, the

---

9 Voltaire, *Lettres philosophiques, ou Lettres anglaises*, ed. Réne Pomeau (Paris: Garnier Frères, 1964), Letter 24, p. 154 (the translation of the passage is my own).

Royal Society deliberately chose to derive its income from members' subscriptions.

'The Royal Society', writes the historian of science Charles Webster, 'purposely avoided entanglement with national policy. Accordingly the Royal Society was freed from state regulation, but it was also divested of a large element of the humanitarianism and utopianism of the "Agency of Universal Learning".'[10] The Society was characterized, as he puts it, by an 'absence of public responsibility'. It is worth adding that, in this respect, the differences between the Paris Académie and the Royal Society correspond to a fundamental difference between pre-capitalist and capitalist societies: while pre-capitalist powers of appropriation are typically inseparable from the performance of certain communal or public functions – jurisdictional, military, political – capitalist property is unique in the degree to which appropriation is separate from the performance of such public functions – in other words, it is notable exactly for 'the absence of public responsibility'.

At any rate, although we should clearly not be misled by Voltaire's observation that the Royal Society was full of amateurs and dilettantes (it had among its active members some of the foremost scientists of their or any other day, from Boyle to Newton), there is an important truth in his observation. The general (not, to be sure, necessarily active) membership of the Royal Society came in large part from the landed classes, especially the gentry: men who did not regard their intellectual pursuits as a kind of professional activity.[11] The active core, including those who would by any standard be called scientists, would certainly not have regarded their scientific pursuits as a form of salaried service, let alone a type of office-holding. Their collective consciousness, if they could be said to have one, was clearly something very different from the corporate consciousness of professional

10   Charles Webster, *The Great Instauration: Science, Medicine and Reform, 1626–1660* (London: Duckworth, 1975), p. 97.

11   On the social composition of the Society in its early years, see, for instance, Lotte Mulligan, 'Civil War Politics, Religion and the Royal Society', in *The Intellectual Revolution of the Seventeenth Century*, ed. Charles Webster (London and Boston: Routledge & Kegan Paul, 1974), pp. 317–46. Mulligan looks at members of the Royal Society who were old enough to have been involved in the Civil War and breaks them down according to such factors as their social rank and occupation as well as political and religious leanings. See, in particular, the table on p. 340, which indicates that 55 per cent of these members came from the gentry and another 18 per cent from the nobility (with those of merchant or artisan background at 14 per cent). In his introduction, the editor points out the flaws in such a purely statistical approach in any attempt to determine the social, political and religious origins of English science – partly on the grounds that only a very small proportion of members of the Royal Society were active. But the figures remain significant, and, as will be suggested in what follows, there were some fundamental commonalities of interest between the grandees of the Society and their less active amateur co-members.

intellectuals in France. More particularly, their different status, and their very different relation to the state, were expressed in the very specific preoccupations of the Society.

This is not to deny that there were many common concerns among academicians in England and France. But in at least one respect the English were distinctive, indeed unique. If, for instance, we consider the concerns of the founders of the Royal Society – distinguished figures, both scientists and non-scientists, such as Robert Boyle, John Evelyn, Robert Hooke, William Petty, Christopher Wren, and the first co-secretaries of the Society, Henry Oldenburg and John Wilkins, not to mention members such as Lord Shaftesbury and Locke – one of the things that stands out is their shared preoccupation with agriculture, and specifically its 'improvement', the enhancement of its *productivity*. One of the Society's earliest projects was a county-by-county survey of English farming, based on what may be the first ever systematic questionnaire on a technical subject – probably compiled by Robert Boyle. This preoccupation was part of a larger trend: the explosion in the seventeenth century of a body of literature devoted to improving agricultural practices.[12] In that respect, even the most active core of the Society

---

12 The study was conducted by the 'Georgical' committee of the Society. Among its members and those associated with its work were not only such dignitaries as Boyle, Evelyn and Wilkins, but also Shaftesbury, Locke's patron, the very model of the early capitalist landlord, whose farms were situated in the heart of agrarian capitalism (see Neal Wood, *John Locke and Agrarian Capitalism*, Berkeley: University of California Press, 1984, pp. 21–2, 26). This gives at least an indication of the convergence between the interests of landlords and the scientific preoccupations of the Society's core members. It is worth noting, too, that founders of the Royal Society such as Boyle, Evelyn, Oldenburg, Petty and Wilkins had in common their earlier involvement in Hartlib's Agency of Universal Learning (Webster, *Great Instauration*, p. 99). As Webster points out: 'Husbandry more than any other subject was used by Hartlib to demonstrate the aims of his Agency to "do good, in love to the Publick"' (p. 472).

One final remark: some commentators have pointed out that the Royal Society underwent a significant transformation, even a decline, in the decades following its foundation. Margaret Espinasse's 'The Decline and Fall of Restoration Science', in ed. Webster, *Intellectual Revolution*, pp. 347–68, associates this 'decline' with the dominance of an aristocratic outlook and the loss of interest in trades and industry in favour of arts more suitable to gentlemen. But there is, perhaps, in this judgment a bit too much of the 'bourgeois paradigm'. There was, to begin with, a significant continuity between the preoccupations of the Society in its golden age and the gentlemanly pursuits of the subsequent century. In any case, the notion of 'improvement' demonstrates that a shift from 'bourgeois' interests in trades or industry to 'gentlemanly' or 'aristocratic' pursuits like farming is no indication of declining interest in productivity or profit. The following century may have been less scientifically distinguished than the first decade or two of the Royal Society, but it was certainly the age in which the culture of improvement came into its own. In that sense (as in others), the scientific preoccupations of the Royal Society in the seventeenth century, and indeed the 'aristocratic' interests of that time, came to fruition in the eighteenth century.

had fundamental interests in common with the less active amateurs from the
aristocracy and gentry.

There is nothing in France, even in the eighteenth century, like the
'improvement' literature of seventeenth-century England, and that cultural
fact conforms to a material reality. Although it is sometimes said that in the
eighteenth century the productivity of French agriculture was more or less
the same as it was in England at the time, this simply means that total output
or land productivity was roughly the same. But it took a larger labour force
in France than in England to produce that total output. What the English
had that the French did not was an imperative to improve labour productivity (output per unit of work), that imperative derived from a system of social
and economic relations very different from those prevailing in France, a
system that already in the seventeenth century subjected English agricultural producers to the requirements of a competitive market – in other
words, agrarian capitalism.

To sum up the comparison between England and France simply and
crudely: where French science in the eighteenth century typically
answered the needs of the state, English science, even a century earlier,
was already answering the needs of property, and property in an increasingly capitalist form.

The principal differences can be brought into sharper relief by means of
an interesting paradox – or something that may look paradoxical from the
vantage point of the bourgeois paradigm and the conception of modernity
that goes with it. If we were to compare the French academicians of the
eighteenth century with English scientists of the seventeenth using our
conventional criteria of modernity, even discounting the time difference,
the French would undoubtedly emerge as the more 'modern': they were the
professionals, in a so-called rational, bureaucratic organization. The
English were amateurs and dilettantes in a more formally irrational
system. The French were by definition largely bourgeois. The membership
of the Royal Society was overwhelmingly landed, mainly from the gentry
but also the nobility.

Yet, seen from a different angle, which one is more 'modern': the corporatist French bourgeois professional academician serving the absolutist
state, or the English improving landlord, member of the Royal Society with
an 'amateurish' scientific interest in a capitalist-style enhancement of labour
productivity?

Progress and the Republic of Letters

The example of the Paris Académie may give us some clues about the ways
in which the material and institutional interests of intellectuals shaped the
culture of the Enlightenment. First, in a society where access to the state, to

the lucrative resources of state salaries, pensions and privileges, was a primary material concern and where access to high office depended on birth or wealth, the question of qualification for office was a very live issue.

It might not be too much to say that a significant part of French Enlightenment culture had to do with redefining the qualifications for office. This redefinition took the form of an ideology that sought to replace an aristocracy of birth or wealth with an aristocracy of talent and intellect. No doubt, intellectuals in general have a material interest in so-called meritocracy, but this would be especially so in a society in which life chances were so closely bound up with the state and public office.

The symbiosis between intellectuals and the absolutist state is visible in other ways too. The bureaucratization of culture in the absolutist state encouraged some distinctive cultural patterns – in particular, the standardization of language that was a favourite project of the absolutist state, or French classicism, with its precise and formal aesthetic and philosophical rules.[13] This cultural configuration helped to promote the sense of intellectuals as a corporate community, with their own internal laws and culture. Under these conditions, where intellectuals had a very self-conscious corporate consciousness, and where that consciousness had very specific institutional expressions, the idea of an intellectual community, a Republic of Letters, acquired a very concrete meaning. It is not at all difficult to see how the idea of a Republic of Letters worked itself out in the Enlightenment, especially in the concept of progress.

The most obvious point about the Enlightenment concept of progress is that its source and its model is scientific knowledge, the cumulative, directional quality of that particular form of knowledge. In the end, that is what the idea of progress comes down to: whatever other evils, reverses and moral lapses have punctuated human history, the mind, especially in the form of scientific knowledge, is, according to this view, the one thing we can count on to advance, however slowly and painfully and however much the perfection of any kind of knowledge is projected into an indefinite future.

Now, in itself, the idea of progress as the advance of knowledge may not be particularly distinctive. It is certainly not enough to distinguish England from France, or the Enlightenment of either one from all the other 'Enlightenments'. Nor would it be true to say that the French had no interest in material progress. For instance, the idea that human civilization has gone through various stages of material organization, or the idea that human history has been characterized by several successive modes of subsistence, from hunting to pastoral through agricultural to

---

13   In my *Pristine Culture*, I contrast these French cultural patterns with the English culture of capitalism – expressed in various domains, from language to gardening.

'commercial' society, owes as much to French thinkers as it does to Englishmen or indeed to the Scottish political economists who theorized the experience of English capitalism. But the corporate consciousness of French intellectuals gives this concept of progress a special flavour. It is not surprising that the notion of progress that we associate with the French Enlightenment in particular conceives of the history of civilization as, above all else, the history of the Republic of Letters. It misses the point completely just to conflate this with the notion of technological progress in the sense we associate with capitalism and the enhancement of labour productivity by technological means.

The culmination of the Enlightenment conception of progress, in a way its last gasp, is Condorcet's *Sketch for a Historical Picture of the Progress of the Human Mind* – published in 1795, after the ideas of the Enlightenment had already been enlisted in two major revolutions, and written while he was hiding from the Jacobins in fear of his life. It can, of course, be argued that Condorcet was not a representative figure; that his optimism, no less than his universalism and egalitarianism (at least in anticipation of progress), was exceptional even among the great Enlightenment thinkers. Optimism was in any case only one side of the Enlightenment picture. The secular view of history that distinguishes this concept of progress from religious millennialism is necessarily two-sided: it does not simply make assumptions about human perfectibility or the historical possibilities available to human agency. It is also, and for the same reasons, shot through with pessimism about the dark side of human life; and the tension between these two is a constant theme in the Enlightenment.

But if Condorcet is exceptional, the very qualities that make him so also make him perhaps the most revealing example. His notion of progress as the universal triumph of human reason over ignorance and superstition may be more uncompromising than others of his time; but it does represent a crystallization, without ambiguities, of the themes that bind all Enlightenment figures together and give the concept of 'Enlightenment' whatever meaning it has. Precisely because his optimism about the beneficence of human reason is so uncompromising, because his universalism is so wide-ranging and cosmopolitan – because, in other words, he takes Enlightenment principles to what critics would regard as their extremes – his *Sketch* provides a clear and simple measure against which to test the standard accusations levelled at the 'Enlightenment project', about the inherent oppressiveness of its rationalism and the imperialism of its universalist principles.

Here, first, is how Condorcet sums up the goal of human progress: 'Our hopes for the future condition of the human race can be subsumed under three important heads: the abolition of inequality between nations, the progress of equality within each nation, and the true perfection of mankind.'

'The final end of the social art', Condorcet says in the most unambiguous terms, is 'real equality'.[14]

Here are his views on imperialism:

> Survey the history of our settlements and commercial undertakings in Africa or in Asia and you will see how our trade monopolies, our treachery, our murderous contempt for men of another colour or creed, the insolence of our usurpations, the intrigues or the exaggerated proselytic zeal of our priests, have destroyed the respect and goodwill that the superiority of our knowledge and the benefits of our commerce at first won for us in the eyes of the inhabitants.[15]

And on sexual oppression:

> Among the causes of the progress of the human mind that are of the utmost importance to the general happiness, we must number the complete annihilation of the prejudices that have brought about an inequality of rights between the sexes, an inequality fatal even to the party in whose favour it works. It is vain for us to look for a justification of this principle in any differences of physical organization, intellect or moral sensibility between men and women. This inequality has its origin solely in an abuse of strength.[16]

Condorcet may not be typical in the degree to which he holds such views, but even postmodernist critics of the Enlightenment may have some difficulty in deconstructing this discourse of equality or transforming it into something evil and oppressive. Nor can we dismiss the many ambiguities in the Enlightenment legacy, or the dangers inherent in excessive optimism about the perfection of humanity, not to mention the evils perpetrated in the name of progress. But it remains significant that here, in the *locus classicus* of Enlightenment optimism, equality within and between nations, races and sexes emerges not in opposition to, or in uneasy juxtaposition with, rationalism and universalism but as their logical conclusion, the final destination of progress.

Condorcet illustrates to perfection how the French preoccupation with the narrative of mind and the Republic of Letters is related to a kind of

---

14 Antoine-Nicolas de Condorcet, *Sketch for a Historical Picture of the Progress of the Human Mind*, trans. June Baraclough (London: Weidenfeld & Nicholson, 1955), pp. 172, 173.
15 *Ibid.*, pp. 175–6.
16 *Ibid.*, p. 193.

universalism and (to a greater or lesser extent) egalitarianism. There is no doubt that French intellectuals (with notable exceptions like Diderot – the Genevan Rousseau is something else altogether) envisaged themselves as an aristocracy of intellect, an elite, which consciously distanced itself from artisans and more vulgar kinds of professionals. Yet in this very particular and fairly short historical conjuncture, intellectual elitism, and even the material interests of intellectuals, had certain interesting and paradoxical effects. In the first place, in its own historical context, this meritocracy, in its commitment to the ideal of 'careers open to talent', had mildly democratic implications. But there were also other, wider implications. These thinkers saw it as their special mission to disseminate knowledge, which is the most distinctive and important feature of the French Enlightenment.

Condorcet, for instance, called for mass education – and he actually devised a plan for the Académie as the institution that would preside over a system of mass education. The kind of egalitarianism he espoused, his insistence on defining progress in terms of increasing equality and social inclusion, was inseparable from his view of the intellectual's mission. In a sense, his egalitarianism and his elitism were two sides of one coin. For him, as for other Enlightenment figures, the intellectuals' special claim to status and authority was their role in educating the world.

There is no intention here of exaggerating the Enlightenment commitment to equality. There were obviously strict limits to the equality envisaged even by thinkers like Condorcet, let alone, say, Voltaire, and much of it was in any case deferred to an indefinite future. But it is still significant as an aspiration, and it is significant how, in these very particular historical conditions, the logic of intellectual elitism impelled Enlightenment thinkers in that direction, into ideas that could be, and were, appropriated by far more radical and revolutionary forces.

No one can doubt that Enlightenment universalism could and did have oppressive, racist and imperialist manifestations; but it is also important to keep in mind something that postmodernist critics systematically forget: the connection between Enlightenment universalism and a critical temper that subjected European knowledge, European authority and European culture to more trenchant critique than any other. Even the conception of progress, which is supposed to be the essence of Enlightenment Eurocentrism, had anti-imperialist implications. The conception of progress as the progress of the human mind and knowledge takes for granted that the advance of knowledge is a very long-term cumulative process, projecting if not into infinity at least into the indefinite future. This conception, to be sure, implies that at some point, if not in the foreseeable future, certain truths can and will be discovered; and it further implies that some cultures are more advanced and therefore superior to others. But it also implies – perhaps even more fundamentally – that any given knowledge is open to question, that all authority is subject to challenge, that no one has a monopoly on truth.

The appropriation of history by intellectuals certainly evinces a far-reaching hubris. But at the same time that these intellectuals are arrogating history unto themselves, they are also taking on the burden of human falli-bility and the whole dark history of human error and evil. A deep pessimism is never very far away from Enlightenment optimism. It is, in fact, just the other side of the same coin. If Enlightenment conceptions of knowledge and progress are founded on a kind of universalism, then it is a universalism that implies open-endedness, flexibility, scepticism. For all its dangers, Enlightenment universalism has provided a theoretical underpinning for emancipatory projects much more effective than anything postmodernists have been able to devise. So, indeed, has the concept of progress. For that matter, it gives us something that postmodernist celebrations of diversity and difference do not and cannot: a *reason* for recognizing and respecting otherness – if only on the grounds that the cumulative and open-ended qual-ity of human knowledge and the progress of the human mind require us to be careful about closing any doors.

Condorcet may not have been typical in the degree to which he took the emancipatory logic of the Enlightenment seriously, but it says something about the complexity of the Enlightenment – and about the vacuity of many criticisms today – that this most classic example of Enlightenment optimism and universalism is also the one that most explicitly attacks the very evils ascribed to that Enlightenment optimism by critics today: racism, sexism, imperialism. Nor is this an accidental or contradictory juxtaposition: Condorcet's universalism and his optimism about human progress rest on the same foundation as his commitment to equality, his respect for the authenticity and integrity of other cultures, his attack on imperialism.

The Ideology of Capitalism

In the French Enlightenment we are approaching the end of a long history in which the inextricable unity of political and economic power is a central preoccupation of Western political thought. In the specific conditions of French absolutism, this preoccupation centred on privilege and access to high office, which gave a special salience to ideas of equality. It is true that, with few notable exceptions, the great Enlightenment figures were generally elitist and took hierarchy for granted – not to mention their own position, or aspira-tions, in that hierarchy. This was true even of Condorcet. Yet, for very concrete historical, even material, reasons, eighteenth-century France produced an ideology of universalism with more or less democratic and egalitarian impli-cations. The Revolution would take that ideology much further than most *philosophes* intended; and the revolutionary legacy, with wide-ranging implications far beyond French borders, would certainly survive. But in the mainstream of Western political discourse, the Enlightenment 'project' would be overtaken by a different cultural formation, producing different notions of equality and shaping modern conceptions of democracy, the roots of which are traceable to early English capitalism.

England, needless to say, shared much with its European neighbours; but it had something specifically its own, a distinctively *capitalist* culture. English culture had certainly inherited some of the same universalistic legacies as had the French – for instance, the universalisms of Christianity and natural law. It was an Englishman, Isaac Newton, who practically invented the idea that the world was governed by certain universal, mathematical laws. As for equality, the English certainly took second place to no one in formulating ideas about the natural equality of men; and, of course, ideas of equality, at least of an ambiguous and qualified sort, did play a part in the ideology of England's ruling class in its battles against monarchical excesses, as in Locke's political theory. For that matter, the whole Enlightenment concept of progress owes a great deal to Locke – though it could be argued that the French conception of progress owes more to his epistemology, while the Anglo-Scottish conception has a greater affinity with his theory of property. But the point here is that, for all this common cultural legacy, English capitalism produced its own very specific ideological requirements. The interesting question is what happened when these universalistic and egalitarian ideas came within the orbit of capitalism.

We have seen how the social structure of France – its forms of appropriation by means of 'politically constituted property', the related importance of corporate principles – gave a particular salience to equality as an oppositional principle. The English situation was very different. In sharp contrast to France, corporate principles were already very weak in the seventeenth century, and they never had been as strong. The development of capitalist property forms was undermining the old extra-economic principles of hierarchy, and old conceptions of natural or prescriptive inequality were already seriously undermined. This made it harder to construct a theoretical case for inequality grounded in classic justifications of corporate hierarchy or appeals to a 'great chain of being'.

There is another point too. The old conception of bourgeois revolution as applied to the French is flawed in many ways, but the flaws have more to do with the conflation of bourgeois with capitalist than with the antithesis of bourgeoisie and aristocracy. There was indeed a conflict between 'bourgeoisie' and aristocracy, and that conflict did have material implications, which certainly would figure centrally in revolutionary ideology. But the bourgeois interests at stake in the conflict had less to do with capitalism than with the system of privilege and access to higher state office. This gave the aspiration to equality a special force. In England, the case was again very different. There was indeed a capitalist interest, but it was no less 'aristocratic' than 'bourgeois'; and in its struggles to maintain its own supremacy, equality was obviously not the objective. In fact, the idea of equality could become a real liability, as it did in the form of seventeenth-century English radicalism. If the theory of natural or prescriptive inequality, of corporate hierarchy and privilege, was the main problem facing the French bourgeoisie, for the English capitalist class the problem was, on the contrary, a theory of natural equality. In the absence of the old corporate principles and hierarchies, they were obliged to find wholly new ways of justifying domination that were compatible with natural equality. The English – although they were, as we have seen, building on a long tradition of Western political thought in combining ideas of natural equal-ity with vast political and social inequalities – were especially creative in constructing a theoretical justification of inequality on a foundation of natural equality.

Here the most instructive example comes from John Locke. What makes him such a revealing object of comparison is the common ground he shares with his Enlightenment successors, which brings their divergences into sharp relief. Locke was certainly a major influence on the Enlightenment, espe-cially through his epistemology. While he never went as far as Condorcet would later go, he had some reasonably enlightened attitudes about natural equality, as well as toleration and opposition to tyrannical government. But he also had some very distinctive ideas which set him apart from the main figures of the French Enlightenment and which are uniquely characteristic of capitalism. In fact, it is striking that, though Locke is writing a century before Condorcet at an early stage of capitalist development, some of his seventeenth-century attitudes have a more familiar ring to those of us who live in advanced capitalist societies.

The central issue for capitalist landlords was something rather different from the questions that confronted a non-capitalist bourgeoisie. In particu-lar, they had to establish a certain kind of right to property, a historically unprecedented kind of right, which excluded and extinguished all other use rights, customary and common. They had to establish the primacy of profit and the market over rights of subsistence. All this created a very distinctive ideological pattern, which emerged in both theory and practice. The culture of 'improvement', which was such a striking feature of the Royal Society, appears not only in Locke's political theory but increasingly in English property law and in court decisions about property rights; in the new science of political economy; in the dispossession of small producers. 'Improvement', in the sense of productivity for profit, trumped all other goods. It would increasingly be cited in favour of exclusive private property: that is, property that excluded not only other individuals' rights to use it, but also communal regulation of production of a kind that would prevail for much longer in

France. Improvement could, in other words, as Locke makes very clear, turn even the most egalitarian ideas into justifications of dispossession.

Let us consider again Locke's famous observation, in the *Second Treatise*, that 'in the beginning, all the World was *America*' (§II.49). America here stands for the quintessentially primitive condition of humanity in the continuum of human development, and it provides a standard against which to judge a more advanced condition. Locke is here making the point that the earliest, and the natural, condition of the earth was effectively 'waste', and that human beings have a divine obligation to remove the earth from the waste, to make the earth *productive*, to *improve* it. His measure of improvement or productivity, as we have seen, is 'profit', not in the older meaning of advantage, whether material or otherwise, but quite simply as exchange value or commercial gain. As we saw in Chapter 7, Locke makes it clear that the issue is not labour as such but the productive – and, more particularly, the profitable – use of property.

This argument has many implications – for instance, that improvement, or productivity and profit, trump any other claims, such as the customary rights of English commoners, or the rights of indigenous peoples. For all the natural equality of men, on which Locke emphatically insists, the requirements of productivity and profit trump that, too. This is, put simply, a warrant for capitalist property. It is also a warrant for appropriating 'waste' land, and so for settler 'plantations'. Locke can even reconcile slavery with his assertion of men's natural freedom and equality: although no one can enslave himself by contract or consent, people can be legitimately enslaved as captives in a just war. This more or less traditional justification of slavery, apparently as a punishment for violation of natural law, would apply to any time and place.[17] Here again Locke's view contrasts sharply with Condorcet's, for whom the abolition of slavery would be a sign of progress.

Having begun his case against absolutism, then, with the unambiguous premise that men are free and equal in the state of nature, Locke goes on to cover his flank by finding ingenious and historically novel ways to justify inequality, deploying radical arguments against absolutism while taking great care to denude them of their most democratic and egalitarian implications. His approach to natural law in the *Second Treatise* – spelling out, with dialectical ingenuity, the conditions in which natural-law restrictions on accumulation of property can be overcome without violating natural law – also nicely illustrates how this supremely universalistic principle could be subordinated, or at least harnessed, to the requirements of private property and capital accumulation. In both cases, 'improvement' is the overriding principle.

We get a fairly clear picture of what constitutes progress for Locke, and

17   See Locke, *Second Treatise*, § 23.

the contrast with Condorcet is striking. Consider the main axis along which each thinker divides the advanced from the undeveloped state of humanity: for Condorcet it is rationality v. ignorance and superstition, equality v. inequality; for Locke it is profit v. waste. Locke certainly identifies rationality as a superior condition, but while for Condorcet the progress of reason is inextricably bound up with the advance of equality, for Locke rationality is paired with 'industriousness' and is very hard to dissociate from productivity and profit. In fact, beginning with the proposition that all men are naturally equal, he turns these principles of productivity and profit into a new and historically unprecedented kind of validation of inequality.

The contrasts between Locke and Condorcet bring into sharp relief the differences between the ideologies of capitalism and enlightenment. For all their qualifications, Condorcet's egalitarian aspirations are striking, and they are in sharp contrast to Locke. If, for Condorcet, equality is an objective for the indefinite future, for Locke it is a reality in an unrecoverable past or, at best, a moral principle conceived as easily compatible with gross inequalities in the real world. Locke's theory of knowledge and his views on education may suggest a fundamental egalitarianism, which attributes differences among human beings in large part not to nature but to experience; and he certainly ascribes to 'industriousness' a greater weight than, say, to aristocratic birth. But he shows little sign of any aspiration like Condorcet's hope for 'the abolition of inequality between nations, the progress of equality within each nation, and the true perfection of mankind'. If for Condorcet the objective is the improvement of humanity, for Locke the objective is the 'improvement' of property. The progress of humanity is subordinated to, or at least subsumed under, the advance of productivity and profit.

In the eighteenth century the 'Scottish Enlightenment' would produce ideas of progress and equality very much akin to those in France, which on the face of it have more in common with Condorcet than with Locke. Yet even here, there are significant divergences. In the French versions, even when they are at their most materialist, the story of progress is the story of the human mind, as a development from barbarism and superstition to reason and Enlightenment. Condorcet's *Sketch*, for instance, presents all kinds of economic, social and political advances as the development of mind and reason. An even more striking example comes from Turgot. His *Discourse on the Successive Progress of the Human Mind* was delivered in 1750, and though he never wrote the universal history he was planning, his ideas on the subject seem to have been influential, not least on his friend Condorcet. The case of Turgot is significant not only because commentators treat him as a pivotal figure in the Enlightenment idea of progress, and even of the socio-economic theory of progress, but also because he is mainly known as an economist, both as a theorist and a state administrator, who might be expected to tell the story in its most materialist or economistic form. Yet for him, too, the principal issue is the 'steps taken by the human mind' in the progress 'from barbarism to refinement', from ignorance to knowledge, from superstition to reason and enlightenment. The principal agents of history are learned men and scholars, even academicians, the kind of people who constitute the Republic of Letters.

On the other side of the Channel, it was Scottish more than English political economists who developed something analogous to the French conception of progress, but they did so against the immediate background of English capitalism. The Scots, in fact, theorized English capitalism more effectively than did English theorists, no doubt because they were more conscious of its difference, its otherness, seen from the vantage point of the Scottish experience. The great Scottish intellectuals were very conscious of the contrast between English prosperity and Scottish poverty at the time of Union in 1707 and the hopes of economic improvement that had motivated many of its supporters. While the Scots more than the English wrote from an intellectual perspective with certain self-conscious affinities to the French, the example of England's material wealth was ever present in their conceptions of history and human development. At the heart of Adam Smith's political economy, like David Hume's history of England, is the English model of progress.

The Scottish Enlightenment was no less interested than the French in the whole range of progress – advances in knowledge, culture, politics, morality – but the distinctive development of the English economy was always at the core. One of the classics of the anglophone literature on progress, Adam Ferguson's *Essay on the History of Civil Society*, is, for example, a very wide-ranging story of progress, with many different aspects, social, political, cultural, as well as economic. The critical turning-point is identified in Part II, 'Of the History of Rude Nations', where Ferguson draws a line between 'Rude Nations prior to the Establishment of Property' and 'Rude Nations, under the Impressions of Property and Interest'. Beyond the invention of property that constitutes the dividing line between savagery and barbarism among 'rude' nations, the minimal condition for moving beyond rudeness to refinement is the division of labour; but it is the advent of commercial society that sets in train a distinctive capacity to sustain progress by directing the pursuit of individual self-interest to progressive development.

Commerce does, to be sure, endanger civic virtue, and political wisdom is required to preserve it; but the mechanisms of the market, and precisely those imperatives of competition that threaten virtue, are for Ferguson the only conceivable engine of self-sustaining progress. He does not attribute to the market quite the same role in integrating selfish motivations as does his friend Adam Smith, who eventually sought a solution in the disciplines of competition; and Ferguson still assigns to the political domain a greater role in preserving social bonds and moral order. But there is no mistaking his conviction, shared by Smith and Hume, that whatever may have been accomplished by the evolution of the human mind, it is commercial mechanisms and the enhancement of productivity for profit that set in motion progress as a self-sustaining process.

The advance of scientific knowledge as the engine of progress seems, then, to be displaced by a different kind of historical mechanism, a self-sustaining economic growth that, in historical reality, existed at that time only in England. Much the same idea of progress appears in the work of Adam Smith, and it is here that we can see the implications of such an argument for conceptions of equality. It may be true that Smith shared Condorcet's commitment to equality, as well as liberty and justice;[18] but for the Scot the burden of progressive development falls unambiguously on the market. The desirable effects of equitable distribution are, above all, a consequence of market mechanisms. The natural outcome of economic growth will be not only to raise the living standards of the poor but also to rebalance the distribution between profit and wages, on the grounds that the greater the amount of 'stock' or capital, the lower the rate of profit in relation to wages.

This is not the place to consider the flaws in Smith's economic argument. Suffice it to say that any mistakes he may have made about the relation between the growth of 'opulence' and the distribution of wealth among classes only made it easier for some of his successors to factor out the benevolence of his intentions and reduce his economics to the ruthless operations of the market. What is significant for our purposes is that, even if we reject conventional interpretations of Smith as a 'free market' theorist in the manner of a Friedrich Hayek or a Milton Friedman, even if we insist on his unrelenting commitment to the 'moral sentiments' and equitable distribution or the role of the state in achieving those ends, even if his advocacy of a 'free' market presumes its contribution to justice and equity, to make the economic mechanisms of a capitalist market the engine of historical advance inevitably risks allowing market imperatives to trump other social goods. In the manner of the Lockean paradigm, the advance of productivity for profit seems to overtake the improvement of humanity as the main criterion of progress.

---

18 For a compelling case that Smith and Condorcet, whatever their differences, shared common ground in their commitment to such ethical and political principles, contrary to conventional caricatures of a coldly unfeeling and rationalist 'Enlightenment', see Emma Rothschild, *Economic Sentiments: Adam Smith, Condorcet, and the Enlightenment* (Cambridge, Mass: Harvard University Press, 2001).

Capitalism and Democracy

The elevation of market mechanisms to moral imperatives was clearly an important development in Western social thought. But capitalism would have even more far-reaching effects in recasting the political terrain. The social map was completely redrawn by capitalism's distinctive configuration of political and economic power; and ways of thinking about rule and domination, about liberty and equality, were accordingly transformed.

We can gain some perspective on these transformations by looking back briefly at the notions of freedom and equality as they had evolved in the history of Western political theory. It had become fairly common to defend the right to rule while acknowledging and even stressing the universal freedom and equality of men (and, of course, it has generally been men). What makes Western political theory particularly interesting and even puzzling in this respect is that it invented a defence of domination not simply combined with, but even based on, a notion of equality, which specifically denies any natural division between ruler and ruled, or any justification of domination on the grounds of natural inequality. Hobbes, who defends an absolutist monarchy on the grounds of a very radical notion of natural equality and a denial that there exists any natural division between ruler and ruled, may be the most extreme and paradoxical example; but he certainly was not alone in combining equality with domination. That paradox has been a staple of Western political thought. This is not to say that ideas of equality and universal human community are exclusive to the culture of what, for lack of a better term, we call the West; and neither is it unusual for such ideas to coexist more or less happily with the realities of inequality and domination. But the Western canon is distinctive in its systematic mobilization of egalitarian doctrines and ideas of a universal human community in the *justification* of both class and imperial domination.

As long as the principle of domination is accepted on its own terms – whether as the 'mandate of heaven' or even simply on the basis of tradition or perhaps hereditary principles, the dynastic principles of royal bloodlines or descent from the Prophet – it can be perfectly compatible with the idea of general human equality. But Western political theory, at least at certain seminal moments in its history, confronted a very specific problem in explicating the juxtaposition of equality and domination. It had to find ways of explaining and justifying domination *on the basis* of equality. Or, to put it another way, it had to find new ways of systematically explaining and justifying domination itself.

The idea of natural equality became a troublesome issue when and because it was coupled with a notion of political equality, a fundamental challenge to the very idea of rule. Before the ancient Greeks invented a wholly new civic sphere and the new identity of citizenship, it had always been clear that the state represented domination, even, or especially, where men were assumed to be naturally equal. But now, the state itself – in fact, the state above all – represented equality. Equality, in other words, was not a simple fact of nature that had no bearing on the right to rule. Equality resided in the political sphere itself, expressed in the political identity of citizenship.

In societies where wealth and dominance depended fundamentally on privileged access to political rights, where economic power was so closely bound up with legal, political and military status, the concept of civic equality posed serious risks to dominant classes. In the case of ancient Greek democracy, the invention of citizenship and civic equality, while it certainly did not eliminate economic and social inequalities, had real practical effects on disparities of economic power, limiting the possibilities of 'extra-economic' exploitation. The citizenship enjoyed by peasants, for instance, spared them the kinds of dependence on lords or a tax-hungry state that have plagued most peasants throughout history.[19]

Yet if the civic ideal seemed a threat to rulers and propertied elites, once the idea had taken root it was difficult to eradicate; and it became necessary to find new ways of justifying domination within a civic community. Hellenistic and Roman emperors preserved the ancient civic principles but found ways of adapting them to serve imperial purposes. Alexander the Great and his successors, for instance, appropriated the principal themes that had emerged from the life of the polis, its notions of citizenship, law, freedom and equality. They then deprived these ideas of their subversive force by transplanting them from polis to 'cosmopolis', the universal polis of the Empire. On the elevated plane of the imperial cosmopolis, all men were equal under the skin; but in the real world of everyday life, some were rich and some were poor, and the emperor ruled over all his imperial subjects. The Roman Empire that followed would perfect this strategy of displacing the civic idea to a less dangerous sphere.

The idea of the cosmopolis did have its own egalitarian possibilities. Hellenistic Stoic philosophy, for example, produced the idea of a universal cosmic order governed by principles of natural reason, a kind of natural law, accessible to all human beings.[20] But Roman Stoics would take the sting out of this idea. Elaborating their own conception of a universal empire, a single world empire ruled by one absolute ruler, the Romans found their own ways of converting the old principles of the polis into imperial ideas. In the Roman concept of citizenship, the ancient civic principles of active political agency were replaced by an increasingly passive conception of citizenship. At the same time, Roman thinkers (like Cicero) put their own distinctive stamp on the idea of natural law, neatly combining a notion of universal moral equality

---

19   The ancient Greeks are discussed at some length in my *Citizens to Lords*.
20   For more on this, see *ibid*., esp. pp. 103–14.

with an explicit commitment to social and political inequality and domination. The old Greek civic community, with its principles of freedom and
equality, was removed to a still higher level of abstraction, still more detached
from the realities of social inequality and political hierarchy.

This elaboration of natural law owed a great deal to the characteristically
Roman duality of state and property, political power and ownership. The
idea of two modes of authority, each with its own distinctive domain, would
be readily adapted not only to asserting the *imperium* of Caesar while
preserving his subjects' *dominium*, their exclusive claims to private property,
but also to acknowledging the dominance of gods while preserving the
authority of Caesar. Even when the lines between property and jurisdiction
were blurred by the parcellization of sovereignty, the Roman legacy survived.
The Romans produced a way of thinking about property and spheres of
authority that made it possible to insist on one universal cosmic *logos,* a
universal and common natural law, the equality of all human beings, and
even a supreme divine authority, while still declaring the sanctity of private
property, the legitimacy of social inequality and the absolute authority of
earthly governments – and that included the authority of governments that
by any reasonable standard defied the ethical principles of divine or natural
law. It was only a short conceptual step to Western Christianity and its
distinctive division of labour between Caesar and God.[21] The Western
Christian tradition, especially its dissenting sects, would, to be sure, produce
its own kinds of radical egalitarianism; but its official orthodoxies took the
final step in relegating human equality to a sphere beyond this world: from
polis to cosmopolis to heaven.

In the Middle Ages, it became more difficult to manage the delicate
balance between equality in one sphere and domination in another. Even the
old Christian dualism could not suffice. Feudal lordship depended unequivocally on a legal and political hierarchy embodied in formal status
differences, and economic exploitation depended directly on that

---

21   The philosopher Seneca (ca. 3 BC–AD 65) nicely illustrates the conceptual se-
quence. Explicating Stoic doctrine, he demonstrates how all things can be considered
common, at least to wise men, while still remaining individual and private property. He
draws a significant analogy with the rights of the emperor: 'all things are [Caesar's] by
right of his authority [*imperio*]', yet at the same time the sense in which everything is his
by right of *imperium* must be distinguished from the way things belong to him as his own
personal property by right of inheritance, 'by actual right and ownership', or *dominium.*
Seneca then goes on to apply the analogy to the gods: 'while it is true that all things
belong to the gods, all things are not consecrated to the gods, and . . . only in the case
of the things that religion has assigned to a divinity is it possible to discover sacrilege'
(*On Benefits,* VII.vi–vii). In other words, just as Caesar's *imperium* does not preclude
the property of others, the *dominium* of the gods over all things does not preclude the
authority of earthly powers in this world.

extra-economic hierarchy. The capacity of landlords to exploit the labour of peasants required a monopoly of political and military power, and a legally formalized structure of lordship and dependence. Feudal ideologies of domination tended to be quite explicit about their inegalitarian foundations, which meant that Christian brotherhood and equality before God were obliged to coexist not only with earthly inequality but with ideas of a divinely ordained cosmic hierarchy, a 'Great Chain of Being'.

The idea of a universal moral equality and government based on the consent of naturally free men would, nonetheless, remain deeply rooted in the Western tradition; and thinkers worked out elaborate conceptions of natural freedom and equality that did not endanger ideas of unaccountable and virtually unconditional rule. Ideas of natural freedom, equality and government by consent could even be mobilized in defence of absolute monarchical power. Still, the strategy was not without its risks, which could be exploited by doctrines of resistance.

There would be a brief moment in the 'Age of Enlightenment' when the structure of privilege and office in the absolutist state gave earthly equality a special salience among intellectual elites. But this would soon be overtaken by a different, specifically capitalist culture, with its own conceptions of equality. With the advent of capitalism, the ideological possibilities and the needs of dominant classes would change radically. Once economic power no longer depended on extra-economic status or privilege, the civic ideal of political equality could be brought back to earth in wholly new ways. For the first time in history, the rhetoric of democracy could become the preferred and systematic ideological strategy of domination, both class domination and imperialism. In the 'early modern' period covered by this book, that ideological strategy was not yet fully viable, but nor was it necessary or even possible completely to suppress the civic ideal. Ruling ideas were increasingly challenged by more democratic aspirations, and new ways were found to renegotiate, in new historical conditions, the relation between civic equality and social inequalities.

Locke's conception of property is a milestone in Western political thought not simply because it represents a novel theory of property rights but because it points to a redefinition of the political sphere. There were, in Locke's time and thereafter, significant political conflicts over the meaning of property; and principles very much like the ones Locke was invoking were being used to underwrite new legal conceptions of property, to say nothing of colonial expansion. The capacity to mobilize the law for such purposes, and to gain the support of the state in redefining property, of course presupposes control of political processes. Privileged access to the political domain gave propertied classes in England huge advantages in shaping the law to their requirements. Yet the effect of redefining property in this way was to shift relations of domination away from politics and into a separate economic sphere. It would be a long time before political rights were more equally distributed; and the state would continue to be used by propertied classes, often with great force, to discipline their labouring subordinates. But by the time democratic rights were finally extended, the disciplines of the market and capital's control of production had made direct coercion by the state less important to the dominant classes: political equality would no longer have the same direct effects on social domination and economic inequality.

In eighteenth-century England, that extension of democratic rights was still a distant prospect, but the formation of an 'economic' sphere distinct from the political domain was well advanced; and with it would come a new conception of politics and democratic rights. The 'economy' became the subject of a new mode of theorizing, the 'science' of economics. The classical political economists were not the first in history to reflect on the processes of production, appropriation and distribution that are the primary subjects of the economic discipline; nor were the English or the Scots the first to theorize about self-propelling economic 'circuits'. But never before the advent of capitalism had it been possible to conceive of economic processes as abstracted from 'non-economic' relations and practices, operating according to their own distinct laws, the purely 'economic' laws of the market, and without the integration imposed by a 'legal despotism' in the physiocratic manner. It had never before been possible to conceptualize an 'economy' with its own forms of coercion, to which political categories seemed not to apply. The 'laws' of supply and demand, the production and distribution of goods, or the formation of wages and prices could, for the purposes of economic 'science', be treated as impersonal mechanisms; and human beings in the economic sphere could be perceived as abstract factors of production, whose relations to each other were very different from the relations of power, domination and subordination that defined the political sphere, the sphere of rulers and subjects or citizens and states.

This new kind of 'economy' would redefine the political sphere. The development of capitalism was making it possible for the first time in history to conceive of political rights as having little bearing on the distribution of social and economic power; and it was becoming possible to imagine a distinct political sphere in which all citizens were formally equal, a political sphere abstracted from the inequalities of wealth and economic power outside the political domain. Political progress, or even the progress of democracy, could be conceived in terms that were socially indifferent, with an emphasis on political and civil rights that regulated the relations between citizen and state, not the maldistribution of social and economic power among citizens, who in the abstract sphere of politics were equal.

If in the 'Age of Enlightenment' intellectual elites, and not only popular forces, had just begun to challenge the long Western tradition of transforming ideas of natural equality into justifications of inequality and domination, capitalism neatly circumvented that challenge by abstracting the political sphere from economic hierarchies and coercion. It made possible not only a neat division of labour between discrete and autonomous 'sciences', which is reflected in both classical political economy and liberal political philosophy, but also a view of the world in which 'economic' forms of power and coercion are not recognized as power and coercion at all. In the political domain, it may be necessary to limit excesses of power or to safeguard democratic liberties; but the political principles of liberty and checks on power do not belong in the 'economy'. Indeed, a free economy is one in which economic imperatives are given free rein. The essence of the capitalist 'economy' is that a very wide range of human activities, which in other times and places were subject to the state or to communal regulation of various kinds, have been transferred to the economic domain. In that ever-expanding domain, human beings are governed not only by the hierarchies of the workplace but also by the compulsions of the market, the relentless requirements of profit-maximization and constant capital accumulation, none of which are subject to democratic freedom or accountability.

INDEX

absolutism: Continental-style 13, 221; culture of 169–73; royal 225, 283–4; transition from feudalism to 14; views on 163, 242. *See also* French absolutism

absolutist monarchy 167

absolutist theory 255, 272

Addison, Joseph 282, 287

Address to the Christian Nobility of the German Nation (Luther) 63

Against the Robbing and Murdering Hordes of Peasants (Luther) 71–2

Age of Discovery 171

Age of Enlightenment 171, 173, 315

Agency of Universal Learning 297–8

agrarian capitalism 29, 188, 280–1, 283, 286

The Agrarian Problem in the Sixteenth Century (Tawney) 82n9

Agreement of the People 233–5

agriculture: Dutch 114–5; English 11–2

Alexander VI (Pope) 47, 92, 93

alienation of power 100n7

Althusser, Louis 53n9, 178n24, 183n26

Americas 87, 92

Anglo-Scottish 25, 26, 138, 306

anti-absolutist arguments 221, 251

Apologie for the Oath of Allegiance (James I) 105

Aquinas, Thomas 67, 106, 124

Aragon, Kingdom of 86

Aristotle 43–4, 51, 101, 103, 166

Arminians (Remonstrants) 112, 120

An Arrow Against All Tyrants (Overton) 237, 270–1

The Art of War (Sun Tzu) 51

Aubrey, John 141

Bacon, Francis 242, 257

Balibar, Etienne 132, 140, 143

Bank of England 280–1

Baron, Hans 37–8

Behemoth (Hobbes) 249

Beza, Theodore 157, 158

Bible 224

Bodin, Jean 161–5; on absolutist monarchy 54; *Method for the Easy Comprehension of History* 162; *Methodus* 162, 163–4; on mixed constitution 23; political philosophy of 150; *République* 162, 163–4; *Six Books of the Commonwealth* 161; on sovereignty 22, 137, 161, 162, 164, 198–9, 220

Bonaparte, Napoleon 15, 16, 17

Borgia, Cesare 42, 92

Bossuet, Bishop 171, 175

Bourbon monarchy 171

de Bourg, Jean 153, 154

bourgeois paradigm 290–5

bourgeois revolution 16, 17, 115, 295–300, 306

Boyle, Robert 299

Brenner, Robert 11n11, 294n7

cahiers de doléances 150, 153–61

calling, doctrine of the 80

Calvin, John 74–80, 84

Calvinism 62, 84, 111, 117, 156

Cambridge School 19, 27, 28, 30

The Cambridge History of Political Thought: 1450–1700 4n2

capitalism: about 289–90; agrarian 29, 188, 280–1, 283, 286; democracy and 311–7; in England 8, 26, 168, 310; ideology of 305–11; modernity and the bourgeois paradigm 290–5; Protestantism and 83; Republic of Letters 301–5; rise of 80–4, 259

Castile, kingdom of 86

Catholic Church 65, 76, 77, 105, 106, 111, 117, 149

Catholic League 150, 155

Cauvin, Jean. *See* Calvin, John

Cavendish, William 241

chambers of rhetoric 111

Charlemagne 171